Dynamic Acting through Active Analysis

Dynamic Acting through Active Analysis

Konstantin Stanislavsky, Maria Knebel, and Their Legacy

Sharon Marie Carnicke

methuen | drama

LONDON • NEW YORK • OXFORD • NEW DELHI • SYDNEY

METHUEN DRAMA
Bloomsbury Publishing Plc
50 Bedford Square, London, WC1B 3DP, UK
1385 Broadway, New York, NY 10018, USA
29 Earlsfort Terrace, Dublin 2, Ireland

BLOOMSBURY, METHUEN DRAMA and the Methuen Drama logo
are trademarks of Bloomsbury Publishing Plc

First published in Great Britain 2023

A catalogue record for this book is available from the British Library.

A catalog record for this book is available from the Library of Congress.

ISBN: HB: 978-1-3502-0518-5
        PB: 978-1-3502-0517-8
      ePDF: 978-1-3502-0519-2
     eBook: 978-1-3502-0520-8

Typeset by Integra Software Services Pvt. Ltd.
Printed and bound in Great Britain

To find out more about our authors and books, visit www.bloomsbury.com
and sign up for our newsletters.

Contents

Part 2 Six Lessons in Active Analysis

List of Illustrations

About the Author

Sharon Marie Carnicke is internationally known for her groundbreaking research in *Stanislavsky in Focus*. She earned her Ph.D. in Russian from Columbia University, while maintaining an active career in theatre as actor, dancer, and director. She began her artistic work with an internship at the American Shakespeare Festival Theatre (Stratford, CT). She performed in New York and has directed in New York, Los Angeles, Moscow, and Oslo. She founded the Stanislavsky Institute for the 21st Century and is currently Professor of Theatre and Russian at the University of Southern California (Los Angeles).

She has published widely on acting for stage, screen, and new media. In addition to *Stanislavsky in Focus*, her books include *Anton Chekhov: 4 Plays and 3 Jokes*, *Checking out Chekhov*, *The Theatrical Instinct: The Work of Nikolai Evreinov*, and the co-authored *Reframing Screen Performance*. Her articles and chapters number more than fifty. She has won many awards, including a citation for translation from the Kennedy Center (Washington, D.C.), and grants from prestigious organizations, including the Rockefeller Foundation, the American Council of Learned Societies, the American Association for Theatre Studies, and the United States National Science Foundation.

As a theatre artist, she has used Active Analysis in her teaching and directing in the United States and abroad. She has conducted intensives at such institutions as the National Association of Acting Teachers (U.S.), the National Academy of the Arts (Norway), *MetodiFestival* (Italy), the National Institute for Dramatic Arts (Australia), the Institute for Puerto Rican Culture (San Juan), and the Moscow Art Theatre School (Russia). Her research with scientists has applied Active Analysis to the study of emotional expression through motion capture and interactive digital storytelling. (For more see www.sharoncarnicke.com.)

Acknowledgments

Every actor who has worked or studied with me and every colleague and friend with whom I have discussed acting have contributed to my book on Active Analysis. A few have played key roles. Years ago, the theatre designer and director John Blankenchip made me promise that I would write this book. Shortly before his death, he asked my close colleague Mary Joan Negro to keep me to my promise, which she has done with grace and generosity. Her talent as an actor and as an exacting teacher inspired me every step of the way. In particular, her careful reading of my drafts, her insightful comments on the dramatic texts that I analyze, and her belief in the importance of my project unquestionably made this a better book. So too did the talented director and teacher, Matt Trucano. His detailed comments and fascinating questions kept my eye on the evolving state of theatrical art. When Professor Michael King at Northern Kentucky University told me that directing *Three Sisters* through Active Analysis was on his bucket list and invited me to work with his cast, he further galvanized my intention to write this book for actors, using my artistic voice.

I thank the prestigious director Anne Bogart for generously introducing me to her editor, Anna Brewer, at Bloomsbury/Methuen, whose enthusiasm for my project kept my spirits high during days of isolated writing at the height of the Covid-19 pandemic. I am grateful to her and the entire Bloomsbury team for making this book a reality.

Over the years, I have also benefited greatly from ongoing conversations with a number of generous people, among them: Dr. Andrew Makarovskiy, who grew up in Knebel's presence; her long-time assistant Natalya Zvereva; the actor Lyubov Zabolotskaia Weidner; Milton Justice, who always reminds me of the professional realities of working actors; Deborah Margolin, who enthusiastically allowed me to hold her up as a model trailblazer; R. Andrew White, who acts as an invaluable sounding board for my ideas; and Maria Ignatieva, whose research on the women of the Moscow Art Theatre is uniquely valuable. I am also grateful to those who initiated the workshops on Active Analysis that inspired Part II of this book: Egil Kipste, Paolo Asso, Gianluca Iumiento, Hanne Riege, Even Lynne, and Juan Vaquer. I also thank those who spent significant time in helping me format my typescript: Juliana Sabo, who is an ongoing member of my Studio; Ryan Zuzulock and Emmanuel Spero, who were my work-study assistants at the University of Southern California; and Morgan Hill-Edgar, who pursued a directed research project on Active Analysis with me, while I was writing and often reminded me of why I wanted to write this book in the first place.

Research was funded by grants from the National Endowment for the Humanities, the National Science Foundation, the American Society of Theatre Research, the Zumberge fund for Advancing Scholarship in the Humanities and Social Sciences from the University of Southern California, and a sabbatical leave that allowed me time to write.

Note on Transliteration and Translation of Russian Sources

In order to make my text reader-friendly, I anglicize Russian names (Stanislavsky, Knebel, Meyerhold, etc.) according to guidelines established by the American Association of Teachers of Slavic and East European Languages. However, in citing from published sources, I retain any non-standard transliterations of names (i.e. Stanislavski, Nemirovitch-Dantchenko, etc.) and mark these with "[*sic*]" to alert the reader to variations in English spellings. In my references and bibliography, however, I transliterate Russian names and titles according to the more scholarly Library of Congress system (i.e. Stanislavskii, Knebel', Meirkhol'd, etc.). I maintain established spellings of names for Russians (i.e. Blyum, Smeliansky, Solovyova, Michael Chekhov, etc.), who have published in English. In my bibliography, when an author's name has appeared in print in different forms, I list their works by chronological order, rather than alphabetically.

All translations from Russian sources including those from Stanislavsky's and Knebel's works are mine unless otherwise specified.

Abbreviations of Frequently Cited Sources

Letopis': Vinogradskaia, I., ed. (2003), *Zhizn' i tvorchestvo K. S. Stanislavskogo: Letopis'* [A Chronicle of the Life and Creative Work of Stanislavsky], 4 vols., Moscow: Moskovskii khudozhestvennyi teatr. Citations to this source include the volume number and date.

SS: Stanislavskii, K. S. (1988–1999), *Sobranie sochinenii* [Collected Works], 9 vols., Moscow: Iskusstvo. Citations to this source include the volume number and date.

Preface: To My Readers

Active Analysis is Konstantin Stanislavsky's most innovative approach to performance. It invites actors to explore the interactive dynamics in plays by enacting them before memorizing lines or setting blocking. The heart of the technique is the etude—a purposeful, improvisatory study of a scene that uncovers the motives, desires, and subtexts that prompt characters to speak and act as they do in the play. Through successive etudes that take actors deeper and deeper into the text, the cast drafts and perfects their performance. As Stanislavsky puts it, you "take yourselves to where your muscles believe" (Vinogradskaia 2000: 488). Named "Active Analysis" by Maria Knebel, this process of rehearsal taps actors' minds, bodies, and spirits simultaneously. "Active Analysis does not work if you don't fall in love with it and it does not work if you are not in love with acting," so said a student of Knebel's (Liadov 1988: 18). In my experience, most actors are passionate about acting and, once introduced to Active Analysis, become its passionate advocates.

I was first introduced to Active Analysis in Moscow at GITIS (the Russian Academy for Theatrical Arts), where Knebel had taught for decades. Her close assistant Natalya Zvereva and the prominent director Leonid Kheifitz had generously opened their classes to me and a small group of international experts. I fell in love with the technique while watching an etude in a bare, upstairs classroom, which was transformed into a rich space by the actors' imaginative work. Since then, I have researched the technique's history, practiced it, and taught its principles to actors in the United States, Puerto Rico, Europe, and Scandinavia. By experimenting with it in classic and postdramatic plays, on stages and motion capture sets, and with beginning and experienced actors, I have come to believe that Active Analysis offers exactly the artistic flexibility that contemporary actors need to work in a range of dramatic styles and across media.

Dynamic Acting through Active Analysis is the first guide for actors in English to the history and practice of Stanislavsky's and Knebel's legacy. In Part I, I bring to life the vulnerable, but courageous people, who created and kept the technique alive during the darkest era of Soviet repression. Three chapters that unfold like a mystery novel tell the hidden stories of how their ideas on acting and the rehearsal process evolved, how they struggled to articulate those ideas in face of unprecedented censorship, and how Active Analysis survived despite all the obstacles. In Part II, I invite you to join a fictionalized company of actors (diverse in age, cultural backgrounds, and acting experience) as they explore Active Analysis. In six lessons, they dust off two classic scenes, rehearse a new microdrama (published here for the first time), probe how the technique fits into Stanislavsky's wider System of actor training, and share applications to professional acting and the devising of new plays.

The Hidden Historical Record in Part I

Because Active Analysis was created during Stalin's regime of terror, when art became a matter of life and death, I begin by recounting the personal costs paid by Stanislavsky and Knebel for their artistic views. My mission to bring this history to light began when I was simultaneously studying Russian at Columbia University and acting at the HB Studio in New York. Knowing that I could read Russian, my acting teacher had asked me to look up a term in Stanislavsky's books that had been puzzling him. While I no longer recall the term, I vividly recall how reading Stanislavsky in his native language opened my eyes to a man whom I liked a great deal more than his English-language persona as a tyrannical patriarch of theatre.

The Russian Stanislavsky brings the wisdom of experience and the humility of a man in love with the messy art of acting to his writing. He sometimes speaks with the confidence gleaned from his long career as actor and director. At other times, he frankly admits that there are questions he cannot yet answer, because there is still so much more to learn about the complexities of acting. While reading, I sometimes laughed aloud, as I did when he compared a play to a roasted turkey that must be eaten bite by bite and not swallowed whole (SS II 1989: 204). Sometimes I cried, as I did when he unknowingly asked a young woman who had recently lost a child to play the role of a grief-stricken mother. His panicked reaction, when he learned of his inadvertent mistake, revealed his compassion and concern for what he called "the mental hygiene" of his actors (SS II 1989: 450–4). Above all, I came to admire his desire to speak plainly and commonsensically to actors, avoiding as much as possible the professional jargon that makes so many acting classes as clear as mud.

As Robert Lewis put it, by the mid-twentieth century the American Method had made a "fetish" of terminology and "created a kind of dogma out of what should have been a freeing principle" (Lewis 1958: 69). To this day, actors, directors, teachers, and even scholars continue to argue about Stanislavsky's words. Sometimes our debates are bitter and long-lived as was the falling out between Lee Strasberg and Stella Adler, dating back to 1934, over the use of "affective memory." Sometimes our discussions are comical, as was the one I witnessed in 2011 at the *MetodiFestival* in Italy, when three English-speaking teachers from the Meisner, Strasberg, and Adler schools were arguing over the use of "if," "as if," and "what if" in the development of character. They finally turned to Natalya Zvereva for a definitive answer. She merely shrugged and said, "In Russian there is only one word, and so your argument is all yours and not ours."

One of the most misunderstood of Stanislavsky's terms continues to be "objective" (*zadacha* in Russian), now ubiquitously used, but variously interpreted, by actors in the English-speaking world. Does this term refer to the character's goal or the desired end result in a scene? Or is it, as Lewis erroneously assumes, a synonym for action? (Lewis 1958: 29) Is the newer translation of "task" any clearer? When reading Stanislavsky's discussion in Russian, I understood perfectly that in every scene the character faces a set of given circumstances that pose a *zadacha*, which the actor (as the character) must attempt to solve by taking action. The actor is like a student in a math class, Stanislavsky explains, who has been given a *zadacha* by the teacher (SS II 1989: 212). This context suggests that the most apt translation is "problem."

In short, my acting teacher's question turned me into a detective. I wanted to know why the Russian and English-language Stanislavsky resembled each other so little and to understand the process that had turned a person into a hardened icon. That quest revealed a complex cultural and political story that significantly distorted information about Stanislavsky's life and actual practice, most particularly with regard to the time in which he was completing his books and experimenting with what would become Active Analysis. While the public in Russia and elsewhere hailed him as the world's most influential actor and director, only his closest family and associates knew how hampered his life had become and how Soviet censorship and disinformation were affecting what could be known about his work. When the Soviet Union fell in 1991, long-buried archives and unpublished records revealed details concerning suppressed aspects of his life and thought. My earlier book, *Stanislavsky in Focus*, tells this complex story and specifically examines how the System and the American Method diverge.

Part I of *Dynamic Acting through Active Analysis* initially focuses on Stanislavsky's last ten years from his heart attack on stage in 1928 during a performance of *Three Sisters* to his death in 1938. During these years, he suffered an unacknowledged house arrest, imposed by Stalin so that the state could manipulate Stanislavsky's name, reputation, and work without his permission. Memoirs, letters, and transcripts of his last classes personalize the man, who suffered so much as he brought forth his most forward-looking rehearsal technique.

But Stanislavsky represents only half of the story. Eyewitness accounts of his last work vary in reliability based upon their authors' politics. Loyal Soviets and others, fearful for their lives, hid information that did not sit well with Stalinist policies. These sources tend to speak of a "Method of Physical Actions" that was said to be in alignment with Marxist materialism, which was, as Stanislavsky himself stated, "required of all" (*SS* IX 1999: 475). In fighting against this Soviet distortion, Maria Knebel renamed his technique "Active Analysis" and offered a clear-eyed account of his last experimental work. Her role in the survival of Active Analysis cannot be underestimated.

Arguably the most influential voice in Russian theatre next to Stanislavsky, Knebel had studied acting and directing with three major figures from the Moscow Art Theatre—its two founders (Konstantin Stanislavsky and Vladimir Nemirovich-Danchenko) and the brilliant actor Michael Chekhov. Over the course of her career, she became a prism for all that was best in the famed company's tradition. She combined this background with a directing career that began in Moscow's alternative theatres, where she worked with avant-garde artists and members of Vsevolod Meyerhold's theatricalist company. In bringing this artistic breadth to her promotion of Active Analysis, she jumpstarted the careers of prominent actors like Oleg Efremov (who founded the groundbreaking Contemporary Theatre in 1957), bold new playwrights like Victor Rozov (who reinvigorated Russian drama in the post-Stalin era), and imaginative directors like Anatoly Vassiliev (Russia's most internationally known director today). Without a doubt, theatrical art would be the poorer without her.

In all she did, Knebel championed Active Analysis. She had learned it directly from Stanislavsky as his assistant at the Opera-Dramatic Studio from 1936 to 1938. Despite a Stalinist ban against the technique during the 1940s and 1950s, she continued to use it in her directing, often teaching it in secret by taking trusted actors into the basement for privacy. When politics allowed, she taught it openly at GITIS and wrote about it, completing six books and nearly a hundred articles by the time of her death in 1985. As she explains:

I understood that the method of Active Analysis strengthens the improvisatory nature of the actor, helps uncover the actor's individuality, and cleans the dust of time off literary works with wonderful images and characters in them.

(Knebel' 1967: 485)

Given her work with Active Analysis in a range of aesthetic styles and for new and devised plays, she is perfectly positioned to light the way forward into and beyond our post-modern and postdramatic world.

Despite my deep research on Stanislavsky, I had not fully understood Knebel's importance until I shared the stage with Natalya Zvereva and Anatoly Vassiliev at the international symposium, *Le Siècle Stanislavski*, in Paris in 1989. While heralded in Russia, Knebel had remained virtually unknown in the West. Of course she had, as had so many others, suffered under Stalinism and endured the vicissitudes of state censorship all her life. But as a woman she also struggled with the invisibility of her gender. As she herself once flatly admitted, "being a woman director is not easy" (Knebel' 1976: 248). While her male colleagues became known outside Russia, she was simply left out of the cannon. For example, Vasily Toporkov's account of Stanislavsky's Method of Physical Actions was translated twice into English, once by Christine Edwards in 1979 and again by Jean Benedetti in 2004. In contrast, Irina Brown's 2021 translation into English of Vassiliev's compilation of Knebel's writings only became available for purchase in January 2022, as I was finalizing this book. Prior to this only four of Knebel's articles had appeared in English (Moore 1973: 44–7; 48–55; Knebel' 1979: 107–35; Thomas 2016: 83–154). In 2010 I was proud to publish the first sustained account in English of her career and work (Carnicke 2010a: 99–116). *Dynamic Acting through Active Analysis* takes another significant step forward in amplifying her voice.

The Fictional Studio in Part II

Ever since falling in love with Active Analysis at GITIS, my artistic mission has included its practice in my own work, its promotion outside of Russia. and its application to new directions in the dramatic arts. I had once thought that I could advance these goals by writing a textbook, but soon found that such a format forced me into describing a paint-by-numbers approach that dismisses the technique's inherent flexibility. While the dynamic principles of Active Analysis provide a sketch for a performance and etudes fill that sketch with colors, I could not capture how the technique encourages actors to paint creatively and ignore the numbers when need be. Yet, the technique's ability to bend to the artistic needs at hand is precisely what makes it so valuable for actors who work across a variety of dramaturgies and go back and forth from stage to screen.

Unlike a textbook, Part II reflects the inherent flexibility in Active Analysis by following a fictional company of actors as they discover creative freedom within the technique's structure. Friends have told me that I have written an homage to Stanislavsky, who wrote his "system in a novel" (*SS* IX 1999: 99). Oddly, I was not thinking about him at all when I decided to risk using my artistic, rather than my scholarly, voice in this book. I had been discussing my frustration with the textbook genre, when my colleague Cynthia Baron recommended that I take another look at Richard Boleslavsky's 1933 *Acting: The First Six Lessons*. While his tone is unarguably outdated, his form suggested that I might be able to write Active

Analysis as a contemporary play, which would allow me to share not only the actor's creative process, but also the joy I take in the technique, which encourages me as a director and teacher to become as improvisatory as the actors with whom I work. In practicing Active Analysis, I bend my approach to the individual strengths, talents, and artistic desires of the actors within the ensemble.

Part II is modeled on the Studio that I conduct in Los Angeles as part of the Stanislavsky Institute for the 21st Century. The diversity of the membership mirrors the actors in my actual Studio, eleven of whom have generously permitted me to borrow their first names for my fictional characters: Louisa Abernathy (who initially founded the Studio as a network for professional actors), Setrak Borghosizian (who graduated from *Universidad Complutense de Madrid* and *Real Escuela Superior de Arte Dramático*, Spain), Keith Day (who does indeed fly in from Philadelphia to attend my Studio), Shari Greene Barrese (a former choreographer who worked in Japan), Anisha Jagannathan (a recent college graduate), Rose Leisner (whose invaluable assistance to me began when she signed on as my work-study student in college and has continued to work with me since her graduation), Grigor Panosyan and Sargis Panosyan (who did begin with improv and do compete in ballroom dancing), Hannah Pierce (as talented a dancer and musician as an actor), Juliana Sabo (whom I had first met as a student in my course on acting theories), and Geo Sityar Sargent (who brings a warm spirit of charity to the ensemble).

The content of the six lessons follows the curriculum I have developed in my intensive workshops, in particular those at the National Institute of Dramatic Arts (NIDA, Australia, 2009 and 2010), the Institute for Puerto Rican Culture at the Victoria Espinoza Theatre (San Juan, 2009), *MetodiFestival* (Italy, 2008 and 2011), and the National Academy for the Arts (KHIO, Norway from 2012 to 2016). I am deeply grateful to Joan Eyles Johnson, my Studio's actual resident playwright, for allowing me to use her play, *The Lie*, as the subject for Lesson 4, to publish it for the first time, and to include her as a character in this book's fictional conceit. Finally, the adaptations of Active Analysis to the work-a-day conditions of acting in Lesson 6 are those shared with me by working actors from my studio, and I am especially happy to quote the words of Louisa Abernathy, Liliana Carrillo, Tiffany Cole, and Teena Pugliese and ideas from Francesca Calvo, Caroline Sanchez, Natalie Peyser, and Bianca Dovarro.

As you will see in the lessons, I teach Active Analysis simply. I emphasize its dynamic principles and apply them to texts of various styles. In Russia there are a number of programs that involve detailed curricula that incorporate adaptations made to Active Analysis by leading directors to suit their own artistry and the Russian repertory system. I have found that such programs of study do not always travel across the borders of time and cultures as easily as do the underlying principles. Some readers, who might be familiar with these programs of study, may think my book simple, but I have found that the more I stress the basics the more flexible the technique becomes and the more complex and moving the performances that result. I take heart from Knebel's reminder that one should not confuse what is simple with what is simplistic (Chekhov 1995 vol. 2: 22). I hope that you enjoy reading this book as much I enjoyed writing it, and that you will find inspiration within it.

Part 1 The People behind the Legacy

"Whatever you want badly and believe in sincerely will come to pass." Handwritten by Stanislavsky on a photograph to Knebel that hung in her home (Liadov 1998: 80).

1 The Mystery on Leontyevsky Lane

A Gala Affair at the Moscow Art Theatre

October 27, 1928: Stanislavsky Speaks

The story of Active Analysis begins with the end of Konstantin Sergeyevich Stanislavsky's career as an actor in October 1928. During that month a whirlwind of events honored the Moscow Art Theatre on its thirtieth anniversary. He had co-founded the Moscow Art in 1897 as an amateur actor in his thirties with the prominent playwright, Vladimir Ivanovich Nemirovich-Danchenko, who headed Russia's only professional acting school. At Nemirovich-Danchenko's invitation, the two men met for dinner at the Slavyansky Bazaar, a popular restaurant in the center of Moscow. Their conversation ended at Stanislavsky's estate outside Moscow after eighteen hours of intense discussion during which they came up with a pragmatic plan for a new theatre, where they began by experimenting with realism on stage. Thirty years later, their company had reformed theatrical production, not only in Russia, but worldwide.

As the years passed, Stanislavsky had become increasingly dissatisfied with the company, which had continued to trade on its early reputation for realism. He wanted to experiment more widely with new dramas and new ways to understand acting. As early as 1904—the year in which their realist production of Chekhov's *The Cherry Orchard* had premiered—Stanislavsky was already eager to try something else. "My God," he recalled thinking, "are we stage artists doomed, because of our material bodies, to serve eternally and portray only crude realism?" (*SS* I 1988: 383). His need to experiment strained the relationship between him and his co-founder, with each man in turn supporting and judging the other.

At sixty-five, he could no longer tolerate drinking, eating, and talking all night long, as he had done thirty years ago at dinner with Nemirovich-Danchenko. Yet, night after night, the company's anniversary celebrations lasted until three in the morning. "Every day I had to raise my glass in a toast to someone else's health, and I couldn't refuse, even though I know wine is bad for me" (*Letopis'* IV 2003: 65). The gala was sapping all his strength. He worried most of all about the banquet for Soviet officials on October 27, where he was scheduled to deliver an official speech. "Speaking in public generally torments me," he recalled (*Letopis'* IV 2003: 65); but anxiety over this particular speech kept him from sleeping for two full nights. Stalin had just announced a radical Five-Year Plan to remake the country from a largely agrarian, illiterate society into a futuristic, industrialized state. This news meant that Stanislavsky also had to say how he would remake his formerly capitalistic theatre into a model for the future of Soviet art. "Somehow I had to make a speech without offending anyone" (*Letopis'* IV 2003: 65), and he feared that he might not find a properly tactful and politically correct tone.

He was "a child when it came to politics," or so said the one staunchly Bolshevik actor in his company (*Letopis'* III 2003: 65). Stanislavsky had greeted the destructive violence of the 1917 revolution with faith and mercy. For example, when the Bolsheviks vandalized Moscow's beautiful Maly Theatre because it symbolized Russia's royal past, Stanislavsky wrote to the company's administrators, advising forgiveness: "The savagery of people who have not been blessed with culture cannot insult us. If we are to be forces of enlightenment, we must be very wise, especially now, when people have gone wild with savagery. Try to answer all insults [...] with compassion and leniency" (*SS* VIII 1998: 473–4).

In facing the cataclysmic changes in his country, Stanislavsky tended to use art as his shield against ideology by insisting that he was an artist, not a politician. Thus, when New York journalists had accused him of playing politics in his selection of plays for the Moscow Art Theatre tours to the United States in 1923 and 1924, "as if we had brought *Tsar Fyodor* to show a weak tsar, *The Lower Depths* to show the strength of the proletariat, and Chekhov to illustrate the worthlessness of the intelligentsia and the bourgeoisie," Stanislavsky flatly denied the charge. "America merely wants to see what Europe already knows," he told them (*SS* VI 1994: 221–2). But by 1928, this shield no longer held. With Lenin's death in 1924, Stalin took iron-fisted charge of the state and its arts. Theatre critics now openly announced that "there is no more important, no higher purpose for all Soviet art than that ordained by the Bolshevik Party" (Simmons 1961: 5). The state had made clear that it viewed theatre primarily as a political platform, with Stanislavsky's long-held belief in acting as a spiritual endeavor becoming, at best, irrelevant and, at worst, a dangerous view. In the Soviet Union, politics and art had become one and the same. Like it or not, Stanislavsky had to speak the language of politics.

On the evening of October 27, 1928, after seemingly endless toasts to honor the country's most influential leaders, Stanislavsky finally rose to give his speech. He had carefully written and memorized his remarks, but he was visibly nervous as he spoke, sometimes losing his place, sometimes forgetting his lines, and sometimes feeling his voice go weak (*Letopis'* IV 2003: 61). He began well, praising Stalin's growing control over the arts as a positive force for change: "Without doubt, there is no government in the world that pays as much attention to theatre as ours, and so, I bow deeply to it for its attention, its continual concern, and its help" (*SS* VI 1994: 294). Other points also rang the right political bells. He thanked the government for creating "a cultural revolution" that was "putting theatre on the path to progress, which extends before us like a highway, beaten smooth by the feet of the workers" (*SS* VI 1994: 294). Soon, he predicted, "Soviet youth will take theatre forward and further develop the art" (*SS* VI 1994: 298).

But when he spoke about his company and his personal views on art, he began to lose his political footing:

> When the events of the revolution at first threw us—the old-timers, the actors of the Art Theatre—into a state of confusion, when we didn't fully understand what had happened, our government did not force us to change our color to revolutionary red, to remake ourselves into something that we were not. Yet little by little we came to understand our epoch, little by little we evolved, and with us, our art evolved too, normally and organically. If it had been otherwise, we could have produced nothing but hackwork. And we wanted with all our hearts not merely to wave red flags, but to look deeply into the revolutionary soul of our country.
>
> (*SS* VI 1994: 295)

Should he have admitted in public that the revolution had initially "confused" him and his actors? No, only whole-hearted enthusiasm was acceptable to this audience of politicos. Then too, his reference to Lenin's earlier policies toward the arts sounded too much like a veiled criticism of Stalin's forced march into the future. Moreover, by using the negative word, "hackwork," Stanislavsky seemed to criticize the quotas for production, recently imposed by Stalin's Five-Year Plan. The slur implied that speed and volume of work would now trump quality.

Even worse, Stanislavsky had dared to use the word "soul" despite the state's strict atheism and the recent ban on all religious rites and spiritual ideas. He should have known better than to remind his listeners of his abiding belief that "art creates the life of the human soul" (*SS* VI 1994: 297). After all, he knew that only three months earlier in July 1928, his talented protégé, Michael Chekhov, had fled the country to escape an arrest warrant that had been issued against him for his religious beliefs and his spiritualized theatrical practices (Chekhov 2005: 136).

As Stanislavsky continued with his speech, he dug a deeper and deeper hole for himself. Instead of praising the Soviet soldiers and workers, who began to attend his theatre after the revolution, he spoke of them as if they were school children, who needed to be taught by the artists:

> Theatre must not ingratiate itself to its spectators. No, it must lead spectators up the steps of a grand staircase. Art must open their eyes to the ideals created by our country's people. But the people's ideals exist in a chaotic state. The writer comes; the actor comes; they see these ideals clearly, clean them of anything superfluous, clothe them in artistic form, and serve them back to the people who created them. In this way, these ideals become more digestible, better understood.
>
> (*SS* VI 1994: 297)

Stanislavsky was sounding less like a forward-thinking communist and more like an elitist, who thought he knew better than his audiences precisely because he was holding on to the pre-revolutionary past. Artists, he said, "need the techniques, [...] passed down to us as traditions, created by the genius of our predecessors throughout the ages. [...] And so, we must above all strive to save these many traditions" (*SS* VI 1994: 297). This statement had surely offended his listeners, whose job had been to sweep away the old traditions by means of revolution. Finally, when Stanislavsky praised the wealthy capitalist, Sava Morozov, for investing in the Moscow Art Theatre during its early years (*SS* VI 1994: 297), Stanislavsky sealed his fate. On October 28 the press launched a vicious campaign against him, calling him a traitorous capitalist and a counter-revolutionary enemy of Soviet arts (Autant-Mathieu 2003: 73).

October 29, 1928: Stanislavsky Leaves the Stage

Despite the attacks, Stanislavsky still had one more official duty to perform on the 29th for his company's anniversary celebration; he had to reprise the role he had created as a young man, that of Lieutenant-Colonel Vershinin in Anton Chekhov's *Three* Sisters. The gala's full program consisted of excerpts from the theatre's thirty-year history. Most notable were scenes from the 1898 production of *Tsar Fyodor Ioannovich* to remind the audience of the

Moscow Art Theatre's innovations in stage realism; Act I from the 1901 *Three Sisters* as a showcase of Stanislavsky's reforms in acting; and selections from the 1927 dramatization of Vsevolod Ivanov's popular novel, *Armored Train 14-69*, primarily staged by Ilya Yakovlevich Sudakov, who was widely regarded as one of the best young directors in the company (*Letopis'* IV 2003: 64).[1] This last climactic excerpt demonstrated that, despite having been founded in Tsarist Russia, the Moscow Art Theatre was now supporting Soviet political art.

Stanislavsky's botched speech two nights ago had made performing his former role in *Three Sisters* no longer seem a good idea. First, the press had just called him a traitor to the revolution and accused him of being hopelessly stuck in Russia's Tsarist past; and now, when playing Aleksander Vershinin, Stanislavsky would have to wear a Tsarist military costume, as if visually confirming the journalists' accusations. Even worse, there was another Vershinin on the bill that night. The villain in *Armored Train 14-69*, Nikolay Vershinin, is an ignorant peasant who leads a guerilla attack against the Soviets. The program made it seem as if Vershinins stand on the wrong side of history. Second, Stanislavsky's subtle and poetic production of *Three Sisters*, when juxtaposed with Sudakov's starkly partisan approach to *Armored Train 14-69*, positioned Stanislavsky as old-fashioned and Sudakov as the face of the future.

How could Stanislavsky have been anything other than wary as he donned Vershinin's pre-revolutionary costume? Did he sit in his dressing room and think about the years that had brought him to this moment in time? His world after the revolution had been turned inside out. When the Bolshevik government had abolished capitalism and private property, he had lost everything: his family's factory that had made him rich by manufacturing gold thread for church vestments; his shares in the Moscow Art Theatre that had been founded as a share-holding company in capitalist Russia; his privately funded studios, where he had forged his now world-renowned System for actor training; and the home in which he had been born. Did he think of August 30, 1919, when he had been arrested and questioned for over fifteen hours by the secret police (*Letopis'* III 2003: 65)?

Did he remember 1920, when he and his family had faced eviction and the real possibility of crowding into a single room within a communally shared apartment? Faced with this personal crisis, he had found an unexpected advocate in Anatoly Vasilyevich Lunacharsky, a talented playwright, appointed by Lenin as the People's Commissar of Enlightenment and Education. Lunacharsky had long admired the Moscow Art Theatre and was distressed to learn that Stanislavsky, "one of the rarest men, both in the moral sphere and an incomparable artist," was about "to sell his last pair of trousers" to feed his family. Lunacharsky had begged Lenin to relent: "I want very much to alleviate his condition," because his ill treatment "will turn the cream of the intelligentsia against us in great disgust, may even create scandal in Europe" (*Letopis'* III 2003: 119). Thanks to Lunacharsky's efforts, Stanislavsky and his family were relocated to a house on Leontyevsky Lane with a number of rooms for their personal use and two large salons for Stanislavsky to use as studio and rehearsal space.[2] Such quarters were unheard of in post-revolutionary Russia. But, even Lunacharsky's support had limits, as in 1923, when the Soviet press lambasted Stanislavsky for forming unacceptable alliances with foreign capitalists while he was touring in the United States, and again in 1924, when he was branded a traitor for having attended a benefit in New York for Russian émigré artists who had fled the Soviet Union (Benedetti 1990: 252).

And what about the changes that the revolution had brought to his career? With the state insisting that all art serve as propaganda, the Soviet Union had slowly but steadily built a comprehensive system of agencies to control artists, with professional theatres like Stanislavsky's called to account for everything. They were now required to expand their audiences to include red army soldiers, factory workers, and peasants, most of whom were illiterate, had never before attended performances, and "came to [the theatre] without removing their hats" (*SS* VI 1994: 296). The actors were also required to spend their free time performing at workers' clubs, schools, union houses, and factories. Not only were they exhausted by the overload, but they found the conditions in these make-shift venues inadequate. As one of them joked, the dirt seemed to have been placed there "as if on purpose" to insult us and our art (Germanova n. d.: 116).

Fig. 1 Stanislavsky as Vershinin in Chekhov's *Three Sisters*, 1928. The Sharon Marie Carnicke Collection.

The level of censorship over plays and productions had inexorably intensified with the establishment in 1923 of the Central Repertory Committee. True Stanislavsky had always coped with some level of censorship. The Russian Tsars banned plays from production if they spoke against the crown or included dialogue that offended the royals' prudish sensibilities. Such censorship had even modified Chekhov's plays. But such strictures seemed mild in comparison to the new Soviet rules. Now theatres had to submit all scripts for clearance in advance of rehearsals. Then, once productions were set to open, censors would attend the dress rehearsals to assess their work. Under this new system, theatres often lost months of work and lots of money when the censors forbade a fully prepared production from opening (Carnicke 2014a: 249–64).

As Stanislavsky sat in his dressing room on October 29, he knew that his life was no longer entirely his own. The state owned the house on Leontyevsky Lane, where he and his family lived. He was no longer in charge of the theatre he had co-founded. He and his partner now followed state directives on budgets, salaries, audience development, the selection of plays, and the scheduling of performances at the theatre proper and in other venues throughout the city. In short, everything that touched his life and the life of the theatre he loved was now the government's business. Nonetheless, Stanislavsky took heart. Acting, not politics, was his proper medium and he was still in control of his acting. "I did not feel at all nervous," he later told a colleague. "Only my costume, which had gotten a bit tight over the years, bothered me. And I hadn't wanted it adjusted out of vanity. But that was nothing much" (*Letopis'* IV 2003: 65).

While waiting backstage for his entrance as Vershinin, wearing his too snug pre-revolutionary uniform for a role that represented his and his company's youth, he peeked around the curtain, but could barely recognize the theatre that had been his artistic home for thirty years. Its modest grays and browns had been painted over in garish white, gold, and red to mark the company's Soviet present. In the audience sat the state's leaders, who now made all the important decisions about his theatre and who had heard him speak two nights ago. The journalists who had accused him of being a traitor yesterday were there too. So too were the new Soviet spectators, whom he had called disrespectful. The curtain goes up.

> I enter, there's applause, I say my lines, and suddenly—I feel faint! I almost fell, but I pulled myself together, fought with myself and continued with the act. But when the blocking took me upstage—I remember it was upstage of the dining table—I sent word to my doctors. I knew that two were in the audience. Finally, we reached the end of the act. I took two curtain calls, and then … fell. I was carried out. The audience didn't notice anything. They were only surprised that I did not come back for more curtain calls.
>
> (*Letopis'* IV 2003: 65)

The volcano of political and personal stress that Stanislavsky had been sitting atop since the Bolshevik revolution had erupted in a major heart attack. No one watching seemed to know what had happened. Spectators saw "an attractive young man with gray hair," who seemed to have "shed the weight of years, as if the calendar had been turned back to 1901, when he had first played the role" (*Letopis'* IV 2003: 63). One of his doctors recalls that he had acted "remarkably well" (*Letopis'* IV 2003: 6). But from this moment on, nothing would ever be the same.

A Soviet Game of Bait and Switch: Recuperating Abroad

March 14, 1930: Stanislavsky's Shocking Premiere

Stanislavsky's life as an actor ended with his heart attack, but nothing could keep him from creative work for long. He would live for ten more years—writing about the System of acting to which he had devoted his career; teaching; and developing an innovative approach to rehearsals, now known as Active Analysis. However, his last years coincided with the reign of terror that Stalin launched upon the country and hampered Stanislavsky in ways that he could not have previously imagined.

His new life started with an extended leave from his theatrical duties. For a year and a half, he lived abroad to recover his health. He left Moscow on May 2, 1929, traveling with his wife and a doctor, employed for him by the state. He stayed in convalescent homes at Badenweiler in Germany (where Anton Chekhov had died) and Nice in France. All the while Stanislavsky received a salary in rubles and an additional stipend in foreign currency from the Soviet government for his medical expenses. One might well applaud the Soviets for generously supporting one of the country's most internationally prominent artists. Indeed, that was exactly what Stalin wanted the world to see. But this generosity masked ulterior motives. After the unexpected fiasco of Stanislavsky's speech for the Moscow Art Theatre's thirtieth anniversary, the government no longer trusted him to say or do what was expected of him. At the same time, he was too famous to disappear entirely from the public eye, as had so many other so-called enemies of the people who were summarily arrested, sent to labor camps, tortured, executed, and never heard from again. With Stanislavsky's health leave, the state found an elegant way to keep him out of the way, while still using his fame to brand Soviet theatre.

With Stanislavsky safely in Europe, 1929 unfolded as a "watershed year" for Soviet theatre (Leach and Borovsky 1999: 327). First, Stalin replaced the liberal Lunacharsky as Commissar of Enlightenment and Education with a former soldier, Andrey Bubnov, who gave orders to artists as if they were his troupes. Even Lenin's widow reported his militaristic tone as shockingly conservative (Leach and Borovsky 1999: 327). Stanislavsky now had to grovel to Bubnov, sometimes for favors as small as the extra thirteen francs in 1930 for medical expenses, dutifully writing, "I am sincerely touched by your kind treatment of me" (*Letopis'* IV 2003: 116).

Second, in September Stalin appointed a communist manager, Mikhail Geits, to run the Moscow Art Theatre. Stanislavsky initially welcomed the appointment, assuming that Geits would handle only administrative matters. "I am sick, and I cannot work as I once did," Stanislavsky told his friend, the actor Leonid Leonidov. "A good manager in such a position can offer the theatre a great deal of help. [… And surely Geits will] leave stage directing, aesthetics, repertory, literary choices, and generally the artistic and acting areas in the theatre alone" (*SS* IX 1999: 353–6).[3] Within a month, however, it had become clear that Geits considered Stanislavsky and his partner, Nemirovich-Danchenko, as irrelevant in their own company.

Geits first completely reorganized the management structure, dismissing in the process the company's head of operations, Nikolay Yegorov, an old man who had formerly served as accountant in the factory that Stanislavsky's family had owned and for whom Stanislavsky felt deep affection. Outraged by this dismissal, Stanislavsky lambasted Geits, calling his decision an unjustified "purge" (*SS* IX 1999: 373),[4] a word that echoed Stalin's treatment of anyone who countered his will. Geits next took firm control of all artistic matters, including the new production of *Othello* that Stanislavsky had begun before his heart attack and was continuing to prepare from his sick bed. This production meant a great deal to Stanislavsky. He had been drawn to *Othello* as a youth, when he watched the great Italian actor, Tomasso Salvini, portray the Moor while on tour to Moscow. As a passionate amateur in 1896, Stanislavsky had tried his hand at directing the play and acting the title role. Now as an old man, he found himself returning to *Othello*. He was using it as a primary touchstone for his book on acting by describing how his semi-autobiographical younger self, Kostya, prepared the title role through a humorous process of trial and error (*SS* II 1989: chapter 1).

Stanislavsky also believed that a new production of *Othello* could reinvigorate the Moscow Art Theatre. On the one hand, he felt that the play captured the present era, when villains and heroes could so easily be mistaken for one another. He envisioned the Moor (perhaps like himself) as vainly attempting to bring justice to a world fashioned by the double-dealing Iago, who slanders the innocents (much like the Soviet bureaucrats who were taking over his theatre) (Ignatieva 1998: 1–10). On the other hand, because the play is a classic, he felt that a new staging of it could bring renewed international attention to the company. "Classic plays can uniquely serve as *model productions*, [...] especially the plays of Shakespeare, to demonstrate our theatre's reputation to foreigners" (*SS* IX 1999: 408).

When Geits took charge of the project, Stanislavsky was in the process of writing a detailed promptbook for the production with full interpretations of the characters, sketches for the sets, and hand-drawn diagrams to show the actors' blocking (Stanislavskii 1943).[5] As he carefully worked through the play, he sent his notes for each act back to Moscow for use in rehearsals, just as he had done three decades earlier in preparation for the company's renowned production of *The Seagull*. But, while Nemirovich-Danchenko had awaited each act eagerly in 1897, Geits found Stanislavsky's process far too slow. Geits needed to step up the pace of production in order to meet the quotas set for the theatre by Stalin's Five-Year Plan and thus turned rehearsals of *Othello* over to a brigade of directors headed by Sudakov, who had proven himself with *Armored Train 14-69* and was always willing to do what was needed. Unlike Nemirovich-Danchenko with *The Seagull*, Sudakov neither waited for Stanislavsky's notes to arrive, nor felt the obligation to follow his plan, especially when it implied criticism of the Soviet regime. Sudakov worked fast and dutifully followed Geits' orders. When Stanislavsky heard about the rehearsals, he wrote to his secretary, calling Sudakov's approach to the play "illiterate." "I took up *Othello* precisely to correct this sort of illiteracy" (*SS* IX 1999: 408).

Othello opened on March 14, 1930, without Stanislavsky's knowledge and after he had completed notes for only three of the play's five acts. Yet, Geits retained Stanislavsky's name as the production's primary director in the program and all the publicity. When Stanislavsky learned of the premiere, he exploded in anger and shame. "I am appalled!" he confided to his secretary. "What has this to do with Stanislavsky's staging? I blush for myself, when I think of it. Can't my name somehow be unobtrusively removed from the posters?" (*SS* IX 1999: 408).

As if fate had taken Stanislavsky's side, the hurried production failed so miserably that it was performed only ten times. Leonidov as Othello had begun to experience uncontrollable stage fright, clinging to the furniture to get him through each act. Then, the production's Iago tragically died when he fell from a window while visiting guests (Smeliansky et al. 1998 vol. 2: 157). Nonetheless, neither Stanislavsky's privately expressed anger, nor the production's public failure could change the fact that Stanislavsky's name had become more important to the Soviet government than his actual work.

Stanislavsky suffered Geits for three long years, until he could tolerate him no more. In 1932, Stanislavsky filed an official complaint with Stalin asking for the removal of the "Red Manager." In an appeal that he had labored over for nearly a year, Stanislavsky argued that political advisors in theatres "force us to give the audience potboilers and they imagine that in such a way we can educate the new spectator. But, that's not true" (*SS* VI 1994: 348). Such an approach to production slowly but surely erodes theatrical art. He predicted the demise of his beloved company. "I do not say that the Art Theatre has already been destroyed and that there are no means by which to resurrect it, but I do say that it is on the eve of catastrophe. [...] My child is perishing" (*SS* VI 1994: 344). He then asked for Stalin's trust by pointedly reminding him that "I decided to give my strength to my country and stay to take part in its new structuring" (*SS* VI 1994: 344) rather than defecting while abroad, as so many other Russian artists had. Such loyalty, Stanislavsky implies, deserves respect. He ends by suggesting that the Moscow Art Theatre report directly to the government instead of to a low-level administrator like Geits, mistakenly assuming that the more powerful the person-age, the more clear-headed the understanding of art. Stalin answered by granting the old man a pyrrhic victory. From 1932 forward, the theatre was required to report to the Central Executive Committee of the Communist Party, which meant that Stalin himself personally approved both the selection of plays and their productions (Smeliansky 1991: 7–13).[6]

Othello's premiere in 1930 signaled the government's new approach to handling Stanislavsky. He was granted generous medical leaves to keep him at a distance from Moscow, while his name was used without his permission to brand Soviet theatre initiatives. This pattern would repeat with small variations until the end of his life in 1938. Thus, a huge gap had opened up between his private despair and the public accolades accorded to him. While the state forbade ordinary Soviet citizens to travel abroad for fear that they might emigrate, it funded two more rest cures to Europe for Stanislavsky, one in 1932 from July 5 to November 17 and another from July 30, 1933, to August 4, 1934, during which signifi-cant theatrical events and initiatives continued to unfold in Moscow.

Despite visits from celebrities (such as Stella Adler, who sought him out in Nice in 1934) and working sessions with his American translator (Elizabeth Reynolds Hapgood, the wife of the prestigious theatre critic Norman Hapgood), Stanislavsky felt marginalized and unable to influence developments in his home country. The events that transpired in Moscow during the second of these two trips hit him especially hard.

Following the disastrous premiere of *Othello*, Stanislavsky decided to turn his full atten-tion to the completion of his book, a project with which he had been struggling for at least half his life. As early as 1899, he had identified the need for an actor's "grammar." In 1904, he had a preliminary draft, but two years later he completely rethought the project. In 1908, he reorganized his massive accumulation of notes into discrete topics in preparation for a more extended manual on acting. In 1909, with his System already in use as a rehearsal technique, he put down on paper some of its now most famous terms like "magic if." During 1910, he generated dozens of new drafts and potential titles, ultimately rejecting all of it. He

Fig. 2 Stanislavsky, *c.* 1934. The Sharon Marie Carnicke Collection.

produced yet another version during his US tours, but abandoned that effort, too, when his American publishers insisted on an autobiography, because they felt it would garner a wider readership.[7]

In order to move forward with the book he most wanted to write, he had to confront the fact that, in order to capture in words what he knew in his bones about acting, he needed a new writing strategy. Moreover, this strategy had to cope with the fact that his constant experimentation had made his subject a moving target. By 1923 he hit upon a solution that would cleverly meet both difficulties. He jettisoned the idea of writing a tract about acting and determined instead to write "the System in a novel" (*SS* IX 1999: 99). By creating a fiction-alized course, he could best mirror acting's most evanescent dimensions and minimize the need for neat theory expressed in expository prose. Moreover, the fictional characters who people his novel would allow him to bring in contrasting perspectives on acting and to give multiple examples and restatements of each of his ideas, thus maintaining the nuanced complexity of the art that he so loved. In short, by writing a novel he could portray, rather than explain, his practice and directly convey the experience of an actor learning how to act. Things now seemed to be moving in the right direction. Even his Russian editor found this new "half-fictional form [...] very well suited to its content" (Dybovskii 1992: 110).

While abroad on medical leave, Stanislavsky had enough time on his hands to make real progress with his book. He was writing feverishly during the summer of 1934, when he unexpectedly learned about the publication in Moscow of a new book, *The Stanislavsky System*, authored by none other than Sudakov! He shared his reaction in a letter to his secretary:

> All day long I walked around feeling like I had been hit in the head with a cane. It's not my authorial vanity that's hurt, but rather the fact that my most beloved creation—what I gave my whole life for—has been cynically raped and launched into the world in such a maimed fashion for the judgement of the crowd. Now they will sling mud at that which is so dear to me, because, given the maiming of my creation, it deserves nothing less.
>
> (*SS* IX 1999: 560)

Sudakov had again done what was needed, getting Stanislavsky's teachings down in writing faster than could Stanislavsky, and without his knowledge or permission.

The New Normal: Internal Exile

November 3, 1930: At Home

When Stanislavsky returned from his first medical leave to the house on Leontyevsky Lane on November 3, 1930, he was applauded by the public as a great man of the theatre and honored by his country as a model artist. He brought with him a suitcase filled with a fat typescript of his book, already so long that he would eventually split it into two parts for publication. At home, he eagerly took up his work again. He continued to write, ending with sufficient drafts for yet a third volume. He also turned his large salon into a rehearsal hall, where he could work with actors from the Moscow Art Theatre on roles that they were preparing for productions. As time went on, he invited young actors and protégés to study with him there as he continued to experiment with acting, rehearsing and direct-ing. All seemed placid on the surface, but in his heart of hearts he must have known that the Soviets would continue to make whatever use of his name and work that they wished.

The 1930s brought unimaginable hardships to his country. Ordinary Soviet citizens endured harsh privations. Whole families lived in single rooms and cooked on portable stoves in communal apartments that the government now owned and requisitioned for use. Electricity and hot water were unreliable. People stood in long lines with ration coupons to buy the bare essentials of life, only to find that, when their turn came, supplies were sold out. Yet Stanislavsky remained comfortable, ate healthy food, and was tended round the clock by medical personnel. He was even allowed to keep the private automobile that the German director Max Reinhardt had given to him as a gift in 1928. Such a vehicle was a luxury, reserved only for the highest-ranking members of the communist party. The government also lavished him with awards: the U.S.S.R. Order of the Workers' Red Flag in 1933, the newly established title of People's Artist of the U.S.S.R. in 1936, and the Order of Lenin in 1937. On his last birthday in 1938, Stalin created five Stanislavsky Fellowships for student actors. But these luxuries and honors ironically isolated him from the world and muted his voice. This was his new normal.

From time to time, he was sent to a nearby convalescent home in the country, where, so it was said, he could enjoy the fresh air. These visits were usually timed to coincide with major theatrical events in Moscow, such as the annual All-Republic Theatre Olympiad, a festival established by Bubnov in 1930 to advertise Soviet theatrical achievements to the world (*Istoriia sovetskogo dramaticheskogo teatra* 1967 vol. 3: 30). While journalists and theatrical notables from across the globe flooded into Moscow, the country's most internationally known theatre figure was nowhere to be found. As Stanislavsky explained when Hapgood asked about visiting him, "I am usually locked up in my rooms or somewhere outside the city in a convalescent home [...] with strict rules on visits." Come if you would like to see theatrical productions, he effectively told her, but don't plan on seeing me (*SS* IX 1999: 671–2).

Stanislavsky had led a busy life before his heart attack. In spring 1928 Stanislavsky's typical day took him from the theatre to various rehearsal halls and to his office. He juggled acting, directing, and administration in a single day.

> What can I tell you about my life? From 10 in the morning to 12:30 I am busy at my Opera Studio. From 1 in the afternoon until 5 I rehearse at the Art Theatre; from 5 to 7 I handle routine business; from 7 to 8:30 I have dinner and rest; from 9 to 11 more rehearsals; and from 11 to 1 or 2 in the morning more routine business. As you can see, life is difficult. And so it goes from day to day with only a month a year to rest and recuperate.
>
> (*SS* IX 1999: 310)[8]

After his first recuperative trip abroad, his days on Leontyevsky Lane fell into a nearly unvarying routine of sleeping, eating, writing, and rehearsing. This schedule was enforced by a live-in nurse, Lyubov Dmitryevna Dukhovskaya, hired in October 1930 to regulate his daily activities and to sleep nearby so that she could hear him during the night. Her care was so continuous that she took only a week's leave in 1935 when her mother lay dying (*SS* IX 1999: 618). Every day Dukhovskaya woke him at eleven in the morning, brought him breakfast, and read to him from his mail and the state-sanctioned newspaper *Pravda*,[9] discreetly skipping anything that was deemed unfit for his ears. In keeping unacceptable news from him, she found an ally in Stanislavsky's wife, the actress Maria Petrovna Lilina, who had noticed that, when he was ill with typhus fever in 1910, theatrical reviews agitated him so much that she feared for his recovery. She had newspapers kept from him then, and now approved of doing so again in hopes of hastening his recovery (Ignatieva 2008a: 52). His day's routine continued at half past noon, when Dukhovskaya took him to his salon for rehearsals or visits with special guests. At eight in the evening, he napped and then dined alone in his bedroom. At half past nine she would take him back to the salon for time with his family. Finally, at midnight, Dukhovskaya would tuck him into bed, where he would work on his book until he fell asleep (Gurevich 1948: 527–30).

Late March 1932: The Old Man's Tears

At first Stanislavsky took the state's proffered generosity at face value. His heart attack had left him ill and frightened of every draft and sniffle. He became "a disciplined and obedient patient," relying upon doctor's orders as if they were law. "Whenever I prescribed a medication," said his doctor, "he would ask about how it worked and would then take it exactly as directed. Whenever he was allowed to stand and walk after a spell of being bedridden, his first question was always: 'How many steps can I take a day?' And after being given a number, you could see him counting as he walked about the room" (Gurevich 1948: 512).

Stanislavsky's fear for his health made it easy for his doctors and nurse to function as his warders, monitoring more than his physical condition for the state. However, he soon began to sense that all was not as it seemed. As early as 1929 during his stay abroad, he had filed an official complaint with the government, calling his health leave an "exile" (*SS* IX 1999: 333). He begged to be sent home: "I know that you do not consider me a flight risk or think I'm feigning my illness, and so please understand my worries and concerns about my theatre. […] Every day, every hour I think of Moscow […]. How I long to sit healthily in the director's chair!" (*SS* IX 1999: 366; 367). During his first stay abroad, he desperately tried to convince his doctor that returning to theatrical practice would be salubrious for him. "Denying me my work only makes me feel worse," he insisted (*SS* IX 1999: 366). And, truly, once back home, his nurse noticed that whenever he worked with actors "color came into his face and he became handsome again" (Gurevich 1948: 528).

As time passed and more constraints shaped his daily life, his suspicions became sureties. "I know little about what is happening now at the Art Theatre. Apparently, they hide it from me. A bad sign," he told a fellow actor (*SS* IX 1999: 584). "I feel insulted that important decisions are made without consulting me," he confided to a trusted friend (*SS* IX 1999: 554). At times, he even let those who kept things from him know that he knew. For example, on June 18, 1936, his friend, the playwright Maksim Gorky, died at the untimely age of sixty-eight. The next morning, when Stanislavsky's nurse brought him his breakfast, but no newspaper, he pointedly asked, "My dear, have you heard anything of Gorky?" "No, Konstantin Sergeyevich," she responded. He persisted. "There's nothing in the newspapers?" She said nothing. Then, after a long pause, he asked again, "Haven't the newspapers come yet?" "No, not yet," she said. Seeing through her lie, he concluded, "Well, then that's that. Gorky has died" (Gurevich 1948: 540).[10]

As surely as he knew that his name was being used without his permission, he also came to know that his words were being actively censored and distorted to suit Soviet policies. By 1932, he bluntly told his American translator that a visit to Moscow to work with him on his book no longer made any sense: "Now, no one is allowed in to see me and this is a new constraint" (*SS* IX 1999: 475). He also told her that he could not yet deliver a complete typescript because "all our work according to the laws of my country must now be checked for its compliance with dialectical materialism; this is compulsory for all" (*SS* IX 1999: 475). He soon became so fearful of losing control over his evolving book that he began to carry all the heavy drafts with him in a small suitcase whenever he moved from room to room within his home.

With greater awareness of his situation came greater despair. In late March 1932, Stanislavsky unexpectedly called a meeting of key members of the Moscow Art Theatre.

One of the company's youngest actors, Vasily Orlov, attended and left a poignant memoir, which describes Stanislavsky as lying saint-like in his bed, "his big head surrounded with a halo of gray hair that spread out on the pillow" (*Letopis'* IV 2003: 192), a literal icon of theatre. But he behaved as a mere mortal, beginning the meeting with an ironic joke: "If the head of the factory cannot go to the factory, then the factory must come to the head" (*Letopis'* IV 2003: 192). His quip refers simultaneously to his capitalist past as the actual manager of his family's thread-making factory and to the present treatment of theatres as factories of art under Stalin's Five-Year Plan. Then he fell silent for a long time. "No words can convey what hung in the air," Orlov remembers (*Letopis'* IV 2003: 192). Finally, Stanislavsky spoke. "I have given my life to you, my theatre! ... I am ill, and you are now destroying my life's work." After these few halting words, he "suddenly burst into tears, crying like an aggrieved child, bitterly sobbing. Tears ran down his wrinkled cheeks. Helplessly he blinked his eyes, his head sinking deeper into the pillow" (*Letopis'* IV 2003: 193).

1934–1938: Internal Exile

Stanislavsky was effectively locked within his own home, and the Soviet game had changed from one of bait and switch to one of strict confinement. From 1930 to 1934, he had occasionally gone out to public places and these excursions had made news. For example, when he attended a rehearsal at the Moscow Art Theatre on September 15, 1931, after an absence of three years, his visit was widely reported by the press (*Letopis'* IV 2003: 161). By 1934, however, there were no longer such excursions and he became a permanent shut-in, only occasionally going for a drive around Moscow, accompanied by a loyal Soviet, or spending some months in a convalescent home outside Moscow. He no longer set foot in any public theatre. He now made news, not by going out, but by being photographed in his salon with prominent visitors.[11] The press reported that illness and old age were to blame for his confinement. After all, he had an enlarged heart and his health was indeed fragile. It made sense to think of him as hermetically sealed away from the weather in order to protect his frail body. However, some who knew him thought that perhaps Soviet reality had simply become too much and that he had voluntarily walled himself up in his rooms to escape.[12] After all, unprecedented terror had taken hold outside his walls.

Stalin was purging the country of all opposition, whether real or imaginary. Massive numbers of people deemed "enemies of the people" were arrested, tortured, imprisoned, and executed in Stalin's labor camps. No one was immune. Highly placed communist and military officials fell alongside prominent artists, scientists, university professors, and ordinary citizens. Arrests occurred anywhere and everywhere by operatives in all sorts of disguises. The novelist Aleksander Solzhenitsyn conjures the horror of the times:

> They take you aside in a factory corridor ... and you are arrested. They take you from a military hospital with a temperature of 102 ... They take you right off the operating table ... In the grocery store ... You are invited to the special-order department and arrested there. You are arrested by a religious pilgrim whom you have put up for the night 'for the sake of Christ.' You are arrested by the meter man ... You are arrested by a bicyclist who has run into you on the street, by a railway conductor, a taxi driver, a savings bank teller, the manager of a movie theatre.
>
> (Solzhenitsyn 1973 vol. 1: 10)

This terror also engulfed Stanislavsky's family in June 1930, when his nephew and his nephew's wife and sister-in-law were arrested. Stanislavsky learned of their arrests only when he returned from abroad in November. He immediately pleaded for their release. "I know them like I know myself. I am certain that they cannot be guilty of any crime. A tragic misunderstanding must have occurred" (SS IX 1999: 436).[13] His letter went unanswered. Then in January 1931, when his nephew's teenage children told him that new tenants had moved into their parents' vacant room, Stanislavsky understood that his relatives had in fact been convicted. He now begged the government to "soften" the terms of their imprisonment by allowing husband and wife to remain together and permitting their children to take possession of their parents' goods (SS IX 1999: 448). In April, Stanislavsky again pleaded on their behalf, this time writing directly to the Party's Central Committee (SS IX 1999: 454). But this letter arrived too late; his nephew had already died in prison of pneumonia. Stanislavsky could now do no more than request that the children be permitted to remain in Moscow to complete their schooling (SS IX 1999: 454). A year later, Stanislavsky again intervened on behalf of his nephew's son, when the young man was denied entry into the Electrical Engineering Institute, because his father had been convicted as an enemy of the state (SS IX 1999: 479). In 1933 he begged for his granddaughter, who had been expelled from the Foreign Language Institute where she was studying English simply because she came from a family of pre-revolutionary factory owners (SS IX 1999: 511).

Neither frail health, nor a desire to escape reality can fully account for Stanislavsky's new house-bound condition. The truth lay elsewhere. Despite his political gaffes and pre-revolutionary, capitalist past, he had earned worldwide fame, which protected him from arrest and execution. His disappearance would be noticed by the international press and thus threaten to expose Stalin's nefarious methods. Stalin therefore handled Stanislavsky differently than other Russians, according to a plan that guaranteed the "isolation and preservation" by house arrest of untrustworthy citizens with high visibility (Smeliansky 1991: 9). If Stanislavsky had not won acclaim and influence throughout Europe and the United States, his fate may well have mirrored that of his younger protégé, Vsevolod Emilyevich Meyerhold, whose story makes the high stakes for artists in these terrible times vividly clear.

As a founding actor of the Moscow Art Theatre, Meyerhold had played Treplev, the young playwright who searches for new theatrical forms in Chekhov's The Seagull. The role eerily predicted Meyerhold's future career. By the 1920s Meyerhold had become a prestigious director, known for his innovative non-realist work with constructivism in production and biomechanics in acting. By the 1930s his radically experimental art marked him as an artist who flew in the face of the Soviet call for socialist realism. Unlike Stanislavsky, however, Meyerhold remained a local artist, primarily known to Russian and Soviet audiences and only to the few foreigners who ventured to the Soviet Union to see theatre.[14]

While theatre scholars have tended to place the two directors at opposite aesthetic poles, with Stanislavsky representing realism and Meyerhold as realism's staunch critic, the truth was more complex. The two men admired and supported each other's work. While Meyerhold criticized productions at the Moscow Art Theatre, he praised Stanislavsky as "a genius of theatricality," committed to persistent experimentation in art. In a journal article from 1921 Meyerhold compassionately reports that Stanislavsky's innovative interests sadly marginalized him in his own company (Radischeva 1999: 78–9). Stanislavsky, in turn, sought collaboration with the younger man. As early as 1905, Stanislavsky had set up a studio for

Meyerhold to stage symbolist plays (Listengarten 2014: 67–81). In 1935 the elder director told a colleague that, in contrast with other theatricalist directors at the time, "Meyerhold is talented, even when he errs" (*Letopis'* IV 2003: 332).

In 1938 Stanislavsky invited Meyerhold to direct a production of Verdi's opera, *Rigoletto* for the Stanislavsky Opera Theatre with rehearsals set to take place on Leontyevsky Lane. The invitation shocked everyone in Moscow's theatrical circle, because Meyerhold had by that time come under fierce attack by the Soviet regime for his aesthetic views. His theatre had been forcibly closed and people literally crossed the street to avoid greeting him for fear that an association with him would mean their own arrests. In short, he was a doomed man. By offering him a job, Stanislavsky effectively used his own high profile to protect the younger man. And Meyerhold clearly understood Stanislavsky's brave generosity. "My dear teacher," Meyerhold writes, "my feelings are such that expressing them with a pen fades and kills them. How can I tell you that I love you?!" (*Letopis'* IV 2003: 421) With Stanislavsky's death, however, this protection ceased.

On June 19, 1939, Meyerhold was arrested, tortured into confessing his artistic sins, and sent to a labor camp where he was executed in February 1940. His family suffered too. On July 14, 1939, his wife, who was the leading actress in his theatre, Zinaida Raikh, was brutally murdered, when two thugs broke into their apartment. They stabbed her repeatedly, leaving blood all over the walls. Days later, Raikh's adult children were ordered to vacate the apartment. Their housemaid, who had also been beaten during the apartment's break-in, was arrested and questioned. While Raikh's murder is still officially deemed a burglary, it is widely thought that the government had arranged it to punish Meyerhold's family for his betrayal of Soviet art (Braun 1995: 302–3).

By contrast with Stanislavsky, whose portrait was retouched but retained in Soviet theatre history, Meyerhold's image was literally erased from Soviet books and historically important photographs. Records about his last work on *Rigoletto* for Stanislavsky's studio also disappeared.

August 8, 1934: The Walls Have Ears

Nothing seemed to make sense anymore in the Soviet Union. The country's laws were so arbitrarily invoked and dismissed under Stalin that those who were accused of being "enemies of the people" could neither protect nor defend themselves. In desperation, citizens began spying upon one another, informing on their friends and neighbors in order to prove their loyalty by denouncing others. For example, Pavlik Morozov, a fourteen-year-old peasant boy who denounced his father for objecting to the state's confiscation of their family farm, was praised for betraying his family and glorified as a Soviet hero (Kort 2010: 225).

Absurd too was the life of confinement that Stanislavsky led on Leontyevsky Lane during the 1930s. As he helplessly faced the fact that his life's work was being tailored to support Soviet policies on art, he also came to realize, slowly but surely, that the walls around him had grown ears. Virtually nothing he said could be considered private. It was one thing to have his nurse and doctors spying upon him. After all, they were state employees. It was quite another thing to admit to himself that some of the actors, whom he had once so freely invited to his home, could no longer be trusted.

The atmosphere of spying and paranoia that surrounded Stanislavsky in his last years is dramatically captured in transcripts of his conversations with Boris Vulfovich Zon, a director from St. Petersburg (then called "Leningrad") who periodically visited Stanislavsky from 1933 to 1938 to observe rehearsals and learn about his latest ideas. Zon initially noticed Stanislavsky's discomfort in speaking about his use of Yoga, a spiritual practice that had been banned under Stalinism. During an opera rehearsal in 1933, Stanislavsky discussed how the radiation of vital energy, called *prana* in Yoga, serves as a vehicle for communication. He believed that rays of energy, better than language, can establish true communion among actors and their partners and audiences. "Reach your hand out to Olga," he coaches a singer. "Completely. So that your hand calls to her, so that it radiates the call" (Durylin and Markov 1955: 445). Stanislavsky then tells Zon that "earlier we naively called this *prana*" (Durylin and Markov 1955: 445). By simultaneously naming and dismissing the yogic term as naïve, Stanislavsky clued Zon into its importance to the System, while staving off potential criticism.

Following the rehearsal, when Zon asks for more information about *prana*, Stanislavsky responds with similar ambivalence. On the one hand, he eagerly demonstrates how energy can travel through his arm like "mercury," citing the recurrent image for *prana* used in the books by Yogi Ramacharaka that Stanislavsky owned and studied. "Now all my energy is in my shoulder! Now further down in my elbow! My wrist! In the hand! The fingers! And now it reverses direction!" (Durylin and Markov 1955: 446).[15] On the other hand, Stanislavsky makes light of "radiation," dismissing it as a shorthand term "in our actors' jargon for a distinctive kind of gymnastics" (Durylin and Markov 1955: 446). By referring to gymnastics he aligns Yoga with the physical, hence materialist, thinking demanded of everyone by the Communist Party. In both the rehearsal and conversation that followed Stanislavsky uses the same tactics in speaking of Yoga that he would later use in his writings to sidestep censorship: he confesses to a youthful idealism that he has presumably outgrown in order to include unacceptable sources and spiritual terms. He then uses Marxist materialist terms to describe ideas that are anything but that. In short, in 1933 Stanislavsky was already engaged in self-censorship (Carnicke 2009: 104–9).

In other meetings with Stanislavsky, Zon found it even more disturbing when they were unexpectedly interrupted by the actor and director, Mikhail Nikolayevich Kedrov. On the surface Stanislavsky treated Kedrov as a young protégé, who had joined the Moscow Art Theatre in 1924 as a member of its new generation of actors and who had garnered public attention in 1927 by playing a Chinese communist partisan in *Armored Train 14-69*. When Stanislavsky began to invite actors for coaching to Leontyevsky Lane, Kedrov was among them. He first visited in 1931 to rehearse the role of an eccentric and greedy landowner for the company's dramatic adaptation of Gogol's satiric novel, *Dead Souls*. In 1932 Kedrov received his first Moscow Art Theatre directing assignment, *Out among the People*, a play adapted from Gorky's short stories. Thus, Kedrov initially won Stanislavsky's trust as "a very talented person, a good actor" and overall "an able young artist" (*SS* IX 1999: 539; 657). By 1934 Stanislavsky thought of Kedrov as "my closest assistant in terms of the artistic part of building my System" (*SS* IX 1999: 611).

But Zon also detected an unsettling subtext, whenever Kedrov entered the room. Over time, the younger man had become an increasingly constant presence on Leontyevsky Lane. At first, he seemed merely eager to learn his craft by attending any and all rehearsals in

Fig. 3 Stanislavsky rehearses *Tartuffe* on Leontyevsky Lane, *c.* 1935. To his left sits Kedrov, whose face is partially obscured. The Sharon Marie Carnicke Collection.

Stanislavsky's salon. Soon, Kedrov was meeting regularly with Stanislavsky to discuss drafts of his acting manuals, offering alternative and politically correct terms for spiritually inflected elements in the System and suggesting deletions of passages about styles other than realism. In short, by 1934 Kedrov was actively reshaping Stanislavsky's books to conform to Soviet expectations. In 1936 Stanislavsky made Kedrov an assistant and cast him in the role of religious hypocrite for a planned production of Molière's *Tartuffe*. Photographs from the mid-1930s almost invariably show Kedrov seated at Stanislavsky's elbow, eyes turned toward the old man and looking like his artistic heir apparent. The relationship between the two might have been genuine, but Kedrov may also have been playing the role of a hypocrite in real life.

In the 1930s the government had identified Kedrov as "an excellent and talented follower of Stanislavsky's System and directorial methods" (*Letopis'* IV 2003: 262). Such a fellow, if invited frequently to Leontyevsky Lane, might be called upon to do the state some service.

In fact, Kedrov's specific intrusions into Zon's conversations with Stanislavsky suggest that Kedrov was indeed functioning as a Soviet watchdog. For example, during a visit in 1934, when Zon again raises the topic of "radiation," Kedrov unexpectedly enters the room, arriving early, so he says, for an appointment to review drafts of Stanislavsky's book (Durylin and Markov 1955: 466–7). Was Kedrov listening at the door so that he could enter when the conversation became unacceptable? Probably so. And was Kedrov's appointment part of the ongoing censorship of Stanislavsky's publications? No doubt. Moreover, Zon notices that with Kedrov's arrival Stanislavsky seems rattled. In fact, during this period, whenever Stanislavsky turned to things that most mattered to him, "he speaks too loudly and strongly, as if he were trying to destroy an invisible enemy" (Durylin and Markov 1955: 445). At another meeting Stanislavsky invites Zon to take a ride in his automobile, presumably to give them some time alone to converse more freely. But when Kedrov joins them, Zon realizes that no such private conversation could take place (Durylin and Markov 1955: 468).

When Zon last mentions Kedrov, he again enters the room at an especially critical moment. It is August 8, 1934, and Stanislavsky has just learned that the Soviet Congress of Writers has adopted socialist realism as its sole and official artistic style. He responds by musing that the "main task of the Soviet writer should be to show the soul of the new people." But Kedrov objects, explicitly voicing communist ideology: "The soul is a figure of speech." Stanislavsky will not concede the point. He pushes back against Kedrov in precisely the same way that he will soon do with the censors of his books. "Think up an equivalent word," he dares the young man, "and I will happily use it." But Kedrov could not (Durylin and Markov 1955: 468),[16] nor could the censors of Stanislavsky's books, when he later demanded the same of them. To this day, the word "soul" appears on nearly every page of his otherwise heavily censored books.[17]

By tracing the changes in their conversations over time Zon demonstrates how Kedrov's role in censoring Stanislavsky had escalated. In 1933, Stanislavsky had expressed fear that his books would not accurately convey how "my new method is a development of what has come before." He begged Zon "in complete seriousness" to "tell actors, tell students …. Please …. Tell them, explain to them, try without fail, and then tell me what comes of it. This is for me terribly important" (Durylin and Markov 1955: 453–4). By 1934, however, when Zon tries to turn their conversation back to the dangers of misinterpretation, Stanislavsky refuses to engage with the topic. Instead, he skirts the issue and "point[s] to Kedrov who was standing to the side," saying, "it is the work of the young to elucidate everything" (Durylin and Markov 1955: 471). In this gesture, the effects of confinement and censorship are palpable.

The System for the Cause: The Opera-Dramatic Studio

September 1, 1934: An Enemy Calls

For all Stanislavsky's international fame, he was, like all Soviet citizens, put to work in the construction of the state. For many years, the noted theatrical critic, Pavel Ivanovich Novitsky, had persistently attacked Stanislavsky's work as "too spiritual," "too subjective," "antiproletarian," and "antirevolutionary." But on September 1, 1934, Novitsky unexpectedly visited Leontyevsky Lane (*Letopis'* IV 2003: 271). Stanislavsky was, to say the least, surprised:

[Novitsky] was always the meanest of my enemies, an incurable opponent of my so-called system. And now, he says, he had previously thought 'a bit too superficially' about it. And more recently, he says, [...] he looked more deeply into the question and found value in the System ... Then he went into ecstasies about it.

(*SS* IX 1999: 605)

At last Novitsky admitted that he had come on behalf of the Committee on Enlightenment and Education—*Narkompros* in Russian—"to ask me to build a school to educate new cadres of theatre workers, [and] this school must be the model for the whole Soviet Union." Stanislavsky thought with uncharacteristic cynicism that "someone must have ordered something!" (*SS* IX 1999: 605).

Clearly, Stalin had finally decided what labor to demand of Stanislavsky in his prison house. He was being conscripted in the creation of a vast web of free educational institutions under the first Five-Year Plan. As Stalin put it:

There are no grounds for believing that the working class of the U.S.S.R. can manage without its own [...] intelligentsia. The Soviet government has taken this fact into account and has opened wide the doors of all the higher educational institutions in every branch of the national economy to members of the working class and laboring peasantry.

(Sakwa 1999: 189)[18]

Novitsky was probably chosen to convey the news because he knew precisely how Stanislavsky's private beliefs would need to change for the cause.

The idea for a national academy of theatre had been brewing for some time. In 1931, Gorky had raised the idea with Stanislavsky. That same year, Stalin positioned the Moscow Art Theatre to house such a school when he transferred its management from Geits to the Communist Party's Central Committee.[19] In 1932, the Committee had tested the idea by offering a pilot course on the Stanislavsky System taught by Sudakov. Stanislavsky "dispiritedly" interpreted this move as just another of the "many slaps hitting me. [...] Soon, we'll have the Sudakov Academy!" (*SS* IX 1999: 503). When Stanislavsky demanded an explanation, he was flatly told that the Art Theatre would eventually "create an Academy which will serve as the seed-bed for new cadres of actors and directors" (*Letopis'* IV 2003: 229). Novitsky's visit signaled that the planning stage was over. An academy would be established with Stanislavsky as its titular head.

September 29, 1935: A New Academy for New People

In 1935, *Narkompros* officially approved the creation of a model theatre academy and Stanislavsky named it "The Opera-Dramatic Studio." He placed his sister, Zinaida Sergeyevna Sokolova, whom he trusted to teach his System, in charge of assembling a team of teaching assistants, which included Novitsky's daughter, Lidia Pavlovna.[20] Classes took place in rooms on Leontyevsky Lane and on the small stage of the Moscow Art Theatre, which Stanislavsky never visited. Students regularly showed their work to him, while he continued to experiment with acting and new ways to rehearse. The state invested generously in the project. "One hundred fifty thousand [rubles] was tagged for the first year of [the school's] operations" and a stipend of 300 rubles was set aside for each student (*SS* IX 1999: 605; 657).

The Opera-Dramatic Studio officially opened on September 29, 1935, with Novitsky and Bubnov as the Commissar of *Narkompros* presiding over the ceremony. Stanislavsky was notably absent! He had been sent out of town to the nearby convalescent home. In a letter he asked his sister to greet the students with words that eerily echo his botched speech at the Moscow Art Theatre's gala in 1928. Again, he starts well. "I want to express personally how much we value the attention paid to us by the government and *Narkompros*, which are so movingly concerned about our theatres and our art, about our old and young cadres of artists" (*SS* IX 1999: 634). Again, he loses his political footing when he turns to what matters most to him. He asks his sister to urge the Studio's students to strive always for artistic integrity and avoid "hackwork."

> Let them not forget that, just as they now seek art through theatre, so too does every spectator seek art. Let them not exchange stones for bread. Let them come to recognize genuine art and distinguish it from counterfeits.
>
> (*SS* IX 1999: 634)

As Novitsky had predicted, students had been recruited "not only from Moscow, but from all over the U.S.S.R." (*SS* IX 1999: 605). By 1936 the student body included "many simple workers, peasants from the collective farms, and red army soldiers. There are homeless among the students, as well as the sons and daughters of famous actors, engineers, and the intelligentsia. When they all come together," Stanislavsky observed, "you can't tell the peasants and the craftsmen from the intelligentsia" (*SS* IX 1999: 656–7). Moreover, since most of the students had been born after the Russian revolution and grew up with communistic values, they embodied the new Soviet mores in ways that often amazed and sometimes puzzled the gentlemanly Stanislavsky. "They are," he mused, "actually 'new people'" (*SS* IX 1999: 656–7).

"Let Them Not Exchange Stones for Bread!"

The official founding of the academy in 1935 brought increased governmental scrutiny to Stanislavsky's classes and writings. There were visitors, like Novitsky, at every turn and official assistants, like Kedrov, at Stanislavsky's side, watching intensely and transcribing his words. An editorial commission was appointed for the publication of his books, which were now considered official textbooks on acting, "required for all schools and theatres" (*SS* IX 1999: 657).

Happily, the government had asked Stanislavsky to do the work that he actually wanted to do. After his heart attack, he had become more and more enamored of teaching, hoping to leave an artistic legacy to his students after his death. In a 1934 letter to Yelizaveta Telyeshova, an actress who had become a leading teacher at the Moscow Art Theatre's Second Studio, Stanislavsky confided that "I am beginning to lose my taste for directing, and, instead, I find the business of pedagogy and young people more and more interesting" (*SS* IX 1999: 551). Since returning from his first health leave, he had already been turning every rehearsal that he conducted in his home into a lesson. In 1933, while directing rehearsals for Ostrovsky's classic play, *Talents and Admirers*, he admitted that "what we are doing with this play cannot simply be called rehearsing. It is more properly a research study, a school that tests and corrects the actors' techniques and examines their creative lines of development" (*SS* IX 1999: 527). He also genuinely wanted to put his System down on paper in a form that would be accessible to future generations. "I believe that all masters of the arts need to write [in order to] systematize their art" (Filippov 1977: 58).

Unfortunately, the circumstances of his internal exile and the imposition of censorship made it hard for him to teach and write freely. He had lost significant control over his work and had begun to refer cynically to "the so-called Stanislavsky System" (*SS* IX 1999: 657). This tongue-in-cheek phrase underlined the fact that he had even lost control of his name. He understood how the dialectical materialism that was "required of all" (*SS* IX 1999: 475) warped what people outside of his most intimate circle could know of him. It was not so much that he couldn't say what he believed about acting; he just couldn't say it all. What the public knew about his work, and especially about his last rehearsal technique, was not so much wrong as incomplete. Moreover, his most innovative and forward-looking ideas were invariably left out of the record.

Despite the public nature of Stanislavsky's new Opera-Dramatic Studio, the story of Active Analysis continued to unfold behind the closed doors of his salon on Leontyevsky Lane, where he took his own advice and honored his own artistic integrity. He offered his protégés the kind of theatrical art that nourishes the soul, like bread nourishes the body. There he examined the complexity of human experience in all its fullness by working on various kinds of dramatic materials: plays in verse, operas, and performances devised from literature and improvisations by the actors. "Human life is so subtle, so complex and multifaceted," he explained, "that it needs an incomparably large number of new, still undiscovered 'isms' to express it fully" (*SS* II 1989: 458). There he exhorted actors to work holistically with body, mind, and soul in concert. That was the most he could do.

As he carried on with his work, he trusted that someone would "tell actors, tell students […] explain to them, try without fail, [… for] this is for me terribly important" (Durylin and Markov 1955: 453–4). That someone turned out to be a tiny woman with unusual looks, whom he had invited to join his Opera-Dramatic Studio in 1936. She in turn made it her mission to keep the legacy of Active Analysis alive.

Notes

1. A brigade of three directors (Stanislavsky, Sudakov, and Nina Nikolayevna Litovtsyeva) were listed for *Armored Train 14-69*, but Sudakov had taken the directorial lead and championed the play's pro-revolutionary stance. The full program also included scenes from Shakespeare's *Hamlet* (1911) and Nemirovich-Danchenko's dramatization of Dostoyevsky's *The Brothers Karamazov* (1910) to testify to the company's versatility with classics.

2. At that time, Stanislavsky's family included his sister Zinaida Sokolova, whose husband had been killed in the civil war, and his brother Vladimir, who was a musician. His brother Grigory and Grigory's three sons were executed for colluding with anti-revolutionary troupes in the Crimea in 1921. For more, see Shevtsova (2020: 52; 49). The building on Leontyevsky Lane is now the Stanislavsky House Museum, which opened in 1948 at the prompting of Stanislavsky's wife and granddaughter.

3. Benedetti (1990) transliterates the name as "Heitz" to reflect its Germanic roots; and Shevtsova (2020) transliterates it as "Geytts."

4. Stanislavsky's persistent defense of Yegorov eventually resulted in his reinstatement in May 1932, a year after Stalin removed Geits from his post at the Moscow Art. Similarly, when Stanislavsky heard in January 1930 that his brother and sister were to be removed from their positions at his Opera Studio, he successfully pleaded with the government to save their jobs (*Letopis'* IV 2003: 195).

5. Stanislavsky's unfinished promptbook for *Othello* was edited by his secretary, R. K. Tamantsova in 1943; it was then translated into English by H. Nowak in 1948.

6. Officially, Stalin put his close colleague and member of the Central Committee, Avel Sofranovich Yenukidze, in charge of overseeing the Moscow Art Theatre, yet Stalin himself often approved both repertoire and productions. Yenukidze fell from favor in 1937 and was executed as an enemy of the people.

7. For more on Stanislavsky's books, see Carnicke (2009: chapters 5 and 6).

8. Even before his heart attack, Stanislavsky was considering ways to lighten his load. "My health no longer allows me to work as I once did, as director, actor and theatre administrator all at the same time. I will have to eliminate something" (*SS* IX 1999: 315).

9. The title means "truth" and registers ironically, because the press was so heavily censored.

10. Gorky had also been confined to his home by Stalin, who most probably ordered the playwright's poisoning.

11. Among Stanislavsky's visitors were the directors Joshua Logan and Norris Houghton, the Chinese actor Mei Lanfang, and the African American opera star Marion Anderson.

12. Shevtsova is among those who stress that Stanislavsky's "frail body kept him housebound" (2020: 69). Anatoly Smeliansky raises the notion of escapism (1996: 42).

13. Their names were Mikhail Vladimirovich Alekseyev, Aleksandra Pavlovna Alekseyeva, and Nadezhda Pavlovna Riabushinskaia. The two women were both doctors.

14. Meyerhold briefly toured to Germany and Paris in 1930, but without generating an "international persona that could have shielded [him] from further attacks back home," writes Stefan Aquilina (2020: 160).

15. For more on Yoga in the System see Carnicke (2009: chapter 9), White (2005: 73–92), and Tcherkasski (2016).

16. Kedrov's objections to the spiritual dimensions of the System register ironically in light of the fact that his father was a Russian Orthodox priest.

17. While "soul" (*dusha*) and "spiritual" (*dushevnyi*) appear in Stanislavsky's censored books and Hapgood's abridged translations, Benedetti eliminates both words in his 2008 translations, consistently translating dusha as "mind" (*um*) and dushevnyi as "mental" (*umnyi*). In the 2021 English translation of Vassiliev's compilation of Knebel's works, Irina Brown restores Stanislavsky's use of "spirit" and "soul" in those quotations from his writings that she herself translates, but retains Benedetti's erasure when she imports his translations of Stanislavsky's books.

18. Under Stalin, free primary education led to a significant increase of literacy and state-supported higher education trained many citizens for the professions. The development of Soviet education was unquestionably one of Stalin's highest achievements.

19. It may have been Stalin's intention to remove Geits before Stanislavsky begged to be rid of him, so that the regime could position the company as a launchpad for the academy.

20. Most of the teaching staff had studied the System with Sokolova prior to their hire. Benedetti uses Lidia Pavlovna Novitskaya's 1984 account of the Opera-Dramatic Studio as the basis of his 1998 book, *Stanislavski and the Actor*.

2 Behind Closed Doors

For the Love of Theatre

Becoming an Actress

In 1917, the year of the Bolshevik revolution, Maria Osipovna Knebel was seventeen and on the brink of choosing a profession. Since childhood, she had dreamed about becoming an actress. Once, when she was six or so, her father had taken her to the Korsh Theatre where he was visiting a friend. As he led her through the rehearsal hall, she thought that the actors seemed "all powerful, becoming any person, old or young, smart or stupid, evil or good. I could never forget the people in that big room" (Knebel' 1967: 30). At age ten, she sat weeping in the auditorium of the Moscow Art Theatre after viewing *The Cherry Orchard*. An usher tried to console her. "There's no need to cry!" he said. "Anton Pavlovich called his play a comedy." When she continued to sob, he whispered, "there's no reason to be ashamed. Everyone cries, even the adults" (Knebel' 1967: 207–8). But "these weren't tears of sadness," she recalled. "The presence of art had stirred my soul even as a child" (Ryzhova 1967: 64).

Concerned, her parents kept her away from theatres. Yet, her dream persisted. Finally, when she was seventeen, her father took her by the hand, led her to a mirror, and asked her to look at herself objectively. She was too short in stature, too lacking in traditional female beauty, and too shy in demeanor to become an actress (Knebel' 1967: 36). Persuaded by him, she chose to study mathematics instead, a subject in which she could exercise her quick mind, her intelligence, and the analytical prowess that had made her passionate about chess. "She loved chess her whole life," recalls a neighbor, "and beating her was never easy" (Liadov 1998: 83).

A year later a friend took Maria to visit a studio, recently opened by the famous actor, Mikhail Aleksandrovich Chekhov, the writer's nephew. Stanislavsky valued Chekhov as an actor of extraordinary talent and in 1911 had chosen him as a founding member of the First Studio, where the System was born. But after a few years of work Chekhov had suffered a serious mental breakdown, causing him to flee the stage in the middle of performances, to fear leaving his home, and to struggle with suicidal depression (Chamberlain 2004: 13). By 1918 he was no longer performing publicly. Persuaded by Stanislavsky and other trusted friends that teaching might prove to be a healing balm, Chekhov opened a studio in his home. Not only were his friends right about his recovery, but his classes also served as a crucial laboratory for his future teaching in England and the United States, where he would become known as Michael.

Maria expected to sit quietly to the side. That plan was turned awry when Chekhov instructed everyone in the room to imagine that they were patients in a psychiatric hospital, each with a single obsession that would condition their behavior during the exercise. She tried tiptoeing out of class, but Chekhov noticed her and made a suggestion: "Imagine that you are made of glass and that you are afraid of getting broken. […] Don't play anything, only imagine that you are glass …." (Knebel' 1967: 54). She lent herself to the suggestion:

> The fear of breaking literally seized me. I don't know how, but I forgot about everything else—that this was an unsanctioned visit to an acting studio, that the famous actor Chekhov was watching me. I carefully walked through the room, avoiding others, trying to step lightly and gently. To this day I remember the joy and freedom that yielding to this imaginary idea provoked in me.
>
> (Knebel' 1967: 54)

That night Chekhov took Maria aside, told her that he admired her abilities to concentrate and improvise, and urged her to join his studio. When she answered that she had decided against acting because of her looks, Chekhov reassured her, predicting that she would find plenty of character roles to play (Knebel' 1967: 56). She dropped mathematics and took up acting.

Chekhov's "little creative laboratory" (Knebel' 1967: 60) used primarily improvisation to investigate aspects of performance that Stanislavsky had called the "elements" of acting: concentration of attention, the harnessing of one's will in readiness to work, the creation of moods and atmospheres, detailing the given circumstances that underlie dramatic situations, using physical tempos and rhythms to make visible their characters' inner states, etc. Following Stanislavsky's lead, Chekhov called these improvisations "etudes," from the French verb "to study." Maria loved and excelled in etudes, the more imaginative the better.

In 1921 Chekhov felt well enough to return to the professional stage and closed his studio. In order to continue acting, Maria auditioned for the school run by the Second Studio of the Moscow Art Theatre. One of four affiliated Studios at that time, the Second was widely considered to be closest to the home company's traditions.[1] It had been founded in 1916 by a Moscow Art director and three actors, who had been teaching Stanislavsky's System at a private school which they had previously created. This educational impulse behind the Second Studio's founding reassured Maria that she would be in good hands.

She entered as a beginning student, but was permitted to perform publicly in crowd scenes and small roles due to her prior study with Chekhov. She attended rigorous classes in acting, voice, dance, and movement, but for the most part, she rehearsed and performed in accord with her teachers' often repeated philosophy that acting cannot be taught, but can be learned. She and her fellow students were expected to prepare etudes and scenes independently of their teachers, who would then critique their work. It was "a tough school," Maria recalled, "demanding considerable courage from us. But if you showed initiative and persistence," she recalled, "you got all the advice and help you needed" (Knebel' 1967: 143–4).

Maria particularly valued classes with Yelizaveta Telyeshova, a seasoned Moscow Art Theatre actor and director. Despite Telyeshova's sometimes "cruel" and always "unsentimental" critiques, she was "a true friend to actors," because "she could see in an ugly duckling, the future swan and help that swan be born" (Knebel' 1967: 145). Telyeshova always stressed the importance of basic technique: "The higher the tower [you build], the stronger must be its foundation," she said (Knebel' 1967: 145). So too did she insist that however imaginative an actor's flight of fancy in an etude might be, its success always depends upon "the strict observation of the given circumstances" that inform the story being performed (Knebel' 1967: 146). These lessons stayed with Maria for the whole of her professional life.

Knebel performed publicly for the first time in a benefit for the hungry on May 29, 1922. Stanislavsky was reprising his role as Dr. Stockmann in Ibsen's *An Enemy of the People*, and the Studio had recommended her for one of Stockman's two young sons. Stanislavsky interviewed her and agreed to the casting. Although her part was small, she was intensively coached on the boy's "inner and outer characteristics" by Vasily Luzhsky, a leading actor of the Moscow Art Theatre (Knebel' 1967: 152). During the performance, she became as deeply absorbed in the play's fiction as she had in her first etude for Chekhov:

> Upon entering, I saw Stanislavsky as Stockmann. His eyes shined with gentleness and affection. He looked at the two of us, as if we were truly his family, his boys. I forgot that I was supposed to 'look around the room as if I were bewildered.' I was aware only of how desperately I wanted to tell him that we loved him and were proud of him [...]. That alone was what I experienced on stage during those brief moments with Stanislavsky-Stockmann.
>
> (Knebel' 1967: 153)

Her description of what had happened to her perfectly matches the kind of acting that Stanislavsky wanted to nurture through his System. Although he had admired actors, like Sarah Bernhardt, who presented to their audiences carefully rehearsed and artistically stunning portraits of their characters, he personally preferred actors like Eleonora Duse, who experienced performance as a creative act which occurs in the presence of the audience. As he had told a journalist in May 1907, "I admire all styles and all trends in art. But I demand one thing from all of them: every moment of the acting has to be experienced anew with sincerity and fervor" (*Letopis'* II 2003: 71).[2] Knebel's artistic instincts and her acting education allowed her not only to fulfill that demand, but also to crave its fulfillment in her future work.

The 1922 to 1923 season represented the Second Studio's bold but unsuccessful flirtation with stylized production. It was, in Stanislavsky's words, "an orgy in futurism" (*SS* IX 1999: 158). The sets featured cubist backdrops, intended to universalize the plays' classic stories for contemporary audiences; the actors wore exaggerated and expressionistic make-up that transformed their faces into masks of their characters' souls. For Schiller's *The Robbers*, Knebel devised a character not found in the text—a mute dwarf, who was servant to the play's protagonist. She envisioned him as a "sinister," "infernal creature," more like a "fantastical animal" than a man, who jumped from place to place like a frog (Knebel' 1967: 167). In Ostrovsky's *The Storm* she played the old, aristocratic woman, gone mad, who haunts the play's provincial town, cursing those whom she suspects of having broken the social norms. Her madness mirrors the town's misogynistic condemnation of the play's heroine, who is ultimately driven to suicide by a loveless and abusive marriage.

At the Second Studio, Knebel crossed paths with two men who would, in years to come, play inimical roles in Stanislavsky's life. First, there was Mikhail Nikolayevich Kedrov, who kept a close eye on Stanislavsky in his last years. Kedrov had joined the Second Studio as an actor in 1922 and, like she, played a small role in *The Robbers*. A decade later, she would meet him again on Leontyevsky Lane, where they both assisted Stanislavsky in his

Fig. 4 Knebel in her youth. The Makarovskiy Family.

Opera-Dramatic Studio. Then, a decade following Stanislavsky's death, she would run afoul of Kedrov, but that part of her story is yet to unfold.

Second, there was Ilya Yakvolevich Sudakov, who seemed an Iago in Stanislavsky's eyes. It was, after all, Sudakov who put political needs over aesthetics in the 1927 production of *Armored Train 14-69*, who ignored Stanislavsky's directorial plan for the disastrous 1930 *Othello*, and who published a book in 1934 about the Stanislavsky System before its true author could complete his own. At the Second Studio, Sudakov directed Knebel in *The Storm* and she felt nothing but "gratitude [toward him ...] for having entrusted me, so young an actor, with a role that I have always thought remarkable" and "for having worked with me so patiently on it" (Knebel' 1967: 169). However, as she watched his career unfold at the Moscow Art Theatre, his willingness to accept any assignment, however distasteful, led her to see him as "a tragic figure" (Knebel' 1967: 180). "Was he to blame?" she asked herself. "Yes, of course," she admitted. "But there are factors difficult to explain in theatre, as when everyone around you, and so you yourself, begin to believe that you are indispensable" (Knebel' 1967: 150). Sudakov's fate became a reminder that good people sometimes trade integrity for advancement.

In 1924, while Stanislavsky was touring in the United States, Nemirovich-Danchenko reorganized the four Moscow Art Theatre studios and merged the Second into the main company. In one swift move, more than thirty young artists—among them Knebel, Kedrov, and Sudakov—became the Art Theatre's second generation, as they came to be called. The merger was well-timed, since many of the company's first-generation actors had remained abroad after the tour. Without this infusion of new talent, the Moscow Art Theatre would surely have been the poorer. Thus, by age twenty-six Maria Knebel had achieved her dream! For the next twenty-five years, she played a range of characters at the Moscow Art Theatre, including the childish "Sniffles" in Maeterlinck's symbolist tale, *The Bluebird*; the society matron, Madame Kartasova, who first notices her friend's adulterous behavior, in Nemirovich-Danchenko's adaptation of Tolstoy's *Anna Karenina*; the society gossip, Sophia Karpukhina, in Nemirovich-Danchenko's adaptation of Dostoevsky's *The Uncle's Dream*; and Charlotta, the eccentric governess, in Chekhov's *The Cherry Orchard*.

In 1934 Knebel had taken advantage of the company's custom, whereby actors could audition for roles they wished to play by preparing a scene for the company's co-founders. She wanted the role of Charlotta, but finding a scene proved impossible, since the governess is so fully embedded in the play's ensemble. Therefore, Knebel decided to prepare an etude instead that would reveal Charlotta's seed by performing a series of magic tricks, inspired by Act III of the play. The "seed" (*zerno* in Russian) had become a central notion at the Moscow Art Theatre. As Knebel explains, "just as a plant grows from a seed, so too does a work of art grow from the author's specific thought and sensibility" (Knebel' [1959] 1982: 32). At the audition, Stanislavsky was so taken with Knebel's etude that he stepped into the audition as Gayev (his usual role in the play), asking Charlotta questions about her life and debating with her about issues that inform the play. Suddenly, Gayev invited Charlotta to play his favorite game (Knebel' 1967: 261). The audition ended with Stanislavsky-Gayev winning at billiards and Knebel winning the role of Charlotta, which she played "incomparably" (Rozov 1977: 60) for more than fifteen years.

Becoming a Director

By the time Stanislavsky had founded the Opera-Dramatic Studio, Knebel had gotten a little tired of playing "midges," as she called her usual roles (Rozov 1977: 60). When the chance to direct came along, she leapt at it. Her then husband, Pavel Vladimirovich Urbanovich, was a director at Meyerhold's Theatre of the Revolution and taught biomechanics—the physical training program that Meyerhold had developed to support his stunning, nonrealist productions (Rozov 1977: 60).[3] Following Stalin's 1934 imposition of socialist realism as the only acceptable style for Soviet art, Urbanovich and his colleagues joined a group on aesthetics to address how best to handle this shift in artistic policy. When Urbanovich hosted a session at his apartment, Maria found herself in a lively debate with one of his colleagues, the director Aleksey Dmitriyevich Popov, who insisted that she join the group "not as a 'wife,' but as an independent, thinking 'individual'" (Knebel' 1967: 290). As time passed, Popov became convinced that Knebel should put her clarity of thought, her analytical skills, and her visual imagination to work as a director.

> "Why don't you take up directing?" he asked, but I could not answer. I simply had never thought about it. Then with logic as sharp as a scalpel, he cut right through to the creative heart of me. I cannot say that I felt comfortable when he "dissected" me in front of everybody. No one other than my father had ever spoken to me as directly.
>
> (Knebel' 1967: 290)

The group arranged for Knebel to stage an Ostrovsky comedy, *Not a Kopeck to Be Had and Suddenly There Are Three,* at the Electric-Energy Institute. Soon she was directing more visible productions at Moscow's alternative theatres, like the notable Yermolova Studio Theatre.

A Tantalizing Invitation

In March 1936 Knebel was happily juggling her acting at the Moscow Art Theatre with her directing at other venues, when Stanislavsky unexpectedly requested that she visit him.

> I went to Leontyevsky Lane worrying, trying to figure out the possible reasons behind his summons. He sat me down in a big, soft, armchair across from him, looked at me searchingly and affectionately, and then apparently satisfied with the fact that I was sufficiently perplexed and excited, finally asked: "Have you heard of my studio?"
>
> (Knebel' 1967: 264)

He then invited her to teach the "literary word" in order to investigate "verbal action" at the Studio. Confused by his request, she protested that she had never taught and knew nothing about that particular subject. "That's even better," he countered, "because that means you will have no false ideas about it" (Knebel' 1967: 264). He continued:

> This is an area [in acting] that still needs much work and much thinking; we need to discover the ways in which words, which now sit passively on the actor's tongue, can become active. [...] What is verbal action? How can speech be action? We need to resolve such questions by working with our students. So, are you willing to teach while learning?
>
> (Knebel' 1967: 264)

For a moment, his question hung in the air.

During this silence, she might well have remembered another occasion when Stanislavsky had also summoned her to Leontyevsky Lane. It had been in November 1930, shortly after he and his wife had returned from abroad. In their absence, Knebel had secured the role of Sophia Petrovna Karpukhina in *The Uncle's Dream*. Knebel liked the role, envisioning Karpukhina as a judgmental gossip in the grotesque style, then popular among Russia's avant-garde artists. She had poured all of her passion and creative energy into developing the character; but as soon as Stanislavsky saw her perform it, he replaced her with Maria Lilina, his wife, whom he had originally hoped to cast as Karpukhina. When Knebel then asked the theatre's administration for an explanation of her removal, she was told that Stanislavsky had likened her Karpukhina to "a circus act" (Knebel' 1967: 258). Knebel genuinely admired Lilina in the role, which she "play[ed] remarkably well, [...] gossiping with inspired fervor, horror-stricken by the vices of [society's] ladies, and amazingly sincere in her righteous judgement of them!" (Knebel' 1967: 258). But, as Knebel also confided to a trusted a fellow actor, "I had dreamed of creating a different kind of person" (Knebel' 1967: 258).

Months passed, until one day, when Lilina fell ill, Stanislavsky requested that Knebel step back into the role. She adamantly refused. Moreover, while she had previously declined Meyerhold's offer to join his theatre, she now decided that, should Stanislavsky insist on her playing Karpukhina, she would leave the Moscow Art Theatre for the Theatre of Revolution.

Upon hearing of her decision, Stanislavsky immediately summoned her to him. As she stood at attention in his presence, she felt like a pupil being questioned by the principal for bad behavior.

> "Is it true, that you want to leave the theatre?"
> "It's true."
> "Is it only because I insist that you play the role I took away from you?"
> "Yes."
> He looked closely at me, then invited me to sit down in the armchair, and gently asked: "What are you thinking? Only tell me the truth."
>
> (Knebel' 1967: 258–9)

She began by reminding him that he had thought her work on Karpukhina a "circus act." She continued by praising Lilina in the role. Then Knebel stopped, sure of being reprimanded. She imagined him saying, "Child, you must learn from the great actresses!" (Knebel' 1967: 259). But instead he simply asked why she had "stumbled" in her explanation. That question emboldened her:

> [You] yourself taught us that we must do only what we can believe in, otherwise we embark upon a path that leads to the copying of others' work. [...] I don't yet have [Lilina's] experience or her technique, but all the same I will not copy her.
>
> (Knebel' 1967: 259)

After a long silence, Stanislavsky asked her to explain how she envisioned Karpukhina. But, he added, speak of her in the first person, as if you were she, speaking from her seed: "So then, I, Sophia Petrovna, drink four glasses of vodka in the morning, and the same number in the evening, and then after my usual appetizers, my soul feels emancipated ... " (Knebel' 1967: 259). As Knebel got more and more absorbed in her improvised monologue, Stanislavsky started to react, as if he were her acting partner, nodding in sympathy and wagging a finger in disagreement. In this way, he met the Karpukhina that lived in Knebel's imagination.

When the exercise was over, Stanislavsky told her that he now understood what she had wanted to create, but reaffirmed that in his opinion she had not succeeded with it on the stage. "The grotesque [with its extreme contrasts and sardonic humor] is the highest level of art, and you are right to want to work with it," he said. But, he admitted, it is also devilishly hard. "I have tried to create the grotesque, but succeeded only once—as Dr. Stockmann" in *An Enemy of the People* (Knebel' 1967: 260). This reference took her back to 1922, when she had played his son. Stanislavsky then praised her first teacher, Mikhail Chekhov, for succeeding with the style as the leading character in *The Inspector General*, a production that she had seen many times in 1921 and 1922. She vividly recalled how Chekhov had consistently amazed her by adding new touches to his role at every performance, proving himself to be "a genius of improvisation" (Chekhov 1995 vol. 2: 28). Stanislavsky then turned his attention to the style's fashionable popularity. "Now-a-days," he said, "we don't get the grotesque, but only the 'grotesque' in quotation marks, and that's awful!" (Knebel' 1967: 260). Was he thinking of the alternative theatres in which she was then directing? Finally, he suggested how she might succeed in the role by relying upon irony: "The next time you perform Karpukhina, find […] something to cry about that the audience will laugh at, and then you will understand the grotesque in Dostoyevsky" (Knebel' 1967: 260).

Something had changed in their relationship during that conversation in 1930. By sharing his struggles with the grotesque, he was speaking with her as a fellow artist, not a student. She now saw clearly that "the very essence of his artistic conviction" lay in his belief that any artistic style, no matter how radical its form, "must be justified from within," not put on like a garment or an ornament. "I left happy," recalled Knebel (Knebel' 1967: 260). The shift in their relationship made it easy for her to return to Karpukhina, sharing the role with Lilina for many years, each of them succeeding with it in entirely different ways.

Now in 1936 Knebel again left Leontyevsky Lane happy. She joined Stanislavsky's Opera-Dramatic Studio in order to assist him in developing a new way to rehearse, which would soon become her primary "path in art" (Knebel' 1967: 485).

Inside the Opera-Dramatic Studio

Learning while Teaching

Knebel entered the Studio in 1936 as one of a new group of assistants who brought fresh perspectives to Stanislavsky's ongoing experimental work. This group also included Maria Lilina, with whom Knebel shared the role of Karpukhina, and Mikhail Kedrov, whom Knebel knew from the Second Studio. Another group of assistants had been recruited a year earlier by Stanislavsky's sister, Zinaida Sokolova. They were directing students, who had previously studied the System under her. Among this initial group were Grigory Kristi, who worked with opera and whom Stanislavsky would trust in 1937 to take charge of editing his books, and Lidia Novitskaya, the daughter of the theatre critic who had so unexpectedly in 1934 told Stanislavsky of the government's decision to establish an academy. These assistants had already spent a year training the Studio's students in the basic elements of the System. Stanislavsky guided their pedagogy, but, uninterested in writing a textbook, he urged them to develop their own exercises (Vinogradskaia 2000: 440).

When Knebel arrived, the Studio's students were advancing to the next stage of their studies, which entailed rehearsing full operas and plays. For Stanislavsky, this stage of work was crucially important. First, he believed that by applying his ideas to rehearsals he would avoid promoting technique for technique's sake. He feared that, without pragmatic application to texts, his theories could too easily be treated as dogma. Sadly, Knebel eventually saw his fear come to pass. Second, he hoped that by giving his students experience with full works they would be prepared to go out and create new professional companies of their own, dedicated to the furtherance of his experiments. Third, he chose works that he knew deeply, in order to better investigate the relationship between text and action, which was, as he had told Knebel, his major area of interest at the time (Knebel' 1967: 266).

Ensembles of opera students, each guided by an assistant, worked on Puccini's *Madame Butterfly*, Verdi's *Rigoletto*, Rimsky-Korsakov's *The Snow Maiden*, and Otto Nicolai's *Merry Wives of Windsor*. The drama students, guided by other assistants, rehearsed plays by Shakespeare, Chekhov, and Griboyedov. Groups also tackled poetry, literary texts, and other experimental projects. Ongoing classes in voice and diction, movement and musicality, singing and dance ensured that the students acquire the skills needed by actors and actor-singers to attain professional levels in performance.

The Studio's work during Stanislavsky's last two years was intense. Even though some classes were conducted on the small stage of the Moscow Art Theatre, most of Stanislavsky's home was turned into rehearsal space, with opera singers and actors working shoulder to shoulder. All the rooms, except for the family's bedrooms and a small sitting room, were stripped of décor to accommodate the work. Students and assistants used every nook and cranny, including the hallways, courtyard, and Stanislavsky's private balcony, when he was well enough to offer it (Knebel' 1967: 280–1). They worked from early morning to late at night.

At ten in the morning students, assistants, and invited guests would crowd into the elegantly columned salon on the first floor to attend Stanislavsky's classes. Fondly called the Onegin Hall, it had been the site of Stanislavsky's innovative 1922 production of Tchaikovsky's opera, *Eugene Onegin*, which he had staged for the singers in his earlier Bolshoi Theatre Opera Studio (Carnicke 2019b: 91–12). Now, the hall rang with opera and drama, acting exercises, poetry readings, and etudes. Each session would begin with the nurse bringing Stanislavsky into the room and settling him in his chair. Then the students would show him their work.

Despite his illness Stanislavsky was "uncommonly handsome," Knebel recalls, always appearing at lessons freshly shaved and meticulously dressed in a suit, fresh shirt, and bow tie (Knebel' 1967: 280–2). His attire signaled his deep respect for theatre and those who dedicated themselves to art. He also struck Knebel as uncommonly generous in his last years. "Take advantage of my being here with you," he often said, "to take as much as possible from me" (Knebel' 1967: 264). His actions consistently proved the sincerity of his words. For example, after Knebel admitted to him that she found it difficult to break plays down into events, as his new technique demanded, he suggested that she practice by analyzing a new play every day. If she were then to bring him her notes, he would, he promised, review and correct them every night. He kept his word (Knebel' 1967: 265).

> He had never before held back, but in those years at the studio, his generosity in sharing his creative ideas took on a particular character. It struck me as courageous, tragic, and sublimely peaceful. It was as if he actually felt that death was close, and it engendered in him one desire—to give away everything while time still remained. I never heard him indulge in the grumbling of old age. He was deeply and joyously focused on what our discoveries could offer to theatrical art.
>
> (Knebel' 1967: 265)

Stanislavsky at Work

A kaleidoscope of memories shaped Knebel's understanding of the rehearsal technique that she would later call "Active Analysis."[4]

April 1937: *Romeo and Juliet*

It is ten in the morning. The cast, their teacher Lidia Novitskaya, Knebel, and the rest of the Studio's assistants and students hold their breath in anticipation as the well-dressed

Fig. 5 Stanislavsky (third from the left) and his Opera-Dramatic Studio assistants, including his sister and Knebel (fourth and fifth to the left), watch a rehearsal in the Onegin Hall on Leontyevsky Lane, c. 1937. The Sharon Marie Carnicke Collection.

Stanislavsky begins the day's lesson. Novitskaya has already explained to him that her students have been rehearsing Act I of *Romeo and Juliet* and are ready to show him their work, including the interaction between Romeo and his cousin Benvolio in the first scene (*Letopis'* IV 2003: 400).[5] Verona's prince has just threatened the feuding Capulets and Montagues with execution, if they should ever fight again. Benvolio and Romeo's parents had taken part in the "fray," but Romeo had not. He was out wandering in the woods, secretly love-sick for Rosaline, an aristocratic lady who spurns him. Worried about their son, the Montagues share their concern with Benvolio, who pledges "to know his grievance, or be much denied." When Romeo appears, his parents leave the cousins alone for a private conversation.

Novitskaya tells Stanislavsky that she has titled the cousins' interaction "Benvolio Drags a Secret out of Romeo" (Novitskaia 1984: 156). She then outlines the actors' process so far: they have studied the circumstances as given in the play; written a list of their physical actions; and told the scene's story to the whole cast "while sitting on their hands," exactly as Stanislavsky had instructed them to do. "Good," said Stanislavsky to Novitskaya, you were correct to have them write down *what* they do. But don't let them decide *how* to do anything before they get up to work with each other. Such "adjustments" will come when they study the scene through an etude. That way the scene "will develop organically and logically." At the start, "the main thing is to find the actor's call to action" (Novitskaia 1984: 157–8). He repeats the main point so that everyone can hear: "It's important to know not *how*, but *what* to do" (Novitskaia 1984: 161).

Turning to the actors cast as Romeo and Benvolio, Stanislavsky instructs them to observe each other closely as they rehearse. Watch what your partner does, consider his state of mind, wonder how his eyes reflect his soul, and allow yourself to adjust to him. "Every scene is like a chess game: one moves this way, the other answers that move, and so one always depends upon the other" (Novitskaia 1984: 161). This image perfectly captures the interactive emphasis in Active Analysis.

Stanislavsky then asks the actor-Romeo[6] to tell him what main events occur in Act I, asserting that this question is important, because you must "learn to parse the play into its big events, so that you can understand how the author tells the story through the play's plot" (Knebel' [1954] 2009: 25).[7] The actor identifies the first event as Romeo's love for Rosaline and the second as his love for Juliet. Stanislavsky nods, "Yes, if Romeo had not been infatuated with Rosaline, he would not have pursued her by going to the ball given by his family's enemies, and so he would not have met Juliet" (Knebel' [1954] 2009: 25–6). But then, as Knebel recalls, Stanislavsky begins "literally throwing questions at the student," as if "his life depended upon his understanding of Romeo" (Knebel' 1967: 271). How can you use "love," to describe both events? "Romeo loves Rosaline, yes, but he feels something different for Juliet; he feels as if he and she were born for each other" (Novitskaia 1984: 154). Stanislavsky continues questioning the actor-Romeo, who continues responding:

"Is Romeo in love with Rosaline?"
"Maybe not really. Maybe he just wants to show off!"
"Show off? Imagine that you are sitting in Shakespeare's chair. Why would you depict a person who is not really in love, but only wants to show off? Maybe Romeo's love for Rosaline is the beginning of his passion for Juliet. In Rosaline, he loves not Rosaline but the idea of love."

(Novitskaia 1984: 165)

Stanislavsky's reference to Shakespeare captures the way in which Active Analysis invites actors to recreate the author's process of writing the play by finding the need for their characters to speak. By uncovering the dynamics in a scene before memorizing their lines, actors paradoxically discover why the words on the page become tools for their acting.

Stanislavsky then turns to the actor-Benvolio, and asks for his "main action," which is Stanislavsky's term in the 1930s to describe the force that drives the scene forward. He expects an active verb in response and the student complies:

"To drag what's happening to Romeo out of him."
"And what kind of action is that—physical or spiritual?"
"There are elements of both."
"That's true. But for the moment, let's agree to call it physical. Psychological and spiritual actions are tricky, because it is easy to go wrong and play the emotion. But in every feeling, there is also something physical."

(Novitskaia 1984: 165)[8]

This statement echoes another rehearsal that same month on *Hamlet*, when Stanislavsky had more explicitly said that "physical actions are necessary because they get your senses, feelings, and unconscious working for you" (Vinogradskaia 2000: 462). In his book, he explains that "in every physical action there is something psychological" (*SS* II 1989: 258) due to the "organic connection between body and soul" (*SS* II 1989: 349). Clearly, Stanislavsky expected the actor to use body, mind, and spirit during performance and his stress on "physical actions" served only as the gateway. Knebel was beginning to think that his calling the technique a "method of physical actions" did not describe very well what he actually wanted the actors to do when rehearsing.

Stanislavsky and the actor-Benvolio are still speaking about the first scene in *Romeo and Juliet*: "Let's say that you will drag something from Romeo. What will you do?" asks Stanislavsky. "I would go up to him; take him by the shoulder, sit him down, lead him into a conversation" (Novitskaia 1984: 165). Stanislavsky shakes his head, unhappy with the actor's naming of "all the little physical actions" that might be possible depending upon what Romeo does. "You sound like you are preparing Romeo," not Benvolio, Stanislavsky tells him, "because you are already creating what you think Romeo needs from you in order to speak" (Novitskaia 1984: 165). In a chess game, you don't decide how to move in advance. You wait for your partner's move and then react. Planning how you will move in advance anticipates how the scene will unfold, and by doing so you limit your own and your partner's creativity. Stanislavsky suggests another way to think about the interaction:

> "Tell me, please, what is the very first thing you need to do when you meet Romeo, or any person for that matter?"
> "I need to draw him in, to get his attention."
> "Yes! Yes! Don't forget about this moment. [...] A process of communion with him begins right there. You must attract his attention in order to start that communion and you need do nothing more. There's no Romeo, no Benvolio. You know as a person what to do. [...] You need to feel your partner out, to use your antennae, observe his eyes, penetrate his mind, take your lead from him. Only then can you fulfill your action."
>
> (Novitskaia 1984: 165–6)

This suggestion brought to mind yet another rehearsal on Act I scene 3 of *Hamlet*, when Ophelia tries to counter her father's advice to spurn Hamlet's love. Then too Stanislavsky stressed communion as a foundational aspect of his new technique. "In the end, it all comes down to communion," he had said, "because that triggers in the actor all the elements of our psycho-physical technique." At that rehearsal, he had even risked referring to the banned spiritual practice of Yoga by telling the actor-Ophelia that communion is the non-verbal "exchange of energy rays—*prana*—between people" (Novitskaia 1984: 190).

Stanislavsky now turns his attention to the character of Romeo. If Benvolio's main action is "to drag the secret out of Romeo," what is Romeo's action? "To not yield to Benvolio," the actor-Romeo responds. "That's correct. You fulfill the counteraction throughout this scene," Stanislavsky agrees (Novitskaia 1984: 172). At this moment in the lesson, the interactive emphasis in Stanislavsky's new rehearsal technique becomes crystal clear. Action and counteraction in communion with each other define the rules of the chess game.

Stanislavsky then asks, "What's the next step?" When the actor-Benvolio responds, "to go to the words," Stanislavsky shakes his head. "No, today we are only working on making action organic and logical in terms of the given circumstances" (Novitskaia 1984: 166). With that goal in mind, he asks the two actors for an etude through which they can engage with each other "today, now, here"[9] within the circumstances of the scene. "Follow elementary logic," he advises, "and keep in mind the simple process of communing with each other." Do not change the story or the problems with which your characters are dealing, but do "allow your fantasies to be flexible" (Novitskaia 1984: 167–9).

The actors get up and play the chess game of the scene. Benvolio draws Romeo out and Romeo resists. They closely attend to each other, with Benvolio trying first one way and then another, until finally he sits Romeo down on a bench, puts his arm around him, and succeeds in getting Romeo to confide in him. Stanislavsky is pleased with their etude. The story unfolded in action. The actors connected the logic of thought with the logic of their moment-to-moment behavior toward each other. Stanislavsky summed it up:

> You don't need the text. You know the scene's theme and that is enough to play your role in accord with organic processes. And if you feel the need to speak, I give you permission to speak your thoughts within the role's theme, using your own words.
>
> (Novitskaia 1984: 171)

As the session ended, Knebel realized that this session had gone to the heart of Stanislavsky's new technique. The actors had analyzed the interaction between Benvolio and Romeo by doing what is required of them by the scene and using their natural impulses to speak in order to help them. In short, they had engaged in the active analysis of the scene.

June 1937: *The Cherry Orchard*

It is eleven at night, when Stanislavsky's wife, Lilina, begins a rehearsal with two actors (*Letopis'* IV 2003: 402),[10] who have been working with her on *The Cherry Orchard*. Knebel has joined them to observe and the four have gathered in Lilina's private room on Leontyevsky Lane, just down the hall from Stanislavsky's bedroom (Knebel' 1967: 273–4), where he is still up and writing. The actors are scheduled to show their work to him in a few days, but they have been struggling with the scene in Act IV when Lopakhin tries but fails to propose to Varya.

For this particular project Stanislavsky had forbidden the actors to read the play, trusting his wife to guide them toward Chekhov's text. Having played both the landowner's youngest daughter and Varya, the adopted older daughter, Lilina knows the play inside out. She would start every rehearsal by describing the given circumstances, then she would read the text to the actors, and finally the actors would play their scenes using their own words (Ignatieva 2016: 3–12). For this rehearsal, she follows the same process. She reminds the actors that from the beginning of the play everyone has expected Varya and Lopakhin to marry, but by Act IV he has still not proposed. The failed proposal scene on which they plan to work takes place after Lopakhin has bought the estate, after Varya has arranged to take a position as a governess elsewhere, and just before the family leaves their ancestral home forever. Her mother has just convinced Lopakhin that if he is to propose, he must do so now. He agrees and she sends for Varya, leaving the room so that the two can have a moment alone. Clearly Varya knows what's up when she enters. Lilina then reads aloud the text of the scene, full of small talk but no proposal.

As the actors begin to rehearse, there is an unexpected knock on the door and Stanislavsky's nurse announces that he will be joining them. Then he enters, leaning on his cane and dressed in a suit and bow tie (Ignatieva 2016: 3–12). Encouraged by Lilina to speak, the actor-Varya complains that Chekhov does not give her enough to say for the audience to understand what is going on in Varya's heart. Stanislavsky agrees:

> In order to appreciate Chekhov's work, you have to understand the enormous place occupied in it by inner monologues, the unspoken thoughts in the lives of the characters.

[…] You will never succeed in creating the truth of your scene with Lopakhin if you don't discover for yourself Varya's actual train of thoughts for every, single second of your being in this scene.

(Knebel' [1954] 2009: 93)

He then asks the actors to try an etude with Lopakhin speaking as Chekhov has written him, but with Varya voicing her unspoken thoughts alongside the unimportant things she says aloud in the text.

The actor-Varya begins in a state of anxious excitement. "Now it will happen, what I've wanted for so long," she whispers to herself, and yet she cannot force herself to look directly at her partner-Lopakhin. "I want to look, but I just can't …" Then aloud, looking away from him and into the corners of the room, she says, "It's strange, I can't seem to find it." As the scene continues with the actor putting herself fully into the play's circumstances, she realizes how much of Varya's future rides on this one moment. The actor knew that this was so before she began the etude, but now this knowledge touches her heart. What if he again says nothing to her? Does she dare propose to him? As a woman, she's not supposed to do that! She feels suddenly very vulnerable. She doesn't know what to say, so she says nothing. Then, when he asks about the weather, she can't believe it. The weather? Really? Why doesn't he ask about marriage? But instead she says aloud in a flat tone, "our thermometer's broken." How stupid to mention the thermometer, how awful! When he then asks about her plans, she feels confused. Does he think that her plans have nothing to do with him? Doesn't he know that if he were to propose, all her plans would change? She would drop everything, stay here on the estate with him, make a home for them. If it has been embarrassing to face her family and friends before this, how much more embarrassing will it be now, if everyone knows that he came to propose and then didn't? As the scene ends, she finds herself still looking for that misplaced item, just for something to do to shut out her thoughts and keep her sense of embarrassment at bay. "Yes," she tells him when he asks, "life in this house is over." Then suddenly he is called away and gone. She is alone. The moment has passed and so too have all her hopes. Varya has experienced so much while saying so little aloud.

"Excellent," Stanislavsky whispers to himself. Raising his voice, he tells the actor-Varya that "the audience will not know what words you say to yourself, but they will understand your character's inner state of mind, her spiritual state, they will grasp the organic process in the unbroken line of your subtext" (Knebel' [1954] 2009: 95). At one in the morning, Stanislavsky left. In the coming years, Knebel would often think about this unforgettable, intimate rehearsal. Inner monologue had always been part of the Stanislavsky System, but Active Analysis more effectively than any other of his experiments uncovers the thoughts which prompt characters to speak.

A few mornings later on June 14, 1937, the full studio assembles to watch Lilina's students perform *The Cherry Orchard*. At the start of the session, Stanislavsky surprises everyone by asking the cast to take ten minutes for preparatory exercises, calling them the actor's *toilette*, the French word for getting dressed. He asks them first to focus on their breathing and to relax their bodies. Next they study the details in the hall's old-fashioned chandeliers and then on the elaborately painted ceilings in order to practice their powers of observation and concentration. When a student questions the value of taking time away from rehearsing the play, Stanislavsky declares that a "*toilette* for *toilette*'s sake" is indeed a waste of time. But, when performed properly, it becomes a necessary step in performance. "It's like tuning an instrument," he explains. "You cannot play on an untuned instrument" (Vinogradskaia 2000: 504). Many decades later Knebel would echo Stanislavsky, telling her students that exercises for the exercises' sake are no good, but "if you treat every exercise like a little piece of art, you will never be bored."[11] In June 1937 such preparation was an entirely new idea. Lilina recalls that "this was the first time I had seen this procedure and I liked it very much. It can help even well-prepared and experienced actors do their best" (*Letopis'* IV: 402).

After their *toilette*, her students showed their work on *The Cherry Orchard* and everyone present was astonished by the depth of their acting. The next day, in confidence, Stanislavsky admitted to Lilina, "Everything was truthful, correct, and full of life. Your students fulfilled my expectations better than the other groups in the Studio" (*Letopis'* IV: 402).

February 1937 to June 1938: *Hamlet*

Valentina Alexandrovna Vyakhireva was conducting the rehearsals on *Hamlet*. Stanislavsky had told her at their first meeting that he had entirely re-thought the play and was "interested in doing something new with [it]" (Novitskaia 1984: 146).[12] Perhaps this revisionist impulse led to his casting of the eighteen-year-old Irina Yurievna Rozanova in the title role. Never shy, she had boldly asked for the male role. After a day's thought, Stanislavsky happily agreed, telling her, "Hamlet will be your university" (Vinogradskaia 2000: 386). He warned her, however, against playing a male stereotype. Approach the role as any other, he advised, by imagining yourself in Hamlet's circumstances (Vinogradskaia 2000: 442). One of her fellow actors recalled that the casting suited her: "The straight line of her nose with a short haircut, bangs covering a third of her forehead [...] added masculinity and sternness to her face. One could imagine Hamlet's face exactly like that!" (Ignatieva 2008b: 122). As she worked, she "emerged as a youth with such invigorating sincerity and purity of heart," said Stanislavsky, that "this young Hamlet was the one I had dreamed of for years" (Chushkin 1968: 288).

Work began with Act I scene 2, when Prince Hamlet confronts three facts: his father is dead; his mother Gertrude has married his uncle Claudius; and Claudius has taken Hamlet's father's place not only on Denmark's throne, but also in his mother's bed. At a morning session in April, Rozanova tells Stanislavsky that she cannot make sense of Gertrude's behavior. It is as if Hamlet has more than one mother, Rozanova insists. Stanislavsky pushes back. You "made up" all those mothers instead of "visualizing" someone in Gertrude's specific circumstances (Vinogradskaia 2000: 463). He then asks Rozanova to name the main problem[13] that occupies Hamlet during the court scene with regard to his mother. She repeats, "I cannot understand Gertrude!" Echoing his earlier question to the actor-Benvolio, Stanislavsky now prods Rozanova to say what actions she would take in order to get a better understanding of Gertrude. When Rozanova says that she would "ask" her mother, Stanislavsky objects. You cannot ask within the public circumstances of the scene, so instead "you need to observe." Rozanova now agrees "to follow" everything that her mother says and does (Vinogradskaia 2000: 455–6).

Stanislavsky's next question also echoes the earlier class on *Romeo and Juliet*: "Does the verb 'to follow' suggest one physical action or many?" When Rozanova answers, "many," he suggests that she play the scene by trying all the various adjustments that Hamlet might use "to follow" what Gertrude says and does (Vinogradskaia 2000: 455–6). While the actors work, Stanislavsky frequently reminds Rozanova that observing Gertrude in order to understand her is like "working out a mathematical problem" (Vinogradskaia 2000: 510).

By May Rozanova was successfully using "her eyes, her ears, her conscious mind" to follow Gertrude's behavior (Knebel' 1967: 268), but Stanislavsky was not yet satisfied. In the book he was then writing, he likens the sequence of images that flash in one's mind as one thinks to a "filmstrip" (SS II 1989: 130). In class, he presses Rozanova to develop just such a "filmstrip" by using her imagination to visualize her thoughts as the scene unfolds.

> Surely in life, when you observe someone, you paint pictures for yourself of what it is that you are following. You see your mother crying, in tears, dressed in black. Then suddenly you see her happy, more than happy, married to this scoundrel, this villain. What will you do if you want to understand this metamorphosis?
>
> (Knebel' 1967: 268)

When Rozanova responds that she would feel jealous, he orders her "to sit down and be jealous." "I can't," she admits. He presses her further to "ask yourself for real," what would a person do in Hamlet's circumstances. In the next etude, Rozanova becomes very still, completely absorbed in following the actor-Gertrude, as she smiles at her new husband and reaches for his hand. Stanislavsky praises Rozanova for this unexpected stillness: "For a second or two, you got to the truth!" (Knebel' 1967: 269) This exchange between actor and teacher brings to mind a hallmark of Stanislavsky's System—that emotion results from our actions, and therefore actors should simply do what their characters do, letting emotion arise of itself.

Rozanova found Hamlet's Act I encounter with his father's ghost even more challenging than the court scene. She begged her friend, Vladimir Fromgold, cast as the ghost, to rehearse with her at night in a local cemetery. Fromgold recalls her as a "very temperamental" actor who threw herself completely into her roles. She had previously studied with Serafima Birman, a founding member of Stanislavsky's First Studio, where Stanislavsky had most actively experimented with emotional memory as an acting technique. Thus, Rozanova's personality and prior training made her feel that rehearsing in the cemetery could unlock for her the emotional underpinnings in the scene. While Fromgold had initially resisted, he eventually gave into her pleas (Ignatieva 2008b: 124–5). Had the site-specific experiment helped her? Whenever they showed the scene to Stanislavsky, Rozanova swooned and sometimes fainted at Fromgold's entrance, overcome by a fear of ghosts and the "eerie" atmosphere of a cemetery at night. Stanislavsky was not pleased with her loss of control and reprimanded her for putting emotion first. Acting, he said, should comprise "90% technique and only 10% emotion." You have inverted that ratio (Vinogradskaia 2000: 442).

Stanislavsky had already alerted Vyakhireva to watch for those occasional instances when actors "walk up to the edge of the ocean of the unconscious" and are unexpectedly "swept away by a wave of emotion." Stanislavsky had emphasized that the actor's "goal is to approach without being engulfed in the ocean" (Vinogradskaia 2000: 443). He advised that she help her actors maintain their balance by directing them "to come on stage in order to solve a problem, to ask themselves 'what would they do in the play's circumstances,' and then to use simple physical actions in order to make it through the entire play" (Vinogradskaia 2000: 443–4). In coaching Rozanova, Stanislavsky followed his own advice. At one morning session he directs Rozanova-Hamlet to "orient" herself to the ghost when he appears. Remember, he tells her, Hamlet's late father has a great deal to say. So you wouldn't want to scare him away before he can confide in you (Vinogradskaia 2000: 463). This prompting helped Rozanova shift her attention away from her fear to Fromgold-Ghost. Her need to gain the ghost's trust becomes more prominent. She begins to adjust to Fromgold's specific behavior within the scene. "By paying attention only to Hamlet's feelings you were playing the result" of his actions, said Stanislavsky, and that is "incorrect." Now, you are beginning "to commune" with your partner. "You must always take your partner in" (Vinogradskaia 2000: 463).

While Stanislavsky's experimental method of rehearsing begins by asking actors to explore their actions and counteractions before memorizing their lines, he always expects the text to serve as the springboard into performance. Therefore, all his rehearsals at the Opera-Dramatic Studio tested his paradoxical hunch that actors can best embody text by initially stepping away from the author's words in order to discover how what they do prompts them to speak. Knebel was beginning to see what Stanislavsky had in mind, when he asked her to teach "verbal action."

At a session in May 1937 the actor playing Claudius questioned this paradox. After using his own words to play the court scene in Act I, he worried that the etudes would lead him away, rather than toward the play. "What if I break down the organic processes and put them into a single line of actions, but later find that Shakespeare's text gets in my way?" (Vinogradskaia 2000: 467). Stanislavsky answers with a question. Given the fact that you must act in accord with the specific circumstances of the king at court, "why would you think that you would choose to speak in coarser language about what's important or beautiful than would Shakespeare? Is it simply the fact that the text is in poetry and that you need to hold on to its rhythm that bothers you?" (Vinogradskaia 2000: 467). Your classes in poetry and rhythm, diction and vocal technique will help you do that. But remember that in the end "the meter of the verse must enter into you so deeply that it will sound in your head at lunch and at dinner" (Vinogradskaia 2000: 467). Put another way, if the actor places himself fully into Claudius' circumstances, his etudes will uncover the need to speak the lines that Shakespeare has crafted for him. "The focus of my method," Stanislavsky states, "is to pull the rug of conventionalized acting out from under you and give you soil that is genuine and alive on which to stand" as you speak (Vinogradskaia 2000: 468).

On June 13, 1938, Stanislavsky met with the cast of *Hamlet*, for what would prove to be the last time. After showing their work, the actors pull their chairs close to Stanislavsky for a conversation, in which he restates many aspects of their work to date. He speaks again of the importance of the ghost scene to Rozanova's character. Hamlet's problem had been ordinary—a young man accepting the death of his father and his mother's remarriage. But the ghost changes everything. His problem now becomes extraordinary—how to set a corrupt world right:

> You, Hamlet, must take up your sword and go through the whole court, cleansing it of corruption; in this way alone will you save your father's soul. Like a mission, you must cleanse the whole world. This is the thought, the problem, which your father entrusted to you, that you must fulfill, and that only you can fulfill.
>
> (Vinogradskaia 2000: 508)

This problem has become a "super-problem"[14] and generates the play's central theme. "Can you now say," he asks Rozanova, "what this super-problem is?" (Vinogradskaia 2000: 508). A chorus of voices respond with "to find the truth of life," but Rozanova roundly rejects this answer as too philosophical. Stanislavsky, however, stands with the cast, telling her that "a theory of existence goes to the very question of why such corruption can occur" (Vinogradskaia 2000: 509). In this moment, he reveals that, in rethinking *Hamlet*, he may have drawn a parallel between the rotten state of Denmark and the terror launched by Stalin on the Soviet Union.

Stanislavsky then prompts the actors to consider what was and was not working in their performances that day. He specifically points to those moments when they performed the results of an emotion or when they preplanned how they would work with their partners. Such moments, he tells them, belong to a conventional way of working that he calls "the school of representation." In contrast, he praises them when they genuinely interacted with each other in the here and now of rehearsal. At these moments, the actors successfully avoided theatrical clichés and experienced the story's fiction as their present reality. All his life Stanislavsky had sought to nurture this "school of experiencing," as he had named his preferred form of acting. This is why his constant refrain at the Studio had become "today, here, now."[15]

Stanislavsky also returns to the importance of verse in their conversation. He observes that in the Act I monologue beginning with the words "Oh that this too, too sullied flesh" Rozanova had ignored Shakespeare's rhythms, robbing the speech of its action and inner conflict. "Do you feel how the text is written like a song? [...] It is a *cantilena*, [the Italian musical term for a smooth lyrical melody, like a lullaby.] There is action in these words, but you do not use it" (Vinogradskaia 2000: 505–7). In her performance, she had distorted the *cantilena* by pausing unnecessarily: "You don't have the right to stop for a single second. You don't have the right to stop the musical flow of the sound. This must be a single, continuous melody," he tells her (Vinogradskaia 2000: 507). The musical structure of Shakespeare's verse embodies Hamlet's urgent need to speak and without accounting for this rhythm the monologue makes no sense. Nor did she use diction to convey the sound patterns, nor did she stress the words that make the meaning clear. "The form must be there," he insists (Novitskaia 1984: 208). He recommends that she practice phrasing, diction, and breath control every day (Vinogradskaia 2000: 507).

> Do not be disconcerted by my criticism. You know you have chosen to work on a role that should be the culmination of an actor's career. [...] If you will succeed in this work, you will be up to speed for a hundred plays. All the work you will have done here, will be useful to you.
>
> (Novitskaia 1984: 209)

He ends the conversation with words of advice to the entire cast.

> Your main problem is technique and technique. Sacrifice some years of your life now to learn the [physical, vocal, analytical, mental and spiritual] techniques that actors need. After this, there will be no time. [...] Art is very difficult. And why is it difficult? Because it demands systematic, daily work.
>
> (Novitskaia 1984: 208 and Vinogradskaia 2000: 512)

January to June 1938: *Higher and Higher*

Stanislavsky had hoped that his Opera-Dramatic Studio might be more than an acting school, but also a seedbed for ensembles of artists, who would create new drama as readily as they would act in plays written by others (Knebel' 1967: 266). Put into contemporary terms, he fantasized about actors devising texts by using his new rehearsal approach as their guide. To that end all students learned to use literature to generate etudes. For example, Knebel's students devised plays based upon short stories that Stanislavsky had selected (Knebel' [1954] 2009: 66)[16] and Novitskaya's group created a sequel to Pushkin's one-act tragedy, *Mozart and Salieri*, by imagining Salieri's life after poisoning his musical rival (Novitskaia 1984: 57–8).

On another front, Sokolova guided the assistants, whom she had recruited, in their attempts to create an entirely new work by means of etudes.[17] They chose as their subject the 1930s Soviet-American race to the stratosphere, which set the tone for the space race that would later play out during the Cold War. In September 1933 the Soviet *Stratostat*, a high-altitude balloon that was fueled by highly flammable hydrogen, rose high enough to see the earth's curvature and broke all aviation records. Its crew of three, who endured the frigid cold and altitude without pressurized space suits, oxygen, or safety devices other than parachutes, returned to earth as heroes. There followed a cultural craving for science fiction; a circus act in which an acrobat, costumed as a stratonaut, was shot from a cannon; a popular film that included the act; and a spate of radio announcers who began their broadcasts with "Mars Speaking!" In November 1933 the United States broke the Soviet record for altitude. In 1934 the Soviet Union developed an even more radically innovative ship, *Osovikhim I*, which launched on January 30 to coincide with the convening of the Communist Party Congress. Tragically the ship crashed, killing all three on board, and turning Stalin's planned triumph into an internationally publicized embarrassment (Smith 2015).

Sokolova's group used etudes to develop *A Flight to the Stratosphere*, in which the pilot (played by Kristi) bids farewell to his fiancée, who supports him in his mission; the crew's physicist confides his fears to his wife (played by Vyakhireva), who reminds him that he is part of history; and the female co-pilot (played by Novitskaya) brushes off her mother's desperate demand that she stay on earth (Knebel' 1967: 277). When they showed their work to Stanislavsky, he was not pleased. "It's too calm, you are not struggling with anything," he said (Knebel' 1967: 278). He challenged them to rethink the play by recounting a story about a physicist, whom he had personally known and who had parachuted from a high-altitude balloon in order to avoid being killed in an explosion. The physicist survived, but the event had changed his entire outlook on life. Their play needed something of life-changing importance. As Stanislavsky allowed his imagination full reign, he began wondering whether their balloon to the stratosphere was enough, suggesting that they might even imagine a moon rocket (Knebel' 1967: 278).

Inspired by Stanislavsky's critique, the actors worked more intensively, probing their characters' strivings for success and their fears of danger and death. Each actor-character asked what values were worth the sacrifice of their lives. Their etudes not only sharpened the conflicts among them, but also their love and admiration for each other. Unexpectedly there emerged a love triangle within the crew of three, which prompted them to question the genre of their play. They retitled their work *Higher and Higher* and showed it again to

Stanislavsky. This time he liked it much more. He asked Kristi to transcribe their text and Knebel to direct. He then promised to look at their work again in the fall, but fall for him would never come (Knebel' 1967: 278).

Learning while Directing

In her free time Knebel had continued to direct at the Yermolova Studio Theatre, and in 1936 she was invited to stage a play of her own choice. Partly inspired by Nemirovich-Danchenko's rehearsals of *Enemies* for the Moscow Art, she chose to direct another Gorky play, *The Last Ones*—a brutal story about police corruption. Banned from the stage after an initial 1917 production, *The Last Ones* had not been produced since.

After a morning session in the Onegin salon, Knebel asked to speak privately with Stanislavsky. She told him of her directing opportunity and asked whether he might be willing to help her identify the main events in *The Last Ones*, as he had been doing for her with other works. He readily agreed, telling her that Gorky's plays are "an excellent school for actors" (Knebel' 1967: 310). In the same breath, he asked her how she would plan for the etudes. When she hesitated, he guessed that she had decided to use the older approach to directing. Her silence provoked him:

> Why are you studying at my studio? Why do I take joy in giving you the opportunity to verify the knowledge that you are acquiring with my students here, if not to verify it as well with other young theatres and actors?

> (Knebel' 1967: 310)

She felt shaken and ashamed. He was right to reprimand her. His generosity obligated her to apply and develop his new method, if she were to stay at his side. "This conversation," she later recalled, "was the true beginning of my work with and my own investigation into Active Analysis" (Knebel' 1967: 311).

Her production of *The Last Ones* opened in 1937. She had rehearsed it entirely through Stanislavsky's new etude process, learning the hard way how much careful preparation Active Analysis demands of the director in order to unleash the actors' individual and collective creativities. It demands developing a shared understanding about the play—its structure, language, overarching themes, and meanings—in order that the entire production team speak to their audiences in a single artistic voice. "This is only possible when the main idea of the production grows from the seed of the play and from the problems posed in it by the author" (Knebel' 1967: 314). Most of all, Active Analysis demands of the director the same generosity of spirit, mutual respect, and disciplined commitment to art that Knebel saw in Stanislavsky.

An Intolerably Hot August

On June 16, 1938, Stanislavsky held his last class on the opera *Madame Butterfly*. He ended the session by telling everyone that he held much hope for the future of theatre because of their commitment to art and the progress he was making on his book (*Letopis'* IV: 450–1). However, his heart was growing weaker and he took to his bed as June came to an end. August arrived in a record-breaking heatwave. On the 2nd Stanislavsky was supposed to go to the nursing home outside Moscow for some relief from the intense heat, but he was too weak to travel. By the 6th he had a temperature of 39.7° Celsius (102° Fahrenheit). The next day his heart stopped (*Letopis'* IV: 456).

There remained in the hearts of his students vivid memories of his talents, such as the one from October 26, 1937, after an actor had presented a futurist poem by Vladimir Mayakovsky, a contemporary Soviet poet of enormous creative passion. Stanislavsky had been speaking about how poetic rhythms, like music in opera, cannot be separated from the work's themes and meanings, when he began to illustrate his remarks with examples from Aleksander Griboyedov's 1823 classic, *Woe from Wit*, which is written in iambic verse. The play centers around a liberal young nobleman, named Chatsky, who stands at the opposite pole from his soon-to-be father-in-law, Famusov—a rich, well-fed bureaucrat. Stanislavsky had played Famusov in 1906, the very year in which he had decided to systematize actor training. Now more than thirty years later he found himself revisiting the role. As he tried to explain how the verse had helped him to embody Famusov's comic pathos, he began to show his students what he meant by reciting a monologue. A young actor bore witness to what happened next:

> [Stanislavsky] started casually and imperceptibly got carried away with the reading. He sat in his chair and seemed to grow progressively older, more bloated, more wrinkled. His eyes bulged and widened. It even seemed to us that he had grown a stomach. In front of our very eyes, he had changed completely without using any make-up and without donning a costume. He recited the lines—no, he acted Famusov's monologue. [… This was] a beautiful illustration of his theory. Here was the organic necessity of the verse. You could not have produced this performance in prose.
>
> (Vinogradskaia 2000: 487)

Stanislavsky was, first to last, an actor, but he had not performed publicly since his heart attack in 1928. A few old-timers at the Moscow Art Theatre remembered him as an actor, but the majority of those who crowded into his Opera-Dramatic Studio knew him only as a teacher. No wonder this impromptu performance seemed "an unexpected and beautiful gift to us who had never seen him on stage" (Vinogradskaia 2000: 487).

This was, of course, not the only time that Stanislavsky had performed a monologue at the Studio. But this time, when he reached the end, everyone in the salon "sat silently, not knowing how to react." Finally, someone felt "bold" enough to applaud, leading others to join in. As the applause built in volume, Stanislavsky "stood up from his chair, bowed to each corner of the hall, and exited like an actor, leaving the stage after a successful performance" (Vinogradskaia 2000: 487–8). Time passed. Everyone waited, unsure what to do, until finally Stanislavsky's nurse appeared to announce that "the lesson is finished for today" (Vinogradskaia 2000: 487–8).

While reliable eyewitnesses, like Knebel, offer glimpses behind the closed doors of Leontyevsky Lane, gaps in information still remain. His published books, however well translated, will forever bear the marks of Stalin's censors. The forty-eight existing transcripts of his classes at the Opera-Dramatic Studio paint only a partial picture of his experimental work. Similarly, while Stanislavsky's archives were fully opened to scholars after the fall of the Soviet Union in 1991, his correspondence and writings still leave questions unanswered. For example, despite strong circumstantial evidence, no explicit records prove beyond a shadow of a doubt that Stalin ordered Stanislavsky's internal exile or that those surrounding him, like his nurse and Kedrov, were other than what they purported to be. But the absence of records means little, given the fact that the Soviet state actively suppressed information about Stalin's evil treatment of his country during the 1930s. While most scholars believe that the archives are complete, the Moscow Art Theatre's long-time dramaturg, Anatoly Smeliansky, believes otherwise:

> We do not know everything that took place on Leontyevsky Lane. The relatives of Stanislavsky affirm that before surrendering Konstantin Sergeyevich's archives after his death, papers were burnt in his home for two days.
>
> (Smeliansky 1991: 13)[18]

Following Stanislavsky's death a commission determined what projects from the Opera-Dramatic Studio would go forward. Kedrov was its chair, and its members included Stanislavsky's sister Sokolova, the Studio's principal who was a government official, the translator of *Romeo and Juliet*, and another Shakespeare scholar (Novitskaia 1984: 218). The commission authorized Lilina to continue with *The Cherry Orchard*, and she carried on rehearsing until Hitler's invasion of the Soviet Union on June 22, 1941, brought the project to an end. Novitskaya's *Romeo and Juliet* went forward as well, but also came to a halt in 1941 due to the Second World War (Ignatieva 2016: 3–12). The cast of *Hamlet* lobbied hard for the opportunity to complete their work, with Rozanova personally pleading with Kedrov who seemed uncomfortable with her and her casting (Ignatieva 2008b: 127). The project never received a definitive answer from the commission. Sadly, Rozanova's career was cut short by her death in a traffic accident in 1943, just after she had been invited to play Hamlet by a rising new director. She was twenty-five at her death (Ignatieva 2008b: 127).[19] Knebel continued working with Sokolova's group to finalize their devised play, *Higher and Higher*, which had won approval for production from the censorship bureau (Novitskaia 1984: 58). Nonetheless, as Knebel reports, Kedrov "showed no interest in this work, and so it [too] came to an end" (Knebel' 1967: 278).

At the time of Stanislavsky's death, *Rigoletto* and Molière's *Tartuffe* were also being rehearsed on Leontyevsky Lane. No longer protected by Stanislavsky's international fame, Meyerhold had no choice but to stop work on *Rigoletto*. His arrest and execution for his sins against socialist realism soon followed (Chapter 1). In contrast, Kedrov took charge of Stanislavsky's rehearsals on *Tartuffe*, which premiered posthumously at the Moscow Art Theatre in 1939. Hailed for the completion of this work, Kedrov became Stanislavsky's most visible heir, advancing the politically correct Method of Physical Actions.

Meanwhile, Knebel went underground to keep her mentor's more holistic version of Active Analysis alive. The time she had spent on Leontyevsky Lane had been life-changing:

> There are a great number of paths in art. For me, the path was a rehearsal process, the method of Active Analysis. Through my many experiences and in my work on Shakespeare and Gorky, I understood that this method strengthens the improvisatory nature of the actor, helps uncover the actor's individuality, and cleans the dust of time off literary works with wonderful images and characters in them. [...] With these convictions in mind, I continued to work.
>
> (Knebel' 1967: 485)

Notes

1. Few sources in English treat the complex history of Stanislavsky's many studios. For more on the Second Studio, see Gauss (1999: 60–87) and Shevtsova (2020: 149–56).
2. Stanislavsky used the word *perezhivanie* to name his preferred form of acting, which I translate as "experiencing" (Carnicke 2009: chapter 7). I do so in order to encompass all perceptual forms of experience including emotional, physical, sensory, intellectual, spiritual, etc. For more on Stanislavsky's admiration of Duse see Carnicke (2017: 56–71).
3. Knebel married her childhood friend Boris Goltsev in 1917; they divorced in 1922. In 1924 she married Naum Frid, whom she had met in Michael Chekhov's studio; they divorced in 1932. She then married Urbanovich in 1933; he disappeared in 1939, most probably arrested for his association with Meyerhold (see Chapter 3). She had no children, but had suffered a miscarriage in 1938. (Abensour 2019: 14–16; 43–5; 261–5) Knebel never bore grudges and consequently she stayed friends with her ex-husbands; both Goltsev and Frid would bring her flowers for her birthday (Liadov 1998: 8).
4. There are forty-eight published transcripts of Stanislavsky's classes from 1936 to 1938 at the Opera-Dramatic Studio. Sometimes there are two or more accounts of the same class. In this section, I have created a collage of moments from the transcripts, using a combination of paraphrase, analysis, and direct quotations from primarily three sources: Novitskaia (1984); Vinogradskaia (2000); and Knebel' ([1954] 2009).
5. Romeo was played by Igor Rozhnyatovsky and Benvolio by Lev Elagin.
6. Stanislavsky thinks of the character as a hybrid of the actor and role, using a hyphen when he writes to convey this understanding graphically. In this book, I use Stanislavsky's format of actor-role throughout.
7. The Russian verb *razbirat'* is generally translated as "analyze," but it can also refer to the parsing of a sentence in grammar. This latter meaning is appropriate within the context of Active Analysis (see Lesson 3 on *razbor*). The use of "story" and "plot" that follows in this quotation suggests the influence of Russian Formalism on Stanislavsky's thinking (see Lessons 1 and 4).
8. Stanislavsky uses the word "action" in a number of different ways in his classes. Here, the "main action" refers to what initiates the scene (its impelling action, see Lesson 1) and "physical actions" identify the ways in which actors adjust their behavior to what their partners do moment to moment in an etude. Here Stanislavsky makes clear that his use of the word "physical" is provisional.
9. In transcripts from the Opera-Dramatic Studio, Stanislavsky uses "now," "today," and "here" in varying combinations. I use the order as given by Novitskaia (1984: 167).
10. There were multiple casts for this project with Varya played by L. Novitskaya and M. Mazur and Lopakhin played by Mozzhechkov, A. Krug, and B. Valikin. The two actors at this rehearsal are not named.
11. Personal communication from Natalya Zverova, *MetodiFestival*, Italy, October 2008.
12. Benedetti provides an abridged translation of Novitskaya's transcripts for *Hamlet* in his book *Stanislavski and the Actor* (1998: 131–48).
13. The Russian word is *zadacha*. See Lesson 2 for a discussion about this term and its alternative translations. I consistently translate the term as "problem," here and throughout the book.

14. The term, *sverkhzadacha*, translated here as "super-problem," is as problematic as its root, *zadacha*. For more on its meaning and alternative translations see Lesson 4.

15. See notes 2 and 9 above.

16. Actor training in Russia to this day begins with students dramatizing short stories, which help them understand the contexts and subtexts that inform rich performances.

17. The group included G. Kristi, L. Novitskaya, V. Batyushkova, Yu. Malkovsky, A. Skalovskaya, V. Vyakhireva, I. Mazur, A. Zenkovsky, E. Sokolova, and E. Zvereva (Knebel' 1967: 277).

18. In a personal email on January 28, 2019, Maria Ignatieva suggested that the burning of documents was unlikely.

19. The director was Nikolay Okhlopkov, who eventually staged *Hamlet* in 1954 at the Mayakovsky Theatre as a "retrospective comment on the Stalinist years" with Denmark depicted "as a prison" (Worrall 1989: 181–3).

3　The Truth Will Out!

A Normal Soviet Life

Stanislavsky's funeral in 1938 was a lavish state affair, its pomp and circumstance another example of the Soviet hypocrisy that honored his body, while burying his artistic soul. For her part, Maria Knebel vowed to keep his legacy alive through the practice and promotion of Active Analysis. But how to do so within the circumstances of Soviet life remained unclear.

As an ordinary Soviet citizen, Maria had to cope with material deprivations and the continuing terror of the Stalinist regime. She was living at 22 Pechatnikov Lane, number 8, a *kommunalka* or state-owned apartment, in which each room was occupied by a different family. She had first moved there in 1924 with Naum Frid, her second husband and a fellow student of acting. The apartment had then belonged to his parents and for several years the young couple enjoyed the entire apartment. But in 1929 when the state requisitioned it for communal living, the two had to crowd into a single room. When they divorced in 1932, Knebel kept the room and a year later her third husband, Pavel Vladimirovich Urbanovich, moved in (Liadov 1998: 81). Urbanovich was a member of Meyerhold's company and a teacher of biomechanics. He had asked Knebel to host the debate on theatrical aesthetics in their cramped quarters, during which his colleague, Aleksey Popov, had insisted that she try her hand at directing (Chapter 2).

As Yelena Vasilyeva Lyadova, a fellow tenant, recalls, Maria's friendly manner and inherent generosity made living together in number 8 more bearable than in many other *kommunalkas*, where grief, greed, and jealousies soured daily life. "When someone needed help, Maria Osipovna was ready and willing. She did what was needed simply and sincerely, as if for herself, and always stood up for the truth" (Liadov 1998: 85). Yelena had been fourteen years old in 1935 when her mother was arrested and sent to a labor camp for two years, leaving Yelena to raise her siblings and maintain her own education. Maria offered food and money when possible, gave Yelena a skirt when the girl's had become too worn to repair, and sent a lovely dress to Yelena's mother, knowing that she would remember it as Maria's. At that time, sending recognizable items to prisoners instead of letters, which would be censored, was a way of letting loved ones know that people at home were thinking of them (Liadov 1998: 81).[1] The same "goodwill, instead of rancor, guided her hand" in professional matters as well. "Although she was in no sense an innocent lamb," observes her biographer, "she preferred not to write about those whom she did not respect and in whose work she did not believe" (Vladimirova 1991: 275). She focused instead on those whom she admired, often without mentioning her own accomplishments. As one of her students said, "there is not a shadow of vanity" in her (Liadov 1998: 76).

With Stanislavsky's death in 1938 Meyerhold had lost his only remaining champion. He was arrested on June 19, 1939 (Chapter 1). Knebel's husband reacted to this news in fear, shutting himself up in their room and drinking heavily. After some time had passed, Knebel was sent on tour with the Moscow Art Theatre and, when she arrived home, she learned that her husband had gone missing and her sister's husband had died on the same day (Liadov 1998: 88 and Knebel' 1967: 122–3).[2] Then, in 1940 during an antisemitic campaign Maria's brother Nikolay was arrested in front of her, her sister, and mother, while they were vacationing (Liadov 1998: 88–90).[3] The branding of her brother as an enemy of the people meant that Maria too was shunned. "In the corridors of the Moscow Art Theatre people would avoid meeting her, so that they would not be obliged to say hello," recalled a friend (Liadov 1998: 100).

Despite her difficulties, Maria would rarely indulge her feelings, only telling others the bare facts—that "her husband had left," or "her brother had been arrested," etc. "She knew how to control herself," recalls a neighbor (Liadov 1998: 88). Years later, after editing Knebel's autobiography, Natalya Anatolyevna Krymova marveled that "Maria Osipovna's life as a woman remained for me such a mystery" that I was taken aback when, at her funeral, a fellow actress called her "the most sexual woman at the Art Theatre" (Liadov 1998: 49). Nonetheless, Maria's words would sometimes reveal the toll that she had paid for living an ordinary Soviet life. For example, she once cynically asked a female directing student why she "would want to raise her son to be an intelligent person, knowing full well that it would only make his life more difficult" (Liadov 1998: 100).

As an actor in the Moscow Art Theatre Knebel continued with her roles in *The Blue Bird*, *Uncle's Dream*, *The Cherry Orchard*, and other plays in the company's regular repertoire. Her acting insured her salary, but offered little chance to put into practice what she had learned from Stanislavsky at the Opera-Dramatic Studio. As a director she had better luck. The Yermolova Studio Theatre allowed her to continue experimenting with Active Analysis, and so she poured her best energy into productions there, even turning down a prestigious invitation in 1937 to join the Moscow Art Theatre's directing team. As she explained, "I felt bolder on the smaller stage" (Knebel' 1967: 316). Members of Meyerhold's company had run the Yermolova when she had first joined, but now Nikolay Pavlovich Khmelyov, widely considered one of the Moscow Art Theatre's finest young actors, was in charge. Knebel had known him since her time at the Second Studio.

Khmelyov invited Knebel to co-direct Shakespeare's *As You Like It* with him at the Yermolova in 1940. She agreed on one condition: that he allow her to use Active Analysis from conception through performance. They divided their work as was customary at that time: she assisted the actors in their creation of characters; he staged the play and worked with the designers. Initially skeptical about her rehearsal process, Khmelyov was completely won over, when the actors performed their first etudes. That rehearsal marked "a joyful day in my life," she recalled (Knebel' 1967: 347). Their acclaimed production created "a world [that] was not entirely good," as one critic put it, "but there was somewhere to run to, away from those places where evil existed. The fairy-tale, lyrical world of the forest of Arden was more real than the real world" (Leach and Borovsky 1999: 338). Moreover, Arden was designed exclusively of natural materials—wood, straw, leather, and feathers—a stark contrast to the repressive world of the court from which Rosalind flees, and which, like Stalin's industrial vision for the country, was made of concrete, metal, and electricity.

By 1941 Knebel felt confident in her ability to persuade others to try Active Analysis, and so joined the directing team at the Moscow Art Theatre. She came to value her new and close association with the company's co-founder, Vladimir Ivanovich Nemirovich-Danchenko, calling him "my university in directing" (Knebel' 1967: 374). Despite the years of tension between him and Stanislavsky, Knebel saw the two men as complementary artists, one brilliant in terms of acting, the other just as brilliant in his approach to dramaturgy. As Nemirovich-Danchenko pushed her to take more and more initiative in her directing, she "felt absolutely free" (Knebel' 1967: 374).

Among her most notable directing assignments was a new patriotic play, *Kremlin Chimes* by Nikolay Pogodin, a journalist and prolific playwright. The story centers around an engineer, who is summoned by Lenin shortly after the revolution and asked to fix the clock in the Kremlin's tower, so that the chimes can bring cheer to the populace. In discussions with Pogodin, Knebel shared the story of how her father had been similarly summoned after the state's confiscation of his publishing company. Lenin was planning to create a new State Literary Press and needed her father's help to succeed. "Will you sabotage us or work for us?" Lenin had asked. This question would later become a pivotal line in Pogodin's play (Knebel' 1967: 26–7).

When the Nazis invaded Russia on June 21, 1941, Knebel was working on *Kremlin Chimes* as one of the "brigade," as directorial teams were then called. Nemirovich-Danchenko and the actor Leonid Leonidov headed the brigade, while she took charge of staging a climactic crowd scene within the production. "I changed the very form of the rehearsals, calling small groups of actors aside in order to work with them individually." Her process won praise from the actors who "took pleasure in the chance to exercise their creative initiative and imaginations" (Knebel' 1967: 366). On August 7 the government decided to evacuate senior members of the company from Moscow for their safety, leaving the younger generation behind to carry on, with air raid shelters provided in the rehearsal halls. At midnight on the eve of August 9 Nemirovich-Danchenko telephoned Knebel. He sounded upset as he asked her to handle all rehearsals in his and Leonidov's absence. "I believe in your strong will," he told her. "And I am asking you to do everything you can to keep *Chimes* going" (Knebel' 1967: 402). He admitted that it would be difficult for her, especially since many of the actors being evacuated held leading roles and she would need to recast. He recommended that Khmelyov play the engineer. He also suggested that she consult with his colleague, Vasily Sakhnovsky, should she need directing advice. Later, Nemirovich-Danchenko would confide to his secretary that "Knebel always clears away my pessimism, if only for a time" (Nemirovich-Danchenko 2003 vol. 4: 116).

The dress rehearsal was set for October 14, 1941, but canceled when fighting reached the outskirts of Moscow (Knebel' 1967: 404). Knebel, together with her sister and mother, Nemirovich-Danchenko's secretary, and the entire cast of *Chimes* were now evacuated to the city of Saratov on the Volga River in Western Russia. There Knebel's mother died. There too the company continued rehearsing without sets or costumes under her direction. Reporting to Nemirovich-Danchenko about conditions in Saratov, his secretary wrote that "our dear sweet [Maria ...] now one of the company's best friends [...] is herself ill and heartsick" (Solov'eva 2005: 690). *Kremlin Chimes* finally premiered in Moscow in 1942.[4]

"Being a woman director is not easy," Knebel once wrote. "There are not many of us" (Knebel' 1976: 248). Her words understate the context of hostility that she faced in this endeavor. Sakhnovsky, whom Nemirovich-Danchenko had suggested that she go to for help, expressed the typical belief that "there are no women directors." He joked that those women who do direct are "not really women" (Liadov 1998: 31). Critics similarly praised Knebel for having "a mind that was truly not a woman's mind" (Liadov 1998: 61) and for displaying the "masculine traits" of clarity and structure in her productions (Vladimirova 1991: 204). Her achievements were often dismissed, because, given the Soviet propensity for brigade work, she had rarely had the opportunity to direct independently. Needless to say, the men with whom she collaborated were also in the brigades, but their contributions were not similarly dismissed.

Fired!

With the opening of *Kremlin Chimes* things seemed to be looking up professionally. Knebel continued acting and directing and was also chosen for the acting faculty at the newly founded Moscow Art Theatre Studio School. Things were also looking up personally, when she and her sister Yelena moved into two adjoining rooms on Vadkovsky Lane. Over the years, Knebel had increasingly come to rely on her older sister for support. "We had a common childhood," Maria wrote, "a common life that spanned two different and decisive periods of history, childhood and the hard years of war" (Liadov 1998: 105). They now also shared a small country house (a *dacha*) outside Moscow, where they enjoyed relaxing and entertaining during the summer months (Liadov 1998: 34). In short, she was doing what she loved, supported by those who loved her.

When Nemirovich-Danchenko died in April 1943, Khmelyov's appointment as Artistic Director of the Moscow Art Theatre reassured Knebel that her experiments with Active Analysis would continue. She was working on a play about early Russia, *The Difficult Years* by Aleksey Tolstoy, in a brigade of directors that included her friend Aleksey Popov and with Khmelyov in the central role of Ivan the Terrible. Nothing, it seemed, could be better than this trio of like-minded artists! The three even risked drawing a subtle parallel in their production between the autocratic Ivan and the "cult of personality" that had grown up around Stalin (Solov'eva 1966: 10–11). All was well, until the dress rehearsal on November 1, 1945, when Khmelyov felt ill, collapsed backstage, and died of a heart attack. He was only forty-four years old. His sudden death triggered a struggle for control of the theatre, which continued with in-fighting for another four years, during which time Knebel retained her standing in the company. But the ground was shifting beneath her feet.

As soon as Knebel's longtime colleague Mikhail Nikolayevich Kedrov was appointed Artistic Director in 1949, everything changed for her. Despite their association that had begun at the Second Studio, included their work at Stanislavsky's Opera-Dramatic Studio, and continued at the Moscow Art Theatre where they had shared the stage in Nemirovich-Danchenko's adaptation of *Anna Karenina*, an administrator pulled Knebel aside on June 8 at the end of the season to tell her that Kedrov would work only with those who considered themselves his students. "Struck dumb" by the comment, Knebel responded by observing that being "the same age, his comrade, and his colleague," she could hardly call him teacher (Knebel' 1967: 477).

At the time, she did not mention this peculiar conversation to anyone, because she was preparing for her sister's birthday party on June 10 at their *dacha*. "We spent the day laughing, joking, playing games." No one, not even Popov, who knew her very well, guessed at her troubled inner monologue. "The next day [...] when I told him the whole story, it was only then that I clearly saw that I was being thrown out of the company" (Knebel' 1967: 477). On September 7, just before the start of the 1950 season, Knebel received a curt letter relieving her of her directing duties. When she then arrived at the theatre to get her acting assignments, she found that her salary had been suspended and that all the plays in which she regularly performed, including *The Cherry Orchard*, had been pulled from the repertory. As she stood in the theatre stunned by the news, only the women of the company dared speak with her (Knebel' 1967: 478). The final blow was learning that she had also been replaced at the school, where her students were mystified by her unexplained absence (Liadov 1998: 140).

The stunning manner in which Kedrov had rid himself of Knebel mirrored Stalin's iron-fisted treatment of those who disagreed with him. But why had Kedrov felt that this move was necessary, when prior administrations had seen Knebel as an asset? The answer lies in the fact that, since Stanislavsky's death, she had been telling a radically different story about what had happened in the Opera-Dramatic Studio than he. Her commitment to the truth and his loyalty to Soviet policies had put them "in furious opposition" with one another (Liadov 1998: 26).[5]

Kedrov had proclaimed himself Stanislavsky's artistic heir in 1939 by staging the post-humous production of *Tartuffe*. Now, as the Artistic Director of the Moscow Art Theatre, Kedrov was promoting himself as "the disciple of the so-called *Method of Physical Actions*, [...] displaying a rare intransigence when it came to [this] working method" (Leach and Borovsky 1999: 356). He was saying that at the Opera-Dramatic Studio Stanislavsky had finally confessed to the idealistic errors of his youth and had jettisoned his prior spiritual practices in favor of a new, scientifically accurate approach to acting. Using Stanislavsky's often reiterated phrase "the method of physical actions" as label and *imprimatur*, Kedrov linked Stanislavsky's last rehearsal technique to recent Soviet discoveries in behaviorism, particularly to Ivan Pavlov's experiments on behavioral conditioning (Carnicke 2009: 162–3). This teleological story allowed Kedrov to filter out of the System everything that was politi-cally suspect and to bring Stanislavsky into alignment with Marxist materialism and Soviet policies on the arts. In practice, Kedrov focused exclusively on logical sequences of simple physical actions, meant to anchor the actor's performance in material reality. For example, in an escape scene the actor walks forward, reaches out a hand, turns the knob, opens the door, and exits.

In contrast, Knebel took Stanislavsky as he was, valuing the holistic way in which his last rehearsals triggered actors' physical, mental, and even spiritual imaginations. In contrast to Kedrov's story, Knebel saw Stanislavsky's last rehearsal technique as "absorbing everything that was discovered earlier; it absorbs [his] entire life and work. Without understanding this, you cannot understand what is new in his last discovery" (Knebel' 1968: 47–8). Knebel's more complex story resulted from her sharp-eyed observations at the Opera-Dramatic Studio and her willingness to tell the full truth about those aspects of the work that ran afoul of Soviet policies. Thus, she held that all styles of art can express the truth of human behavior, despite the state's imposition of socialist realism. "Why must one stylistic vision exclude another?" she asked (Chekhov 1995 vol. 1: 17). She also spoke of Stanislavsky's belief that art is by its very nature a spiritual activity, despite their country's imposition of atheism on its populace. She stressed that whenever Stanislavsky spoke about "physical actions," he simultaneously referred to their "psychophysical" underpinnings, because anything expressed through the body begins in the actor's mind and soul. In practice, Knebel emphasized how physical activities arise from a constantly changing trajectory of intentional actions that collide with the counteractions of others. For example, in an escape scene, the character might strive to avoid an uncomfortable meeting or personal embarrassment. Alternatively, the character might beat a hasty retreat, or abscond, or cut and run, etc. The descriptive verb necessarily affects the way in which the actor walks forward, reaches out a hand, turns the knob, and opens the door in order to exit the room. The scene is composed of the same sequence of physical motions but grounded in the character's rhythmic energy and trajectory of desire.

When Soviet repression made Knebel's story dangerous, she told it in secret only to those whom she could trust. When political conditions relaxed, she taught about it more openly. Eventually, she would call Kedrov's practice a "vulgarization" of Stanislavsky's work, coining the term "Active Analysis" in order to differentiate his holistic practice from the politically correct, bloodless "Method of Physical Actions" that was being taught in the Soviet Union (Knebel' 1971: 109).

In 1949 Knebel's story was particularly dangerous, because it defied the post-Second World War theory of conflictlessness, which proposed that, since Soviet reality had successfully transcended class conflicts, Soviet art should also do away with all conflict except that between Communism and Capitalism. From its inception socialist realism had enjoined artists to reflect a varnished Soviet reality, but in the late 1940s, when the government was cracking down especially hard on the arts, drama critics and playwrights reacted defensively with this latest and absurd theory, based upon the false assumption that in the allegedly perfect society created by Stalin's five-year plans, all interpersonal conflict had become irrelevant. Only competition between the better and the best was appropriate in Soviet life and art (Bown 1998: 221–301). "Conflictlessness" willfully ignored not only the "conflictual processes" of history (Scott 1999: 5, 7, 9, 25), but also the social and interpersonal dynamics upon which dramatists have historically relied. With conflict now banned, so too was Active Analysis, which depends upon the collision of actions and counteractions (Lesson 1). Clearly, Knebel and her story about Stanislavsky's last years had to go.

A Company of Her Own

Knebel's abrupt firing from the Moscow Art Theatre did not mean her abandonment of Active Analysis. She vowed to keep "the secret cult of knowledge" alive (Knebel' 1968: 46), finding an unexpected haven in children's theatre. By the 1940s theatre for young audiences had become an established Soviet institution, fully subsidized and professionally staffed with well-trained adult actors and directors. These theatres could sometimes escape the bounds of strict socialist realism by staging fantasies in theatricalist styles, because their audiences expected fairy tales. As the Russian theatre scholar Anatoly Smeliansky observes, during the darkest of times "the artistic flame [...] was kept alive in various theatrical catacombs," not the least of which was Moscow's Central Children's Theatre, where Knebel began directing in 1950. There, "immediately after the death of Stalin, the revival of the Russian stage would begin," due largely to her efforts (Smeliansky 1999: 5–6).

Moving out of her former and into her new artistic home, however, proved more challenging than she had expected. Nothing was familiar: not the walls, not the stage, not the company of actors, and certainly not the audience.

> Finding myself for the first time in the auditorium of the Central Children's Theatre, I did not feel tenderness, but confusion and fear. After the stern and respectful public at the Moscow Art Theatre, these screaming, agitated spectators would stun anyone. [...] They laughed loudly when, as it seemed to me they should cry. They burst into ecstasies that took me off guard, and then remained cold when I expected bursts of applause.
>
> (Knebel' 1967: 483)

After every performance she questioned spectators, paying special attention to the "twelve year old skeptics," who taught her that the ideological context that had threatened her security had also provoked in them strong emotions. Full of fear, hating authoritarianism, and conscious of the lies told them at school, "their laughter [..] hides their need for tears" (Knebel' 1967: 483). She rejected the romantic notion that children are tender and innocent. She decided that, just as theatre should level with adults, so too should it level with young people.

> We undervalue the enormous spiritual work that occurs minute by minute and hour by hour within them. What an awful sentiment, "Children won't understand!" I fought against it with teachers and playwrights. I strove to speak with children through the language of great art, without the babbling condescension that could be heard loudly in other children's theatres during those years when the "theory of conflictlessness" was blossoming.
>
> (Knebel' 1967: 484)

On March 5, 1953, Stalin died. His role in having helped defeat Hitler and his transformation of the Soviet Union into a world power through the country's industrialization argued strongly for his place in the pantheon of national heroes. During his regime he had so successfully hidden his personal role in the terror that people believed him a savior, blaming only his underlings as devils. Even Stanislavsky, who suffered internal exile and strict censorship, had fallen for the ruse, as proven in his 1932 complaint asking Stalin to remove the Communist Manager and take personal charge of the Moscow Art Theatre in order to save it (Chapter 1). When Stalin died, men, women, and children openly wept in the streets for the leader, whom they believed to be a hero. By 1956 Nikita Sergeyevich Khrushchev had consolidated his power as the new Soviet premier, and in February he gave a so-called "secret speech" to the Congress of the Communist Party in which he denounced Stalin for his egregious crimes against humanity. Suddenly Stalin was no longer a hero and the state had launched a program of reforms that undercut his most stringent policies.

However, a "thaw" had already begun within the artistic community.[6] In 1952 an editorial in the Communist newspaper *Pravda* attacked the notion of conflictlessness in drama. In 1953 the censorship agency that controlled theatres was closed and theatrical oversight was transferred to the Ministry of Culture. In 1955, in an effort to diversify Soviet aesthetics, the state rehabilitated a number of leading avant-garde artists who had been purged by Stalin, including Michael Chekhov and Vsevolod Meyerhold. Their names now cleared, they could be discussed, studied, and even admired. In short, theatre was relatively free for the first time since the 1920s to experiment with non-realism.

In 1955 Knebel was also appointed Artistic Director of the Central Children's Theatre. She now trained her actors in Active Analysis and they appeared in a broad-ranging repertory of classics, including Griboyedov's *Woe from Wit* and Molière's *Bourgeois Gentilhomme*; dramatic adaptations of novels, among them Gogol's *Dead Souls* and Dickens' *Oliver Twist*; and contemporary plays on current issues, like Pogodin's controversial treatment of Khrushchev's agricultural reforms in *We Three Went to the Virgin Lands*.

She also used Active Analysis to devise new works. As a director she had already used Active Analysis for her 1952 production of *The Little Humpbacked Horse* to assist the playwright Pavel Malyarevsky in writing his dramatic adaptation of the famous 1834 poem by Pyotr Yershov (Knebel' 1967: 500–8). As Artistic Director she went even further with her 1958 dramatization of a Chinese fairy tale *The Magic Blossom*, for which she had no formal text. "If Active Analysis had been able to help us as directors and actors with analyzing classical works and Soviet plays, and if for *The Little Humpbacked Horse* it had helped not only us but also the playwright," she reasoned, then why not "in this instance, use it to create an entire play"? (Knebel' 1967: 508) After each rehearsal Knebel and her assistant director would record dialogue that had emerged from that day's etudes. In addition, Knebel hired a specialist in Chinese theatrical dance to inform the company's work. As the cast learned the new physical vocabulary, they incorporated its style into their etudes. "As we got to the essence of the fairy tale," she observed, "we tried bolder and more varied forms of expression" (Knebel' 1967: 509). The resulting production employed a unique interweaving of language, dance, and pantomime. As critic Pavel Markov wrote, "theatrical stylization had become fairy tale reality" (Vladimirova 1991: 133).

By making honest theatre for youth Knebel came into her own, creating productions through Active Analysis that parents flocked to see along with their children. Throughout her tenure as director she strove for consistently high artistic quality and nurtured outstanding actors, directors, and playwrights. A roster of those she hired to work at for the Children's Theatre reads like a who's who of Soviet theatrical talent in the latter half of the twentieth century. No wonder Knebel's seemingly modest children's enterprise became one of the most popular theatres in Moscow. In 1958, this body of work earned her the title of National Artist of the Russian Republic of the U.S.S.R.

Spreading the Word

Over the years Aleksey Dmitriyevich Popov had supported Knebel at pivotal moments in her life. Without his prompting, she would not have tried directing. When her husband disappeared, Popov had helped her stay calm. When she was fired from the Moscow Art Theatre, she confided first in him. Some, who knew her personally, felt sure that Popov had been her greatest, although unrequited, love. For example, her friend and editor, Natalya Krymova, "had no doubt that [Maria] loved him deeply, loved him as a woman, a passionate, intelligent woman who was no longer young, had never been beautiful, and who acknowledged that Popov had a family of his own with its own complications" (Liadov 1998: 49–50). Popov's daughter, Natalya Zvereva, who became especially close to Knebel, called the relationship a "friendship, not a romance as many had thought. I witnessed how much she needed my father's friendship and how their work together fed Knebel's artistic soul" (Zvereva 2014: 11).

In 1948 Popov invited Knebel to co-teach with him at the State Institute of Theatrical Arts (GITIS),[7] and she happily agreed. Her primary mission had become promoting Stanislavsky's Active Analysis. While the Central Children's Theatre had offered her the opportunity to practice it, GITIS would significantly expand her ability to reach future theatre artists through a student body that was both national and international. Popov and Knebel forged a teaching partnership that soon became legendary. Fellow faculty members and students saw them as complementary in their talents. Popov "was a poet when it came to directing. He always strove for poetic imagery. [...] She was a poet when it came to pedagogy, [...] with a unique ability to work with the person in every artist" (Liadov 1998: 28). When Zvereva decided upon a career in directing, she went to Knebel for support, explaining that "where my father made things complicated, [Maria Osipovna] brought clarity (without ever making what is complex simplistic)" (Liadov 1998: 34).[8]

In 1961 Knebel got news of Popov's death while she was working on her autobiography with Krymova, who witnessed "a storm of tears that no one else but me would ever see" (Liadov 1998: 50). In a calmer moment, Knebel would write that "Popov and I became like-minded through our passionate arguments and creative discussions. And I have rarely experienced better minutes than those spent with him, full of artistic sincerity and mutual understanding" (Knebel' 1967: 430). With his death, Knebel resigned from the Central Children's Theatre in order to accept the chairmanship of the directing program at GITIS, where she developed the current curriculum, in which directors and actors train together. Based in Active Analysis, her program also includes important elements of directing that she learned from Nemirovich-Danchenko and of acting from Michael Chekhov (Carnicke 2010a: 99–116).

As a teacher, Knebel believed that artistic technique must not be confused with aesthetic styles. Technique is a means to an end and not the end. Therefore, she never imposed her tastes on her students. Instead, she taught Active Analysis as a set of flexible principles to guide artists as they explore their own talents and tastes. As Zvereva explains, Knebel "was free from all dogma, not only professional. She was surprisingly free in her thinking and the breadth of her opinions" (Zvereva 2021: 98). Consequently, the roster of her students include major artists of differing stripes, each with a unique artistic vision, ranging from those who loved realism to those who experimented with new forms. She attributed her ability to nurture such a range to her practice of Active Analysis:

> The etude puts the actor's individuality at the center of the event. In doing an etude, the actor and director both know that you cannot hide—not behind the text, the blocking, your partners, nothing. When interacting with my partner, it is only me—my eyes, my ears, the train of my thoughts, my words, my reactions to what's happening. [...] All this uncovers the student's individuality.
>
> (Knebel' 1976: 360)

Just as Knebel brought clarity to Popov's thinking, so too did she make clear Stanislavsky's insights into the complexities of acting. In the 1960s when the Latvian director Adolf Shapiro enrolled in her class, he expected to find the usual Stanislavskian "psychological" method. Instead of this "insufficiently vivid [...], even boring" approach, Knebel's teaching "unexpectedly took me prisoner for life" (Shapiro 1999: 133–5). Similarly, the innovative director Anatoly Efros frankly writes that, having studied the Stanislavsky System elsewhere for years, "it was only after encountering Maria Knebel [at the Central Children's Theatre] that I properly and practically understood what this method is" (Efros 2007: 139).

Knebel kept teaching for as long as she had life with the same generosity that she had observed in Stanislavsky so many decades earlier. When she could no longer climb the stairs to her third-floor classroom, her students carried her. Her lively spirit during her last years can be felt in an anecdote told by the prestigious director Leonid Kheifits, who was at that time her student. One day, he noticed a small tear in her sleeve and mentioned it. At the next class she donned a stylish outfit and French perfume, mischievously eying him, while telling her students that she had replenished her wardrobe. She was eighty-six at the time (Kheifits 2001: 156–7).

As she taught, she also wrote. Her sister Yelena kept house, allowing Maria uninterrupted time to work. When intrusive visitors called, Yelena turned them away. Every evening Yelena would read and review the pages that Maria had written that day (Liadov 1998: 106). In 1954 Knebel published *The Word in an Actor's Creative Work*, her first book-length study on Stanislavsky's experiments at the Opera-Dramatic Studio. The title recalls his initial request that she help him investigate the literary word as verbal action (Chapter 2). Her next book in 1959, *On the Active Analysis of the Play and the Role*, was "a revolutionary event in theatrical art, inciting the careers of many theatrical artists" (Melik-Pashaeva and Turchkin 1999: 271).[9] In 1966, she published *Nemirovich-Danchenko's School of Directing*. Her 1967 autobiography, *All of Life*, came next. In 1971 she assembled her most salient journal articles and portraits of her mentors in an anthology fittingly entitled *What Seems Most Important to Me*. Despite repeated requests, she had long resisted writing about her own teaching, which she experienced as an improvisatory art much like acting that is as mutable as mercury.

Fig. 6 Knebel at the State Institute for the Theatrical Arts (GITIS), *c*. 1980. The Makarovskiy Family.

When she finally overcame her reluctance, she published in 1976 *The Poetry of Pedagogy*, which is at once a useful manual that traces her curriculum at GITIS and a deeply personal account of what teaching meant to her. Its first edition was richly illustrated by her favorite set designer, Yury Pimenov, and instantly became essential reading for Russian actors and directors.

Knebel's last publishing project was as the editor for the two-volume *Literary Heritage* of Michael Chekhov's collected writings, which appeared in 1986, one year after her death. This edition was like a theatrical earthquake in Russia, because Chekhov's writings had never before been published in his native language. He had fled from the Soviet Union in 1928. In that year, two apparently enthusiastic actors had joined his classes, where he was teaching, but carefully avoided naming, the artistic methods of Rudolf Steiner, whose spiritual practice of Anthroposophy had been officially banned in the U.S.S.R. since 1924. Chekhov soon discovered that his new students' enthusiasm masked a darker intent. Following their attendance in class, he received a deceitfully friendly letter from the People's Commissariat of Education and Enlightenment directing him to cease teaching Steiner. In this letter, verbatim quotations from Chekhov's classes were placed next to "the relevant quotations from Steiner's works," proving that the two alleged students were actually spies, "hiding behind the door curtains" in order to record "the phrases that to their mind were suspect" (Chekhov 2005: 135–6).[10] Chekhov then learned that a warrant for his arrest had been issued. He and his wife immediately left the country on a previously approved two-month medical visa to Germany to escape arrest, never to return.

Like those who disappeared into Stalin's labor camps, those who emigrated also disappeared. While Chekhov's directing and teaching in the West brought him international renown during his lifetime, his achievements went virtually unknown in his native land. As theatre scholar Inna Solovyova explains:

> For most of the people who stayed in Russia those who had gone abroad actually did cease to exist. All ties were severed. There was no way of finding out whether an émigré was alive or dead. Historians of the arts had to fight for the right to mention that émigrés had actually existed even before their departure: the inroads of official propaganda went that far.
>
> (Soloviova [*sic*] 1992: 70)

Knebel had long harbored a desire to bring her first teacher's legacy back home. She owed him not only her start in theatre, but also the improvisatory mindset that had allowed her to understand the full complexity of Active Analysis. By 1967 Khrushchev's thaw made it possible for her to devote a full chapter to Chekhov in her autobiography. In 1971, she included this chapter in *What Seems Most Important to Me*. In 1976 she names Chekhov as the source for many of the exercises given in *The Poetry of Pedagogy* (Knebel' 1976: 36–9; 220–6). "You can do any exercises as an exercise. But raising it to the level of art—that I got from Mikhail Chekhov," she said (Zvereva 2021: 103).

In the last decade of her life, which coincided with Mikhail Gorbachev's liberal *perestroika* (or reconstruction) of the Soviet Union, Knebel worked diligently, collecting Chekhov's letters, memoirs and essays; sifting through them to select the most representative texts; and fighting with the censors to retain as much as possible about the still-forbidden topics of his emigration and his religious beliefs.[11] Her editor, Krymova, remembers how they read "in secret" Chekhov's "painfully bitter" account of the events that led to his flight (Liadov 1998: 56). Once Knebel became so frustrated with the censors that she exploded in anger, calling herself an "anthroposophist" in order to preserve intact Chekhov's passages on his religious beliefs (Liadov 1998: 57). As she lay dying, Krymova did not have the heart to tell Knebel that despite their best efforts Chekhov's religious views had been cut from the edition by the censors (Liadov 1998: 57).[12]

Over the course of her life Knebel authored six books and more than a hundred articles on her teachers, their pedagogies, and her own career. While she had escaped the extraordinarily stringent censorship under Stalinism that had hampered Stanislavsky in his final years, she still had to navigate the changing tides of censorship during Khrushchev's "thaw," the artistic stagnation that Brezhnev instigated with stricter controls, and Gorbachev's *perestroika*. Knebel responded to each new tide with cagey strategies to ensure publication. Without betraying her principles, she walked a political tightrope of what could and could not be said. She quoted Marxist philosophy and used political rhetoric when necessary to shield her divergent ideas from the censor's eye (Carnicke 2015: 191–206). Like all Soviet authors, she did so, knowing that her readers would look between the censored lines for the innuendos. This kind of Aesopian reading had become a normal part of Soviet culture, making the translation of Russian books into English a particular challenge (Carnicke 2009: chapter 6). In the same spirit, when she received an award from the Red Army, she thanked, not the Army, but her teachers (Liadov 1998: 8). Her students would have understood her veiled dig against the government.

In short, the "sober idealism" (Liadov 1998: 9) that helped Knebel survive as an actor and director in the Soviet Union also sustained her as a teacher and writer. In her sixties, when appointed chair of directing at GITIS, she pragmatically joined the Communist Party for the first time. She needed this credential for her new job, because, as a colleague explains, "A party membership was like a school child's corridor pass, like a legal residence permit, like proof of loyalty" (Liadov 1998: 55).

"My Own Cherry Orchard"

In the mid-1960s Maria Knebel was writing her memoirs, when she received an invitation that she could not resist from Popov's son, Andrey, now the Artistic Director of the Central Theatre of the Soviet Army in Moscow. He wanted Knebel to direct a new production of *The Cherry Orchard* for the 1965 season. Major memories of her long-time relationship with the Moscow Art Theatre had coalesced around Anton Chekhov's last play. At age ten she had wept at the art in the company's 1904 production; as an adult she had auditioned for Charlotta by improvising a magic act and playing an impromptu game of billiards with Stanislavsky in his role as Gayev. "I can recall the M.A.T. production not only in my mind, but in my muscles" (Knebel' 1967: 569). She last appeared as Charlotta on the Art Theatre's stage before being fired by Kedrov. In rereading the play, she came to think of the loss of her long-time artistic home as "her own cherry orchard" (Knebel' 1967: 569).

She allowed these autobiographical memories to shape her production. In this "deeply philosophical play," she writes, Chekhov confronts us with the "cruel truth" that loss is always part of the human condition. "He understood very well what it means to lose that which you infinitely love. [… And] each of us has lost and will lose our own 'cherry orchard.'" But, such losses also open new doors, she affirms. "In the moment, when we lose our 'cherry orchard,' it seems to us that we have lost everything. But," as she had herself learned, "ahead of us is a life that is a thousand times richer than what we have lost" (Knebel' 1967: 570).

Knebel embodied this reading of the play most visibly at the end of Act III. Paralyzed by the news that the family's orchard has been sold, the landowner Ranyevskaya is physically pulled by her daughter, Anya, and her late son's tutor, Trofimov, into a slow, meditative waltz. As the young couple, who represent the future, whirl Ranyevskaya around the stage to the calming rhythm of the waltz, the curtain drops slowly, obscuring their ongoing dance (Vladimirova 1991: 113). The audience is left with the image, painted on the curtain, of "a still-life of things—a candle, gloves—[...] that outlive the people" who once owned them (Knebel' 1967: 571). Through this performative moment Knebel suggests that the way to cope with the inevitability of loss is to join the swirling vortex of the present, which is, in itself, brief and precious.

The autobiographical dimensions in Knebel's 1965 production depended upon her radical shifting of the play's "centrifugal force" away from the ensemble of characters and toward "Ranyevskaya's drama" (Rudnitskii 1974: 143). In this way, the play becomes an analogue of Knebel's dismissal from her artistic home with Ranyevskaya as the director's self-portrait. Knebel chose for this role Lyubov Ivanovna Dobrazhanskaya, "an actress of such variety that [her work was like] a cut crystal, turning to reveal all its facets. [...] Without her," Knebel recalled, "I would not have risked launching the project" (Knebel' 1967: 571).

Dobrazhanskaya played Ranyevskaya as a complex woman, on the one hand, "courageous, well-bred, pure, strong and strong-willed" and on the other, "inconsistent and sinful, a vulnerable woman in need of protection, who exhibited swift changes of mood" (Rudnitskii 1974: 143). But what Knebel most admired was Dobrazhanskaya's unsentimentalized portrayal of a woman who "know[s] that misfortune is unavoidable and inevitable" (Vladimirova 1991: 116). This knowledge kept Ranyevskaya from entertaining Lopakhin's ironic plan to save the orchard by chopping it down. It also kept her from bearing a grudge against him when he proceeded without her.

Dobrazhanskaya hit the mark as evidenced by the fact that Knebel's friends and colleagues recognized her through the performance. For example, as her biographer remembers:

> One can't say of Knebel that she was a gentle angel, she was sharp and sarcastic, unflagging in her convictions, but she understood that it is stupid to bear a grudge, to nurse it, if one can overcome it, and at the same time create something equally dear to the offended and the offender.
>
> (Vladimirova 1991: 20)

Similarly, a colleague at GITIS warned against "idealizing" Knebel. "She was not at all a simple person," he writes (Liadov 1998: 38).

Knebel used the set of her *Cherry Orchard* to embody her artistic philosophy: that theatre must always speak to the present. It therefore looked nothing like the Moscow Art Theatre's 1904 production. The designer, Yury Pimenov, surrounded the massive stage of the Central Theatre of the Soviet Army with a curtain of white tulle, which, in Knebel's words, became a "glimmering haze" under the lights (Knebel' 1967: 568). One reviewer compared the backdrop to "clouds in the sky," another to "blossoms on the trees of the cherry orchard" (Vladimirova 1991: 119). The few pieces of furniture on stage were covered with white dust cloths, and so appeared to fade into the white tulle. The actors, costumed in period clothing, emerged from this white environment as if they were a "mirage" (Vladimirova 1991: 119). After Act III the furniture was replaced with a "still-life" of suitcases and packing crates (Knebel' 1967: 572), echoing the "still-life of things" painted on the front curtain. "The set evoked the ephemeral, as if life were about to disappear," according to one reviewer (Vladimirova 1991: 119). It also suggested a blank canvas, upon which the characters can paint their futures. Many critics, who expressed nostalgia for the Moscow Art Theatre's famous realism, criticized Knebel's work as "ultra-contemporary" (Knebel' 1967: 568), a comment that she took as a compliment. When asked why she did away with the orchard, she responded by saying that "the cherry orchard must be in [your] soul" (Knebel' 1969: 162).

In 1968 Ireland's Ambassador to the Soviet Union saw Knebel's *Cherry Orchard* and asked that it represent Russia at the next Irish international Theatre Festival (Abensour 2019: 162). But rather than bring her production to Ireland, it was decided that she should restage it for the Abbey Theatre in Dublin with Irish actors. This work thrust her willy-nilly into the role of cultural ambassador at the height of the Cold War. No Soviet artist was at that time immune from politics. As one scholar put it, "With the onset of the Cold War, artists metamorphosed into frontline soldiers in the ideological showdown between East and West" (Ezrabi 2012: 137). Conditioned by Stalinism, Knebel was gripped by fear when the Communist Party's Central Committee summoned her for an interview shortly before her trip. She sent a coded message through the elevator operator to the production's composer, Grigory Samulovich Frid, who lived in her apartment building and was a nephew of her second husband. Alarmed by the mysterious note, Frid hurried to her and found her shaking in fear, her head wrapped in a scarf with only her eyes visible. He struggled to convince her that the meeting was a formality for anyone traveling abroad. Only when he agreed to play the role of interrogator and rehearse the interview with her did she calm down (Liadov 1998: 126).

There is no record of what was said at her meeting with the authorities, but Knebel arrived in Ireland ten days earlier than expected, which sent her hosts into a tail spin. Another production was running at the Abbey; her two star actors were on tour—one in New York, the other in Rome; and the rest of the company was leaving on the next day for a different tour. Márie Ní Ghráine, cast as Dunyasha, recalled:

> We were smothered up the stairs to meet [Knebel] in the office and [told …] not to tell anyone she was in the country. You see, [it was a matter of] Russian secrecy. There was the Iron Curtain and she was from a restricted area. But why this was, I never found out.
>
> (Abbey Theatre Oral History Project 1968)

In a magazine article, Knebel would later describe her early arrival merely as a happy accident that allowed her to see the sights of Dublin, but it is hard to imagine that this could be so, given the tight control under which Soviet artists traveled abroad during the 1960s. Yet again there is no evidence to suggest that there were ulterior motives beyond the general anxiety prevalent during the Cold War.

Pressure for Knebel to succeed as a director in Ireland was intense, because Soviet art "had to be clearly differentiable from—and superior to—art produced under democratic capitalism" (Ezrabi 2012: 137). On this front, her artistic process was her greatest success. In the first week of rehearsals at the Abbey Theatre, Knebel was taken aback when she realized that the Irish actors expected her to block the play physically from beginning to end and also tell them how to say their lines. As a proponent of Active Analysis, this was anathema to her. She expected actors to collaborate on the creation of their performances. The company "told me that this was the first time they had a director, who discussed with them the inner paths of their roles" (Knebel' 1969: 163). Her Russian approach to rehearsing made the Irish actors "love" her. As Niall Buggy, who played Trofimov, recalled, she "loved acting and actors" and "created an atmosphere, which lent itself to creativity. I don't think I've ever seen the actors so happy doing any other play." Kathleen Barrington, who played Varya, put it more simply: working with her "was just magic." (Abbey Theatre Oral History Project 1968)

Maria Osipovna Knebel had accomplished much in her career after losing her own cherry orchard. Despite the fact that her "personal and professional lives were very difficult, [...] the strength of her spirit in meeting adversity was enormous," so writes her artistic daughter, Natalya Zvereva (Liadov 1998: 39). When Knebel's sister died in 1980, Maria was bereft. She felt alone for the first time, as she moved in with her brother's son and his family. "I have grown terribly old," she told a friend in 1983 (Liadov 1998: 103). Yet, as in her youth, she kept her spirits up by working until the bitter end. By the time of her death in 1985, she had become arguably the most important voice in Russian theatre, second only to Stanislavsky. At the centenary celebration of the Moscow Art Theatre, her protégé Anatoly Vassiliev placed her legacy on the same high level as those of Stanislavsky, Grotowski and the controversial director, Yury Lyubimov (Smelianksy 1999: 215). That legacy, based upon her practice and promotion of Active Analysis, now serves as a bridge from the past to the future.

The Future Is Today, Now, Here

Active Analysis acknowledges that change is a normal part of our artistic lives. Stanislavsky begins his autobiography by recalling everyday items from his nineteenth-century Russian childhood that were no longer in use—candles made from lard, the *tarantas* (a rough-hewn, horse-drawn cart), flint-lock muskets, and the like (*SS* I 1988: 53). Such things were unknown to the young actors, who crowded into his Opera-Dramatic Studio during the 1930s where he was developing what would become Active Analysis. By 1938 when he died, the artistic revolutions that had occurred during his lifetime died with him. The 1890s turn to realism and the 1910s craze for symbolism were long out of fashion. The Russian theatricalist avant-garde of the 1920s had also been snuffed out prematurely by the Soviet state, which imposed a bloodless form of socialist realism on all Russian artists. At his last Studio, Stanislavsky consciously chose a range of dramatic texts from different eras—classic plays in verse, Chekhov's modernism, operas, and even a scenario based upon space travel—in order to disassociate his new rehearsal technique from any one particular dramatic style. He was especially concerned about uncoupling his System from the realism of his early career, because the Soviets were using it to argue that he was on the front lines in the "battle for [socialist] realism." No, he insisted, "human life is so subtle, so complex and multifaceted, that it needs an incomparably large number of new, still undiscovered 'isms' to express it fully" through art (*SS* II 1989: 458).

In her turn, Knebel discusses in her autobiography the now-forgotten everyday conditions of Soviet life—her room in a *kommunalka;* coffee made from used grounds due to food scarcities; the witnessing of her brother's unwarranted arrest; the unexplained disappearance of her husband (Knebel' 1967: 27; 81). Her artistic life spanned all but five years of Soviet theatrical history from the heady days of the early Soviet avant-garde; through the stultifying atmosphere of socialist realism, when "brigades" of directors produced works that met the required political standards; to the revitalization of Russian drama in the last half of the twentieth century. Her personal tastes in art were even broader than Stanislavsky's. On the one hand, because her father was a famous pre-revolutionary publisher of art books, she grew up surrounded by Russia's most famous artists, many of whom Stanislavsky also knew and admired. Her father's friends included the landscape painter Levitan; Dobuzhinsky, an impressionist who designed sets for the Moscow Art Theatre; and the mystic and symbolist painter Roerich, who designed for Diaghilev's *Ballets Russes*. She even recalls sitting on the lap of the great novelist, Leo Tolstoy, when she was very little. As one of her protégés explained, Knebel brought the "aroma of [Russia's past] culture" into the room with her (Shapiro 1999: 135). On the other hand, she also loved what was new. She experimented with the popular style of the grotesque in her acting at the Moscow Art Theatre, collaborated with members of Meyerhold's company at the Yermolova Studio Theatre, and produced new and sometimes controversial plays at the Central Children's Theatre during the post-Stalin era. Her embrace of different trends in art ensured that, as times changed, she remained "a contemporary person, never 'old-fashioned' even in her eighties" (Liadov 1998: 43).

Today, changes are occurring at a dizzying pace in all spheres that affect actors' work from the types of plays we enact to the technologies that frame our performances and from the business of auditioning to the development of new audiences. If Stanislavsky's and Knebel's experimentation had been confined to those types of plays that they themselves staged, then we might find ourselves admiring both of them as interesting figures from the past, with little relevance to us. But that is not the case.

Fortunately, Stanislavsky and Knebel saw Active Analysis as a flexible rehearsal technique that is not intended to be in and of itself constitutive of style (Carnicke 2004: 46–54). Consequently, they left a legacy that is as relevant today as it was in the past. Stanislavsky always insisted that "the System is not a trend or a style," making Active Analysis a pragmatic technique, "like voice placement" (Stanislavskii 1986 vol. 2: 254). Lee Strasberg, guru of the American Method, offered a different, more familiar metaphor for thinking of acting technique as separate from style, when he said: "The technique with which we play the piece of modern music is the same technique with which we play a piece of Tchaikovsky" (Strasberg 1956-1969: Tape A1). The prestigious director, Georgy Tovstonogov, who had studied with Knebel's co-teacher Aleksey Popov, created moving productions of new plays in Leningrad during the Cold War, by reinterpreting the basic principles of Active Analysis to suit his own aesthetics. His version of the technique is currently taught at the Theatre Academy in St. Petersburg. Similarly, in Moscow, where Knebel's curriculum is still taught, her protégé Anatoly Efros created productions of great subtlety, by capturing the ambiguous complexities of human life in his radical re-interpretations of Chekhov's plays during the 1960s and 1970s. By the end of the twentieth century and continuing into the twenty-first, Anatoly Vassiliev took the principles he had learned from Knebel and again reshaped the legacy to suit a newer, postmodernist sensibility. He uses Active Analysis to create stunning productions that entirely escape the bounds of psychological realism through a "ludic" (*igrovoi*) theatre that explores metaphysical issues. With the fall of the Soviet Union in 1991, Vassiliev moved his artistic revolution from the local onto the global stage, first to Paris and then to Italy, where he continues to direct and teach his approach to Active Analysis through periodic workshops.

In short, Active Analysis (which dates back to the 1930s) remains as vibrant and valuable for contemporary acting as are the principles of classical ballet (developed in the fifteenth-century) which now serve as a common language and foundational training for dancers who work in a variety of styles from contemporary ballet to modern jazz and from postmodern dance to hip hop. Tovstonogov, Efros, and Vassiliev use and adapt the principles of Active Analysis, just as the great contemporary choreographers, George Balanchine, Mark Morris, and Matthew Bourne, use and adapt the principles of ballet, to suit their own artistic goals and to interrogate contemporary cultural issues through their works.[13]

Active Analysis not only acknowledges, but also prepares actors to embrace change by nurturing an improvisatory mindset. When Michael Chekhov stopped teaching and returned to the stage, Knebel often went to see her former teacher perform the role of Khlestakov in Stanislavsky's production of Gogol's *The Inspector General* at the Moscow Art Theatre. She noticed that Chekhov invariably added something surprising at each performance without ever changing text or blocking. He was, to quote her, "a genius of improvisation" (Chekhov 1995 vol. 2: 28). She came to understand that "one of the secrets of his art, and, in fact, the most important principle behind creativity, is the actor's improvisatory state of mind in the role" (Chekhov 1995 vol. 1: 17). In bringing this insight to bear upon Stanislavsky's work at the Opera-Dramatic Studio, she saw clearly how Active Analysis "creates for the actor this same improvisatory state of mind and body within the rigid framework of first-class dramatic material," within new plays, and when devising new works (Knebel' 1967: 276).

In Stanislavsky's final years, he was hemmed in by censorship, spied upon, and hampered at every turn. Yet, he still hoped that his work would become a living legacy and inspire new generations of theatre artists. He feared that his work would die if it were treated as dogma. In a recurring nightmare, he would often see a typical acting student of the future standing before a stern teacher, who continually checks the student's work against the "rules" in Stanislavsky's published books. "This is terrible, a fraud, the murder of talent," Stanislavsky cries out. "Shred, burn my books, dismiss the students, and tell them I have committed a crime!" (Stanislavskii 1986 vol. 1: 209–10). In the light of day, he more soberly wrote: "What is most dangerous for my technique, for the whole 'system,' […] and finally, for all of art, is a formulaic approach to our complex creative work, a narrow, elementary understanding of it" (*SS* II 1989: 252).

Maria Knebel's non-dogmatic approach to teaching proved to be an antidote to Stanislavsky's nightmare. By focusing on the broad dynamic principles of Active Analysis, she advances it as a living legacy that flexibly supports changes in dramatic and theatrical art. As a director, she herself used it for productions ranging in style from classic realism to theatricalist fantasy. As a teacher, she appreciated the distinctly different aesthetics of Tovstonogov, Efros, and Vassiliev, proving the adaptability of Active Analysis.

It is now our turn to apply the principles of Active Analysis for our own times.

Notes

1. Lyadova eventually became a doctor and maintained a lifelong friendship with Knebel.
2. According to Abensour, a year after Urbanovich went missing, Knebel was forced by the state to divorce him. She was told that he was on a secret mission and needed the divorce to protect his identity. She later learned that he had been in a labor camp and, when released, he was permitted to work in a theatre in Siberia, but not allowed to return to Moscow (2019: 261–5).
3. Knebel's brother was released, but according to her grand-nephew, Andrew Makarovskiy, in a private conversation in Boston during July 2007, Nikolay Knebel died in a suspicious automobile accident in Soviet-occupied Berlin in 1946.
4. In 1956 Knebel headed a new team of directors to revive *Kremlin Chimes* (Knebel' 1967: 525–31) with a revised text that no longer treated Stalin as a revolutionary hero. This revival was included in the 1965 tour of the Moscow Art Theatre to the United States, but was pulled from the repertory following objections in the press (Robinson 2021: November 8).
5. The relationship between Kedrov and Knebel eerily echoes the bitter relationship between Lee Strasberg and Stella Adler, which created a rift in American actor training over the place of personal emotion in acting that continues into the twenty-first century.
6. The "thaw" took its name from the novel by Ilya Ehrenburg (Beumers in Leach and Borovsky 1999: 358–81).
7. The school's name was changed to the Russian Academy of Theatrical Arts (RATI) after the fall of the Soviet Union, but most theatre practitioners still use GITIS.
8. Zvereva would eventually become Knebel's assistant and join the faculty at GITIS.
9. Knebel's student Anatoly Vassiliev published slightly abridged editions of Knebel's first two books, along with other selections of her writings, in French in 2006; this compilation has been translated into English (2021) by Irina Brown.
10. The behavior of these students reminds me of Kedrov's at the Opera-Dramatic Studio (see Chapter 1).
11. Andrew Makarovskiy in a private conversation in Boston during July 2007.
12. Much of what was censored in the 1986 edition was restored in a second edition in 1995, published before Putin again imposed censorship in Russia.
13. Stefan Aquilina and Maria Shevtsova examine the ways in which the transmission of Stanislavsky's practice necessitates evolution. Aquilina discusses "transmission bias […] through which receivers select useful techniques, while discarding others" (2020: 23), and observes that neither scholars nor Stanislavsky is exempt from such biases (2020: 107–8; 56). Shevtsova sees "generational transmission" as a "mediated legacy, whose instances accumulate practical adjustments and necessary socio-cultural 'interferences,' since transmission is a living process between people" (2020: 238). As a scholar and artist, I too am part of the evolving process of transmission.

Part 2 Six Lessons in Active Analysis

"A person stands on a stage. That person must do something, because a person is not a table that only stands there. So, why does the person stand there?" Stanislavsky to the cast of *The Bluebird* (Novitskaia 1984: 90)

Lesson 1 The Dynamic Principles of Performance

Prelude

I enter from the side door and cross through the dark to turn on the lights. My Studio meets here in an American Legion Hall, built more than a century ago in 1912. The electrical light switches are never quite where you expect them to be. Once lit, the fluorescent lights reveal an expansive oak floor that is marred by age and the tapping feet of the kids who also meet here to learn to dance. At times, I have asked my actors to stretch their imaginations by visualizing events that might have taken place in this hall over the decades. Looking up to the ceiling through heavy wooden beams, you can see the heating and cooling system that the Legion has recently installed and, further up, the antique grating that covers an attic fan that rattles and whines in hot weather. There are also holiday lights in the rafters. When turned on, they create a twinkling glow for renters who hold dinner dances and celebrations here. We use them to create atmospheric lighting effects.

At one end of the space is a narrow stage, stairs at each end with metal railings and little latched gates. The stage is much too narrow. We use it when we want a balcony, a change of level, or a grand, wrought-iron entry way. Mostly we work on the floor, sectioning off areas that suggest whatever environment we want to create—sometimes we use the windows, the entrances, or the side and back areas of the room opposite the stage. We carve out prosceniums, thrust stages, and arenas. I love this open, flexible, humble space.

Shari follows me, her high heels clicking. She's a retired dancer, turned actor with a substantial career. We car-pool to class because she no longer likes to drive at night. As always, she is well-manicured and neatly outfitted. She's carrying a colorful bag, tied with a bow. Inside are some heels that no longer suit her and she's hoping that our youngest member might like them.

Louisa arrives next with shopping bags full of food that she unpacks and arranges on a folding table. She has worked successfully as an actor for over thirty years with stars of all stripes in movies and television shows. At times, I and the others unexpectedly catch her on television. Laughing, she once told me that she has played her share of nurses and grand-mas, but never allowed herself to be stereotyped by her race. She found this space for us and brings her generosity to it in food, talent, and intelligence. In fact, she co-founded this Studio in order to support networking and training among actors.

Juliana brings in more shopping bags with paper plates and cups. She carpooled with Louisa, who never learned to drive and always needs a hand with the food. Juliana pushes her long dark hair back and smiles as she steals a cookie. I can see Juliana's quick wit in that smile. She's here to build her career, network, and solidify her craft.

Grigor, Sargis, Geo, and Hannah make a noisy, happy entrance. Grigor and Sargis are proud Armenian brothers who fell in love with performance by studying improv. They work by day with computers and perform in the evenings. They auditioned for me because they wanted to move into serious acting. Grigor is the shorter of the two, a kind of young Sal Mineo (as Louisa says) with dark thick hair. He reads incessantly. Sargis is a bit taller, with less hair, and a warm smile that lights up his face. After working in the Studio for a few months, Sargis surprised me with the news that he had won a ball-room dance competition! Then Grigor admitted that he too was hooked on dance. Geo is older, graying at the temples. He acted in his youth and then worked with the filipino community charities as an event organizer. He joined the Studio to renew his passion for acting. As he once told us with tears in his eyes, life without art is just not enough. Like Juliana, Hannah is working at her career. Her blond hair is long, and her spunk is tattooed in the geometric design on her left arm. She carries with her a battered guitar case, because she loves singing as much as acting. As the actors share stories about their week, they set up a circle of folding chairs, some black, some red with chipped paint, and a few with leather cushions.

I become aware of someone standing behind me. "Hello," he says. I turn and see a middle-aged man with a face that changes expression rapidly from shy to eager. He is dressed in a jacket with pockets stuffed with things and a scarf. "I heard about this Studio and I would like to join." He tells me that he was born in Aleppo, that his Armenian grandparents had fled from the Ottoman genocide, and that after high school, he moved to Spain to study acting at the Royal Academy in Madrid. "I had one teacher, Angel Gutierrez, who was sent to Russia as a child to keep him safe during the Spanish Civil War. He had studied acting in Moscow's main theatre institute, and had become a famous actor. As an adult he returned to Spain and taught us. He was very strict, and I learned a lot. Of course, I also learned a lot from the other teachers, too, but when I heard that this Studio is Russian-based, I thought of my former teacher. Would you consider allowing me to join?" I smile and nod. He continues speaking. "I worked for many years in Spain, in classic stage plays, then on television and in films. Acting is my passion Even as a child in Aleppo I was following local theatres and Armenian and international actors. I started acting then and never stopped. When I came to Los Angeles, I started acting and directing here too." "Wonderful," I say. "What's your name?" "Oh, I forgot to say. I'm Setrak." He takes a seat off to the side, pulls a bottle of water from his pocket, takes a sip, and returns it to his pocket. After a while, I see him shaking hands with Sargis.

Next to arrive is Rose, tall and agile with short red hair, followed by Keith, an ex-marine and professional pilot, who lugs in a case of water for the group. These two actors, now in their thirties, have been with my Studio for nearly as long as Louisa has. Rose studied with me in college and assisted me with a number of projects since then. She still comes here to work on her acting, even though her career is taking off, because she, like Louisa, values the constant process of exploration that happens when actors come together as an ensemble. She continually delights us with her vivid imagination.

Keith's entrance testifies to his disciplined commitment to his acting. When he moved across the country to Philadelphia, he organized his flight schedules in such a way that he could fly back once a week for our sessions. He lands a commercial on television here and there, too.

Fig. 7 Members of the Studio of the Stanislavsky Institute for the Twenty-First Century, 2017. Appearing as characters in this book are: Keith Day, Liliana Carrillo (top row, first and second from the left); Teena Pugliese, Hannah Pierce, Sargis Panosyan (top row, sixth, seventh, and eighth from the left); Grigor Panosyan (first to the left in the bottom row), Louisa Abernathy, Sharon Marie Carnicke, Joan Eyles Johnson, Rose Leisner, and Geo Sitjar Sargent (bottom row third to seventh from the left). Teena Pugliese, photographer.

As we settle down into our chairs, Anisha flies in. She is our youngest member, the child of a family from India. Having recently graduated from college, she's juggling a bunch of odd jobs and classes to get her closer to her dream career in acting. She grabs a chair and sits next to Shari, who silently slips Anisha the shoes! Her ardent apology for being late matches her equally ardent enthusiasm to put on her new shoes and get down to work. Everyone laughs! We are a company of actors, an ensemble!

This evening is the first lesson in an intensive course on Active Analysis. Louisa and Rose have already worked with the technique; Keith and Juliana have too, but still feel confused by aspects of it; the others have asked me to teach the practice, step-by-step from the beginning, so that they can better apply it to their auditions, their work as actors, and their own creations. I start with the theory.

Stanislavsky's Changing Concepts of Action

If I were to throw a baseball, and if there were no such thing as gravity, where would the ball fly? Basic physics suggests that it would fly forever in the same direction in a straight line, without curving and without slowing. It would travel freely, because nothing would resist its flight. While I am personally fascinated by physics, the actor in me sees little drama in this scenario. If I were to write a play founded upon the imaginary circumstance that the earth lacks gravity, throwing a baseball in the first scene would ensure a boring story. The baseball's action would not change or fluctuate, and the play would unfold without the possibility for development, surprise, or a satisfying finale.

But, in fact, there is gravity on earth. Under this circumstance, from the moment that a ball begins to fly it also begins to slow down and curve toward the earth, eventually hitting the ground. From the first to the last moment of its flight, gravity distorts its trajectory. The ball's forward motion is altered by the force of gravity. This dynamic interplay of forces produces a more interesting scene with the ball's action modified by the earth's counteraction. This scene has dramatic potential. It unfolds as a competition between flight and gravity that an audience might interpret as an exploration of freedom, hampered by the limitations of reality. The scene becomes interesting, because the dynamic interaction between the ball and the earth's pull makes it possible for something to happen.

When the ball finally hits the ground, the scene ends with an event that is historic in the life of the baseball. This ball now has a past; its flight has been curtailed. This event also suggests a future in which something else might happen. Perhaps a dog will come along and steal my ball. I might chase her to get it back, thus beginning a new scene between me and the dog. My play now unfolds in earnest.

In this extended analogy, the three main components of Active Analysis are at work. First, a scene starts with an impelling **action**—a force, a drive, a desire that is described by an active verb. The ball *flies*. Second, the scene develops, because this action meets resistance from a **counteraction**—a force, a drive, a desire that is also described by an active verb. Gravity *pulls down* on the ball. Third, the counteraction operates simultaneously with the action and continuously resists the forward motion of the scene until such time as one force overcomes the other. When that happens, an **event** occurs that contributes to the development of a story. In my analogy, the baseball flies until gravity overcomes its flight. When the ball then hits the ground, that event allows for the possibility of a next scene that begins with a new action (the dog steals the ball) and a new counteraction (I chase her).

In short, Active Analysis conceives of a scene as the dynamic interplay between an **action** and a **counteraction**, which results in an **event,** and of a play as **a chain of events** that tells a story. This conception has always reminded me of vector analysis in physics, which assesses the direction and intensity of forces. Consequently, when the prominent performance scholar, Patrice Pavis, called for "a theory of vectors that group together and dynamize entire moments of performance" (Pavis 2003: 23), I realized that what he wanted was right at hand.

Active Analysis, as we know it today, emerged from Stanislavsky's lifelong investigation into the nature of acting. In the late nineteenth century, when he was fourteen, he began keeping personal journals in which he recorded detailed observations of the performances he saw in Moscow's professional theatres. He also wrote meticulous analyses of his own experiences as an amateur actor and director. At the turn of the twentieth century, when he co-founded the Moscow Art Theatre, he began to develop what he then called a "grammar" of acting by experimenting with the production of realist and symbolist plays. When the theatre's co-founder and seasoned actors pushed back against his avid experimentation, he set up a private laboratory, where he could investigate more systematically with willing actors. At this First Studio, founded in 1911, he broke acting down into its various elements: relaxation, concentration of attention, observation, etc. He also developed exercises for each of these elements from a variety of practices, including Yoga, modern dance, and vocal training. Thus, a System, as he now called it, began to emerge.

By the 1920s Stanislavsky was emphasizing the importance of action in drama, following a path laid down by the ancient Greek philosopher Aristotle. In *The Poetics*, Aristotle argues that all art is "imitative" of human experience, but each art is unique in its means and materials. Poetry and prose "imitate" human experience through the medium of words; the visual arts "imitate" what we see through the media of paint, clay, or stone; music "imitates" the sounds we hear; and dance "imitates" movement. While Aristotle observes that theatre borrows liberally from all these arts, he positions drama as the only art that "imitates action" through the medium of the human actor. Thus, he defines action as drama's most distinctive feature (Aristotle 1958: 3–12).

When Stanislavsky wrote and spoke about acting, he often cited Aristotle in order to stress that "on stage one must always take action. Action, the active state—that is the foundation of both drama and the actor's art" (*SS* II 1989: 88). Stanislavsky also pointed to the etymology of the word "drama" from the Greek verb "to do" and to the Russian words for a play's main divisions (*deistvii*, the "acts") and the cast (*deistvuiushchye litsa*, the "acting persons") as reflective of Aristotle's insight (Vinogradskaia 2000: 496).

In the 1930s while experimenting with a new way to rehearse, Stanislavsky's understanding of dramatic action became more nuanced. He had started down a path, cleared by prominent Russian critics, known as formalists, who were persuasively arguing that a work of art communicates meaning and emotion not only through the semantics of its words, images, and sounds, but more importantly through its forms and structures. A story (or *fabula*) is just a story, but a work of literature, like a novel or play, has a plot (or *siuzhet*) that is constructed by the author's selection and arrangement of the story's details (or *facts*). In short, how the author tells the story by means of a plot impacts the work's meaning. (Steiner 1984: 51)[1] Since the formalists believed that meaning in a literary work can only be discovered by examining how it is made, they promoted and excelled at close, forensic analysis. They deconstructed literary plots by examining the facts in order to uncover underlying patterns and artistic devices in their construction, much like one might seek to understand houses and skyscrapers by examining their engineering.[2]

Formalism first emerged in the 1910s, when a group of linguists and scholars became interested in studying the difference between literary and everyday language. Their ideas flourished in Russia until banned in the 1930s, when Soviet policies insisted that propagandistic content, not form, be the sole criterion for judging the value of art. In fact, the Soviets used "formalist" as a pejorative for any artist or critic whose work cut against the realist grain (Erlich 1969: passim).[3] This ban makes it difficult to find explicit references to Formalism in what Stanislavsky wrote during his last years. Nonetheless, traces of formalist thinking can be found (Carnicke 2009: 200–2).[4] For example, Victor Shklovsky had made the term "device" a key marker for Formalism, when in 1921 he wrote that "a work of literature is the sum-total of all the stylistic devices employed in it" (Erlich 1969: 90). In a letter from December 1936 Stanislavsky tells his family about his latest experiments on acting using this very word:

> I am setting a new device in motion now, a new approach to the role. It involves reading the play today, and tomorrow rehearsing it on stage. What can we rehearse? A great deal. A character comes in, greets everybody, sits down, tells of events that have just taken place, expresses a series of thoughts. Everyone can act this, guided by their own life experience. So, let them act.

> (SS IX 1999: 655)

The practice of what would eventually become known as Active Analysis also betrays Stanislavsky's formalist thinking through its incorporation of interactive patterns in scenes and its treatment of plays as structures of events. First, Stanislavsky complicated Aristotle's definition of drama by adding the notion of counteraction to that of action. Like a baseball flying in the absence of gravity, actions without resistance cannot create drama. In August 1934 he told the visiting director Boris Zon that "the course of a play is like a fabric woven from actions that collide with counteractions. Othello goes after one thing, and Iago tries to influence him to go in the other direction" (Durylin and Markov 1955: 464). With this observation, Stanislavsky was doing for drama what the formalist Vladimir Propp had done for fairy tales, when in 1928 he had identified common patterns in tales from different eras and cultures (like the consistent use of three trials to test heroes). Second, when Stanislavsky envisioned the overall structure of a play as a chain of events, he was also thinking like a formalist. For example, in a 1937 rehearsal of *Romeo and Juliet* (Act I scene 1) at the Opera-Dramatic Studio he used formalist terminology, when he asked the actor (cast as Romeo) to break the play down "into the big events that trace the story (*fabula*)" in order to "understand how the author constructs the play's plot (*siuzhet*)" (Knebel' [1954] 2009: 25).

As you think about the theory and history behind Active Analysis, you might associate aspects of it with other acting techniques and terminologies with which you are familiar. Perhaps when you prepare a scene, you ask yourself "What's my action?" or "What does my character do in this scene?" Stella Adler's training particularly focuses on such questions (Adler 1988: chapter 5). Perhaps you ask instead, "What's my objective?," assuming that "objective" is another term for action as do so many English-speaking actors.[5] You might also associate the notion of counteraction with reacting to what your acting partners say and do. Certainly Sanford Meisner's training and his centrally important Repetition Exercise emphasize acting and reacting in an actor's work (Meisner and Longwell 1987: chapter 3). Perhaps, if you have run across a technique called "Actioning," you might even be familiar with the notion of using active verbs to underscore the lines you speak on stage (Caldarone and Lloyd-Williams 2004: introduction). You may have other associations that I cannot guess. Therefore, to demonstrate how action, counteraction, and event are used in Active Analysis, we must get out of our heads and up on our feet.

In Practice: Action, Counteraction, Event

Active Analysis teaches that every event in a play results from an action meeting resistance from a counteraction. But how does this idea translate into acting? And why do I want you to fall in love with this notion of action encountering counteraction? The only way I can convey what I know in my bones about Active Analysis as practice is to improvise a few scenes with you. Let's start with a single scenario.

Improvisation 1

Me I'm going to pick on you Keith, since you're sitting in my easy eye. I hope you don't mind, but I notice that there are eleven actors here, and I had auditioned for ten. There is one too many, so Keith, because everyone except you happens to be wearing green, you should be the one to leave. (*Keith looks confused.*) I'm throwing you out, understand? Please leave right now! (*He looks around in confusion, then gets up and leaves.*)

Assessment of Improvisation 1:

Me (*I go to the door and hold it open.*)   Thank you, Keith. Come on back. (*Turning to the whole ensemble.*) What kind of scene was that?

Keith   Oh, we're done? (*Laughter ensues.*)

Me   Yes, we're done!

Keith   You didn't mean to throw me out!

Me   Of course not. I simply initiated a scene with an action—to throw Keith out—and Keith obeyed by leaving. Since Keith offered no resistance, it was a short and rather boring scene, over in the blink of an eye. Am I right? There was an impelling action (me throwing Keith out) and an event (when Keith left the room), but, without a counteraction. I got my way far too easily.

Over time, I have come to understand that the counteraction in a scene effectively determines the length of a scene and how interesting it might become. Let me show you what I mean. Hannah, I think you can provide a stronger counteraction, when I try to throw you out.

Improvisation 2

Me   Hannah! You're the one who's … um … the eleventh actor. And what is it precisely that you are wearing? Is it black? Or blue? I can't tell.

Hannah   It's gray.

Me   Gray! Well that's not green, so leave the room!

Hannah   I just don't understand why we have this rule? About wearing green!

Me   It's not a rule. I simply need ten actors, not eleven. (*Pause.*) Goodbye!

Hannah   Is it a personal preference?

Me   It's just a random moment of … of authoritarian bullshit.

Hannah   Ohhh.

Me   So out of the room! (*Hannah just smiles.*)

Me   Out of the room, I say! (*Hannah doesn't move.*) Now!

There is a long pause in which I and Hannah stare each other down.

Hannah   Um, okay. Okay, well you know what?

Me   What?

Hannah   You know what? Fine. For now, I'll leave the room. But I will come back in a bit.

Me   Is that a threat?

Hannah   I will come back, yes.

Me   Well, we'll see about that with Rose blocking the door and keeping you out. Rose, take your position.

Rose (*Saluting as she walks to the door.*) Ay, ay, sir, I'm on it!

Hannah (*To Rose, who is now standing at the door.*) You won't keep me out. (*To me.*) I'll be back. (*Hannah brushes Rose aside.*) Goodbye! (*Exits.*)

Assessment of Improvisation 2:

Me (*Opening the door.*) Come on back, Hannah. None of this is personal, right? I'm not picking on you, Hannah. We're acting. (*Turning to the ensemble.*) Was this a more interesting scene? (*Everyone nods.*) Why?

Rose Because she questioned your action.

Me Exactly, Hannah provided a counteraction. We were matching each other pretty deftly, a little like dueling. In fact, I stumped her at one point with my line about "authoritarian bullshit." But then she stumped me, when she smiled so placidly without moving. We each had to work a bit harder to stay on track. But, ultimately, Hannah backed down and left. Yet, even as she yielded, she laid down a new condition—that she would come back—as if she were setting up a scene to follow. The main point is that her questioning prolonged our scene. Only when she chose to back down, did an event take place that ended the scene. Notice that it was Hannah as the counteraction, who controlled the timing of that event, not me, even though I had initiated the scene as the action and eventually got my way.

To sum up thus far, an event occurs when either the impelling action (like mine with Hannah) or the counteraction (like gravity's with the baseball) overcomes the other. That event then contributes to the overall story of the play. But, in both cases, the resistance from the counteraction conditions how long the scene takes to get to the event.

Let's go one step further and look at the strength of the counteraction. Hannah used a direct counteraction, because she engaged with my action head on by questioning me. The scene continued as long as she matched the force of my action with the force of her questions. But eventually she weakened and left the room. What would happen if the direct counteraction were even stronger and more sustained? Grigor, you are "it" and I don't want you to back down.

Improvisation 3

Me Now, Grigor, leave!

Grigor No.

Me Yes.

Grigor No.

Me YYeSSS …

Grigor NnoOO …

Me Yes!

Grigor No!

Me Yes, yes.

Grigor   No, no.

Me   (*Glowering at him and pointing toward the door.*)

Grigor   (*Glowers back and folds his arms. Laughter from the ensemble.*)

Me   YES!

Grigor   NO! (*More laughter from the ensemble.*)

Assessment of Improvisation 3:

Me   (*Laughing, while interrupting our improvisation.*)   Okay, Grigor that's enough. You've got a strong, direct counteraction. We are using our words as tools to act and counteract. I also made a face and pointed to the door, gestures which you turned right back at me with your glowering and stance. Your "no" countered my "yes" with equal energy throughout. (*To the ensemble.*) Notice, however, that no event can occur between us as long as we match each other's energies equally. This "yes—no" could go on for a very long time …

Rose and Keith   … forever.

Me   Our story has very quickly gotten stuck and cannot unfold unless something else were to happen.

Hannah   You or Grigor might have done something to push toward a concluding event.

Me   What might that be? Think about the events we have already seen today. Keith had jumped right to it by leaving obediently. Hannah, you prolonged the scene by questioning me, but ultimately gave in and left. Grigor and I reached a stalemate instead of an event, because neither one of us was able to change the other's mind.

Keith   Either you or he could have backed down. Come to think of it, Sharon, you actually did back down by stopping the scene!

Me (*Laughing.*)   So I did!

Rose (*Continuing to think about the improvisation.*)   If you had stayed with the scene, one of you might have raised the stakes in order to force the other into an event.

To sum it up, the full structure of action-counteraction-and-event is necessary for a story in Active Analysis to progress. If there is no counteraction, or if the action and counteraction are of equal force, such that no event can occur, the story cannot unfold.

The Qualities of Counteraction

The more I have worked with Active Analysis, the more fascinated I have become with the power of counteraction to condition how a scene develops. Not only does the counteraction largely determine how long a scene goes on and its complexity. It also conditions the play's overall dramatic style. Let me show you how …

Geo   Wait! I have to stop you right there. I definitely get *action*, and I also see how drama develops through *events* that tell a story, but I still don't get *counteraction*.

I was always taught that acting is reacting. So, isn't counteraction the same as reacting to your partner?

Me I admit that it's tempting to substitute "reaction" for "counteraction." The classic translations of Stanislavsky by Elizabeth Reynolds Hapgood do just that (Stanislavski 1936: 263). But, think about the difference between these two words. "Reaction" is inherently passive. Something has to happen before you can react. In contrast, "counteraction" names a force that exists independently, like gravity that pulls toward the earth whether or not a baseball gets thrown. Counteractions have agency. You don't have to wait for something to happen to initiate a counteraction. Gravity doesn't wait for a baseball to be thrown.

Geo (*Thinking it over.*) Uh huh. Maybe … (*Pause.*)

Rose Geo, I had that same thought when I first got into this technique. But now that I use "counteraction" instead of "reaction," I see the advantages when I work. (*Turning to me.*) Tell him about the different types of counteractions, and he'll soon understand.

On one count, there can be no scene without a counteraction, as Keith demonstrated. On a second count, as Hannah and Grigor showed, the strength of the counteraction conditions how long and complicated the scene might get. Lastly, and most astonishingly, the quality of the counteraction—whether direct or oblique—can even determine the play's overall dramatic style.

Direct Counteraction

Hannah and Grigor both used **direct counteractions**, because they met my action head on. In fact, Grigor countered me so directly and so forcefully that no event could occur, unless something were to happen that would shift the balance of power between us. Grigor, let's say that we were to pick up our scene where we left off and try out Rose's previous suggestion. I might raise the stakes physically. If I got frustrated with your stubborn refusal to back down, I might, out of that frustration, start tapping your shoulder with every "yes." If you pushed back at me (although I know you are too gentlemanly for that, but let's just say you did), we could eventually end up on the floor, pushing and pulling at each other. You'd probably win as the counteraction, because you are physically stronger and could probably overpower me fairly easily. Such down and dirty fights, when a physically executed action is met directly with a physically executed counteraction, tend to be the stuff of action-flicks, melodramatic brawls, and shoot-outs in Westerns, gangster films, and thrillers.

Direct counteractions also often drive emotionally powerful scenes, such as the one in Sophocles' classic tragedy when Antigone stands firm against King Creon's demand that she leave her traitorous brother unburied. Whenever you find heated, impassioned, confrontational scenes, you will also likely find direct counteractions.

A beautiful example of direct counteraction can be found in Wayne Wang's indie film *Smoke* (1995), when Thomas Cole (played by Harold Perrineau, Jr.) reveals himself to his estranged father, Cyrus (played by Forest Whitaker). Cyrus had abandoned his baby son, following a car accident in which his wife was killed. Because he had been driving drunk, he could not bear the guilt of her death and had fled. Years later, Thomas searches for his father and finds him at a rural gas station. After observing for a time from afar, Thomas signs on to work at the station as a handyman under an assumed name. Finally, Thomas admits his true identity (the action), thus impelling a climactic scene of great emotional depth. Cyrus explodes in an angry denial of the truth (his direct counteraction) by physically lashing out and striking his son. Thomas responds by tackling his father around the waist, turning the punch into a wrestling match. Whitaker's choice of attack is visceral and sharp, expressing the immediacy of Cyrus' refusal to believe Thomas. Perrineau's choice of attack seems as much a hug as a wrestling hold and thus embodies the love-hate ambiguity of Thomas' relationship with his father. Significantly, the characters' confrontation cannot reach a resolution (as was the case in the improvisation between me and Grigor). Neither rejection nor reconciliation can emerge, because Thomas' action and Cyrus' counteraction are equal in force, both fueled by deeply rooted anger and hurt. Instead, the scene ends when Cyrus' new wife intervenes and forcibly stops their fight. Her intervention is the event that ends the scene (Baron and Carnicke 2008: 166; 175–81).

In summary, direct counteraction meets an impelling action head on, creating an obvious conflict at the heart of the scene. Such counteractions often produce debates, arguments, fights, and confrontations, sometimes verbal and sometimes physical.

Oblique Counteraction

But not all counteractions are direct, nor are all counteractions easy to identify in a play's text. Juliana, I'm going to ask you to help me out by giving you a little direction before we improvise. When I try to throw you out, I don't want you to talk to me at all. I want you to turn and talk to Louisa. Talk to her about anything that comes to your mind, no matter what. Ready?

Improvisation 4

Me Juliana, would you please leave the room, because we are one too many, and you are all dressed in black, no doubt "in mourning for your life"! (*The ensemble laughs, remembering Masha's famous first line in Chekhov's* The Seagull.)

Juliana (*Turning to Louisa.*) I was walking my dog, Zelda, down the street and it was snowing and really foggy, but we had a really good time, especially when she started sliding down the street on her stomach …

Me (*Attempting to interrupt.*) Hey, I said leave the room.

Juliana Can you imagine? My brother was actually there too and he filmed Zelda sliding down, and it was the cutest thing ever. When was the last time you had so much fun in the snow?

Louisa (*Glancing at me and then turning toward Juliana.*) Well, I can't say exactly …

Me (*To Juliana.*) Hey, I said leave the room! What is going on here? (*Raising my voice.*) HEY! I said leave the room. (*To myself*). This is infuriating.

Juliana I asked you, when was the last time you saw snow?

Louisa Let me think … It's been about three years.

Juliana (*Continuing with Louisa.*)   So you didn't get out into the snow yesterday at all? It was such a great day!

Me (*To Juliana.*)   Have you heard a word I've said? Have you?

Juliana (*To Louisa.*)   But cold … It was really cold!

Me   All right, I give up!

Assessment of Improvisation 4:

Me   Yes, my resolve weakened. My giving up was the event that ended this scene, and so, Juliana, your counteraction overcame my action. (*Turning to the ensemble.*) Do you all see that Juliana countered me, even though she never directly spoke to me? She used an oblique counteraction, making our scene evolve in a completely different way than my improvisations with Grigor and Hannah.

Anisha   When Juliana ignored you, she acted as if you weren't even in the room.

Sargis   Passive aggressive, if you ask me.

Me   This improvisation exemplifies the notion of **oblique counteraction**. Juliana is not fighting me, but she counters me by side-stepping a fight.

If our dialogue were written down and if someone, who had not seen us perform, were to read the text, the reader might think our lines come from an absurdist play. Sharon says, "Get out of the room." Juliana says, "I've been walking my dog." We don't appear to be speaking with each other or following normal logic. A scholar might even interpret our written scene as a profound statement about a failure to communicate. But, in fact, our improvisation is very Chekhovian.

A beautiful example of oblique counteraction can be found in the near absurdist Act II scene from Anton Chekhov's *The Cherry Orchard*, when the merchant Lopakhin tries to persuade the estate-owner Ranyevskaya to chop down her orchard and rent out parcels of land for summer cottages in order to establish a reliable income to pay the interest on her mortgage. Lopakhin and Ranyevskaya, accompanied by her brother Gayev, enter in mid-conversation after having had lunch in town. Lopakhin says: "You must decide once and for all. Time will not wait for you. There's no point in questioning it. Do you agree to rent your land for summer houses or not? Answer in one word. Yes or no? Only one word!" He is clearly the impelling action in the scene. She, in turn, says: "Who's been smoking those revolting cigars here …" Then Gayev talks about their lunch, a topic that she continues by criticizing his behavior in the restaurant. Lopakhin is entirely left out. (Chekhov 2009: 265–6) While their lines appear to jump illogically from one topic to another, the logic of their interpersonal dynamics makes it crystal clear that Ranyevskaya is the counteraction in Chekhov's scene, as surely as Juliana was in our improvisation. Moreover, Gayev becomes his sister's alliance, just as Louisa was Juliana's, helping Ranyevskaya shut Lopakhin out. If, as an actor, you recognize Ranyevskaya's change of topic as an oblique counteraction and Gayev as her alliance, you can play the scene easily. If you do not, you will miss what's really going on in the scene.

Of course, Chekhov does not have a patent on oblique counteractions. You will find them in many plays from different eras. Whenever you are confused by the flow of a conversation, or whenever you play a weak or passive-aggressive character, a manipulator or hypocrite, check for oblique counteractions.

Sargis Juliana and Ranyevskaya both had someone else to talk to! Can an oblique counteraction ever happen in a scene with only two people?

Me Oblique counteractions are more difficult in such scenes, but they can be used. If Geo were to ask his boss for a raise, and she were to talk instead about the weather or continue answering her emails, then she would be countering him obliquely. But your question also leads me to the next main principle in Active Analysis, the creation of alliances among characters.

Forging Alliances in a Scene

Because Active Analysis focuses on how an impelling action collides with a counteraction to produce an event, applying it to scenes with two characters is fairly straightforward. One actor carries the action, the other the counteraction. The only difficulty lies in figuring out which is which. When there are more than two characters, things become more interesting.

In our exploration of the interactive principles of Active Analysis, there were two moments when a third actor was pulled into the improvisations. I asked Rose for help with my action by guarding the door to keep Hannah out. Juliana got assistance from Louisa, and that alliance strengthened the counteraction. These instances already suggest how Active Analysis deals with ensemble scenes through the forging of alliances.

In theory, no matter how many characters may be involved (two, three, four, or more), every scene develops through one main action colliding with one main counteraction. This collision forms the central focus in the scene, its center of gravity if you will. In practice, this means that actors in a scene with more than two characters begin by determining which character carries the impelling action and which the counteraction. Once this central focus is established, the other actors can ally themselves with either the action or counteraction, thus assisting or resisting the scene's forward momentum. These alliances, like actions and counteractions, are also described with active verbs.

If a strong wind were added to my baseball scene, the wind might help the ball fly by blowing with its flight, thus allying itself with the scene's action. Alternatively, the wind might impede the action by blowing against the ball in alliance with gravity's counteraction.

A good example of Stanislavsky's use of alliances in his directing can be found in transcripts of his rehearsals on Molière's *Tartuffe*, conducted at the Opera-Dramatic Studio from March 1936 to April 1938.[6] Stanislavsky divided the cast into two camps: one led by the religious hypocrite Tartuffe with his staunch followers (the patriarch, Orgon, and Orgon's mother); the other camp composed of those who see through the hypocrisy (Orgon's wife, daughter, brother-in-law, and their clever maid Dorine). In other words, Stanislavsky identified the play's center of gravity in Tartuffe's main action—to con Orgon and his family—and the main counteraction of Orgon's family—to unmask Tartuffe as a hypocrite. The play's final event lies in Orgon's recognition of Tartuffe's villainy and hence a return to normal family life. At times, Stanislavsky would experiment in rehearsal by asking the cast to improvise face-offs between the two camps and to create skirmishes between the forces of hypocrisy and integrity. The actors exchanged insults across the room and played tug-of-war with a rope. As rehearsals progressed, Stanislavsky was careful to ensure that every scene in the play embodied a central collision between these two camps (Carnicke 2009: 198–200).

> **Rose** So, there is one action and one counteraction in every scene, but there can be many alliances, each one siding with either the action or the counteraction.
>
> **Me** Right.
>
> **Rose** And everyone in the scene, whatever role they play, has a verb of their own, even the alliances.
>
> **Me** Right. I find the handling of ensemble scenes through the creation of alliances extremely valuable. Most of you during your careers will likely work in ensembles with roles that have few lines. When you play an alliance, you will always listen to what is happening around you with a clear point of view, making it easy to stay engaged and active during the performance. In other words, if you know what your dynamic function is within a scene (be it action, counteraction, or alliance), you will never find yourself twiddling your thumbs as you wait for your next cue.

In addition, alliance also helps you know when to take the focus of the audience and when to yield focus to others in the scene, because you will understand how the story unfolds at every moment. As a director, I find alliances especially important in bringing clarity to a production, especially when there are lots of people on the stage. When actors work only with their own actions, as is commonly done, all the characters on stage seem equally important and the audience does not know where to look. Forging alliances helps frame the work of the actors, very much like a camera lens that directs the spectators' eyes in a film to what is most important in any given shot.

Counteraction or Conflict

I first learned about "counteraction" from Maria Knebel ([1954] 2009: 25 and [1959] 1982: 35–6),[7] but the term had been hiding in plain sight since the first Russian publication of Stanislavsky's *An Actor's Work on the Self, Part I* in 1938. Stanislavsky was completing this volume in 1935 and 1936, while simultaneously experimenting with his new approach to rehearsing. It is therefore unsurprising that he slipped some of his latest experimental ideas into his book and past the Soviet censors. In Chapter 15 he writes that "every action meets an opposing counteraction, and the latter provokes and strengthens the former" (*SS* II 1989: 425). He introduces this novel idea, when explaining that some actions run throughout the entire play (what he calls "throughactions") and that "in conjunction with every throughaction, there is also a counterthroughaction that travels in the opposite direction" (*SS* II 1989: 425).

This passage is brief and therefore easily missed, particularly since he does not refer to "counteraction" anywhere else in the book. Yet, he includes in this brief discussion an interesting argument on the importance of counteractions:

> This phenomenon is good and we should welcome it, because counteractions naturally provoke new actions. We need continuous collisions that give birth to struggles, arguments, all kinds of corresponding problems and solutions. This phenomenon provokes in the actor an active state of being, a dynamism, which is the basis of our art. If there

were no counteractions in a play and everything were to work out of its own accord, then the characters and the actors, who portray them, would have nothing to do on stage; and the play would lack dynamics and therefore be unstageworthy.

(SS II 1989: 425)

This tantalizing reference to the dynamic structure of drama suggests how Stanislavsky went beyond Aristotle to develop a rehearsal technique that emphasizes interaction.

Geo   Okay, I get *action* and now I also get *counteraction*. But why don't we just call it "conflict"? After all, we've all been taught that good drama depends upon conflict. Why do we need another word?

Me   Do you think that "conflict" and "counteraction" are synonyms? Many people do. In fact, my Russian colleagues often use "conflict." It is also true that direct counteractions result in conflict. But think about the difference between these two words.

In my experience, there are many scenes that do not present themselves as obvious conflicts. Consider scenes involving negotiation or collaboration. Think about love scenes. Think about scenes that show the texture of life within a richly imagined world. Such scenes would be uninteresting without the tension that counteractions provide; yet outright conflicts seem entirely beside the point. Characters in such scenes tend to engage in subtle interactions, like intricate dances, that are often fascinating to watch. As playwright Cynthia Joyce Clay observes, the "theory of conflict" does not help explain plays, like Synge's *Riders to the Sea*, in which atmosphere dominates the story; or those that are poetic and symbolic, like the short plays by Maurice Maeterlinck (Anton Chekhov's favorite playwright); or about subjects other than strife and struggle. Emphasizing conflict is too limiting, Clay writes, because it tends "to produce shallow, violent [dramas] with lots of hollering during dinner scenes […] and to foster interpretations of contention in stories that are not about contention" (Clay 2014: 54–5). The same can often be said of new plays that break away from past conventions.

I love the word "counteraction," precisely because it prompts us to think outside of the usual box of "conflict." It suggests fresh takes on all kinds of scenes, particularly those in which characters want the same thing and move in the same direction. All interesting scenes develop through collisions of actions with counteractions, but not all scenes necessarily need outright conflict. In my experience, using the term "counteraction" elicits more interesting and nuanced work from actors than does "conflict," which can prompt scenes of forced anger.

Let's test this notion of "counteraction" as distinct from "conflict" through a new scenario. Can we devise a scene in which two characters want the same thing? Let's suppose that two people are in love and about to be married. They want to start their life together in a new place to live. In fact, let's make this experiment even more interesting by asking two of our most seasoned actors to step into it. Shari, Geo, let's imagine that you are both widowed and have decided to get married and share your sunset years with one another. I want to see an action (expressed as a verb), a counteraction (expressed as a verb), and an event that occurs between the two of you.

The scene will likely go better if, before you begin, you discuss the given circumstances that you share in the scene, and then take a private moment to think about your individual attitude toward those shared circumstances. Finally, use the principles of Active Analysis to plan what you will do when you get up to work. Who is the action and who is the counteraction? What verb do you want to try? But don't work out exactly how your scene will unfold. Plan only the *what*, not the *how*. When you get up to work, improvise the scene by focusing on your verb and on how what you do impacts your partner.

> **Sargis** I don't understand what you mean by having an individual attitude toward their shared circumstances.

> **Me** Well, both of them want the same thing—to get married—but each of them may want it for different reasons, or may place a different value on marriage. In other words, they want the same thing, but Shari in her way and Geo in his.

Geo and Shari step aside to talk, as the rest of us reset the chairs, turning our circle into a couple of rows, facing the back of the hall. Shari asks Keith to drag a bench to the center of the space. Geo rifles around in his briefcase and finds a large manila envelope, which he places under one arm. Shari nods that they are ready.

Devised Scene

> **Geo** (*Strolling arm in arm with Shari.*) You have a such a beautiful garden here.

> **Shari** Yes, but it's full of old memories. Don't you like any of the places that the real estate agent showed us today?

> **Geo** I can't say that I do, honestly. They are all so normal.

> **Shari** Well, if we are going to start a new life, we can't stay here, where I keep thinking about my last marriage. I really like the small place near all the shopping and cafes.

> **Geo** Not for us.

> **Shari** Then the large one, with the bright sunny windows.

> **Geo** Not for us.

> **Shari** (*As they sit down on the bench to enjoy the sun, she takes his hand.*) Should we look at some other places, then?

> **Geo** Nope. (*Opening the envelope that he has been carrying and presenting her with a colorful brochure.*) I have the perfect place for us!

> **Shari** (*Reading.*) A chateau in Provence!

> **Geo** Yes, refurbished. It will be a real adventure, seven rooms to rent out as a B and B.

> **Shari** We won't have any privacy. (*She pats his arm affectionately.*) I want to enjoy being alone with you, after all the years of having a full house, raising children, and putting others first.

> **Geo** We'll have a whole wing to ourselves. And you always said you loved Paris.

> **Shari** I love France, yes I do. (*Cradling his face in her palm.*) But I don't speak French.

> **Geo** Neither do I. But we can learn.

Shari France? Traveling there is fine, but living there is completely different. I have family here, grandkids … So do you. We'll miss them.

Geo That's the point, a chance to get away from it all.

Shari It's one thing to start a new life, but France … (*Again patting his hand*.) I just can't do it, love.

Geo Well I can move in here. Your place with this garden is better for the two of us than my cramped apartment.

Shari No. I have terrible memories here.

Geo So then to France …

Shari Why not that house in Glendale, up in the hills with the lovely view?

Geo Glendale is a very convenient place to live. But where's the adventure? At the mall?

Shari Well, we could always travel. I love to travel.

Geo How about spending half the year in France and half the year here?

Shari How about a month? Six months away from my family, my friends? I'd miss them.

Geo I want to live there and I want to live there with you and I am tired of the grind—work, home, sleep, then get up again for work, home, sleep, every miserable day.

Shari I love France and I love you. I just don't want to live there.

Geo I see. You are not willing to compromise.

Shari Yes, I want to compromise. Why not?

Geo (*Getting down on his knees in front of her, as if to propose*.)   Then let's get that little romantic house on Silverlake …

Shari Yes, I did like that house overlooking the lake. And we'll live there and travel to Provence every year for a month. (*He takes her hand*.) Can we afford it?

Geo I am sure we can. Our life together will become our adventure, living and traveling …

Shari Why don't we switch our honeymoon plans and go to Provence after the wedding for a whole month.

Geo I'm game, dear, if you are! (*She reaches toward him and they hug*.)

Assessment of the Devised Scene:

Me What a sweet scene! Geo, I loved the surprise brochure and your character's expansive imagination. Shari, your character's affection for him, even as he exasperated you, was strong throughout. But most of all, I loved the moment when you, Geo, got down on one knee, as if you were proposing all over again! That physical choice opened the door for Shari to agree to a compromise plan. Her agreement was the event that brought the scene to its end. Let's pull this scene apart even more. Who was the impelling action?

Keith I'm not sure. It could be Shari, because she started the conversation about the places they'd seen that day. But Geo really drove the scene forward, once he started in on his plan to move to France.

Me Whenever you are unsure about who carries the action in a scene, you can ask yourself who is most necessary to the scene. Without this person, the scene could not begin. In this case, it seems to me that your first instinct is right, Keith. Shari threw the baseball that started their wrangling about a house.

Hannah But Geo became so active, when he took out the brochure. I think he'd been waiting to spring this on her from the beginning. Doesn't that make him the action?

Me The sequence of the scene makes it hard to see Geo as the impelling action. Shari first raised the topic of houses. But don't forget that counteractions have agency that is independent of the action. So, like gravity, Geo's desire to move to France existed before the scene began. Geo, you played a counteraction beautifully. You did not merely react to Shari. In fact, you pushed her in a direction that she could not have anticipated, making it necessary for her to react to you by adjusting her desires. In fact, you were sneaky in playing your counteraction, when you suggested that, should she reject a move to France, you could simply move in with her, knowing full well that her house was the one place she most wanted to leave. The collision between action and counteraction in this scene was like a roller coaster ride rather than a game of ping pong. (*Turning to the group.*) So, did they succeed in creating a counteraction without an obvious conflict?

Keith I'm actually amazed that they never actually fought. Fighting would have been so easy, because Geo was so insistent on France and Shari was so opposed to it. But I also saw Shari looking at him and trying to find something to say that was gentle. She was definitely the more affectionate of the two, always patting Geo's hand, cradling his face. She clearly loved him and wasn't willing to jeopardize this marriage due to his stupid idea! (*Geo laughs.*) And when he got down on his knees, we saw him renew his commitment to her, too. They both wanted this marriage, although I think she wanted it more than he.

Me What is it exactly that drives each of you to want this marriage?

Geo I'm a dreamer. My verb was "to get her to dream."

Shari And I'm more practical. My verb was "to take control of the practicalities in life."

Geo But, for both of us, marriage represented a fresh start. It's a whole new adventure that will keep me feeling young.

Shari Yes, I wanted a fresh start too, just not in France!

In an odd way, your devised scene reminds me of the balcony scene in *Romeo and Juliet* (Act II scene 2). While the play as a whole depicts the long-lived feud between the lovers' families, the balcony scene brings the two title characters together in an intimate, late-night tryst that occurs when Romeo impulsively jumps over the wall of Juliet's home in order to catch a glimpse of her. He is madly in love with her and she with him. The scene could be so simple and direct, but instead, their interaction is subtle and prolonged. Why is this so? Is it enough to assume that they simply want their time together to go on as long as possible? Maybe, but Active Analysis suggests that a better answer might be found by searching for the scene's counteraction. Shakespeare depicts Romeo as a romantic, given to flights of fancy that find expression through poetry. He wallows in metaphors and imagery. The first time he sees Juliet at the party in Act I, he says: "Oh, she doth teach the torches to burn bright!" He continues to heap image upon image in admiration of her. From first to last, Romeo is as much in love with poetry as with Juliet. Geo, you had something of Romeo in you through your expansive desire to move to France! In contrast, like Shari, Juliet is down to earth, in touch with reality, and aware of the consequences of things.

The difference between Romeo and Juliet is immediately apparent in the balcony scene. He jumps over her wall with his usual romantic flourish, following "his heart" in order to "find [his] center out." As soon as she realizes that someone has been eavesdropping, she asks logical questions in straightforward language: Who are you? How did you get here? Why did you come? When she learns that Romeo has come to see her, she warns him of the real and present danger due to their parents' feud: "the place [is] death, considering who thou art, if any of my kinsmen find thee here." Still, he continues with poetry, sweeping aside her worries: "With love's light wings did I o'er perch these walls" (as if love could overcome the force of gravity)! In short, the poetic Romeo impels the scene and the pragmatic Juliet counteracts by resisting his poetic impulses.

As the scene develops, the two readily agree on their love but not on its expression. He wants poetry and she a solution. The interactive dance between them reaches a stalemate when Romeo attempts to "swear by yonder blessed moon" and Juliet cuts him off: "O, swear not by the moon, the inconstant moon, that monthly changes in her circled orb, lest that thy love prove likewise variable." Action and counteraction are so equally balanced at this moment that there seems no way forward. Frustrated by this impasse, Romeo baldly asks: "O, wilt though leave me so unsatisfied?" (Whenever I read this line, I cannot help humming the Rolling Stones' song, "I can't get no satisfaction." Romeo is, after all, a teenager with strong, impatient drives!) In her turn, Juliet seems puzzled. What more can he possibly want from her now? She risks taking the next logical step: "If that thy bent of love be honorable, thy purpose marriage, send me word tomorrow …" Her frank proposal certainly escalates the stakes of the scene, but still the scene does not end. There remains something as yet unsatisfied between them. And then Juliet compares Romeo to a pet bird on a leash. While she begins with her usual pragmatism, she soon shifts into poetic imagery:

'Tis almost morning; I would have thee gone.
And yet no farther than a wanton's bird,
Who lets it hop a little from her hand,
Like a poor prisoner in his twisted gyves,
And with a silk thread plucks it back again,
So loving-jealous of his liberty.

Her poetic flourish is the kind of embroidered metaphor that we have come to expect from Romeo. He, in turn, accepts her image with a short and simple statement that echoes her usual directness: "I would I were thy bird." She has offered him a gift of poetry and he has accepted without poetry. They each have been changed by the other's love and this change registers in the way they speak. Their agreement at this moment in the scene marks the event that brings the scene to an end with a sense of satisfying closure. The dynamics in Shakespeare's scene about young love are not so far from the dynamics that Shari and Geo created for older lovers through the power of counteraction.

In my opinion, actors do not get enough practice in acting classes with scenes that do not erupt into obvious conflicts, despite the fact that such scenes are more numerous in plays than the big, climactic confrontations we crave as actors. In my teaching, I have also found that using the term "counteraction," rather than "conflict," helps actors avoid the trap of angry fighting and encourages them instead to deal confidently with interactive nuance.

Armed with the dynamic principles of Active Analysis—action, counteraction, alliance, and event—we put away the chairs, clean the table, gather our things, and go our separate ways home. As I lock the door, I tell everyone that next time we will roll up our sleeves and get to work on some written texts.

Notes

1. Current scholars translate *fabula* and *siuzhet* differently, but Steiner's "story" and "plot" are more pragmatic when working with actors.
2. For examples of formalist analyses see Lemon and Reis (1965) and Balukhaty (1967).
3. With their work banned, many formalists fled to Prague, where their ideas influenced Structuralism and Semiotics.
4. Formalist theories were based on prose works, making Stanislavsky's adaptation unique. Only Sergey Balukhaty studied plays, particularly those of Anton Chekhov. For more on Stanislavsky's use of Formalism see Lesson 4.
5. For information on misleading translations of *zadacha* see Lesson 2 and Carnicke (2009: 89–91).
6. The loyal Soviet actor Mikhail Kedrov played the title role. Following Stanislavsky's death, Kedrov completed the production, which premiered in December 1939. For more on Kedrov see Chapters 1–3.
7. Irina Brown retains these references to "counteraction" in her translation of Vassiliev's edition of Knebel's writings (2021: 50; 103). Brown is less consistent with her translation of the formalist terms *fabula* and *siuzhet*.

Lesson 2 Scene Study through Active Analysis—Shakespeare

Prelude

Nearly everyone has arrived. Louisa and Juliana have finished setting out tonight's feast. Why is it, I wonder, as I catch Shari taking a bite, that acting and eating seem to go together in Los Angeles? Our table always makes me think of the food trucks that park next to the equipment trailers and the stars' vans when movies film on location. Food, woven into the fabric of our profession, was just not part of Stanislavsky's or Knebel's classes! Sargis and Grigor have already circled the chairs. Louisa and Juliana have chosen seats next to each other. Shari has a festive package on the floor next to her. Grigor seems absorbed in reading his volume of Shakespeare. Hannah is across from him with her guitar case stashed behind her chair. Geo still stands at the table, holding a cheese plate in his hand and arguing passionately with Rose and Sargis about something or other. Setrak is sitting to the side, his jacket draped around the back of his chair and a scarf wrapped around his neck. He takes a bottle of water from his jacket, sips and puts the bottle back. After a while, I see him shaking hands with Grigor, who has moved to the chair next to Setrak.

I join the circle, mentally noting who is missing when Anisha rushes in breathless. "Sorry, the traffic …" She takes her usual place next to Shari, who hands over the package. Anisha pulls out a long, beaded necklace, gasps and slips it over her head. "I'm ready now." I start to speak, just as Keith arrives with a cake. "Sorry, all," he says. "My wife baked this for us, but I was held up in Philly because of the fog, so I landed a bit late. Wow, Anisha, nice necklace!" "Thank you, Keith. I love it, Shari. It's so mid-century!"

"All right," I say, "We are all here. Let's go!"

An Overview of Rehearsing through Active Analysis

"Active Analysis" refers, of course, to the interactive principles that we explored last time. In this sense, the words emphasize Stanislavsky's belief that drama is first and foremost an art that explores interaction.

But "Active Analysis" also refers to the process of rehearsal, through which actors analyze texts actively. You read a scene; you think about its dynamics; you get up and try acting what you think. These trial runs are called "etudes" and make Active Analysis unique. The rehearsal continues with re-reading the text, assessing what happened in the etude, and making any adjustments you think will take you closer to the scene the next time you get up to do another etude. This process of reading, trying, and assessing continues until the scene begins to unfold of its own accord. You begin to know it in your bones. Only then do you memorize the text, set the blocking, and move toward a polished performance. A rehearsal in Active Analysis "is not about preparing for a production" by perfecting your lines and blocking, but rather "a process of analysis," says Knebel (1968: 48), through which you actively discover what you need to know in order to bring the scene to life. As Stanislavsky taught her, "knowing" for the actor means "knowing how" (Knebel' [1954] 2009: 65).

Acting depends upon tacit knowledge that we carry in our bodies. Like riding a bicycle, acting is easier to do than to explain through words. We use metaphors, similes, and images to express what we know. Like acting itself, rehearsing through Active Analysis is also easier to do than to explain. If what I say about it sounds too simple or, alternatively, too complicated, know that I can only hint at the richness I experience when I practice the technique. Therefore, my goal in the next few sessions will be to guide you through a few rehearsals using Active Analysis, so that you can experience it for yourselves.

This session and the next will focus on scene study. I will guide you through the active analysis of Act I scene 7 from Shakespeare's *Macbeth* and an excerpt from Act II of Chekhov's *Three Sisters*. While we won't be able to take the scenes from first readings to polished performances, you will begin to understand the process and its advantages.

I imagine that some of you might think my scene choices are old-fashioned or irrelevant to your desire to work commercially. I admit that I could have chosen different texts: a post-dramatic piece, a comedy of manners, a Japanese Noh or Indian Sanskrit play, an ancient tragedy, an absurdist or symbolist work, a screenplay, a sitcom, etc. But I have decided on Shakespeare and Chekhov for three reasons. First, production data show that they are still the most produced playwrights worldwide. Second, their plays can demonstrate how Active Analysis "cleans the dust of time off literary works with wonderful images and characters," to quote Knebel (1967: 485). And last but not least, I selfishly want to share with you my admiration for their talents. Later, I will challenge you to apply what you have learned from actively analyzing these classic scenes to a brand new play.

The Play as a Score for Performance

Before getting down to work, however, I want to share with you the abiding assumption about written plays upon which all of Stanislavsky's work depends, including his last experimentation at the Opera-Dramatic Studio. As he told the director Boris Zon in 1933, "My new rehearsal method is a development of what has come before" (Durylin and Markov 1955: 453). Therefore, it is necessary to begin with "what has come before."

Me Hannah, have you ever learned to sing a song you had never heard by reading the music?

Hannah I once got interested in protest songs from the American Revolution and found one in the library that I especially liked, "The Liberty Song" from 1768.[1]

Me Can you play it now?

Hannah gets out her guitar, tunes it, and begins. Her voice is clear, the melody stirring. She gets stronger and faster with every repetition of the refrain—"In freedom we are born and in freedom we live." She embodies a growing sense of urgency in the call to arms as she continues to sing. When the last note dies down, the room explodes in applause.

Me   Where does the song you just sang exist—in the notes on the page or in the air around us when you sang?

Hannah   I needed the notes, so I suppose it's in the sheet music.

Louisa   I disagree. I started out in musical theatre and, believe you me, reading printed music is like putting a puzzle together in your mind. You have to imagine what the song will sound like, but you won't know for sure until you perform it. Reading music takes work.

Hannah   Yes, that's true. For this song, I had to figure out how to phrase the lyrics, especially in places where the words didn't fit the tune. I also noticed that there were a lot of repeated phrases. Unless I could somehow emphasize the actual refrain, the song would become a muddle. So I sang the refrain stronger with every new repetition to create a crescendo.

Me   It's interesting that you say "puzzle," Louisa. Knebel's protégé, the prominent director Anatoly Efros, called every play a "puzzle" and told actors that their work starts with "puzzling it out."[2] But, I don't think either of you have yet answered my philosophical question. Where does the song exist—on the page or in performance?

Geo   Absolutely in her performance! (*Everyone now nods in agreement.*)

Me   Stanislavsky would also agree. The notes on the page encode the music, but are not themselves the music. Stanislavsky saw written plays as scores for performance, with the printed words functioning like musical notes. Unlike poetry or novels that are intended to be read and can therefore be considered finished on the page, plays are finished only when actors perform them. Thus, every production of a new play is a discovery and every production of an old play is new for its times. This makes theatre a timeless art that is always recreating itself and evolving.

A great deal of evidence proves that Stanislavsky compared written plays to musical scores. In volume 2 of *An Actor's Work on Himself*, he writes: "Actors must create the music of their feelings based on the play's text and learn to sing this music using the words of the role" (*SS* III 1990: 82). As a young man, he had aspired to a career in singing and studied with a leading member of the Bolshoi Opera. In 1887 his performance in Russia's premiere of Gilbert and Sullivan's comic operetta, *The Mikado*, earned him his first professional review as a brilliant singing actor (Benedetti 1990: 22–3). Ultimately, however, his voice proved too weak to sustain an operatic career. Yet, even as he turned his attention to spoken drama, he continued to take inspiration from music. For example, in his opinion, the famous singer Fyodor Chaliapin could reach with his voice beyond "the material and coarse" aspects of life and embrace the ineffable. Why shouldn't actors be able to do the same? "In inspired moments of performance," Stanislavsky writes, "when you understand not only the surface meaning of spoken words but also their deep, hidden resonances, then you too can find the same sonority, simplicity, and nobility within speech" (*SS* I 1988: 356–7).

Stanislavsky brought his knowledge of music to his lifelong experimentation with acting. As early as 1905 he founded the Studio-Theatre on Povarskaya Street with the young avant-garde director, Vsevolod Meyerhold (Chapter 1). Joining them in their work was the prominent composer, Ilya Sats, who argued that the primary responsibility of directors, like conductors, should be the creation of artistic ensembles from the varied talents of individual performers (Kristi 1952: 54–5). Many years later, Stanislavsky recalled Sats as "the first in the history of theatre to prove how necessary music is for our dramatic art" (*SS* I 1988: 388).[3]

In 1918 at the Bolshoi Theatre's invitation, Stanislavsky founded an Opera Studio to improve operatic acting. His student production of Tchaikovsky's opera, *Eugene Onegin*, which was performed in 1922 in the salon on Leontyevsky Lane with Stanislavsky himself operating a makeshift curtain, was called "one of the most significant productions in contemporary theatre" (Sobolevskaia 1988: 5).[4] The singers, wearing street clothes and accompanied by a single pianist, entered, exited, and sometimes waltzed through the spectators, breaking realism's fourth-wall. Most importantly, however, they stunned audiences with their "remarkable, unforgettable acting" (Sobolevskaia 1988: 5). Notably, Stanislavsky formulated his first comprehensive statements on actor training for the singers in the Bolshoi Theatre Opera Studio. Alongside the many now-familiar elements in his System, he also articulated lesser known elements, such as tempo and rhythm in acting; the pragmatics of clear diction, intonation, phrasing, and vocal control that derive directly from his belief that drama and music are kindred forms (Carnicke and Rosen 2014b: 120–38 and Magarshack 1961).

In 1935, three years before his death, while deeply involved with experiments that would eventually lead to Active Analysis, Stanislavsky again linked spoken drama with musical works. Not only did he emphasize this link by naming his last laboratory the Opera-Dramatic Studio but he again invited Meyerhold to collaborate. While Stanislavsky now rehearsed Molière's *Tartuffe* in the salon, where he had previously directed *Eugene Onegin*, Meyerhold worked nearby with singers on Verdi's *Rigoletto* (Carnicke and Rosen 2014b: 126).[5]

Following from the assumption that words in a play are like notes on sheet music, Stanislavsky prepared detailed promptbooks for rehearsals that he labeled "scores" (*partitury*). He put the play on the right-hand side of the page and his directorial notes on the left, using numbers to relate the notes to the text, much as orchestral scores mark measures of music.[6] He used this format with promptbooks for most of his productions from the groundbreaking 1898 *The Seagull*, co-directed by Nemirovich-Danchenko, to the 1930 debacle of *Othello,* staged by Sudakov (Chapter 1).

Stanislavsky's musical approach to directing also extended beyond the format to the content of his notes. For example, in his promptbook for *The Seagull* he frequently gives time signatures for the tempos of pauses and physical activities. Thus, Treplev kisses Nina for a shy five seconds in Act I, but Trigorin kisses her more aggressively for ten seconds in Act III (Stanislavskii 1981 vol. 2: 65, 133). Even more intriguing are places in the score where Stanislavsky uses contrasting performance styles as if in counterpoint with each other. Thus, in Act III, the *"keenest* realism" for Arkadina's bandaging of her son's wounded head contrasts with her extravagantly histrionic "melodrama" in the next scene as she pleads with her lover to give up his infatuation with Nina (Stanislavskii 1981 vol. 2: 121; 125). The Russian theatrical scholar, Konstantin Rudnitsky, observes that "this was the first time in the history of theatre that the development of dramatic action was construed on the musical principle of *counterpoint*" (Stanislavskii 1981 vol. 2: 21).

Stanislavsky abandoned writing promptbooks only when he redefined rehearsal as an active process of analysis in which director and actors together uncover the inherent music in the play. From the founding of the Moscow Art Theatre in 1897 to his creation of the

Opera-Dramatic Studio in 1934, he had gradually transformed his approach to directing from that of an overseer in charge of all aspects of a production to that of a collaborative leader, who guides an ensemble of equals in the devising of a production. While he still thought of plays as scores for performance, he now shared the responsibility for puzzling them out with his actors. Preplanned "scores" were no longer appropriate, because the imposition of the director's will threatened collaborative work with the cast. When the leading formalist scholar, Sergey Balukhatyi, sought permission to publish the 1898 promptbook for *The Seagull*, Stanislavsky refused in a letter:

> Keep in mind that the *mise-en-scène* for *The Seagull* was prepared in the old method, now no longer used, of imposing upon the actor my own feelings, and not according to the new method that teaches actors to prepare the materials themselves in order that they find on their own what's necessary for the *mise-en-scène*.
>
> (*SS* IX 1999: 177)[7]

As Knebel has observed, the director's role as the leader of a creative ensemble better reflects Stanislavsky's lifelong respect for actors as artists than had his earlier directing method (Knebel' [1959] 1982: 6).

In short, the practice of Active Analysis rests upon the assumption that, like sheet music, a play is a score for performance. Consequently, our rehearsal process in the next few sessions will be similar to Hannah's approach to "The Liberty Song." We'll define what in the score is clear and what needs puzzling out. We'll figure out how the words on the page point to the dynamics of performance. And then, we'll bring the score to life through our performing of it.

In Practice: Rehearsing Shakespeare's *Macbeth* (1606), Act I scene 7

Sargis and Juliana, I want you to take on the roles of Macbeth and Lady Macbeth. While the scene starts with an extraordinary soliloquy by Macbeth, I want you to focus on the interaction between husband and wife that follows, so that we can build upon the interactive principles of Active Analysis that we explored last time. Let's …

Geo Wait, wait, you just said *it* three times! Don't you know that "the Scottish play" is cursed!

Shari He's right. I once played the first witch in an avant-garde production and things went so badly that we held an emergency meeting after the dress rehearsal to decide if we should open or not! You see, actors had started falling down due to a newly installed stage floor. Our Banquo broke his arm. Our M sprained his ankle! Lady M bruised her forehead! And I was limping from painful blisters all over my feet, because I had to dance barefoot around the cauldron.

Geo You see!!

Anisha Did you open?

Shari Yes, after a few days delay. Turns out that the floor had been installed upside down, with the slick side up …

Rose That's not a curse, Shari. That's incompetence.

Geo Same thing.

Grigor   I'm a history buff, and I once looked into this particular theatrical superstition. It dates back to the first production of the play when the boy actor playing Lady Macbeth died backstage. In fact, there are almost as many disasters connected with this play as there are productions (Hay 1987: 322–3).

Geo   I heard that the play is cursed because Shakespeare used actual incantations for the witches' lines, so by speaking them, you call forth ….

Keith   Luckily, guys, we are not working on the witches' tonight, so I say, let's get on with it.

Me (*Laughing*.)   Thank you, Keith.

Step One: Reading for the Facts

Let's begin by reading the text as a score for performance. If Stanislavsky were here, he would warn you that doing so is difficult. He always told opera singers that they are "luckier" than actors:

> The composer gives you everything: the rhythm for your feelings, the right intonations for each word, and a melody which is the pattern of your emotions. All you have to do is find a true basis for the notes given to you and make them your own. How much easier this is for you than for us dramatic actors, who have to create our own rhythms, compose the music of our spoken words, and provide true feelings out in the vacuum of the stage!
>
> (Rumiantsev 1969: 81–2)

Knebel echoes this idea more simply: "The playwright gives us only dialogue, only words. We have to create everything else" (Knebel' 1976: 217).

As your guide to this work, I warn you of another difficulty. The history of drama over the centuries and within the world's diverse cultures presents such a rich and varied tapestry that establishing rules for reading plays is, to my mind, futile. The possibilities in dramatic storytelling are too great for any single checklist to apply to every instance. Moreover, I believe, as did Knebel, that the best strategy is to let each text suggest the questions that you need to ask. Therefore, starting with this lesson, I will point toward possible avenues of investigation, rather than insisting upon a single route that might limit your critical and creative thinking about plays.

I like to call the first step in Active Analysis "**reading for the facts**." Following Stanislavsky's lead, Knebel called it "mental reconnaissance," by which she means that we initially use our intellects to "probe" or "mine" texts for the kind of information that will help us use the words on the page as tools to advance our actions and counteractions (Knebel' [1954] 2009: 29).[8] Her protégé, Anatoly Efros, put it more simply. We read in order to "clear up" not only the meaning of the lines, but also "what is really happening in the scene" (Efros 2006: 44).

Stanislavsky used the term **facts** to name those textual details that encode the dynamic interactions that actors will eventually perform. They include the play's given circumstances, the words that the actors must speak, and the roles' distinctive speech patterns. Facts can also include physical activities, such as Arkadina's bandaging of her son's head in *The Seagull*; environmental details like the cold, dark midnight at the opening of *Hamlet*; and visual details like the green color that Molière's *Misanthrope* persistently wears. In short, facts can be anything in the text that must be incorporated into the performance of the play.

When Hannah studied the melody and the rhythmic structure of "The Liberty Song," she knew what she had to sing. When actors identify the facts they know the basics of what they will need to act.

Once you get the hang of reading for the facts, it becomes a quick process. Thus, step one in Active Analysis represents a radical break with Stanislavsky's earlier practice of spending long periods of time with his actors "around the table," examining every facet of the play, not only those that contribute directly to performance, but also literary and scholarly concerns. Actors would conduct extensive research on the manners and historical era of the play; write detailed autobiographies for their characters; imagine their houses, professions, passions, clothing, food, everything, whether such details appear within the play or not (*SS* IV 1991: 48–173). After twenty years of working this way, however, Stanislavsky admitted that such table work can cause "the actor to come on stage with a stuffed head and an empty heart, and act nothing" (*SS* IV 1991: 325–6). In his last years, he distilled reading for the facts into a more compressed process that targets the information most needed by the actors to perform the scene (Lesson 4).

THE PLAY'S GIVEN CIRCUMSTANCES

Because facts, when taken out of context, can mislead, it is especially important in any scene study to start by defining the broad circumstances in the play as a whole. However, I also want you to know that by limiting our discussion to the play in this lesson we are also narrowing the scope of Stanislavsky's definition of *given circumstances*. He took the idea from the Russian poet Aleksander Pushkin, who wrote an essay in 1808 "On National-Popular Drama," in which he argued that "authenticity of the passions, verisimilitude of feelings in the play's proposed circumstances, that is what our intellect requires of a dramatic author" (Carnicke 2009: 218). Stanislavsky expanded Pushkin's definition from what is "proposed" by the author to what is "given" to the actor, not only by the author but also by other theatrical artists. Thus, according to Stanislavsky, given circumstances include:

> the story of the play, its facts, events, the era, the action's time and place, the conditions of life, the actors' and directors' understanding of the play, what you yourself add to that understanding, the blocking, the staging, the designers' sets and costumes, the props, the lights, sounds, etc., etc., everything that is given to the actors that they must account for in their creative work.
>
> (*SS* II 1989: 104)

This extensive list means that if we were to produce *Macbeth*, we would need to take into account the circumstances that Shakespeare creates and also your interpretations of the roles, the director's concept for the production, and the designers' set, props, and costumes. I wouldn't want you to make the mistake that Michael Dorsey does in the film *Tootsie* (dir. Sydney Pollack, 1982). As played by Dustin Hoffman, Dorsey is a Method actor who is hounded out of the business because he ignores circumstances given to him by the production team. For example, while filming a tomato commercial in which vegetables behave like humans, Dorsey refuses to sit down as the director requires. Tomatoes can't sit, Dorsey argues: "it's not logical." His agent counters with, "You are a wonderful actor, [...] but you are too much trouble." While Dorsey thinks he acts with Stanislavskian integrity, Stanislavsky would likely have been appalled.

For our scene study today, know that we are limiting ourselves to only those circumstances given to us by Shakespeare.

Geo   I beg to differ. I think we can also afford to consider the circumstances given to us by this hall—two doors, a small stage, and a few random chairs.

Me   Spoken like a true actor. But all the same, let's start with those circumstances in the play that condition the specific interaction that occurs between husband and wife in Act I scene 7.

Juliana   Let's see. (*Cautioning Geo before she starts.*) Macbeth is a Scottish noble, who has been fighting on behalf of King Duncan in a war that was begun by a rebel, Macdonwald, who is backed by Norwegian forces. So, I take it that the country has been engaged in a major civil war that also has international repercussions.

Grigor   Actually, in history there were two different wars, but Shakespeare puts them together.

Me   True, but since we are doing the play, the fictional facts as crafted by Shakespeare are more pertinent to our work.

Juliana   Macbeth has been particularly heroic in the battle that finally ends the war, when he overcomes Macdonwald in hand to hand combat.

Sargis   Wait … Wasn't there another Scottish traitor? The Thane of Cawdor? He was caught in that last battle and executed for treason. What is a "Thane"?

Grigor   It's a royal title, like a duke or earl.

Sargis   I see. That's why Duncan rewards Macbeth for his bravery with "Thane of Cawdor."

Rose   That is so ironic! Macbeth gets the title of a traitor, then kills the King and anyone who resists his rule, so by the end of the play, he has turned into a traitor himself!

Anisha   We still haven't mentioned the witches! (*Geo and Shari look at each other.*) On his way back from battle, Macbeth and another general named Banquo meet three witches, who predict that Macbeth will first become the Thane of Cawdor …

Sargis   A prediction that comes true, by the way, without him doing anything …

Anisha   … and then king.

Juliana   Why does Macbeth become the king after killing Duncan?

Grigor   Historically speaking, Duncan had no immediate heir and Macbeth was his cousin, so he was next in line to inherit the throne. It's easy to miss, but Macbeth does refer to Duncan as a "kinsman" in the soliloquy at the top of scene 7.

Juliana   Ah, yes. But then shouldn't they just wait until Duncan dies a natural death and get the throne that way?

Hannah   If they wait, they might be very old, when Duncan dies. But if they kill him now, they will still be young enough to enjoy the power!

Louisa   Hmm. Duncan is childless. That's interesting. So too is Macbeth. Don't forget that the witches predict that Banquo's future children will become kings, not Macbeth's! So both Duncan and Macbeth die without heirs. What a dark childless world!

Rose   And the few children who do appear in the play are murdered by Macbeth! Only Banquo's son escapes. This play is bloody and dark!

Me   What else do we need to know about the context of our scene within the play?

Hannah   Well, Macbeth writes to his wife about the witches' predictions, and she immediately decides that the quickest way to get the throne is to assassinate the king. When Macbeth comes home, she persuades him, too. Then, when Duncan surprises them with a visit, he gives them the opportunity they need to carry out the assassination. On the eve of the murder the Macbeths host a banquet in Duncan's honor, and just before scene 7 begins, Macbeth abruptly leaves the table, so that he can be alone to confront his doubts about proceeding.

Me   You have brought us to the soliloquy, which unlocks the most immediate circum-stance that conditions the Macbeths' interaction. (*The group pulls out their scripts and finds the spot.*)

Macbeth begins by saying that the sooner the assassination of Duncan can take place the better: "If it were done when 'tis done, then 'twere well/ It were done quickly." Then he shifts to a kind of cost/benefit analysis. On the one hand, if the deed results in "success," which he sees as gaining the throne without negative consequences, then the plan is worth the risk. On the other hand, since his faith deems murder a mortal sin, assassinating Duncan will send him and his wife to hell for eternity. Yes, they will enjoy the throne while they live "here, upon this bank and shoal of time," but they will "jump the life to come." In this case, the short-term gain is not worth the long-term risk! They would be condemning themselves: "This even-handed justice/ Commends th' ingredients of our poisoned chalice/ To our own lips." Finally, Macbeth lists the arguments against the assassination. First, as Duncan's "kinsman," "subject," and "host," Macbeth should protect the king from murder, "not bear the knife myself." Second, Duncan is such a good king that his "virtues […] plead like angels, trumpet-tongued, against" the murder. These thoughts lead Macbeth to conclude that in the final analysis the only reason to kill Duncan is crass ambition: "I have no spur/ To prick the sides of my intent, but only/ Vaulting ambition."

Notice the progression of our conversation. We started with the broadest outline of the story and progressively focused in more narrowly on the specific aspects of the play's plot that lead to this scene. Now we can put the text of the scene under a microscope.

THE WORDS ON THE PAGE

Me   Sargis, Juliana, please read the text, starting just after Macbeth's soliloquy. Do not act anything! This is not a cold reading or an audition. You are reading for the facts. If you rush into the acting before having identified what you need to know for your performances, you risk getting stuck in an interpretation that may not serve you well. Focus only on making clear the meanings of the words and observing any interesting features in the text.

Sargis   May I start with the soliloquy's end, since Lady Macbeth interrupts it, when she enters?

Me   Yes, good idea. Hannah, please read the stage directions.

Sargis-Macbeth

                                I have no spur
To prick the sides of my intent, but only
Vaulting ambition, which o'erleaps itself
And falls on th' other—

Hannah   *Enter Lady Macbeth.*

Sargis-Macbeth

                          How now, what news?

Juliana-Lady Macbeth

       He has almost supped. Why have you left the chamber?

Sargis-Macbeth

       Hath he asked for me?

Juliana-Lady Macbeth

                        Know you not he has?

Me   Notice how the words make the facts clear. The banquet for King Duncan is occurring offstage; Macbeth has left the banquet without telling his wife; she has come looking for him. Notice, too, the shared lines in the text. If you have previously worked with Shakespearean verse, you will remember that a single line of iambic pentameter verse can be shared between characters. When this happens, Shakespeare directs you to pick up your cues, because the rhythm demands that the characters speak the words as a single line.

Keith: "Iambic pentameter." Hmm. That means five measures of two syllables each. And in every measure there is a stressed and unstressed syllable. Right?

Hannah (*Beating the rhythm with her hand.*)   Da DUM, da DUM, da DUM, da DUM, da DUM.

Me   In shared lines, the analogy with music is especially apt because the verse establishes the rhythm of your interchange. Sargis, you start by sharing a line with yourself! "And fall on th'other—/How now what news?" This sequence suggests that your wife's physical entrance stops your thoughts, and that you speak to her before she can open her mouth.

Sargis   Then, when I ask about Duncan, Juliana shares that line with me.

Juliana   Her answer—"Know you not he has?"—is a negatively phrased question, as if she assumes that he should know better than to ask.

Me   Yes, facts are found not only in what characters say, but also in how they speak! Shared lines, statements, questions, etc. are facts because the way people speak is as important as what they say.

Sargis-Macbeth

       We will proceed no further in this business.
       He hath honored me of late, and I have bought
       Golden opinions from all sorts of people,
       Which would be worn now in their newest gloss,
       Not cast aside so soon.

Rose   There's a big fact right there! He tells her that he has changed his mind about the plan.

Sargis   Yes, oh yes! "We will proceed no further in this business."

Me   He also states this decision in a single line of iambic pentameter with a full stop at the end. The regularity of the rhythm and the finality of the statement suggest that this decision is firm.

Sargis   As if I'm putting my foot down!

Me   If so, then why does Macbeth continue to speak? Does he pause to give his wife a chance to react? When she does not, does he take her silence as judgmental, prompting him to justify himself? Does he, instead rush ahead without waiting for her reaction? And if so, why? These lines confront us with one of those puzzling moments that makes reading for the facts simultaneously "very simple and not so simple," to quote Efros (2006: 44).

FACTS AND OPEN CLUES

Puzzling moments, like this one, remind us that written plays, like musical scores, are unfinished works. Consequently, while they encode some concrete information about performance, they also leave a great deal out. There will always be places where, no matter how attentively we read, gaps in information remain. Thus, **facts** combine with what I like to call "**open clues**" that raise questions but offer no clear answers. Hannah confronted such gaps when she puzzled over the mismatches between verbal and musical melodies as well as the overly repetitive lyrics in "The Liberty Song." By deciding how to handle these, she completed the score through her performance. While facts lay down the form and structure of a play, open clues invite the actor to collaborate with the author. When you make decisions about the gaps in a text, you exercise your artistic freedom.

My favorite example of an open clue occurs in Shakespeare's *Antony and Cleopatra*, Act III, scene 3. The scene takes place shortly after Antony has married Caesar's sister, Octavia, in order to cement the two men's political alliance. As the couple depart from Rome, Antony bids a reassuring farewell to Caesar, but the tearful Octavia seems unable to speak aloud and instead asks to whisper something to her brother. Her tears and her request to "tell you in your ear" are facts, fixed by the text, as is Caesar's response to her: "No sweet Octavia/ you shall hear from me still." But what she actually says to her brother is an open clue. Should the actor playing Octavia take Caesar's response at face value? If so, she will ask that her brother write to her when she is gone. This choice creates a naïve Octavia. Should she instead reprimand her brother for having heartlessly married her off to a man who will surely prove unfaithful by returning to his lover Cleopatra? If so, Caesar's response now becomes a cover-up, intended to reassure not her, but Antony. This choice creates a wiser Octavia and a Caesar who cares more about politics than his sister. Both options fit the facts, and the actor who plays Octavia has the power to shape the performance of this scene by choosing.

As Stanislavsky's comment about opera asserts, singers are luckier than actors because they do get more facts about their performances from operatic scores. But, as my example above suggests, actors enjoy more freedom as artists, precisely because plays leave more open to our creative imaginations.

Me   Sargis, you will have a chance to investigate why Macbeth continues to speak after putting his foot down, when you and Juliana try this scene on for size. For now, let's just observe this gap in the text and continue with our reading for the facts.

Sargis   I see another important fact in Macbeth's listing of the reasons for his change of heart, like being honored by Duncan and "all sorts of people." These reasons are different from those he gives in his soliloquy. Those were moral and spiritual. These are more worldly. They mostly deal with his reputation, which makes me wonder whether he is taking his soliloquy in a new direction in front of his wife or choosing reasons that he thinks she will buy.

Juliana   Do you think that his newfound fame is something his wife can appreciate more than his integrity? Doesn't that then also say something about his opinion of her?

Me   Good questions. So many open clues to investigate in our etudes! Read on!

Sargis-Macbeth

We will proceed no further in this business.
He hath honored me of late, and I have bought
Golden opinions from all sorts of people,
Which would be worn now in their newest gloss,
Not cast aside so soon.

Juliana/Lady Macbeth

          Was the hope drunk
Wherein you dressed yourself? Hath it slept since?
And wakes it now, to look so green and pale
At what it did so freely? From this time
Such I account thy love. Art thou afeard
To be the same in thine own act and valor
As thou art in desire? Wouldst thou have that
Which thou esteem'st the ornament of life
And live a coward in thine own esteem,
Letting "I dare not" wait upon "I would,"
Like the poor cat i' th' adage?

Juliana   I'm sorry, but I just don't understand this line about a cat!

Grigor   I looked that up! It refers to a story (or "adage") about a cat who wants to eat fish, but is afraid to get his paws wet.

Juliana   I see. I'm saying that Macbeth wants the throne, but doesn't want to get his hands bloody.

Juliana-Lady Macbeth

          Wouldst thou have that
Which thou esteem'st the ornament of life
And live a coward in thine own esteem,
Letting "I dare not" wait upon "I would,"
Like the poor cat i' th' adage?

Sargis-Macbeth
>   Prithee, peace.
> I dare do all that may become a man.
> Who dares do more is none.

Juliana-Lady Macbeth
>   What beast was't, then,
> That made you break this enterprise to me.

Anisha   Three more shared lines! Why so many?

Hannah   Do they interrupt each other more and more as they speak because each of them wants to have their say, like people who are arguing? Or are they feeding off one another, like people who know each other so well that they can finish each other's thoughts?

Juliana   What Lady Macbeth says in these lines is also huge. She undermines his manhood, saying that his decision to stop the plan is proof of his cowardice, and she does so by questioning him. In fact, nearly everything she says is a rhetorical question.

Sargis   He tries to stop her with this strong statement   "I do all that may become a man." But her questions just keep coming!

Me   You are getting the hang of this now. You are observing what they say and also how they speak, treating the verse as a score for performance with the words, like notes, encoding the melodies, rhythms and harmonies of their interaction.

Juliana- Lady Macbeth
>   What beast was 't, then,
> That made you break this enterprise to me?
> When you durst do it, then you were a man;
> And to be more than what you were, you would
> Be so much more the man. Nor time nor place
> Did then adhere, and yet you would make both.
> They have made themselves, and that their fitness now
> Does unmake you. I have given suck, and know
> How tender 'tis to love the babe that milks me.
> I would, while it was smiling in my face,
> Have plucked my nipple from his boneless gums
> And dashed the brains out, had I so sworn as you
> Have done to this.

Me   This speech contains the toughest language in the scene. What do these words mean? "Nor time nor place did then adhere, and yet you would make both./ They have made themselves, and that their fitness now does unmake you."

Hannah   I think she's saying that when he first told her about becoming king, they could not have done anything about it because "the time" was not right and they weren't in the right "place." But now Duncan is under their noses—so the time and place "have made themselves" without their doing anything! Then she underlines the irony—when they couldn't do it, he was ready, but now that they can, the opportunity "unmakes" him. Wow, that is sharp! She reads him like a book! What a role!

Juliana   But this image of her dashing her baby's brains out is so horrible that she sounds like a monster.

Louisa   She doesn't say she did it, only that she once nursed a child. Maybe the baby's an open clue, with the fact buried in what she actually says   that if she had "sworn" to kill her child, then she would have done it. In other words, if she had made her husband a promise, even if it were the worst thing that she could possibly imagine like killing her child, then she would keep that promise no matter what it cost her. I think she is reprimanding him for letting her down!

Juliana   I see, yes. She wants to shock him into understanding what it means to break his word.

Juliana-Lady Macbeth
> I would, while it was smiling in my face,
> Have plucked my nipple from his boneless gums
> And dashed the brains out, had I so sworn as you
> Have done to this.

Sargis-Macbeth
> If we should fail—

Juliana-Lady Macbeth
> We fail?

Hannah   Those last three phrases are a single shared line: "Have done to this.- If we should fail—/ We fail?" Wow, that is cool! The rhythm of their communication has really gained speed.

Juliana-Lady Macbeth
> We fail?
> But screw your courage to the sticking place
> And we'll not fail. When Duncan is asleep
> (Whereto the rather shall his day's hard journey
> Soundly invite him), his two chamberlains
> Will I with wine and wassail so convince
> That memory, the warder of the brain,
> Shall be a fume, and the receipt of reason
> A limbeck only. When in swinish sleep
> Their drenchèd natures lie as in a death,
> What cannot you and I perform upon
> Th' unguarded Duncan? What not put upon
> His spongy officers, who shall bear the guilt
> Of our great quell?

Anisha   I think these lines are harder to understand than the earlier one you pointed to, Sharon. What are "spongy" officers? What's a "limbeck"?

Grigor   Yup, I looked that up too! A limbeck is a still for making alcohol. (*Anisha looks confused.*) A "still" is a machine that distills liquor. She's saying that she will get Duncan's guards so drunk that their bodies will soak up the alcohol like sponges; that's why they are "spongy officers." Their brains will be as full of alcoholic fumes as stills. As a result, they will be unable to remember anything or to think straight.

Juliana   I get it. I am using these images to paint a picture for Macbeth to show him how fool-proof our plan is.

Juliana-Lady Macbeth
>   When in swinish sleep
> Their drenchèd natures lie as in a death,
> What cannot you and I perform upon
> Th' unguarded Duncan? What not put upon
> His spongy officers, who shall bear the guilt
> Of our great quell?

Sargis-Macbeth
>   Bring forth men-children only,
> For thy undaunted mettle should compose
> Nothing but males. Will it not be received,
> When we have marked with blood those sleepy two
> Of his own chamber and used their very daggers,
> That they have done 't?

Sargis   Yet another shared line! It's as if Macbeth steps back to admire her courage—her "undaunted mettle"—which is so manly that she should be the mother of men. Is he picking up on the image of the baby here? Might she hear that as a dig, since they are in fact childless? Or as a promise to give her another child?

Juliana   Or is it a request that she give him a male heir, who will keep the throne in the family?

Sargis   Whatever the case, the fact is that he is still unconvinced that their plan will work, because he continues to question it.

Juliana   Don't worry, I'll quickly put your mind at ease by picking up on the next shared line.

Sargis-Macbeth
>   Will it not be received,
> When we have marked with blood those sleepy two
> Of his own chamber and used their very daggers,
> That they have done 't?

Juliana-Lady Macbeth
>   Who dares receive it other,
> As we shall make our griefs and clamor roar
> Upon his death?

Sargis-Macbeth
>   I am settled and bend up
> Each corporal agent to this terrible feat.
> Away, and mock the time with fairest show.
> False face must hide what the false heart doth know.

Hannah   *They exit.*

Me   In the end Macbeth changes his mind again and renews his promise to his wife. Notice how the last two lines, which rhyme, give the scene a satisfying sense of closure.

Step Two: A Paraphrase Etude

We have now arrived at the creative heart of Active Analysis. Having read the scene for the facts, you now have enough information to get up and try the scene. True, you haven't yet learned the lines, and perhaps you recall some facts more vividly than others. Nonetheless, I feel confident that you can create a pretty good draft performance. Stanislavsky and Knebel call such drafts "**etudes**" from the French verb *étudier* to study—a word that perfectly describes how Active Analysis studies texts by performing them. In an etude, you act what you think by juggling facts from the text and allowing the underlying dynamics to unfold in real time. By lending yourself fully to the play's circumstances and to the interactive behavior that emerges during your etude, you come to understand why your characters speak as they do and what they might be unable or unwilling to say. In short, etudes trigger your tacit knowledge. What you know in your bones as both actors and human beings will guide you to new discoveries about the scene and your characters. Stanislavsky explains, "The best way to analyse a play is to take action in the given circumstances" (*SS* IV 1991: 332–3). Efros more graphically writes that "the actor should understand not only with his head but also with his guts" (Efros 2006: 40).

> **Shari**   I'm sorry, but acting the scene without having memorized it goes against all my former training.

> **Me**   Yes, Active Analysis turns the usual way of rehearsing inside out. Traditionally we learn the lines, get the blocking from the director, and then use rehearsals to justify both lines and blocking. Yet, when you memorize by rote, you risk, at worst, a recitation of the play instead of a dynamic performance, and, at best, a performance that skims the surface of the text. In contrast, Active Analysis confronts you with the dynamics that prompt characters to speak and move before you memorize anything. In all our etudes, I want you to think of words and movement as "tools" (Knebel' [1954] 2009: 24) to help you push and pull at one another, as you explore the scene's human interactions.

In summary, the purpose of an etude is to study "what is really happening in the scene" (Efros 2006: 44) by doing it. By embodying the collision between action and counteraction, you rehearse the scene's "music" with your whole being—mind, body, and soul. When this interaction leads to the event that ends the scene, the etude takes the cast one step further toward a polished performance.

MAPPING THE SCENE TO THE PRINCIPLES OF ACTIVE ANALYSIS

> **Me**   In order to get up on your feet, however, you still need to map the scene's facts against the interactive principles that we explored last time. Let's start with the event, because journeys often benefit from knowing something about the destination. So tell me, what is the main event that occurs in Act I, scene 7 of *Macbeth*? Remember, like a baseball hitting the ground, the event is what happens to bring the interaction between the characters to an end.

> **Juliana**   That's easy! Macbeth renews his promise to his wife. Clearly Lady Macbeth wins in this scene. (*She grins broadly at Sargis.*)

Sargis   I agree. The event occurs on this line: "I am settled, and bend up/ Each corporal agent to this terrible feat."

Me   And where does the journey start? Who carries the action? In other words, who throws the baseball to get the scene going?

Anisha   Lady Macbeth, because she persuades her husband to get back on track and murder Duncan.

Keith   No, it's Macbeth! He tells her he's changed his mind and that's the driver.

Anisha   No, it's Lady Macbeth, because unless she comes looking for him there is no scene.

Keith   But if Macbeth doesn't break his promise, she wouldn't need to persuade him about anything. So, I still think Macbeth's the action. Without him, there is no scene.

Anisha   I still think it's Lady Macbeth.

Keith   I still think it's Macbeth.

Me   Would it help to ask the next question? Who carries the counteraction? Remember, like gravity that changes the trajectory of a flying baseball, the counteraction resists the forward motion of the scene.

Anisha   Well, if Lady Macbeth is the action, then Macbeth must be the counteraction. She comes to bring him back to the banquet, but he won't go.

Keith   And if he is the action, then she is the counteraction. He puts his foot down, as Sargis said, but she refuses to accept his decision.

Shari (*Laughing*.)   It takes two to tango, is what I say!

Me   Would it help if I ask what the quality of the counteraction is in the scene? Is it direct or oblique?

Anisha   It's definitely direct.

Keith   Finally we agree on something! (*Everyone bursts into laughter*.) They definitely go head to head in this scene.

Louisa   In fact, this scene reminds me of you, Hannah, in that improvisation with Sharon, when she tried to throw you out and you countered her with questions? Lady Macbeth uses that same strategy.

Hannah   You're right. "Was the hope drunk wherein you dress'd yourself?" And on and on. Lady Macbeth shoots one question after another at her husband.

Me   The scene also reminds me of my improvisation with you, Grigor, when we couldn't get to an event because the force of my action equaled the force of your counteraction. In such cases, it is often hard to distinguish the action from the counteraction. That may well be what's going on here between Macbeth and his wife.

Grigor   That's right. I remember you saying that the only way that we could get to an event would be if one of us were to up the stakes or change tactics.

Juliana   That's exactly what happens when Lady Macbeth turns the tide by challenging Macbeth's manhood in this flat-out statement: "When you durst do it, then you were a man."

Sargis   Yes, that's when he wavers. By asking whether they might fail, he gives her a way in.

Me   You are now describing the trajectory of forces in the scene, which, like a baseball flying through space, changes course as it nears the event.

Louisa   But we don't yet have one a clear map; we have two. Anisha, you propose that Lady Macbeth is the action, making her husband the counteraction. Keith, you see Macbeth as the action with Lady Macbeth as the counteraction. Neither of you will give in …

Me   I suggest that we settle this quandary by trying both ideas and seeing which one works best.

Geo   Like dueling etudes. (*Rubbing his hands together.*) This will be fun!

SETTING UP THE ETUDE AND CHOOSING A VERB

Let's try a classic form of etude, in which you play the scene using your own words. First, we'll do one with Lady Macbeth as the action.

As you interact with each other, use whatever you remember from the text—the sequence, facts, exact phrases, and specific images, even full lines, if they come to mind as you work. The point of a paraphrase etude is not to avoid what you know about the text, but rather to study it by enacting its underlying dynamics. Don't force your etude into the parameters of the scene either! Follow the logic of your map, using speech and movement as your tools. The goal is to explore the interactive forces in the scene as fully as you can. Follow your impulses as they arise to see where they lead. If the etude takes you to the author's scene, then it's productive. If the etude goes off the text, it may be just as productive. You will learn through your etudes what you know and what you don't yet know about the scene.

I always recommend that, immediately before you begin an etude, you take a moment to clarify the map that you will follow: (1) Re-read the text for the facts, keeping an eye out for anything you might have missed earlier. (2) Name the event that needs to occur in order for the story to unfold. (3) Confirm who will play the action and the counteraction. (4) Finally, describe your action and counteraction with strong, playable verbs.

In many ways choosing a playable verb is the most important factor in preparing for your etude. First, your verb should describe something you can do to or with your partner. For example, "to ignore" your partner is better than "to stare out the window." The one anchors you into the scene, the other takes you out of it. Next, avoid verbs that name a state of mind or an emotional mood. Such choices are not active; they describe the results of having done something active. You become happy when your verb accomplishes what you want. You become angry when your partner frustrates your efforts. So tell yourself "to lash out" rather than "to be angry," or "to steal a kiss" rather than "to be in love." Last, do not confuse a physical activity with the action or counteraction in a scene. While "setting the table" might be something you and your partner do together, your verb describes what you do to initiate or resist the interaction that takes place between you and your partner, not between you and the dishes. You might ask your wife for a divorce or confront your mother with the fact that you are moving out of the house. "Setting the table" is the context for you "to break up" with your spouse or "to confront" your mother.

Most importantly, pick a verb that seems tasty to you, something that makes your imagination work, something that you want to get up and try. If you like your verb, you will likely be able to stick with it for the entirety of the etude. Pursuing a single verb in an etude can be challenging, because your partner's job is to push you off track. In fact, the best partner is one who makes it hard for you to stay on track. As the etude proceeds, observe your partner's reactions closely in order to figure out whether your verb is working as is or whether you should go about it in a different way. But whatever you do, do not change your verb during the etude. Change only how you go about doing it. Otherwise, you will never know if what you chose would have worked. You can always try a different verb in the next etude.

Geo   Why choose only one verb? In my training, we always broke the scene down into beats and had a different action for each beat.

Me   Ah yes, "beats"! That term harkens back to Stanislavsky's earlier approach to rehearsing, when he asked actors to identify all the strategic steps that might occur within an interactive scene. He called these segments "bits" (*kuski*) that American actors heard as "beats" when their émigré teachers pronounced the English word with heavy Russian accents (Carnicke 2009: 214). Later, when Stanislavsky realized that pre-planning every twist and turn in a scene kept actors at the table far too long, he shifted attention away from "bits" to "events" (Knebel' 1976: 298–9).

Shari   But how can you ignore the beats?

Me   You don't. You just find them differently. Active Analysis differs from other Stanislavsky-based methods, because you stick with one verb during your etudes, but allow yourself to change how you go about it whenever your partner does not respond as you would like. In this way, the "beats" (if you like that term) arise organically out of the interaction between you and your partner. You may set out "to steal a kiss" but as the etude develops, you will do so by "sidling up" to your partner, then "cajoling," "teasing," "flattering," and finally "charming" him. In Active Analysis, you plan *what* you will do, but not *how*. Let's see the first of our dueling etudes in order to clarify which character carries the action.

Juliana and Sargis go to the back of the hall to plan, while the rest of us move the chairs into a couple of rows facing the stage. I hear Shari and Geo talking with Grigor about the curse of *Macbeth*. Hannah and Rose are at the table snacking on grapes, while Setrak takes a sip of water. As Anisha asks Louisa for advice about finding an agent, I walk back to check on Juliana and Sargis. They have reread the text with an eye to Lady Macbeth as the action. They tell me that they are ready with their verbs and I call everyone back.

ETUDE 1: PARAPHRASE

Sargis sits on the steps at stage left, his head in his hands, lost in thought. Juliana enters from the back of the hall with a purposeful step and goes to Sargis, startling him into looking up. He turns away from her, pulling his knees to the side and clasping his arms around them. He is curled up against the wall in a fetal position.

Juliana What are you doing here? Don't you know that Duncan is asking for you? It was all going so well, until I suddenly realized that you were nowhere to be seen. Come back to the banquet before everyone leaves.

Sargis He has honored me of late. And that is enough.

Juliana What do you mean by that? Stand up and tell me to my face.

Sargis (*Moves to a sitting position, but does not stand.*) I mean that we should leave it as is.

Juliana No.

Juliana's "no" sounds like a slap, and Sargis reacts by standing up abruptly. He freezes for a moment. Then, after taking a deep breath, he tries to get past her. She blocks his path.

Sargis Let me pass. Being honored by him is enough. I am the Thane of Cawdor, I am his honored cousin, you and I are well off. Let's just enjoy it.

Juliana From where I stand, you look like a coward. You made me a promise and you will keep it. Are you a coward now? Is that it?

Sargis It's not cowardice to enjoy my reputation as a war hero. Let me pass!

Juliana A war hero? You don't even have enough courage to go back into that banquet hall where Duncan is asking for you?

Sargis And what are you? Do you call yourself a woman? Women are supposed to be gentle. Women were made for breeding, not for bossing their husbands around.

Juliana Oooh, how dare you! You need to come with me and re-join the banquet now. If you don't, he'll know that something is off. He'll get suspicious.

Sargis Nothing is off except your plan.

He forcibly pushes her to the side and exits through the side door of the hall that leads outside. Juliana stares after him in amazement. She slaps her fists on her thighs, and turns away from the door. Geo jumps up and applauds. The others sit quietly, looking as perplexed as Juliana.

Step Three: Assess in Order to Repeat—The Problem and the Verb

Geo (*Applauding madly.*) That was fantastic! What passion!

Louisa Yes, the acting was terrific, but where was Shakespeare? If you were doing the whole play, you would get stuck right there. Without Macbeth agreeing to the murder of Duncan, which is the event in this scene, the play would be over.

Me Good point. (*Sargis comes back into the room and sheepishly stands at the door. I smile at him and he takes his seat.*) Louisa's comment reminds me of an anecdote that Knebel tells about a rehearsal of Pushkin's *The Gypsies*, concerning a woman, who tires of her marriage and takes a lover. Knebel's cast had explored each scene of the play through etudes and had come to the climactic moment when the husband catches his wife with her lover in the woods and kills them both. The actors got so carried away in this etude that, when the husband arrived brandishing a knife, the lover bravely defended the wife before they were both killed. Knebel's ensemble burst into excited applause, as did Geo just now, while Knebel, like Louisa, quietly observed that in the play the lover tries to escape. In short, the actor had "stepped out of the author's fictional story." "Etudes," Knebel said, "should take actors toward the play, not away from it" (Knebel' [1959] 1982: 60–2). What Juliana and Sargis planned took them away from their scene. Our assessment now must look to the reasons for that having happened in order to get back on track.

Sargis (*Sheepishly.*)   Sorry, Juliana. I just couldn't continue with the scene. I just wanted out.

Me   Did you exit because you, as the actor, stopped the scene midway?

Sargis   No. I left because, Juliana made me feel like I wanted a divorce.

Me   So, you left as an honest reaction to what your partner was doing? Then there is no need to apologize. You allowed the interactive dynamics to play out logically …

Sargis   Yes …

Me   If so, then you learned that this map does not lead to the event that the text requires!

Shari   So let's go to the next of our dueling etudes with M as the action!

Me   Not quite yet, Shari. We have reached step three in the process of rehearsing through Active Analysis. In order to ensure that the next etude is productive, we need to assess what happened against the facts in the text. Of course, as Louisa has already pointed out, Lady Macbeth's action did not take us to the event that we were targeting. But there are also other questions to consider. What facts did Juliana and Sargis remember? What did they forget? How did their verbs help or hinder them? Were there any new discoveries about the scene that came as a result of having done the etude? Juliana and Sargis, please read the scene for the facts, recalling in your minds as you read what happened while you worked.

As they read aloud, everyone follows along in their own scripts.

Juliana   I see that Keith is right about Macbeth carrying the action. If Lady Macbeth is the action, all she can do is insist that her husband return to the banquet. She can't go further until he says he's backing out of their plan.

Me   What verb did you choose?

Juliana   To shame him. But again, until he says the plan is off, I can only shame him about his behavior at the banquet and the way he was cowering in front of me when we began.

Me   And you did that well. Sargis, what was your verb for the counteraction?

Sargis   To sever from her and her plan.

Hannah   I saw you doing that from the very beginning. You rolled yourself into a ball to get as far away from her as possible and then you physically severed from her when you left the room.

Sargis Thank you. But when Juliana kept insisting that I go back inside, I lost all taste for the fight. I had absolutely nothing else to say to her. It was a dead-end, so I left.

Juliana To be honest, I didn't like my verb at all. Once I started shaming him, I felt like I had to turn everything he said and did against him. It turned me into the cliched monster that most people think Lady Macbeth is.

Sargis That's right, no discussion, just barbs!

Me Then let's go back to the basics! In his acting manual, Stanislavsky offers advice on choosing verbs for the bits within a scene, but we can easily adapt his suggestion to choosing verbs for etudes. He recommends that the actor ask how the given circumstances at the opening pose a problem (*zadacha*). Name that problem with an adjective or adverb, and then ask what the character might do to solve it. My character feels "trapped" or "lonely." She might "open the windows," "look for an escape," "call a friend," "go to a party," etc. Your answer is your verb! (Carnicke 2010c: 14–15).

Rose I love the word "problem." Whenever I get stuck, just asking myself about my character's problem unlocks the scene.

Geo But "problem" is such a negative word.

Sargis If characters don't deal with problems, plays wouldn't be very dramatic, would they?

Me Hapgood's translation for *zadacha* is "objective" and Benedetti's is "task."[9]

Rose But "objective" makes me think about how the scene should turn out and so encourages results-oriented acting. "Problem" helps me think about what drives my character to take action.

Keith "Task" makes me want to write a "to do" list.

Me To be fair, if you look *zadacha* up in a dictionary you will find that its multiple meanings include "objective" and "task." But translation is never as easy as swapping an English word for a Russian one. My translation is based upon the context in which Stanislavsky introduces the word in his acting manuals. He explains that the circumstances in a scene present the character with a *zadacha*, just as a mathematics teacher presents a student with a *zadacha* to solve (SS II: 88–9). Given Stanislavsky's analogy, translating the Russian word as "problem" makes the most sense. I agree, Rose, that "objective" looks to the end result and thus can short-circuit the actor's journey from problem to solution. And, as you say, Keith, "task" sounds in English like a chore.

Juliana So, if Lady Macbeth's problem is that she thinks her husband won't do what's necessary to get the crown, then my verb needs to deal with that.

Sargis And if Macbeth thinks of himself as a man of integrity, his problem is how to reconcile the image of himself with his ambition.

Anisha That's all very interesting, but can we go back to the etude? I see that the map I proposed does not work. But I also noticed that Juliana and Sargis forgot a lot of facts. Where was the baby? What happened to the careful planning and the "spongy officers"?

Me   Luckily, we have a different map to try and another chance to revisit the scene, so …

Juliana   Sorry to interrupt, but I have another question. When Sargis and I planned our etude, we shared our verbs. Was that the right thing to do?

Sargis   Would it have been better to keep them secret?

Geo   Ah, yes, withholding knowledge from our partners! I once had a director, who would pull me aside, tell me to do something extreme and warn me not to tell my partner beforehand, because he wanted to provoke a certain reaction through the shock of surprise. That kind of thing always felt, I don't know … manipulative.

Rose   It's disrespectful, even cruel! Active Analysis is about collaborating, and if you don't share your verbs, you can't do that.

Me (*To Juliana*.)   Did sharing your verbs interfere with your work during the etude?

Juliana   I don't think so. Even though I knew what Sargis was planning, I stuck to my verb and was genuinely shocked when he walked out on me.

Me   Let me clarify something! When I say "plan *what* you will do," I expect you to share your map and your verbs. When I say, "do not plan *how* the etude will unfold," I expect you to observe your partner closely and modify continually how you do your verb, based upon your observations. You may well be surprised by what happens, leading to new discoveries about the scene, because you are actively analyzing it. Such discoveries help you correct or refine your plan for the next etude. In my opinion, this process treats you respectfully as equals, who collaborate in the creation of a performance.

Rose   Sharon, do you remember that time in our experiments on emotional expressivity, when the scientists asked Juliana's question? (*Speaking to the group*.) We were using Active Analysis on all kinds of texts and recording our etudes with motion capture technology in order to investigate how physical movements communicate emotion (Carnicke 2012: 321–38).

Me   You're right! The scientists wanted to know whether the actors' sharing or withholding of verbs would make a difference in the outcomes, so we tried it both ways. When the scientists debriefed the actors, as I recall, they concluded that it didn't make much difference.

Rose   As one of those actors, I can report that their conclusion was correct. The only thing that ultimately mattered to me was whether or not my verb was having an impact on my partner.

Shari   And what about the audience? I notice, Sharon, that you tend to ask actors for their verbs, only after we have begun commenting on their work.

Me   Audiences serve as actors' mirrors, and the less we know about their plan, the more objectively we can watch. If what we see in a performance matches what the actors are trying to do, then they know they are on the right path. If what we see does not match, the actors can be guided to better choices.

Juliana   Makes good sense to me!

Me   Then, let's get back to our dueling etudes and try one with Macbeth as the action.

Another Round of Active Analysis

Step One: Reading for the Facts Again

Juliana and Sargis step aside to re-read the text for the facts and discuss the new map. They choose verbs and are soon ready to work.

Step Two: Another Etude

ETUDE 2: PARAPHRASE

Sargis is standing on the floor in front of the stage, near the side door. Juliana enters from the rear of the hall, as if the banquet is taking place behind the audience. Her gait is measured and calm. Hearing her steps, Sargis turns sharply and goes forward to meet her.

Sargis   We will proceed no further with the plan.

Juliana stops moving and remains silent for a long time. It is hard to tell whether she has heard Sargis. When he repeats his words more loudly, she still does not acknowledge his decision. She walks past him toward the stage, brushing away his words with a gesture of her hand.

Juliana   Duncan is almost finished with dinner. What are you doing here?

Sargis seems momentarily shaken by her calm demeanor, but he quickly recovers his resolve.

Sargis   We can't go through with it. I've gained the court's respect. He's a friend, a kinsman, family. We can't sully my reputation now …. Our reputation.

Juliana   It is not me, but you, who sullies our name. Are you telling me that you are a coward? You made a promise. We made a plan. Are you backing out? Are you setting yourself up to spend the rest of your life regretting this? Will you look back and remember that there was once a time when you were brave?

Juliana has fallen into an interesting pattern of speech in which she makes a statement of fact, and then asks a series of questions. It is a strategy that pushes Sargis into defending himself, much as Lady Macbeth does in Shakespeare's scene.

Sargis   I was brave in battle. I was brave …. (*Pausing as if searching for words.*) I watched my men die. I accepted the title of Thane of Cawdor, yes, but that is as far as I will go. (*He stamps his foot, as if marking a boundary that he will not cross.*) This is as far as any man should go.

Juliana approaches him, her hand extended, but, instead of taking it, he grasps her firmly by the shoulders, his voice growing in strength as he speaks.

Sargis   If I were to overstep … If I were to do this, I wouldn't be a man. I would be a beast.

Juliana (*Smiling.*)   Were you a beast when you told me about this? I saw a man then. (*She takes his hand from her shoulder, pulls him toward her, embraces him, and continues speaking in a whisper.*) I am a woman, I know the joys of womanhood, of motherhood, but if I had made a promise to you, as you did to me, to kill our child, I would do it for you. You need to man up.

Sargis (*Playing with her hair and whispering in her ear.*)   What if we get caught?

Juliana (*Walks away from him, sits down on the edge of the stage as if enthroned, smooths her skirt, and speaks as if she were laying down an edict.*)   We won't get caught. Just man up!

She proceeds to lay out the plan, as if it were failproof, hitting all the major facts in the text.

Sargis (*Laughs out loud.*)   You should be the man in this relationship. (*He sits down beside her.*)

Juliana (*Kissing his cheek.*)   And what do you think?

Sargis (*He smiles and takes her hand.*)   I'll man up! Let's do this.

Juliana stands and he follows suit. They exit, hand in hand in the direction of the banquet hall.

Step Three: Assess in Order to Repeat

As Juliana and Sargis return, everyone applauds. This etude took them to the event that Shakespeare required and, along the way, they unlocked many more interactive possibilities within the score than they had in their last attempt.

Anisha   I see now why Macbeth is the action. In the very first moments, when Sargis walked toward Juliana, I knew that the scene had gotten off to a good start.

Geo   Juliana seemed so calm and regal. She resisted him, no question, but last time she was like a bulldozer. Now she seemed like his worthy partner.

Keith   And his wife. I saw the love between them.

Sargis   In fact, I was utterly surprised by how she seduced me. I never would have expected that from reading for the facts. She bewitched me into agreeing to the murder.

Keith   When you laughed and said she should be the man in the family, I was right there with you! At that moment, I heard in my head "bring forth men-children only."

Hannah   I loved the way this etude brought out the gender issues. He's a man who's not man enough. She's a woman who is more man than he. When Juliana said "man up!" she said it all.

Sargis   In the last etude, I felt offended by her. This time, when she embraced me and whispered in my ear, it was pleasant. No need for a divorce now. (*Everyone laughs.*)

Geo   When I applauded for your first etude, I thought the acting was terrific. This time, I got caught up instead in their story and their relationship.

Me   What verbs did you choose this time?

Sargis   I liked "to sever." But I thought that something stronger would better solve his problem of needing to see himself as a man of integrity. So I decided "to put my foot down." It had come to me, if you'll remember, when we were first reading for the facts.

Louisa   And you physically did that in the etude when you stamped your foot!

Juliana   Re-reading for the facts made me realize how badly she wants to be queen. Her problem is, that as a woman, she can't go after the crown herself. She needs her husband to do it for her. Hannah, you actually gave me the idea for my verb.

Hannah   I did?

Juliana   You said that if they didn't kill Duncan, they would probably be old when they got the throne. That made me wonder whether Lady Macbeth might fantasize about being queen. I picked "to reign" over him, as if acting out her fantasy would bring him around to her way of thinking!

Louisa   And you physically behaved like a queen! I saw it in your calm movements, your poise, the way you sat on the stage like on a throne and smoothed you skirts …

Sargis   Even the hand gesture that you made when you brushed away my concerns … I have to admit that when I came over and sat next to you, I felt like a king.

Me   You have made some productive discoveries in this etude that can inform your performance. In fact, Shakespeare's score supports much of what you did. Look at the rhythmic patterns. (*Everyone reads for a moment.*) Do you see that Lady Macbeth's speech is much more regular than Macbeth's? (*Juliana nods "yes."*) Juliana, your calm movements and steady confidence matched the verse perfectly. In contrast, Macbeth sometimes has extra syllables in his lines and sometimes reverses the stress—DUM da instead of da DUM. Sargis, the way Juliana's confidence threw you off your verb matches the way in which Macbeth struggles to stay on point with the verse. (*Sargis opens his mouth in amazement, as does Anisha.*)

Repeat

Me   But there is still more to discover. For example, I don't yet see how the shared lines are influencing your work. Juliana, Sargis, please read for the facts again, make whatever adjustments in your map and your verbs that you think might get you even closer to Shakespeare's text, and try another etude. As Knebel taught, multiple etudes function as successive "drafts" of the scene's performance (Knebel' 1971: 52).

Anisha   Keith, can we try an etude on this scene as well?

Hannah   Setrak, are you game to try one with me?

Grigor   Rose? What do you say? We'll make a good pair.

Shari   Geo, it takes two to tango …

As Juliana and Sargis find a corner to read the text again, the others do the same. Louisa and I are left alone, looking at each other.

Me   It's going to be a long session!

Louisa   And a good one.

Notes

1. Dickenson, J. (1768), "The Liberty Song" [Song], accessed November 6, 2020, at https://www. youtube.com/watch?v=RGPUCyghEww.
2. Recollection of actor Lyubov Zabolotskaia Weidner in a personal video call on June 6, 2020.
3. The Maly Theatre's Vera Pashennaia observed that Stanislavsky's actors differed from those in competing theatres, because they always play a "symphony," in which each instrument gets lost in the whole (1954: 104–5).
4. The production was later re-staged and moved to Moscow's larger Novy Theatre.
5. Unlike the posthumous staging by Mikhail Kedrov of *Tartuffe*, which is well-known among theatre scholars, Meyerhold's 1939 *Rigoletto* disappeared from theatre history, when he was arrested and executed as an enemy of the people.
6. While Stanislavsky's "scores" provide records of how he read and directed plays, few scholars have analyzed them. Notable studies include Hristić (1955: 175–283), Merlin (2003: chapter 3), and Carnicke (2019b: 91–112).
7. Balukhatyi eventually published the plan in 1938 after Stanislavsky's death.
8. James Thomas refers to this step as "mental analysis" (2006: 97).
9. Irina Brown in Knebel (2021) adopts Benedetti's translation of *zadacha* as "task."

Lesson 3 Scene Study through Active Analysis—Chekhov

Prelude

Louisa and Juliana have opened the hall and set everything up before I arrive with Shari. The chairs stand empty in a circle. No one hovers around the food either! Instead, small groups of actors, here and there, excitedly chatter about "etudes," "actions," "counteractions," "verbs," and "events." While I survey the room, Shari has filled a plate with snacks and settles down on a chair, waiting contentedly for the others to join her. I notice Sargis, Grigor, and Geo in a passionate tussle over something or other, their words lost in the noisy buzzing of voices throughout the space. I cannot get anyone's attention, so I walk up the stairs, take center stage, and loudly proclaim: "*Vnimaniya, moi druzya!*" Everyone goes silent and turns to look at me. I drop my voice and continue: "I asked for your attention, my friends. My verb was 'to get you to look at me'! Please take your chairs." Everyone laughs as we settle down to our work.

The Difference between Improvisations and Etudes

Sargis   Before we begin, Grigor and I have a question. As you know, we got interested in acting after taking improv classes, and it seems to us that "etude" is just a fancy word for improvisation. Right?

Me   I admit, I used to catch myself using the two words as synonyms. (*Sargis and Grigor smile.*) But I soon questioned this slip of tongue when I noticed that my Russian colleagues never equate the two. So I did some research (Carnicke 2019a: 17–35).

Stanislavsky was under house arrest and subject to strict censorship while developing Active Analysis. Moreover, the Soviet regime considered aspects of his experiments to be subversive. Therefore, he wrote little about them (Chapter 1). There are some unfinished drafts and some rehearsal transcripts from the 1930s (Chapter 2), but I found nothing specific in them about how improvisations differ from etudes. In the first volume of his published book on acting, he writes only that "in our art, much can be done by way of improvisation on one or another set theme. Such creative work gives freshness and spontaneity to performance" (*SS* II 1989: 68). Neither is Knebel particularly helpful. She never uses "improvisation" to describe what happens in an "etude," although she occasionally refers to the "improvised text" that emerges from paraphrase etudes (Knebel' [1959] 1982: 45). Instead, she consistently refers to the etude as a "search" (Knebel' [1959] 1982: 62) for the interactive possibilities within a play's text, thus emphasizing its purpose as analysis.

This absence of clarity in the classic sources meant that I needed to dig deeper. I turned to Lyubov Zabolotskaia Weidner, a Russian actor who has worked extensively with two of

Knebel's most prominent directing students, Anatoly Efros (whom I mentioned last time), and Anatoly Vassiliev, whose productions dramatize metaphysical questions about human existence. Lyuba thinks of improvisation as an exercise in imagination, in which an actor chooses an object of attention or a theme and plays with it, following any creative impulse that arises in the moment. In contrast, her teachers always tied etudes to written texts, even though the actor uses a "free reading," rather than a memorized "hard reading" of the lines. Lyuba took these last two terms from Vassiliev and pointed me to a passage from one of his transcribed master classes. In fact, I was planning to share this quotation with you today, so I have it right here. (*I pull out my notes. Everyone draws a little closer.*)

> Improvisation is freer than an etude. One can say that in an etude, an actor improvises. That would not be a mistake. But an etude is located, say, in Africa. It is always a matter of geography, of mapping the play; and we move around within the confines of that map. We are guided by the map when we improvise in an etude. But an improvisation may go entirely elsewhere!
>
> (Vassiliev 1999: 40)[1]

Now you know why I ask you to prepare your etudes by "mapping" the scene against the dynamic principles of Active Analysis, as Juliana and Sargis did last time. A map that is "true" and "accurate" with regard to the text (Knebel' [1959] 1982: 44) can guide you to a dynamic performance. Alternatively, if you stray from the scene in your etude, as Juliana and Sargis initially did, you will discover gaps in your understanding of the scene and you will need to redraw your map. Vassiliev says more of interest:

> During an improvisation, the actor creates action from a given theme. During an etude, the actor moves according to the map. [Therefore, …] in an improvisation there are two freedoms: the actor creates both the action and the text. In an etude the actor has only the freedom that can be found within the text. This means that the one is not at all the other.
>
> (Vassiliev 1999: 40)

Juliana I have always felt uncomfortable when improvising, but loved doing the etudes. Maybe, because I'm an actor and not a writer, one freedom is enough for me. In fact as Lady Macbeth I felt the freest I have ever felt as an actor in our second etude, because I let the words come from what needed to happen, and I didn't worry about being clever. I just did the work of acting!

Me Notice something else, as well. When Vassiliev assumes that freedom can be "found within the text," he operates from the assumption that a play is an unfinished score for performance. To put it into our terms, the actor finds the map in the play's facts and enjoys creative freedom in the open clues. Active Analysis does indeed foster freedom, but always within structure. As another Russian teacher of Active Analysis reminds us, "freedom is the reward for knowing the play," but warns that "arbitrariness results from the scorning of knowledge," and leads to "dilettantism" (Malochevskaia 2003: 33).

Grigor If I were to serve as devil's advocate, I would argue that comedy improv is not quite as free as Vassiliev thinks. There are rules, the most important one being that whatever your partner offers, you must accept. Such rules are a kind of map too.

Sargis Point well taken! But, after working with Juliana last time, I experienced something quite different than what I generally feel in an improv. I don't know how to put it into words. (*He looks up at the ceiling as he tries to recall what happened.*) I focused on my verb. I saw how Juliana was trying to push me around. I reacted to her. Here's the difference! I said "no." Only at the end did I agree. I also felt completely absorbed in the moment, like I was riding a wave. I was thinking only about my verb and how Juliana was reacting to what I was doing. I wasn't even thinking about a map. Yes, Juliana, I think you are right! I felt freer in that second etude than I would have in an improv, (*turning toward Grigor*) because I could say "no." I don't think I am expressing what I feel very well …

Me Well, I'm not an expert in improv, but I am fascinated with the complex dance that occurs whenever human beings interact with one another. In my experience, the principles of Active Analysis offer actors and directors a great deal of flexibility, as they explore the range of interactive dynamics that can occur within performances.

But, to return to the original question, Stanislavsky may not have been clear on the line between improvisations and etudes because his ideas were constantly evolving. Long before developing Active Analysis, he had been experimenting with improvisations. For example, in 1905 at the Studio-Theatre on Povarskaya Street, he and his protégé Meyerhold innovated a rehearsal technique that went directly from a first read-through to an improvised performance of the play (Chapter 1). Clearly, the seeds of Active Analysis were first planted in this early "laboratory for actors" (Syssoyeva 2013: 37). Also in 1905 Stanislavsky applied this experimental process to the Moscow Art Theatre's planned production of Knut Hamsun's symbolist drama, *The Game of Life*. The company's appalled co-founder, however, shut down the rehearsals. In an extremely long letter, Nemirovich-Danchenko explained to Stanislavsky that "such a way of working would create an all too familiar chaos, dissatisfaction, loss of time, even destroy the play, so I gathered all my energy in protest" (Syssoyeva 2013: 42). The Studio-Theatre on Povarskaya Street was as short-lived, as were the rehearsals for *The Game of Life*, due as much to the disruption caused by the failed Russian Revolution of 1905 as to Stanislavsky's "capricious" and "stubborn" insistence on using improvisation, as Nemirovich-Danchenko had said (Syssoyeva 2013: 42). When Stanislavsky finally resumed rehearsals for *The Game of Life* in 1907, he dutifully prepared a prompt-book in order to avoid his partner's ire. Nonetheless, his desire to create an improvisatory rehearsal technique did not die.

At the height of his directorial career, Stanislavsky also used improvisations as a way for actors to explore their characters' lives, personalities, and behaviors. However, Knebel would not refer to these as etudes, because they do not work on specific interactions within the play, but instead enact imagined moments from the story or the characters' autobiographies that lay beyond the frame of the play. By embodying the habits and behaviors of their characters under such broadly imagined circumstances, actors can develop their roles more deeply. In my own practice, I have sometimes found that such background etudes, as I have come to call them, can be helpful.

In re-reading Harold Clurman's memoirs about the Group Theatre, where the American Method was born during the 1930s, I found an especially interesting passage that describes how he and Lee Strasberg sometimes asked the Group to "improvise situations similar, but not identical to those found in the play" and, at other times, to use "improvisations based on the doing of the actual scenes in the play with the actors using their own words" (Clurman 1994: 47). While the former type reflects Stanislavsky's use of improvisation to explore the characters' backgrounds, the latter comes closer to Active Analysis. Actor Ruth Nelson recalls this work more explicitly:

> We read the play once, each reading his or her own role. The improvisations began. That went on for weeks and weeks. After a very long time, we'd come back and read the play again. The improvisations got closer and closer to the situations in the play until we found ourselves using the words of the author.
>
> (Chinoy 1976: 528)

Her account harkens back to Stanislavsky's experiments with etudes in 1905 and antici-pates those at the Opera-Dramatic Studio in 1936. Unfortunately, Clurman's and Nelson's descriptions are brief, no doubt because, as Clurman also observes, the use of improvisa-tion at the Group Theatre was short-lived in view of the fact that "the commercial theatre is unfamiliar with this method and scornful of it" (Clurman 1994: 47).

Only during the last four years of his life did Stanislavsky find a productive way to explore plays through improvisations that had become, more properly speaking, "etudes." He was no longer a director who controlled performance by writing prompt-books for the actors, nor was he "clutching at straws" in the midst of "chaos," as Nemirovich-Danchenko had described him at rehearsals for *The Game of Life* (Syssoyeva 2013: 37). He now used actions, counteractions, and events to harness "chaos" and unleash actors' creative freedom.

In Practice: Rehearsing an Excerpt from Act II in Chekhov's *Three Sisters* (1900)

For our second scene study I have selected a brief interaction among three characters in Act II of *Three Sisters*,[2] the first play that Chekhov wrote specifically for the Moscow Art Theatre. We will repeat everything we did last time, but in a different key because Chekhov and Shakespeare are different writers. Shakespeare's characters usually say what they mean; even the liars (like Iago) frankly admit to the audience that they lie. Chekhov's char-acters rarely speak their minds; often they do not themselves know their minds. In fact, they more frequently lie to themselves than to others. In describing a typical Chekhovian scene, Stanislavsky conjures up the image of "a man and woman [who] exchange almost meaning-less words that do not express what they feel," adding that "Chekhov's people often behave that way" (Carnicke 2013: 192).

While Shakespeare loves dramatic conflict and direct counteractions, Chekhov's charac-ters tend to interact obliquely. Over the course of his career, Chekhov wrote fewer and fewer scenes of confrontation. You will recall that when I first introduced you to oblique counter-actions, I referenced *The Cherry Orchard*, which includes a stunning image of how Chekhov handles interaction in his plays through Gayev's obsession with billiards, which is a game of angles and indirection.[3] Rarely does a billiards player use the cue ball to hit the target; instead, the player reaches the target by hitting a by-standing ball that sets other balls into motion, one of which eventually reaches the target to score points. Events do occur in Chekhov. Ranyevskaya loses her orchard and returns to her lover in Paris; Lopakhin loses Varya and buys the cherry orchard. Yet these events come about in much the same way that billiard balls score points: through indirection, leaving characters feeling sideswiped and audiences wondering what the characters' actual targets of desire really were.

Unlike Shakespeare, who gives actors so much help with their performances, Chekhov buries his facts in seemingly trivial or irrelevant details. For example, during rehearsals for *Uncle Vanya*, Chekhov criticized Stanislavsky for assuming that the title character wears boots and work clothes simply because he manages the estate. "'Listen,' [Chekhov] said, getting annoyed, 'everything is written down. You haven't read the play.'" Stanislavsky searched through the text, but could find nothing more than an apparently off-hand comment in a stage direction in Act I about a stylish tie. When the puzzled director asked the author to explain, Chekhov said, Vanya "has a wonderful tie; he is an elegant, cultured man. It's not true, that all landowners go around in muddy boots. They are educated people, they dress well, they go to Paris. I wrote all that" (*SS* I 1988: 300). This anecdote demonstrates how important the smallest fact, like a tie, could be to Chekhov. His plays are indeed puzzles.

These traits make reading Chekhov much harder than reading Shakespeare. The words on the page seem like the placid surface of a lake, where very little of interest seems to occur; but life teems below in the depths of the water. Too often, actors look at the surface and miss the drama underneath, as did Stanislavsky when he first read *The Seagull*. "Reading [Chekhov] one says to oneself: 'It's good, but … nothing special, nothing amazing. […] In fact, the first acquaintance with his works is often disappointing. There seems little to say about it" (*SS* I 1988: 289). However, after grappling with Chekhov, Stanislavsky soon came to realize that "not a single performance [had gone by] in which I did not discover some new feeling in my soul, and new depths and subtleties in the works themselves which had escaped me earlier" (*SS* I 1988: 290).

Step One: Reading for the Facts (*Razbor*)

Let's start by reviewing the circumstances in *Three Sisters* that lead to our scene. Geo, please tell the story up to Act II.

THE GIVEN CIRCUMSTANCES

Geo   Let's see. *Three Sisters* is the story of the Prozorov family—Irina, Masha, Olga, and their brother Andrey. They moved from Moscow to a provincial town in the south of Russia, when their father, who was a general, was posted there. The play starts one year after their father's death, and the Prozorovs still live there, despite the fact that they long for a livelier life in Moscow. I don't know why they just don't go. I suppose it's because Olga works at the local school with Masha's husband, so moving would be hard for the older sisters. Then Andrey proposes to a local girl, Natasha, and joins the town council, so he's not going anywhere fast. Only Irina, who is the youngest and just starting her adult life, could move, but instead she takes a job at the tele-graph office and after a while hates it. Of course, she has another option. One of the officers, named Tuzenbach, who serves at the nearby military base, wants to marry her. But she's not interested. She wants a more exciting life …

Shari   … and a fairy tale prince. Humph, the young always want flowers and romance.

Anisha   Well, why not?

Shari (*Patting Anisha's hand*.)   You'll learn, dear.

Juliana   The most exciting thing that happens at the beginning of the play is the arrival of a new officer, Vershinin, who comes from Moscow. He brings the atmosphere of the big city with him. Masha finds him especially attractive and ends up having an affair with him.

Shari   But he's no fairy-tale prince either! He's married with two young daughters! And clearly his wife is unhappy. She tries to commit suicide in Act II! Oh, by the way, Masha's not the only one having an affair in this play. So is Andrey's wife, Natasha, who is going around with the big muckety-muck Protopopov, who heads the town council! That affair started even before her marriage to Andrey. Everyone knows about it except for the husband. These small towns!

Hannah   Well, maybe Andrey knows, but looks the other way, afraid to confront his wife.

Rose   I think Masha's husband, Kulygin, knows about her affair, but, he loves her too much to say anything. Look at how he treats her, just after Vershinin has left. She's crying inconsolably and Kulygin tries to make her smile. His behavior says that he loves and forgives her. He wants them to move on with their lives. That moment makes me fall in love with him! He starts off seeming so pedantic and silly, but in the end he reveals how kind and loving he is.

Louisa   Did anyone notice how close the old military doctor, Chebutykin, feels to Irina? Buying her extra-special presents and sitting near her. Then too he often reminisces about the sisters' mother. When he gets drunk in Act III, he drops their mother's precious clock! It's like he smashes the past. Put two and two together and maybe, when he was young, he had an affair and maybe Irina is his child!

Anisha   Oh my! This is not a fairy tale at all!

Me   Let me set the scene for the interaction in Act II that I want us to study. It is evening, the night before Lent, or as we generally call it *Mardi Gras*—a time to eat, drink, and be merry, for tomorrow fasting begins and continues for forty days until Easter. The characters are gathering in the Prozorov house, waiting for the party to begin. Some have arrived, but not all. No food, not even tea, has yet been served. It is the kind of in-between moment that Chekhov so often creates.

Geo   But the act ends without a party. Natasha sends everyone away because her baby is not well, or so she says!

Louisa   And then she abandons her sick baby to go for a ride with her lover! She has her fun, even if the others don't.

Me   Yes, but that's later. As our scene begins, Chebutykin, who lives with the family, has entered the parlor and sits at a table, reading a newspaper. He beckons Irina to come sit next to him. (*Anisha giggles*.) Irina joins him at the table, where she plays solitaire. In Russia, solitaire is sometimes used to tell one's fortune, so I imagine that Irina is contemplating her future. In another corner of the room, Tuzenbach, Vershinin and Masha have a chat. Their chat is our scene!

Keith   Finally she tells us which scene we're doing! (*Everyone laughs*.)

Me Setrak, you have been quiet since you joined us. You told me last time that you studied with a Russian teacher in Madrid, is that correct?

Setrak He wasn't Russian, but was educated in Moscow. He was very strict and taught me a lot about Stanislavsky. I also learned a lot from my other teachers, especially about "*expresión corporal*"—that's Spanish for "body expression." I still do those exercises every day.

Sargis You know, Setrak, I think I saw one of your productions for the Armenian community in Los Angeles. You are a director too, right? (*Setrak beams and nods.*) It was a wonderful play about a department store in the middle of the night when all the mannequins come to life and dance ....

Setrak ... *expresión corporal*!

Me Setrak, you will play Vershinin, whose name means "pinnacle" or "summit." Chekhov wrote the role for Stanislavsky, who was over six feet tall, naming the character for the actor!

Setrak I'm five foot six!

Keith Height doesn't matter. Vershinin is also a lofty thinker. His head is in the clouds as he dreams about the future, so the name fits him in that sense too.

Setrak Sorry, but I think Vershinin talks to make others around him think he's important. He's always puffing himself up. That makes his name ironic.

Grigor In Act I, Tuzenbach says Vershinin is "patient," because he stays with his wife, even though she is unbalanced and "only says grandiloquent things" and "philosophizes."

Setrak But in this scene, it's Vershinin himself who's saying "grandiloquent things" and philosophizing!

Keith True, but I still don't think that he's arrogant. He's a lieutenant-colonel and outranks Tuzenbach, who's only a lieutenant. Why shouldn't Vershinin be proud?

Me Well, all opinions aside, when we work on the scene, we have to pay close attention to the facts in the text before interpreting them.

Setrak I am very happy to take on the role and reach for the summit!

Me Keith, you will play Tuzenbach. *Tuz* in Russian names the "ace" in a deck of cards and "*bach*" is "bang."

Shari Interesting, given the fact that he's in love with Irina. The ace can be either the highest or lowest card, depending upon the game, so when his lady-love plays solitaire to tell her fortune, the Tuz is the lowest!

Keith The "bang" predicts his fortune! In the end, he's killed in a duel over Irina.

Me His name also sounds Germanic, which Tuzenbach mentions when he tells Vershinin that, "I'm Russian, and I don't even speak German." Chekhov originally wrote this role for Meyerhold, whose name is also Germanic, again suiting the character's name to the actor!

Keith Sorry, Shari, but in this scene Tuzenbach doesn't sit with his lady-love, but with her sister and his ranking officer Vershinin. So, does it really matter at this moment in the play that he loves Irina? And pardon, Sharon, do his Germanic roots matter here?

Me True, not all circumstances are equally important at all moments in a play. In reading for the facts, we have to focus on those things that help us with the scene at hand, while being careful not to violate facts elsewhere in the play. You are correct, Keith, we can't and shouldn't play everything in the play all at once. Regarding Irina, however, Chekhov does place her on the stage, so it might be relevant.

Keith I'm game for the role! Vershinin may outrank me, but, at least in this Studio, I am the taller man! (*Setrak laughs*.) But joking aside, Tuzenbach is a pragmatic man and I like that.

Grigor Tuzenbach may be pragmatic, but he also has a poetic soul. In Act IV, when he is about to risk his life in a duel over Irina, he tells her … Wait, I'll find it. (*He opens his play to a marked page*.) "What beautiful trees and actually, that's just how beautiful life should be near them! […] Look there, that tree has dried up, but it's still waving in the breeze with the others. So I think that if I die, I too will still participate in life in some way or other." That moment in the play made me cry.

Me Rose, you will be Masha. What's her story?

Rose She married Kulygin, when she was eighteen. At that time, he was her teacher and seemed very smart. But as she got older, he seemed less smart. At the start of the play, she's tired of him and the marriage. She's tired of her life in the provinces too. She wants something better. So, Vershinin interests her. He's not only from Moscow, but like her father he's an officer in the military.

Shari Naturally she has an affair with him, knowing full well that he will not leave his wife! She heard it from Tuzenbach like everyone else did! Ah, hope springs eternal. (*Looking straight at Anisha*.) No, I'm not being cynical. I'm being realistic!

Me I'll add one pertinent historical fact. In pre-revolutionary Russia civil service carried ranks in parallel with military service. As a school teacher Kulygin holds the same rank as that of a lieutenant-colonel. That means that he and Vershinin are equal in rank. Masha does not trade up, but laterally when she chooses her lover! Additionally, notice that none of the cast comes anywhere near her father's rank of general! The only one who holds an equivalent rank is Protopopov as the head of the town council; and he, like their late father, never appears on stage!

Louisa So in terms of hierarchy, Natasha's affair outranks Masha's! Ha! I'd love to play Natasha.

Me Yes, Chekhov clearly has fun playing with civil service and military rankings in this play!

Grigor Wow, what a great historical fact! I'll have to research that some more.

Me But, as Keith will remind us, we have to figure out whether the men's ranks are relevant to the scene at hand.

PARSING THE TEXT

It's time to read the text of *Three Sisters* for the facts and open clues that will guide you to your performances. But, before taking that step, I want to deepen our initial discussion about reading plays as scores for performance, because Chekhov so often hides facts in plain sight and thus demands especially careful attention.

While I call the first step in Active Analysis "reading for the facts," Russians call it *razbor,* a word that is devilishly difficult to translate. Russian-English dictionaries usually give "analysis" as its meaning, but, since another Russian word, *analiz*, names Active Analysis, translating *razbor* as "analysis" confuses things. Russian-Russian dictionaries offer explicit descriptions of the various meanings for *razbor* and examples of its usage. There I found one option that struck a chord. In grammar, *razbor* refers to the parsing of a sentence into its grammatical components. For example, when you parse a sentence, such as "the dog ate the treat," you identify the subject (*dog*), the verb (*ate*), and the object (*treat*). Aha, I thought, this is exactly it! Reading for the facts maps the interactive principles within a scene just as grammatical parsing maps a sentence. In effect, we "parse" the scene for its action, counteraction, alliances, and event. Even the association with grammar makes sense, since Stanislavsky had initially called his System "a grammar" for acting (Stanislavskii 1986 vol. 1: 55)!

My Russian colleagues tell me that *razbor* implies a more targeted process than does "table work," a term that refers to Stanislavsky's earlier approach to analyzing plays that kept his actors at the table for long periods of time, discussing every conceivable aspect of the play. In Active Analysis actors search instead for the specific kinds of information needed for performance, just as miners seek for gold. Thus, *razbor*—parsing the text—gets actors up and performing more quickly than standard table work.

While reading for the facts, many topics arise that dovetail with literary analysis: the play's overall story, the given circumstances, historical era, meanings and themes, class and power structures within the society it presents, the style of its language, genre, etc. But parsing the scene differs from broader paths of analysis in that it emphasizes the textual information most necessary for performance. Individual topics may become more or less important in *razbor* depending upon what actors most need to know. As Stanislavsky always said: "to know" a play, actors must "know how" to step into it (Knebel' [1954] 2009: 65).

> **Sargis**   My grandfather grew up in Soviet Armenia. And every time he got really angry with someone, he'd nod toward the door and say *"razberyomsya"*—"let's take it outside." Is that word related to *razbor*?
>
> **Me** (*Laughing*.)   That's the verb form of *razbor*! And yes, the verb, like the noun, implies getting to the bottom of things. Although we're not duking it out when we examine a scene, we do try to get to the bottom of what's going on. I love how Efros once explained it. He was complaining about theatre artists who "see what is *obvious*, but do not want to feel what lies *beyond the obvious*" (Efros 2007: 140–1).[4] Parsing the scene by reading for the facts takes us "beyond the obvious," something especially important when working on Chekhov.

MAPPING THE WORDS ON THE PAGE TO THE PRINCIPLES OF ACTIVE ANALYSIS

Let's parse Chekhov's little scene in *Three Sisters*, starting with Vershinin's invitation to philosophize. Grigor, please read the stage directions.

Setrak-Vershinin   Well? If they won't serve tea, let's philosophize a bit.

Keith-Tuzenbach   Let's. About what?

Setrak-Vershinin   About what? Let's day dream … For example, about the life that will come after us, in about two hundred, three hundred years.

Keith-Tuzenbach   What about it? After us, people will fly in balloons, change the cut of their jackets, perhaps discover a sixth sense, even develop it, but life will remain essentially the same—hard, happy and full of mysteries. And after a thousand years, people will still sigh and say, "Ah how hard life is!" Besides that, they'll still fear death, and not want to die, just like now.

Anisha (*Interrupting.*)   Vershinin is the action. He starts the scene by inviting Tuzenbach to "philosophize a bit." What is that anyway? It's like talking politics, right? So he must be entertaining himself and the others while they wait for tea. That's how I see it anyway.

Hannah   Notice the pause, indicated by three dots in the text. That's called an ellipsis and Chekhov is famous for them! Vershinin is taking a moment right there to choose his subject.

Keith   When Tuzenbach says "What about it?" he doesn't seem very interested. I think he's more concerned with watching Irina across the room.

Shari   I disagree. He says, "Let's." I think he's eager for the talk! He's probably bored, waiting for the party to start. When Vershinin offers a topic, Tuzenbach jumps right in and talks a lot.

Keith   I see what you mean. I bet he's the counteraction in the scene too, because when he gets going, he actively disagrees with Vershinin.

Anisha (*Smiling.*)   I agree, Keith. In fact, his counteraction is direct, making his main partner Vershinin, not Irina.

Juliana   I think that these two have had the same argument before! I get that from the way that Tuzenbach jumps in, even before Vershinin lays out his position.

Me   The facts so far seem to support the hypothesis that Vershinin is the action and Tuzenbach is a direct counteraction. You have also made some strong factual observations pertaining to the ellipsis and to the length at which Tuzenbach first speaks. Other ideas—like how much Tuzenbach is aware of Irina or whether the two men have had this conversation before—may be open clues. For now, we need to find more facts. So, read on!

Setrak-Vershinin   How shall I put it? I think that everything on earth must change little by little, and people are already changing before our very eyes. After two hundred, three hundred, finally a thousand years—the point is not how long it takes—there will come a new, happy life. We won't participate in that life, of course, but we're living for it now, working and suffering to create it. This alone is the goal of our existence, or, if you like, our happiness.

Grigor   *Masha laughs softly.*

Keith-Tuzenbach   What's wrong?

Rose-Masha   I don't know. All day today, since morning, I've been laughing.

Hannah (*Interrupting.*)   That is a weird moment, when Masha laughs. Is that a fact? Or is it an open clue?

Me Remember Octavia's whispered words to her brother in *Antony and Cleopatra* (Lesson 2)! The same thing applies here. Masha's laugh is a fact. If the three actors do not account for it when they perform, a note in the musical score will be skipped. But why she laughs is an open clue that needs more investigation.

Louisa Chekhov is famous for subtexts, so I bet that, when Masha laughs, she is thinking about something entirely different from anything said in the scene. After all, in Act I she was reading, while everyone else was conversing. She often seems to be off in her own world.

Me That's one possibility. Are there others? Would it help to consider that this is the first time we've heard from Masha, even though she has been present from the scene's beginning. Let me remind you of the principle of alliance that we explored in our first lesson.

Rose That's right. The center of gravity in any scene revolves around the collision between an action and a counteraction. So, if there are more than two characters in the scene, the others align themselves with one or the other.

Me Like the wind in our baseball analogy. The ball flies, gravity pulls against its flight, and the wind can either help or hinder its flight. Masha's laugh is the first clue we have in order to determine her alliance within the scene's dynamics, but we need more. Read on!

Grigor *Masha laughs softly.*
Keith-Tuzenbach What's wrong?
Rose-Masha I don't know. All day today, since morning, I've been laughing.
Setrak-Vershinin (*Looking at Keith.*) I finished the same school as you did, but didn't go to the military academy. I read a lot, but don't know how to choose my books, and so perhaps I read a lot that's unnecessary, but anyway, the more I live, the more I want to know. My hair's turning gray, I'm almost an old man, but I know so little, ah, so little! But all the same, I think that what's most important and real, I do know and know well. But how can I prove to you that we won't have, and don't even need happiness ourselves … We must only work and work, but happiness—that's fated for our descendants, far in the future.
Grigor *Pause.*
Setrak-Vershinin Not for me but for the descendants of my descendants.

Geo Stop right there! I want to go back to something Setrak said. I don't think Vershinin is arrogant. He's self-deprecating in what he says. He even says that he knows very little.

Juliana The man doth protest too much, methinks. Don't you know people, who put themselves down in order to fish for compliments? I do. (*Geo shrugs.*)

Me Go on.

Grigor *Fedotik and Rodé appear in the hall; they sit down and sing quietly, playing a guitar.*

Hannah Well, that's interesting. They play music in the background, almost like a soundtrack in a film. Hmmm …. I wonder why Chekhov would do that? For the party atmosphere? We know that the music is quiet, but that's all.

Me More to explore in an etude! Go on.

Keith-Tuzenbach According to you, we shouldn't even dream of happiness! But what if I feel happy!

Setrak-Vershinin You don't.

Keith Now that's positively rude. Why would he say that? Why insult his comrade?

Grigor *(Reading.)* Tuzenbach "*throw[s] up his hands and laugh[s].*"

Keith-Tuzenbach Obviously we don't understand each other. Well, how can I convince you?

Grigor M*asha laughs quietly* and Tuzenbach *gestures to her with a finger*.

Keith-Tuzenbach Laugh!

Grigor *To Vershinin.*

Keith-Tuzenbach Not only in two hundred or three hundred, but even in a million years, life will remain exactly the same as it is. It does not change, it stays constant, following its own laws, which you'll never discover, or at least over which you'll never have any control. Migratory birds, cranes for example, fly and fly and whether great thoughts or small ones wander through their minds, they all still fly, not knowing where or why. They fly and will fly, no matter what philosophers may come among them. Let them philosophize as they will, so long as they fly ...

Anisha Interesting ... Tuzenbach reacts as if Masha is laughing at him, which makes him repeat his opinion more passionately. He gets almost poetic with his image of birds flying. Does he start arguing with Masha now? Are Vershinin and Masha ganging up against Tuzenbach? I think they are. I definitely see this scene as a philosophical debate. No, it's more than that, it's an out-right argument!

Rose And Masha allies herself with Vershinin in terms of the argument. Although I'm not sure I'd say the two are "ganging up" on Tuzenbach. They're not bullies.

Me Keith, please pick it up again with Tuzenbach's words.

Keith-Tuzenbach Let them philosophize as they will, so long as they fly ...

Rose-Masha Still where is the meaning?

Keith-Tuzenbach The meaning ... Look, it's snowing. What meaning does that have?

Grigor *Pause.*

Rose-Masha I think that one must be a believer, or must search for beliefs, otherwise life is empty, empty ... To live and not to know why the cranes fly, why children are born, why there are stars in the sky ... Either you know why you live, or it's all nonsense, just tinsel ...

Grigor *Pause.*

Rose Finally, Masha gets into the debate! In fact, she takes the broadest perspective of all them. She thinks about the entire cycle of life from birth onward. She takes Vershinin's ideas further. He talks philosophy, but she talks about metaphysics. The meaning of life!

Me What a terrific observation! I can honestly say that I never noticed Masha's leap from philosophy to metaphysics! There is always something new to see in Chekhov's work, no matter how familiar his plays!

Hannah I also want to go back to Chekhov's ellipses. He uses them in so many different ways. First an ellipsis shows that Masha interrupts Tuzenbach. Next, there are several that show how she takes time to find the best way to articulate her thoughts, and then at the end, her words trail away into a moment of shared silence, marked by the stage direction, "pause." I am guessing that "a pause" lasts longer than an "ellipsis," right?

Me   That's what I understand.

Hannah   During that "pause" they might have gotten lost in their own thoughts …

Rose   Or maybe Masha's metaphysical idea has stumped the two men and they are literally speechless! Masha seems really intelligent.

Anisha (*Rubbing her hands together.*)   Oooh, I like that option!

Grigor   If Shakespeare directs actors through the rhythms of his verse, then maybe Chekhov directs them through ellipses and pauses! The Moscow Art Theatre was famous for pauses in acting. I looked it up! Some admired how realistic the pauses made the performances seem. Others thought the performances were too slow and made fun of the silences.

Me   Nemirovich-Danchenko used to say that "a pause is not something that is dead, but is an active intensification of experience" (Nemirovitch-Dantchenko [*sic*] 1956: 163). He taught that characters' words emerge from hidden thoughts the way an iceberg's tip sticks up out of the ocean. These hidden thoughts are now commonly called "subtexts" or "inner monologues." During the Studio era in Hollywood, when acting coaches taught a form of Stanislavsky's System to film stars of the 1930s and 1940s, they called what one thinks during a pause a "silent line" (Rosenstein and Sparrow 1936: 61–2). I rather like that term, because it reminds actors that silence is not empty. Whenever you are on stage, whether speaking or not, you are embroiled in the interactive dynamics of the play. Words are facts, but so are silences. Go on with your reading!

Setrak-Vershinin   Still it's sad that my youth has passed …
Rose-Masha   Gogol said, "It's boring to live on this earth, ladies and gentlemen!"
Keith-Tuzenbach   And I say, "It's hard to argue with you, lady and gentleman."

Grigor   That's the scene! You know, I love Russian literature and so does Masha. In Act I she reads a poem by Pushkin, the father of modern Russian literature. Now, she quotes the last line from another classic, a story by Gogol, entitled *The Tale of How Ivan Ivanovich Quarreled with Ivan Fyodorovich*, about two neighbors who fight without end. Masha is clearly telling Tuzenbach and Vershinin that, if they don't stop, they might end up like Gogol's neighbors!

Rose   That's quite funny! And that's also where the scene's event occurs. Masha shuts down their argument.

Me   Makes sense to me, Rose. (*Everyone nods in agreement.*)

Keith   But if that's the event, why does Tuzenbach get the last word! His final line sounds like a quotation too, as if he's mimicking Masha. Maybe it's because he's like a bulldog, who just doesn't want to let go of the argument. I'll have to see how it works in the etude.

Step Two: A One-Sentence Etude

Me   You have your map. Setrak as Vershinin is the action. Keith as Tuzenbach is the Counteraction. Rose as Masha allies herself with the action. The event occurs when Masha shuts down the argument between the two men. It's time to test your understanding of the scene and, because Chekhov's characters do not always say what they mean, I want you to try a different kind of etude. After re-reading for the facts, choose not only a verb, but also one sentence from your lines that you feel goes to the heart of what your character is trying to do within the scene. During your etude, investigate the scene by speaking only that sentence. You can use it in any way that serves you: speak it whole, withhold it altogether, or split it up into single words or phrases. You can repeat the words as many times as you like and in whatever order you like, as long as what you say helps you do the work of your verb. Of course, you can also use other means to investigate the dynamics of the scene: movements, sounds, touch, etc. Acting is a holistic endeavor in which speech is only one of many resources, upon which to draw. In fact, this etude is designed to limit language so that you can better uncover the underlying dynamics.

The three actors take their scripts and sit on the stage to read and confer with each other as the rest of us reset the chairs, stretch our legs, and take a moment to relax.

Keith (*Without moving from the stage.*)   Sharon, we have a question.

Me   Ask away!

Everyone stops to listen

Keith   Now that there are three of us, don't we need two verbs each? As Tuzenbach I want to fight with Setrak but I want to entertain my future sister-in-law. Rose insists that we get only one verb each.

Rose   That's right. I was thinking about "to tease" because I can do that with both Keith and Setrak, just in different ways based on Masha's different relationship to each.

Me   Active Analysis sides with Rose on this one! The idea is to have a strong and specific verb that anchors you into the core dynamics of the scene and takes you from beginning to end. Setrak, you'll need a verb that impels the scene forward. Keith, you'll need one that resists that forward motion. And Rose, you'll need a verb that assists the action. If our map is accurate, you will also need to shut the scene down in the end. In short, each of your verbs should contribute to the scene's center of gravity. Remember too, plan *what* you will do during your etude, but not *how*. You have the freedom to change how you go about doing your verbs as the interaction develops. So let your imaginations guide you.

Keith   Got it!

The actors continue planning, as Geo and Juliana build a set for the scene. They pull some chairs together to create a sofa on the floor in front of the stage, add a piano bench as a coffee table, and place two lovely wooden chairs with high backs and arms on either side of the sofa. To stage left, the door leads outside and to stage right there is a window. When the actors are ready to work, we settle down to watch.

ETUDE 1: ONE SENTENCE

Rose and Keith sit on either side of the sofa, leaving space between them. Rose has a book open on her lap and reads. Keith tries to catch her eye. When he can't, he looks around the room, twiddling his thumbs. Setrak enters from the outside door, walks purposefully over to Keith and shakes his hand. Rose shuts her book and smiles. Setrak sits in the armchair closest to her.

Setrak (*Looking straight at Keith and speaking in a rousing manner.*)   If they won't serve tea, let's philosophize.

Keith (*Frowning.*)   Life will remain essentially the same.

Setrak (*Smiling in encouragement.*)   Philosophize, philoso-phize, phil-o-so-phize. (*He pronounces the word differently every time and sounds like he is giving a lecture.*)

Keith (*Frowning, in a monotonous tone.*)   The same, the same, the same.

Setrak (*Stands up and circles back behind the chair.*)   If they won't serve tea ... (*He puts his hands on the back of his chair as if on a podium.*) ... let's philosophize! Phil, phil, phil ... (*He lifts his eyes and arms up to the sky as he continues. Rose sits up attentively and listens raptly to Setrak.*) Phil, osophy, phil, o, soph, yiiiiy. Philosophy! Let us, let us philosophize. Phillllllll, ooooooo, sophyiiiiiiiiy!

Rose laughs, enjoying the sound of Setrak' s deconstructed words. Keith swivels away from the other two, sinking into the corner of the sofa. He looks staunchly at the door to the outside, as if he wants to escape.

Setrak (*Rhythmically.*)   Philo-sophy, no tea, sophy!

Rose giggles at the rhyming of tea and philosophy

Keith (*Grumbling to himself.*)   Life will remain essentially the same.

Setrak makes a sound, something like "tsk, tsk, tsk," as if taking a student to task.

Rose (*Reaching out to touch Keith's shoulder.*)   Where's the meaning?

Setrak (*Nodding his approval to Rose.*)   No tea, philo-sophy.

Keith (*Pulling away from Rose and glowering at Setrak.*)   Life will remain the same.

Setrak (*Losing his temper.*)   Let's philosophize!

Setrak makes a fist with his right hand and pounds it into the palm of his left hand. He moves out from behind the armchair to the corner of the coffee table. Looking straight at Keith, Setrak stamps his foot. A short silence ensues.

Rose (*Looking first at Keith and then at Setrak.*)   Meaning?

Keith stands up, circles around to the back of the sofa away from Setrak, and then walks quickly, as if fleeing, to the window. Both Rose and Setrak shake their heads in amazement.

Step Three: Assess in Order to Repeat

After a moment of silence, some in the audience applaud politely. Others sit still, thinking.

Setrak   I don't get it. Keith, why didn't you fight with me!

Keith   Yes, I did.

Setrak   No, you didn't.

Me   What were your verbs?

Setrak   "To inspire" Keith and Rose!

Keith   I didn't feel inspired! I felt like you were lecturing to me like a school boy!

Grigor   Wow! Tuzenbach is a lower-ranking officer than Vershinin. Remember? Setrak you embodied that fact in what you did. That is so funny!

Setrak   I didn't think about that. I just felt that Keith wasn't listening. He was frowning, grumbling to himself … He even turned his back on me! I had to get his attention somehow. I can see, how what I did could be interpreted as teaching.

Rose   You even used the back of the chair like a podium! My verb was "to enjoy an intellectual conversation." I had thought about teasing both of them, but I changed my mind.

Keith   I saw you enjoying Setrak's lecture, yes I did, but that made me feel even less inspired,

Louisa   Rose, I believed that you enjoyed listening. When you closed your book and paid attention to Setrak, I also saw the alliance. You even tried to pull Keith in with your hand on his shoulder.

Keith   My verb was "to burst his balloon."

Louisa   (*Laughs good humoredly.*)   But Keith … (*Still chuckling.*) You know we all consider you a talented actor, part of our family, an amazing person, but, honestly, this time, I didn't see you trying to burst anybody's balloon. You were trying to escape both of them. You swiveled away; you pulled away; you walked away. You also put an end to the whole conversation when you went to the window. That's a different event than the one in the text.

Keith   Yeah, yeah, I guess I forgot all about my verb, the map, everything, once we got started. I just went with the flow. (*Thinking over what just happened.*) Setrak pissed me off, the way he was strutting around, the way Rose was admiring him … There was one moment when I wanted to stand up, tower over him, and stare him down, but I didn't.

Me   In my experience, the most important aspect of Active Analysis involves choosing an appropriate verb for the scene that excites your creativity and then actually doing it. As Louisa just observed, there was a gap between the verb you chose and what we saw you doing. I remember watching Knebel's assistant, Natalya Zverova, teach. She expected actors to do whatever they set their minds to do. If an actor said he would "beg" and he didn't, or if an actor said she would "persuade" and didn't, Zverova would point it out.[5] That's when I realized that her actors were like singers singing off-key! And once you become aware of hitting a wrong note, you can correct it. In this etude, Keith, you played off-key. You chose a great verb, "to burst his balloon," but you didn't actually do it. You did something else that looked to us like trying "to escape." Maybe if you had followed your impulse to stand up, you might have gotten yourself on track with your verb. That's why I advise actors to follow their impulses while working in an etude. If you don't, you'll never know what might work.

Keith   Oh, Sharon, I've been at this, you know, for a while, and verbs are hard! They just are!

Me   No need to be discouraged, Keith. The hardest thing about teaching Active Analysis, in my opinion, involves helping actors experience what it means to get up and do something at will. I can't get inside your skin and show you how it feels to pursue a verb fully. Actors must learn by trial and error. We, as your audience, can only guide you by sharing what we see as honestly and respectfully as we can. You need to measure your experience against our observations. Then get up and try again. Trust us and try again!

Keith   Yeah, it's true. I sank into the corner of the sofa. I got up and walked away, but I know I can burst his balloon! Let me try it again!

Me   And you will! But I want to reassure you that you are not alone in struggling with verbs. Actors often think that they are doing one thing, but audiences see something else. It happens all the time! The hard reality is that, as actors, we can never see ourselves working. Even on film we can't, because editing and technology mediates what can be seen. We have to trust our audiences as mirrors to gauge what we have accomplished. When your internal experience matches what the audience sees, you can pat yourself on the back! In the next etude, just focus on your verb! Lend yourself to it and let it play you!

Keith   I'll give it another try!

Another Round of Active Analysis

Anisha   I'm sorry to take our conversation in another direction, but I don't get this scene. (*Everyone turns to look at her.*) Why are we doing it? It's an argument about philosophy. So what? Vershinin starts it; Tuzenbach counteracts; and Masha steps in and stops it. So what?

Shari (*As if lecturing her.*)   My dear, Chekhov is a classic!

Anisha   I know that. But all the same, why do it now? What does this have to do with anything that's going on out there in the street?

Me   Anisha, you are right to ask this question. Knebel always insisted that directors and actors ask "Why do this play today?" (Knebel' 1976: 228). With all due respect, Shari, it's never enough to say that a play deserves to be staged because it's a classic. Yes, Anisha, on the surface, this scene obviously depicts a philosophical argument that, given what happened in the last etude, seems relatively uninteresting. (*Anisha smiles.*) But I want to remind you that Chekhov is not always what he seems. There might be something "beyond the obvious," to borrow Efros' words.

Step One: Reading for the Facts Again

Let's go back to the text, rethink the facts, and get to the bottom of "what is really happening in the scene," to quote Efros yet again (2006: 44). Everyone pulls out their texts and reads silently for a moment.

Louisa   Something happened in Act II shortly before this chat that we have forgotten.

Juliana   Wait. Didn't Vershinin tell Masha that he loves her? Oh my, they started their affair in the scene just before this one!

Shari   You're right! (*Laughing at the realization*.) Now Tuzenbach is sitting there, and the lovers have to bite their tongues!

Me   Rose, take a look at the words that Vershinin uses before your first laugh.

Rose (*Skimming through the text*.)   "Day dream;" "life that will come;" "everything will change little by little;" "people are changing before our very eyes;" "there will come a new, happy life;" we are "suffering" now; but there will be "happiness."

Setrak   He is talking to her in code! Making love to her in code!

Rose   Yes, I think so. And later in Act III, they also communicate in code by singing a melody together. This puts a whole different spin on the scene!

Setrak   I'm making love to Masha right under Tuzenbach's nose!

Rose   And he never gets it. But Masha does! That's why she laughs!

Keith   I see. Tuzenbach thinks he's having an honest argument, when he's really the third wheel in a love scene! No wonder he thinks it's hard to argue with them!

Anisha opens her mouth in amazement and everyone laughs.

Louisa   I admit, Anisha, that I didn't see that coming either!

Me   Masha is in alliance with Vershinin. (*Everyone in the room nods*.) Once she figures out what is going on, she starts speaking in code. It's time for another etude to see if our new idea works.

Step Two: A Silent Etude

Let's review the map: Vershinin is still the action, but that action is directed at Masha rather than at Tuzenbach. She allies herself with Vershinin by playing along. Tuzenbach is still the counteraction, because he resists the forward movement of the scene, but he operates from a false assumption about what is at stake in their conversation. Tuzenbach is the only one in the scene who is genuinely philosophizing!

Let's try my favorite sort of etude, a silent one! This time you will investigate the dynamics of the scene without using any words. Rose, Keith, I know that you both have done silent etudes before, so trust yourselves and follow the map using your verbs. Setrak, I am assuming that your work with *expresión corporal* will make this work easy. But let me warn all of you to avoid miming! Don't translate the lines into gestures that substitute for words. Don't point to the window and then to your eye to mean "Look at the window!" Don't beat your breast to show that you are upset! Such movements belong to classical story ballets, like the sequence in Act I of *Sleeping Beauty,* when the evil fairy predicts that the baby princess will grow up, prick her finger, and die! To convey this prediction, the dancer first uses her flexed hand to show how the baby grows from short to tall; then pricks her own finger in warning; then shivers as if the poison were traveling up into her arm; and finally uses the conventional gesture for death, by passing her right fist along the length of her left arm. (*I demonstrate the physical sequence and everyone laughs*.) Such gestures do not belong in drama, but I used to love doing them when I danced.

The point of a silent etude is to treat the scene as if it were unfolding as a "naturally silent" interaction, to borrow Stanislavsky's words (SS III 1990: 404–5). Use the gestures of everyday life and trust that, if you understand what is happening, we will see the scene.

The three actors retreat to their perch on the stage to re-read for the facts, review the map, and adjust their verbs. They signal that they are ready. We take our seats and lean forward in anticipation.

ETUDE 2: SILENT

Setrak enters and sees Rose sitting with Keith on opposite ends of the sofa. Keith twiddles his thumbs and Rose reads a book. Setrak straightens his jacket, smooths his hair, and saunters over to the sofa. As he approaches, Keith springs up, straightens his jacket, and gives Setrak a military salute. Setrak does not respond in kind. Instead, standing behind the sofa, he reaches across its back, his arm nearly brushing Rose's hair, as he offers his hand to Keith in a friendly manner, as if to say that their ranks don't matter here.

Keith hesitates a moment, shakes Setrak's hand, and then salutes again, as if suddenly uncomfortable with relaxing protocols. (The spectators laugh.) Setrak waves his hand in a gesture that tells Keith to relax. Rose closes her book, places it on the coffee table, and smiles at Setrak who smiles back. As she looks at him, he stretches to his tallest height, and salutes Keith, making sure that Rose sees. Clearly, he recalls Masha's admiration for the military. Confused, Keith springs up again to answer the salute, unsure whether rank matters or not in this house. (Laughter from the spectators.)

As Keith salutes, Setrak grins from ear to ear at Rose. Setrak then circles around the corner of the sofa where Rose is sitting, and relaxes into the nearby armchair. Keith, who remains standing, frowns, as if wondering whether he has been undeservedly dismissed. He then sits in the armchair directly across from Setrak and leans forward, as if in challenge.

Setrak now mirrors Keith's posture by leaning forward toward the coffee table. (Geo nods approval). Setrak looks at Keith but traces a finger slowly around the edges of Rose's book. (Anisha inhales in surprise.) Rose laughs at Setrak's suggestive gesture. Keith reacts to her laugh by glaring at her. She shrugs and sits back, sinking heavily into the sofa. Setrak sighs and stands up. In response, Keith also stands.

As if debating Keith, Setrak pulls himself up to his full height, straightens his jacket, and grins from ear to ear. Setrak now circles around Keith and ends up behind the sofa. As Setrak places his hand on the sofa's back near Rose, he continues to look squarely at Keith. Rose looks first at Setrak, then follows his gaze to Keith.

Obviously uncomfortable with being stared at by the two, Keith paces back and forth, pointing one finger at Setrak, while waving his other hand in a broad gesture that encompasses the whole room. Keith ends his pacing at the window, looking to the outside with his back to Rose and Setrak. The entire time that Keith moves, he frowns and shakes his head vigorously as if in disagreement. (Geo lets out a whispered "yes.")

While Keith moves, a game takes place at the sofa. Keeping his eyes on Keith, Setrak walks the fingers of his left hand along the back of the sofa toward Rose. Whenever Keith looks toward them, Setrak gives a wave with his right arm, mirroring Keith's broad waving gesture. Whenever Keith looks away, Setrak gets a bit closer to

Rose. When Keith reaches the window and looks out, Setrak glances quickly around and then kisses Rose's cheek tenderly. Startled, Rose laughs. (Everyone watching laughs and leans forward toward the stage.)

At Rose's laugh, Keith turns abruptly back to face them. (We all laugh more loudly.) *Rose gets up and walks serenely over to the window, where she joins Keith. As she walks, she glances back over her shoulder to smile briefly at Setrak. Keith returns to the armchair at the right of the sofa and sits. He is now positioned between Setrak, who leans upon the back of the sofa, his eyes drifting up to the ceiling as if dreaming, and Rose, who stands with her back to the window. Keith turns to look at Rose, who smiles sweetly at him. He then turns toward Setrak and shakes his head in confusion. Rose saunters back to the sofa, picks up her book, and begins to read, as if nothing much has happened. Keith reacts by sinking into the chair and sighing.*

Everyone laughs and bursts into enthusiastic applause.

Step Three: Assess in Order to Repeat

Hannah   We saw it! We saw the scene with its philosophical argument and its hidden seduction!

Shari   It was a delight!

Geo   Keith was active and completely engaged!

Grigor   I also saw them as military men! I even got that Setrak outranked Keith in the way that they were playing with their salutes and their jackets as if they were in uniforms.

Anisha   That kiss! It took my breath away.

Shari   The event was exactly right when Rose went right back to her reading!

Me   What made this etude unfold so effortlessly?

Setrak   I wanted to change my verb to something that went "beyond the obvious," so I asked Rose what she thought of me trying "to steal a secret kiss."

Rose   I loved the idea and couldn't wait to try it! I'm so glad that this way of working expects us to talk with each other, so that there won't be any disrespectful surprises.

Keith   I know you said you liked my last verb, Sharon, but, since I had trouble doing it, I decided to choose something easier, "to fight back." I got the idea from what you said, Setrak, about what you wanted from me. Remember?

Geo   Yes, yes, I saw it! That was a smart move!

Louisa   But Tuzenbach is such a nice guy in the play. He's no bully, like that other fellow who loves Irina.

Keith   No, no, he's no Solyony. Maybe, "to fight back" is still not it. I'll have to think about that …

Rose   I rethought my verb, too. I wanted to put my alliance with Vershinin front and center, so I chose "to conspire."

Shari   No wonder you let him kiss you!

Setrak   She didn't "let" me. I stole it!

Rose   But it was a very nice kiss!

Me   We are getting close to understanding this scene, but there remains more to investigate.

Yet Another Round of Active Analysis

When we first discussed the scene, Grigor had suggested that maybe Tuzenbach was distracted by Irina, who is sitting in the room with Dr. Chebutykin. Hannah also drew attention to the fact that Fedotik and Rodé play music during the scene. I suggest that we now actively analyze these aspects of the scene.

Step One: Reading for the Facts Again

Me   Let's go back to the play and look at what happens just before the chat we are enacting.

Everyone pulls out their scripts and pages through Act II.

Hannah   After Masha and Vershinin confess their love for one another, they are interrupted by Irina, arriving home from her job, accompanied by Tuzenbach, who always walks her home.

Me   So Vershinin is already on stage. Setrak, you did not need to enter. Go on.

Hannah   Irina complains about her job. "No, I don't like the telegraph office, I don't like it," she says. Then Tuzenbach observes how she has changed. "When you come home from work you seem so young, so unhappy …" He's obviously in love with her, but she seems oblivious to him, only focusing on how tired she is.

Louisa   Maybe she's avoiding a conversation … She doesn't want him to start talking about love.

Hannah   Then they hear "a knock on the floor." Chebutykin's room must be below the parlor, because he knocks on the ceiling to get their attention. Irina asks Tuzenbach to answer by knocking back. Interesting. Yet another coded communication! Does everyone in this household use code? Chebutykin takes it as an invitation to come up and join them and, when he enters, he looks a bit rumpled. The stage direction says that he "took a nap after dinner." He sits at the table and takes a newspaper out of his pocket.

Grigor   Since Act II takes place on the same set as Act I according to Chekhov, the doctor must be at the dining table where Irina's name-day party took place.

Louisa   But before Chebutykin enters, Masha mentions his and their brother's gambling debts. "Yesterday, the doctor and our Andrey lost at the club again. They say, Andrey lost two hundred rubles." Then Irina says, with a laugh, that he hasn't paid his rent in eight months! Money must be tight.

Hannah   Yet the doctor bought Irina an extravagant present for her name-day. This information is like the rumbling of an earthquake. And yet here they all are, assembling for a party ….

Louisa   They laugh too, when Masha makes fun of how "importantly" the doctor sits at the table.

Geo   It's such a strange, understated atmosphere of anxiety mixed with laughter. There's also another "pause," right there. Maybe each of them drift off, thinking about their own troubles.

Rose   Or, in Masha's case, about love …

Me   Let's read the few lines following that pause that lead up to our scene. Anisha and Geo, will you please read Irina and Chebutykin.

Anisha-Irina   Why are you so quiet, Aleksander Ignatyevich?
Setrak-Vershinin   Don't know, I'd like some tea. Tea! Half my life for a glass of tea! I haven't eaten since morning.
Geo-Chebutykin   Irina Sergeyevna!
Anisha-Irina   What do you want?
Geo-Chebutykin   Please come here. *Venez ici*.
Grigor   That's French for "come here." And so, *Irina goes and sits at the table*.
Geo-Chebutykin   I can't do without you.
Grigor   *Irina lays out a game of solitaire on the table*.
Setrak-Vershinin   Well? If they won't serve tea, let's philosophize a bit.

Step Two: A Paraphrase Etude

Let's finish this session with a paraphrase etude that brings all the characters onto the stage and see what happens. The map we used before will suffice. Setrak, Keith, and Rose, get ready for another round! Anisha, please play Irina. Geo, take Chebutykin. Hannah and Louisa, will you help out as Fedotik and Rodé? The seven actors retreat to the back of the hall to re-read the text and plan the etude, while Juliana and Sargis drag a table and chairs up on the stage and place them in the center, above and behind the sofa. We take our seats and Hannah gets her guitar.

ETUDE 3: PARAPHRASE

Anisha and Geo sit at the stage left end of the dining table. Anisha shuffles cards and Geo reads a newspaper. Keith stands at the bottom of the stairs, stage right, trying to catch Anisha's eye. She lays the cards on the table. Geo pats her hand affectionately as he reads. Setrak and Rose sit on either end of the sofa on the floor in front of the stage, their hands folded primly on their laps. He looks at her, then reaches for her hand. She looks back, smiles, but nods towards the others instead of taking his hand. Unable to get Anisha's attention, Keith sighs loudly and crosses to join Setrak and Rose. Setrak rises to shake Keith's hand.

Setrak (*Glancing down at Rose*.)   Well, if they won't serve tea … (*Back to Keith*.) Let's philosophize.

The men sit down simultaneously, Setrak at the end of the sofa farthest from Rose and Keith in the nearby armchair.

Keith (*Eager for something to do.*) Let's. About what?

Setrak (*Straightening his jacket.*) About what ... (*He stands up and circles around to the back of the sofa, all the time looking straight at Keith.*) Let's daydream ... (*A moment of silence, as Setrak glances again at Rose.*) ... about what life will be like in one hundred or two hundred years.

Keith looks toward the window to gather his thoughts. Setrak takes this opportunity to place his left hand on the back of the sofa close to Rose's left shoulder. She looks up at him and then toward Keith, as she relaxes back into the sofa, getting closer to Setrak. The audience laughs.

Keith (*Looking back at Setrak.*) What about it? After us ... (*As if searching for the proper words.*) People will fly in balloons, change the color of their jackets .... Perhaps even discover a sixth sense and ... they'll even develop it. But life will remain essentially the same, hard, happy ... Full of mystery. And after a thousand years, people will still sigh and say "How hard life is." Just like now.

During this speech, Keith leans forward in his chair, his tone gaining conviction and passion. Setrak nods his head, as if listening intently to Keith, while also sliding his left hand along the back of the sofa until it reaches Rose's right shoulder. He now stands directly behind her, and she snuggles even more deeply into the sofa. The audience laughs.

Keith (*Dropping the register of his voice to emphasize his next point.*) Besides that, people will still be afraid of death and not want to die.

Setrak How should I put it? (*Silent for a moment, as if searching for the perfect answer, he leans more heavily into the back of the sofa.*) I think that life must change, little by little. (*He lifts his eyes upward, and simultaneously puts his right hand near Rose's other shoulder, encircling her with his arms without actually touching her. He speaks more and more gently.*) In fact, I see life changing around us, even as we speak. I just think that, as life changes, we may not find happiness for ourselves, but we can certainly work for it now. And maybe our descendants will find it in the future.

During this speech, Rose closes her eyes as if lulled by Setrak's voice, while Keith seems to analyze each word that he hears. The audience too leans forward attentively.

Setrak (*Shifting his attention to Keith, with a more confident tone.*) Well, that's our goal. That's what we're working for, and suffering for. That's ... That's, how should I say it, that's our ... (*Looking up and speaking gently.*) ... happiness.

Rose laughs as she sinks her head back even further into the sofa, as if trying to lean her head against Setrak. Startled by Rose's laugh, Keith stands up abruptly.

Keith What's wrong?

Rose (*Sitting up.*) I don't know all day since morning, I've been laughing.

Setrak (*Still standing with his arms to either side of Rose, Setrak looks Keith squarely in the eye, and speaks as if man to man.*) I went to the same school you did, and

I like to read books. I read them all the time. I just don't know how to pick them. So perhaps I read a lot of books that are unnecessary.

At this moment, Hannah and Louisa enter from the outside door, Hannah strumming a lilting tune with Louisa humming along. They sit on the edge of the stage to the left and rehearse in preparation for the upcoming party.

Setrak (*In a lyrical, lilting tone, as if inspired by the music.*)   The older I get, the more I want to know. And the more I realize how little I know, oh how little! (*Looking lovingly at Rose, who sinks back into the sofa.*) But what is important, my dear, I do know. (*Back to Keith.*) How can I convince you? That we in this lifetime will never need happiness.

Also lulled by the music, Keith looks lovingly at Anisha, who remains absorbed in her card game.

Keith (*Still looking at Anisha.*)   According to you, we shouldn't even dream of happiness, but … But what if I feel happy?

Setrak (*Nodding his head toward Anisha, flatly.*)   You don't!

Sargis laughs out loud in the audience. Keith gets up and walks toward the window, his back to Setrak. Unseen by Keith, Setrak begins to sway back and forth to the music, as Rose hums along. Suddenly, Hannah plays a minor chord and launches into a passionate Gypsy song, "Dark Eyes."[6] Hearing the change in music, Rose seems to recall that she and Setrak are not alone. She stands up abruptly and takes a few steps away from Setrak toward Keith. Setrak responds by straightening his posture and his jacket.

Keith (*At the window, his back still toward Setrak and Rose.*)   Obviously we don't understand each other. So how can I convince you? (*Rose laughs and Keith turns to face her.*) Laugh! (*He now speaks quickly and passionately.*) Not in two or three hundred, not even in a million years, life will remain exactly the same … just as it is. Everything stays constant, following its own laws, which you'll never discover, or … over which you'll never have any control. (*Setrak and Rose both laugh, prompting Keith to advocate his views even more strongly.*) Migratory birds, for example, fly and fly and whatever thoughts go through their minds, big ones or small ones, they still fly. Not knowing where or why. They all still fly. It doesn't matter what philosophers may come along. (*Gesturing first at Setrak, then at Rose, as if they are the philosophers.*) They can philosophize all they want. As long as they fly.

While Keith speaks, Setrak again sways to the music and looks longingly at Rose, who returns his glance without moving.

Rose   But still, where is the meaning?

Keith   The meaning? (*Chuckling as he looks from Rose to Setrak and back again.*) Look! (*Gesturing to the window.*) It's snowing! What meaning does that have?

Keith looks toward Anisha who is still absorbed in her game.

Rose (*Passionately.*)   I believe that one must be a believer, or at least have some beliefs, because … Why would cranes fly? Why would children be born? Why are there stars in the sky? If we don't have these answers, then everything is just empty, just tinsel, just decoration.

Setrak (*As if begging for a kiss.*)   Still it's sad that my youth has passed.

Rose (*As if saying "later."*)   Gogol said it's boring to live on earth, ladies and gentlemen!

Rose turns her back on both men, goes up the stairs and sits down next to Anisha, taking the cards and laying out a game of solitaire for herself. Geo pats Anisha's hand. Hannah and Louisa continue to play and sing.

Keith (*Raising his voice so that Rose as well as Setrak can hear.*)   And I say, it's hard to argue with you, lady and gentleman.

We in the audience laugh and explode in enthusiastic applause

Step 3: Assess in Order to Repeat

Shari   At one point, I thought that Tuzenbach figured out what was actually going on, but was too much of a gentleman to say anything. It was towards the end when Rose and Setrak were looking at each other. Keith, I want to see the whole play with you in this role.

Keith   Wow, I would love to do this play! I changed my verb again. Louisa's comment earlier made me think that fighting back was too much like the mean-spirited Solyony, who kills Tuzenbach in a duel. When I thought more about it, I realized that Tuzenbach's problem is thinking that he's in a debate. When he gets mixed signals from Vershinin and Masha, he's confused. I decided that the only way to handle the situation was "to tell my truth" whatever anyone else says. They have their truth, that's fine, and I have mine. This time, as I told my truth, I started to feel that Vershinin and I weren't so very different, despite our different views. We are both human beings, trying to give and get some love …

Sargis (*Laughing.*)   And neither of you are getting what you want. Irina won't give Tuzenbach the time of day and Vershinin couldn't even steal a kiss this time! By the way, Setrak, I liked it better this way. I was on the edge of my seat the whole time, cheering you on.

Setrak   Keith was trying so passionately to get his point across that I thought he'd never turn his back. Then, when I was about to move in, Rose stood up! I couldn't succeed.

Rose   Well, Masha will happily kiss you … Just not in public.

Everyone laughs

Juliana   What fascinated me is how Rose and Keith reacted to Setrak's words so differently. They heard the same thing at the same time, but from the expressions on their faces I knew that their interpretations were radically different. In fact, Rose seemed as enamored with Setrak's voice as with his words …

Rose   … I felt like I was conspiring with his lovely voice.

Juliana   And Keith was analyzing Setrak's ideas.

Keith   Yup, if I am going "to say my truth," I realized I needed to understand his too!

Juliana   That kind of thing happens all the time in our lives. We say one thing and our listeners hear something else!

Me   Another new discovery about Chekhov's play!

Grigor   I want to talk about adding Anisha, Geo, Hannah and Louisa to the mix. The acoustics of the scene were so much richer. Even though Keith's verb was focused on Setrak, you could see how aware he was of Anisha, and how unaware of him she was! That was as heartbreaking as Setrak's cozying up to Rose was funny. Having Anisha there made me think about how Vershinin's and Masha's relationship contrast with that of Tuzenbach's and Irina's.

Sargis   In fact, that contrast made me laugh, when Setrak told Keith "you're not happy."

Hannah   Realistically speaking, Louisa and I were rehearsing a song for the party, so we did not really care about anything else, but the actor in me got a kick out of the fact that we were inadvertently underscoring the scene! Then when I saw Setrak and Rose flirting, I couldn't help commenting on it with that Gypsy song!

Rose   Your first tune made me feel very mellow as I looked at Setrak. I loved listening.

Setrak   It made me want to dance, and so I swayed in time with the music!

Sargis (*Laughing*.)   Maybe you should have invited her to dance. Maybe you could have stolen a kiss that way.

Setrak   Maybe …

Rose   But the Gypsy song embarrassed me, because I understood that Hannah was making fun of our flirtation.

Me   Anisha, Geo, Hannah and Louisa deepened our experience of this little scene. So often in scene study classes, actors focus on the speaking characters and cut those without lines. We did that when we started working on this scene, but if we had ended there, we would have missed the "acoustics" in the scene, to use Grigor's word. I remember once working on the scene in which Ophelia is sent by her father, Polonius, and King Claudius to confront Hamlet in order to find out whether love for her has caused his recent madness. Actors often treat this scene from Act III scene 1 of Shakespeare's iconic play as the break-up of two lovers, but in fact it involves an ensemble of four with Polonius and Claudius as unspeaking spies. Our etude began with Polonius giving Ophelia her marching orders — "walk you here" and "read on this book" — then literally pushing her into the room to wait for Hamlet. This prelude made clear Ophelia's position as a young woman caught between love and duty. As the etude unfolded, Ophelia continually shifted her attention between Hamlet and those who watched, further embodying her difficult situation. Finally, after Hamlet leaves, her concluding words to Polonius and Claudius sounded very different to us than when we had earlier read the text. She seemed to be speaking, not only about Hamlet, but also about herself, when she described "the observed of all observers," with a "noble mind o'erthrown," being "quite, quite down!" We, who watched, knew in a flash that the duality of the actor's interpretation of these words predicted Ophelia's later turn to madness. The scene became all the more chilling, when Claudius callously dismissed her by concluding that Hamlet's "affections do not that way tend" and that "what he spake [...] was not like madness." He had seen only Hamlet and missed the enormity of Ophelia's experience. Such are the discoveries that can come from the embodied analysis of a scene through an etude.[7]

Grigor   In that case, your actors discovered Ophelia's deep tragedy. In this case, we discovered Chekhov's sense of humor.

Me   To hear that makes me happy! This little chat is a brilliant example of Chekhov's comic sensibility, and yet the scene is easily overlooked. At first read, you might think it creates a realistic atmosphere and not much more. Or you might see it as one of those esoteric and impossibly boring passages of Russian philosophizing that people erroneously associate with Chekhov. (*Anisha nods "yes."*) By using Active Analysis we took Knebel's advice and "brushed the dust off" this scene, to find a comic gem.

Juliana   I want to compliment the actors on getting so close to Chekhov's lines. Did you memorize the text?

Setrak   No, we had read it for the facts so many times, that the words were there in my head when I needed them. (*Keith and Rose nod in agreement.*)

Me   In three rounds of Active Analysis, you were able to uncover the interactive dynamics in this scene successfully. The next step would be to memorize the text, set the blocking, and polish your performance, but it is now too late to take this final step together. Yet, I feel confident that you can.

The actors nod and start to clear the set, clean the table, and gather their things. They chatter happily, patting each other on the backs for a job well done. I lock the door until next time, and shoo Shari into my car.

Notes

1. My translation is from the Russian transcript.
2. All quotations from *Three Sisters* are from A. Chekhov (2009: 168–241 with the Act II excerpt on 196–8). Stanislavsky first staged Chekhov's plays without Active Analysis, but used it in the 1930s to revisit them at the Opera-Dramatic Studio. The Active Analysis in this lesson, however, is from my Studio and does not represent Stanislavsky's work.
3. The first to write about Chekhov's "plays of indirect action" was Magarshack (1952: 159–73).
4. The italics are Efros'.
5. Personal observation at the *MetodiFestival* (Tuscany, Italy), October 2008.
6. A version of this song, *Ochii chernyi*, is sung by Yevgeniia Grebyonki, accessed on March 14, 2021 at https://www.youtube.com/watch?v=dE-AjoelWBM.
7. This etude took place at the University of Southern California, in *Acting Shakespeare* (Fall 2017) with the following cast: Ophelia—Jordan Medina; Hamlet—Charles Junkins; Polonius—Joseph Harlan; Claudius—Michael O'Malley.

Lesson 4 Rehearsing a Play through Active Analysis— Johnson

Prelude

It is ten in the morning on a Saturday and I am pacing anxiously back and forth near the door to the parking lot. All the actors have arrived, except for Keith, who has generously offered to drive our playwright-in-residence, Joan Eyles Johnson, to the Studio in the truck that he keeps at the airport. The table is set for breakfast and the actors are milling about the hall, balancing cups of coffee and plates of food. They chat noisily about their weeks, recent events in the news, and even Active Analysis. We cannot begin without Joan, because she has written a new play for our session today. Joan lives in a mountain cabin to the north and Keith took an overnight flight to make sure that they would be on time, but any number of things could have gone wrong.

My mind drifts back to my first meeting with Joan. Our Studio was then meeting in the basement of St. Mary's of the Angels, a small gem of a church, built in the Spanish style. Its Anglican parish was founded in 1918 in a store-front by Father Neal Dodd, who made it his mission to prod film studios into depicting religious ceremonies respectfully. Over the years, Dodd not only consulted with directors (including Cecil B. DeMille on *The Ten Commandments*), but also acted the role of cleric in over 300 films (among them *Mr. Smith Goes to Washington* starring Jimmy Stewart). By 1930 everyone who was anyone in Hollywood (from studio heads like Samuel Goldwyn and Louis B. Mayer to stars like Mary Pickford and her husband Douglas Fairbanks, Sr.) had contributed to the building of the church, which is now a Hollywood Landmark.[1] I still remember seeing Pickford's wedding portrait in the hallway leading down to the basement. We were privileged to work there because one of our actors, V. C. Pat Jones, Jr., was the parish deacon and later its priest.

One evening, a woman with a round face and pixie haircut appeared as if from nowhere. She attended St. Mary's, had heard about our group, loved actors, and wondered if she might watch for a while. Of course, I said, actors need audiences! She then handed me an envelope, admitting that she also wrote plays. "Oh dear," I thought, "would I find myself in the awkward situation of having to say something tactful at the next session?" But I soon learned that her diffident manner conceals an extraordinary career. She is an award-winning writer of poetry, fiction, and more than forty plays.[2] Her awards include the Maude Adams, the Robert-Shiras, TheatreWorks, the Phelan (seven times), and the 2016 Ernest Hemingway Prize for Short Fiction. Her full-length play *The Magic Hand* was a top pick from a field of 5,500 entries in the CBS/Dramatist Guild contest. She founded the Arrowhead Readers Theatre in San Jose. She produced and hosted *Joan's Show* (televised by Teleprompter/Viacom), where she interviewed major American performers and activists including Johnny Carson, Joan Baez, Johnny Mathis, and the legendary Jazz musician Cab Calloway. Now she writes and supports other writers in her cabin in the woods. All these facts emerged higgledy-piggledy because, as Joan also once told me, "I have never been organized or made much of my writing career."[3]

The minutes tick by—five, six, seven ... Finally, at quarter past the hour I hear Keith's truck pull into the parking lot. Louisa and I rush out to greet Joan. She clutches at her jacket with one hand and holds onto a worn leather tote with the other, as Keith ushers her toward us. "Look who I found along the way!" Keith jokes. "What a treat to have a chauffeur drive me down the mountain!" says Joan. "And later, up the mountain too," Keith reassures her. "I don't want you handling those sharp turns in the dark."

As we enter the hall, Hannah lets out a squeal of joy. "Oh my, it's Joan. Rose, look who's here!" "Hannah and I did a play of Joan's not long ago, called *Dancing to the Epistle*," Rose tells Setrak as she introduces him to Joan. "Yes," Hannah adds, "the hardest but best experience ever!" "You know," Joan says after taking a good look at Setrak, "I wrote that play for two brothers, and when Sharon asked Rose and Hannah to do it as sisters, I loved it that way too! But, I can also see you in it. Maybe with Grigor." Setrak leads Joan by the arm to the chair next to mine, as the others find their places in our usual circle. We can now begin!

The Lie (2020) by Joan Eyles Johnson: The Play as It Makes Itself Felt

Scene studies, like ours on Shakespeare and Chekhov, are wonderful opportunities to master the basics of Active Analysis. But to go further with it, we need to tackle a full play. Two aspects, in particular, are impossible to explore through scenes taken out of context: the way that Active Analysis conceives of a play as a chain of events, and how actors can use that chain to develop dynamic and interesting characters. I have chosen a new play by Joan, *The Lie*, to serve as a vehicle to explore these next steps in Active Analysis for two reasons.

First, I wanted a "microdrama," to borrow John H. Muse's term for extremely short plays that explore the nature and compression of time in theatre. Such plays date back to the late nineteenth century, when symbolists like Maurice Maeterlinck inspired writers like Chekhov and directors like Stanislavsky and Meyerhold to break away from realism. In the twentieth century, writers as different as Tennessee Williams and Samuel Beckett experimented with brevity, while director Jon Jory celebrated the ten-minute play in annual festivals at the Actors Theatre of Louisville. More recently, playwrights Caryl Churchill and Suzan Lori-Parks have challenged themselves to write cycles of microdramas (Muse 2017). Joan's play is at once complex enough and short enough to offer you a fair idea of the benefits of using Active Analysis to prepare a full play within the time available to us.

Second, I wanted something entirely new. So far, we have been using Active Analysis "to clean the dust of time" off classics (Knebel' 1967: 485). But more than time affects the way we approach published and well-known plays. We often bring ready-made interpretations to them, derived from seeing productions, reading reviews, studying them in literature classes, discussing them with friends, or working on them in other circumstances. Stanislavsky felt that such "preconceptions, thrust upon us by the opinions of others," are "dangerous" to creative work. "Let actors first feel the play as the play makes itself felt!" (*SS* IV 1991: 49; 50).[4] *(Hannah looks at me with a challenging smile on her face.)* Of course, those of us who know other plays by Joan will bring that familiarity to this one. But even so, a new play offers us the best chance to approach it without preconceptions.

This morning, we'll meet Joan's play, exchange first impressions, and begin to read for the facts. Along the way, I will deliver three mini-lectures to fill in knowledge that you will need for today's work. In the afternoon, the active analysis itself will begin in earnest. We will dig deeper into the text and move forward toward performance. Be prepared for an exciting day's journey.

Joan (*Pulling a packet of typed pages out of her tote and laughing.*)   I was surprised when Sharon told me she liked this ugly little play. I started with a vision of a man in a coma, lying in a shroud, neither alive nor dead ....

Me   Don't say anything more, Joan. Following Stanislavsky's and Nemirovich-Danchenko's lead, I would like you to read *The Lie* to us, so that the actors can fall in love with the entire play before falling in love with any particular role.

Grigor   I learned somewhere that Chekhov read *The Cherry Orchard* to the Moscow Art Theatre company before their rehearsals started, and the actors fell so much in love with the play, that they didn't care how large or small their roles would be, so long as they were part of the production. Imagine that! Joan, you will be our Chekhov.

Joan (*Aghast.*)   You want me to read?

Me (*Reassuring her.*)   Don't worry. Just read the play as it formed itself in your head. We promise to listen attentively, because, as Stanislavsky also advised, "it is important for actors to see a play first from the author's point of view" (*SS* IV 1991: 51).

Joan   Well, all right ... (*Louisa hands Joan a bottle of water, as the rest of us sit back to listen. Some look straight at her and others close their eyes. Joan begins.*) "The Lie. SCENE 1: A hospital room. Ty labors to breathe under a white shroud that almost covers his face. His eyes are closed. Rafe, on old man, sits quietly beside the bed for a few seconds, then speaks softly, afraid to be heard. RAFE: You can't hear me. Can you? (He looks around suspiciously.) Nobody's here but us. Ty. Ty. (Whispers.) Can you hear me? (Sighs.) Lilly's doing fine ...*"

As Joan continues, I invite my readers to read The Lie *as printed in the Appendix.*

Joan (*Continuing on to the last page.*)   "POLLY: I'm leaving now. I'm locking you in here. I can't trust you for one minute. You are a demon-lover. You'll be letting them in here the minute my back is turned. *Polly exits and we hear the key in the lock. Lilly weakly gets up and turns off the music, sits down and starts to rock slowly, wiping the tears from her eyes.* END OF PLAY."

Everyone sits quietly for a long moment. Then suddenly lavish words like "beautiful," "awesome," "magical," and "amazing" fill the room.

Me   Thank you, Joan. (*Turning to the actors.*) It is now our turn to share our first impressions with each other. What makes you say "beautiful," "awesome," and "amazing"?

Juliana   It's "beautiful," because it's ... (*Searching for another adjective.*) It's sharp.

Me   What does "sharp" mean to you?

Juliana   First the play goes in one direction and then turns sharply in another. For example, at the start we think that Rafe will put Ty out of his misery in a mercy killing, but at the end the hospital calls to say that Ty is coming out of his coma!

Hannah   That's exactly why I said "amazing." The play amazes, that is to say, surprises us at every turn. For example, Lilly's daughter, Polly, grows up to be a religious fanatic! Nothing prepares us for that! Polly would be a great character to play!

Grigor   I said "awesome," because Joan packs so much human experience into such a tiny package, it left me in awe of her talent. For instance, Ty, Rafe and Lilly are old, but in scene 3 they transform to their younger selves in the flash of an eye! What an awesome acting challenge!

Geo   That transformation is "magical." I think Joan is writing magic realism.

Keith (*His hand on his chin, in deep thought.*)   I do like the play. Thank you, Joan. But I have a question! Actually I have a lot of questions, but I don't want to sound stupid, so I'll ask just one. Is something fishy going on between Rafe and Lilly? Help me out here, guys. Polly is Lilly's daughter. I get that! But what's the time-line? We start in the present with Ty in a coma. A coma? How did that happen? But I'm getting off track from my main question. In the middle of the play, we go back in time to Ty coming home from the war. He's exhausted, and believe you me, having been in the marines, I know what that feels like. You fall asleep on your feet while talking. Naturally, Ty just wants to pick up where he left off. So he's coming home to his wife, expecting everything to be the way it was, and suddenly he's a father! He was gone "almost two years," right? In the navy, right?

Joan (*Nods.*)   I always loved the look of a white dress uniform on a good looking man!

Keith   Lilly tells him that their baby is two weeks shy of one year old. So, do the math! Nine months for the pregnancy plus one more year, give or take a couple of weeks. That's about three months short of the time Ty's been deployed. It doesn't add up.

Louisa (*Offering a hint.*)   What's the title of the play?

Keith (*A long pause.*)   Are you suggesting that Rafe's the father and that Lilly and Rafe lie to Ty about the baby?

Anisha   I think so. In fact, I think Lilly also lies, when she says that Rafe's been home for only a month. She says that twice!

Grigor   The lady doth protest too much, methinks!

Keith   Home? From where?

Anisha   From what Ty says in the third scene, I think both men shipped off to war. Also, in the first scene Rafe talks like a soldier about "passing the ammunition."

Louisa   But no one ever says that Rafe went to war. Lilly says that he came home earlier than Ty. Maybe Rafe was away on a job, like the one in Albany that he mentions in scene 3. In any case, he could not have been gone for long, because Lilly says that when she was pregnant he "helped me every step of the way." I think Rafe stayed with her, while Ty was at war.

Anisha   My point exactly. If Rafe was back for only a month, he could not have been with Lilly during her pregnancy. Both those statements cannot be true. Put that together with the fact that the baby is staying with Rafe's mother and I think it's pretty clear that Rafe is the father!

Rose What if Lilly slept with both men close to the same time? If so, she might not know who's the father. I remember Lilly referring to Polly as "my" daughter, but never as "ours."

Keith No, Rose, the math is off by three months, two at the very least. (*Rose shrugs*.)

Juliana With Lilly and Rafe lying to Ty in the flashback, there's irony in Ty saying that "nothing's changed" and joking with Lilly about her being faithful. Everything has changed! She's slept with his best friend!

Shari Are you saying that Ty is being ironic?

Juliana No, Joan is being ironic. (*Joan laughs and nods*.) Ty doesn't seem to get it at first, but the audience does. When Ty thanks Rafe for taking care of Lilly, he sounds genuinely grateful. When he leaves to go see the baby, he seems happy.

Rose But somewhere along the way, he must have figured it out, because near the end of the play, Lilly reminds Rafe that Ty never wanted Polly to live with them!

Juliana I guess this play is not particularly beautiful, is it?

Hannah But it is "amazing." In fact, given Keith's reaction, I would also say it's "mysterious." Take Polly, for example. We know almost nothing about her. If Ty didn't want her to live with them, where did she grow up? With Rafe's mother? Does she know who her father is? Was she ever loved? All we really know is that she has become a religious fanatic. When she sees a vase of flowers in the last scene, she accuses her mother of letting a demon into the house. She insists that her mother play religious music to purge the evil. Then she locks the door to keep the demons out! Wait … (*She turns her head to the side, thinking.*) Rafe has a key. He can come and go as he pleases. He probably brings Lilly flowers. Maybe he's the demon! Does Polly suspect that Rafe is Lilly's demon lover?

Sargis And here's another mystery … When Ty finally guesses that the baby is not his, why doesn't he confront his wife and best friend?

Geo He's in a coma, Sargis! He can't confront anybody about anything!

Sargis (*Shrugs*.) He could have done it before the coma. Ty probably tried to look the other way for a while, but eventually he banned Polly from his home.

Geo No wonder Polly has gone mad!

Sargis The coma does keep Ty quiet. You may have something there, Geo.

Me Look at what has just happened, Keith's question inspired everyone to dig into the puzzle of "what is really happening" (Efros 2006: 44) in this complex little play.

Keith I don't think we've gotten to the bottom of it yet. By the way, Joan, what war is it?

Joan Any war you like—World War II, the Korean or Vietnam war, Desert Storm, Afghanistan, the Ukrainian war—you name it!

Keith I get it. All wars separate lovers and friends and all soldiers who make it home have to pick up the broken pieces of their lives.

Me You are now moving on to the question of what this play might mean, so it's time for the first of my mini-lectures.

Three Overarching Perspectives on the Play (*Sverkhzadacha*)

Stanislavsky and Knebel used a single word to describe three different points of view on any given play: the author's, the ensemble's, and the role's. Because the Russian term shifts emphasis when used in these different contexts, it is difficult to translate with a single English word. *Sverkh* means "super" in the sense of "overarching" and *zadacha* refers to the "problem" in any given scene that the character confronts, as you will recall (Lesson 2). I could translate the Russian word as "super-problem." Elizabeth Reynolds Hapgood and Jean Benedetti respectively render it as "super-objective" and "supertask," reflecting their translation choices for *zadacha*.[5] However, none of these options make the meaning particularly clear. They sound to me like professional jargon, and run counter to Stanislavsky's stated desire to speak to actors in plain language. As Knebel put it, "one shouldn't stifle the actor with terms, [… but] simply follow the logic of the analysis" (Zverova 2021: 112). Therefore, rather than use a confounding term, I usually ask appropriate questions: What is the play about? Why should we stage it for today's audiences? How does each character develop over the course of the play? Nonetheless, the three perspectives named by *sverkhzadacha* are valuable when rehearsing a full play.

First, the author's *sverkhzadacha* refers to a play's central meanings or themes. For example, when Keith wonders whether *The Lie* explores the impact of war on all soldiers who return home, he is speculating about Joan's perspective on her work. Personally, I think we will find other themes more central to her play, but that is as yet to be determined.

Second, the ensemble's *sverkhzadacha* refers to the meanings or themes communicated to the audience by the play's production, which may or may not coincide with the author's intentions. In the professional theatre, this second perspective is often referred to as the director's concept. Knebel believed every performance reinterprets the text for its own culture and times. She vividly recalls a recording of a single sonnet by Shakespeare as performed by actors from different decades. Each performance was unique from the others and "bore the imprints of its own time" (Knebel' 1976: 276). Thus, she felt that answering a single foundational question—Why stage this play today?—is essential to ensure the success of any given production (Knebel' 1976: 41). Before this day is over, I will ask you: "Why stage *The Lie* today?"

Finally, Stanislavsky and Knebel also speak of each role as having its own *sverkhzadacha*. In this case, the actor seeks an overarching problem with which the character grapples over the course of the play. This perspective zeros in on how characters change as they journey from the play's beginning to its end. Perhaps, you refer to this notion as the character's arc. If the character is central to the play, as is Lilly in *The Lie*, the role's *sverkhzadacha* might well coincide with the author's and the ensemble's, but this coincidence may not hold for secondary characters, like the nurse, who deal with problems that are less central to the author's main concerns.

The Author's Perspective

Me But I am getting ahead of myself. We will tackle the role's and the ensemble's *sverkhzadacha* later. For now, let's go back to the author's perspective. Are there themes other than the one raised by Keith in *The Lie*?

Everyone looks at Joan.

Joan   As I said, I began to write with the image of a man in a coma, neither alive nor dead. To be honest, I can't say much more than that.

Anisha   Maybe Ty represents everyone who lives but does not feel alive.

Louisa   Do you mean he's a kind of "every man"?

Anisha   Or, how about this? Science knows very little about what a person in a coma experiences, so maybe the coma suggests that none of us can ever know what's happening inside another person.

Me   You seem to be pulling ideas out of the air. What do the facts of the play suggest?

Juliana   I think that the coma is an image of being trapped and that all the characters are trapped in some way. Ty is in the coma. Lilly is locked in her home. Rafe seems paralyzed because he doesn't make any actual decisions, whether it's to leave Lilly or to put Ty out of his misery. And Polly? She's trapped in a world of fantasy demons. Everyone in this play except for the nurse is in a kind of coma.

Keith   Maybe, but, as I said earlier, I connect with the way the war impacts these people. When Ty was away, Lilly was desperately alone. She took comfort from her husband's best friend. What she did may not have been right, but it is understandable.

Setrak   What about the love triangle at the heart of this play? I think the play is about love. Lilly lies about her affair, because she loves Ty. She doesn't want to hurt him. That's also why she tells Rafe that their affair is over. Rafe goes along with her lie, because he also loves his best friend. That's why he visits Ty in the hospital day after day. And Rafe definitely loves Lilly. Even though he tells her that he will move away in order to end their affair, he is still there taking care of her in their old age. As for Ty, he doesn't confront his wife and best friend, because he loves them. He doesn't want to risk losing either one of them. In my opinion, this is a play about lies told out of love!

Keith   Wow I see that! And setting it against the hate of war makes the three of them all the more desperate to hold onto their love for each other!

Joan   War and love! That's interesting. As I said, I started with the image of the coma, but, while I was writing, I also kept asking myself "who is the better lover—the man who marries Lilly and goes off to war or the man who stays with her while her husband is away?" I think a man who fights for his country is a hero and so is a man who stays with a pregnant woman. In any case, I thought of Lilly as the force that draws them all together. I also thought of the men's relationship as male bonding.

Keith   When I was in Iraq, I certainly felt one with my men.

Geo   But Ty and Rafe have not served together. They are best friends, but they don't fight side by side. (*Keith shrugs*.)

Anisha   I see what Joan means about both men being heroes. But I think Lilly is also a hero. She's strong and admirable when she tells Rafe that she is still Ty's wife. She doesn't cry or whine or resort to anger. She reminds me of my grandmother, whom I very much admire.

Rose Don't confuse your grandmother's story with Lilly's. She stays married to Ty, but she never stops seeing Rafe. That's two-timing, if you ask me, and that's not heroic! (*Anisha shrugs.*)

Juliana (*Jumping into the conversation.*) This play is not all hearts and flowers and heroic sentiments. Love is only part of the equation. Don't forget the lies! I think that the play is about how lies trap you. Lilly says something about consequences ....

Joan Yes, it's in scene 2. (*Reading.*) "We have suffered enough. Look at us! A life of irony. A life of one big lie and all its consequences."

Setrak Polly's madness is definitely one of those consequences.

Juliana Like I said earlier, they are all trapped.

Setrak Polly is more than trapped. She is the most damaged character in the play. I would say that she is both the subject and object of her parents' lie.

Hannah I see her as the embodiment of the lie and its consequences. She also remains outside the triangle of love. In fact, her birth threatens to break the triangle apart by exposing the truth. No wonder she felt unloved as a child. What happens to her proves that lies, even when told with good intentions, cause real damage. This play is like a moral tale.

Geo But Polly is not just a victim. It's she, not the lie, who locks Lilly in and Rafe out. Polly is like a jailer, who imprisons her mother.

Shari And don't forget the nurse in the first scene. She's a kinder version of a warden, who's there to enforce the rules.

Geo Two jailers—the kindly one starts the play and the villainous one ends it! It's like a fairy tale! Who will undo the spell that entraps them all? Will it be Ty, our sleeping beauty, when he comes to?

Joan (*Laughing out loud.*) Fairy tales often resemble nightmares, you know. They are full of ugliness too.

Anisha I'm sorry to shake things up, but we're still missing something. Everyone lies all the time. Lying is a normal part of life. We lie to others to get out of things, to save our skins, to flatter people, and to be kind. We lie to ourselves about our failings, so as not to damage our self-esteem or overturn our illusions about ourselves. The truth is that we all lie all the time! This play might as well be titled *The Truth about Lies*.

Joan I find your conversation very interesting, because you are raising serious questions and I think that is exactly what plays need to do.

Me You are kind, Joan, but let me intervene. While intrinsically interesting, this conversation is far too general to uncover the author's perspective on the play, its *sverkhzadacha*. We are circling around a lot of possibilities—lies, love, war—but we need more facts to get any farther, so it's time to move beyond first impressions and start digging into the text.

Grigor (*Rubbing his hands together in anticipation.*) Reading for the facts, *razbor*!

Joan hands each of us a hard copy of her play, and the room goes quiet as we read. I invite my readers to join us by rereading The Lie *in the Appendix.*

The Balance of Facts and Open Clues in *The Lie*

While re-reading *The Lie*, I found myself considering the balance between what we can know for sure about these characters and what remains shrouded in mystery. Therefore, I propose that we take a closer look at how Joan manipulates facts and open clues in her microdrama. I have long been fascinated by the different ways that playwrights treat the relationship between facts and open clues. Shakespeare provides a myriad of facts, encoded in both words and rhythms, that make performing him relatively easy. Open clues are rare. Thus, his plays come close to operatic scores in their careful directing of the actors' performances through verse. In contrast, Chekhov's facts are often elusive, demanding actors pay close attention to everything in order to understand what is going on. But, even so, he plants enough facts in the text to unlock the secrets of his plays. When it comes to Joan Eyles Johnson, she revels in open clues. No matter how closely we read *The Lie* we cannot know for certain why Ty is in a coma, what cult Polly has joined, or …

Joan I consider myself an acolyte of Harold Pinter,[6] and, like him, I love including more questions than answers.

Shari (*Harumphing*.) You sure leave a lot to the imagination in this play, Joan.

Joan The only question I might be able to answer involves Polly. She is based on a street kid, who became an addict by the age of thirteen. To kick her habit, she turned to religion. She replaced heroin with fanaticism. I remember visiting her once, when she started playing a recording of music from her church. Then she started chanting along with it and worked herself into a trance as she clapped her hands and cursed the devil. (*A pause.*) That really happened.

Geo (*Clasping his hands in front of him and leaning toward Joan.*) How wonderful, then, to have you here with us, Joan! You can answer all our questions as we go.

Joan (*Bursting into laughter.*) No, Geo. I said I can tell you only about Polly. Authors are the worst people to ask about their plays. Most of us don't know where the stuff comes from. My plays are products of my experience and observations, of course, but when I'm writing I feel like my characters just fall off the edge of the page …. (*Geo scrunches his eyebrows together as if he can't believe what he's hearing.*) My dear, the author is the worst person to ask.

Grigor Fair enough. Here's what I think. *The Lie* covers decades in just ten minutes. No wonder there are so many open clues! It could not be otherwise! Searching for reasons beyond this pragmatic one seems a waste of time.

Me That is too easy an explanation, Grigor. Active Analysis has taught me to look harder. If, after digging deep, we find nothing more than the pragmatic reason you offer, then so be it. But, if we don't ask why a play is composed as it is, we might miss something of real importance. My instinct tells me that we need to ask another question about *The Lie*: Do the majority of open clues fall into the realm of story or do they pertain to the plot? But before you say anything, I need to give my second mini-lecture.

The Formalist Concepts of Story and Plot

You will recall that I introduced the terms "story" (*fabula*) and "plot" (*siuzhet*), while speaking about the influence of Russian Formalism on Stanislavsky's thinking (Lesson 1). The leading Dostoyevsky scholar, Robert Belknap, defines the two terms in this way: "The *fabula* [story] arranges the events in the world the characters inhabit; the *siuzhet* [plot] arranges the events in the world the reader encounters in the text" (Belknap 2016: 17).

When applied to drama, the "story" (or "backstory," if you prefer the word used in cinema circles) refers broadly to everything that happens and has happened to the characters in their fictional world. For example, Tennessee Williams' story in *A Streetcar Named Desire* (1947) includes the way that Stella and Blanche grew up in the South on their family's plantation and all that that connotes; how Stella moved away, met, and married Stanley; his Polish background and his time in the military; Stanley's and Stella's lovemaking and the moment that she realized she was pregnant; how Blanche stayed on the plantation after Stella left; Blanche's marriage to a gay man, who committed suicide after she inadvertently found him in bed with his lover; how she desperately tried to hang on to the plantation as its debts mounted; the many deaths in the family that further drained her resources; the bank's foreclosure on the estate; how Blanche numbed her pain through sexual encounters with strangers and young boys; how she was fired from her teaching job due to her scandalous behavior; etc. Much about this story becomes clear when the characters speak about their pasts and share memories.

In contrast, "plot" refers only to what happens within the play itself. Put into the language of Active Analysis, the "plot" is the chain of events that actors perform when the play is staged. For example, Williams limits the plot for *A Streetcar Named Desire* to the five months from May through September when Stella and Stanley await the birth of their first child and Blanche, homeless and jobless, stays with them. The specific events that occur on stage move from Stella's welcome of Blanche; through Stanley's rape of her, while Stella gives birth in the hospital; to Blanche's forcible commitment to a psychiatric hospital. I could, of course, mention other events that occur in the play, but I think that this broad summary is enough to give you the idea.

While formalists presume that stories unfold haphazardly and chronologically (as do our lives), they conceive of plots as constructs, made by artists who select and arrange details from the story in meaningful structures and patterns. As Belknap explains, "plots [are] the purposeful arrangements of experience" that arise from the artist's "need to select and omit [in order to create] peculiarly vivid and examinable form[s]" (Belknap 2016: 4; 7). When applied to drama, plot refers not only to what happens in the play, but also to the exact sequence (or chain) in which the selected events occur during performance. While the chain might be chronological, causal, logical, or realistic, it need not be. A plot can ignore life's natural laws because it is art. It needs only to respond to the playwright's creative goals and aesthetics. For example, in *Betrayal* (1978) Harold Pinter tells the story of an adulterous affair through a plot that moves backwards in time, starting two years after the affair ends, when the ex-lovers meet in a pub. The last scene depicts their first flirtation. This inverted sequence allows the audience to consider the beginning of the affair with the wisdom of hindsight, a perspective on the story that the characters, who live their lives in normal time, cannot share.

If one assumes, as did the formalists, that the inclusion and exclusion of details in a given work of art are intentional, then what we don't know is as important as what we do. Similarly, if one assumes, as did the formalists, that meaning emerges from the specific ways in which artists construct their plots, then we can probe the author's perspective by paying close attention to how the plot is made, or in other words, how the story gets told.

Story and Plot in *The Lie*

Me   With this information in mind, how would you describe the story in Joan's play?

Geo   Let me take a jab at it! It goes back at least forty years. Rafe and Ty were best friends and both are doctors. Maybe they met in medical school.

Me   No speculating, please. Stick to the facts.

Geo   All right, we don't know how they met, only that they are colleagues and friends, as Rafe says in scene 1. The story also includes Lilly marrying Ty; the start of the war; Ty joining the Navy and Rafe maybe signing up for military service … Sorry, that's not for certain. We only know that he was away from home for a while and got back before Ty did. Going on, Lilly slept with Rafe while Ty was deployed; Rafe stayed with Lilly during her pregnancy; and then when Ty gets back, Rafe pushes Lilly to tell Ty that he is the father of Polly. The story also includes the daughter's upbringing; Ty's decision that Polly should not live with him and Lilly; Polly's decision to join a cult; her taking care of her aging mother. Somewhere in there Ty falls into a coma and Lilly sells whatever she can to support his hospital care. I must say Grigor is right, Joan. You do pack a lot of human experience into your microdrama. The story is extensive.

Sargis   At the same time, there are a lot of gaps in information. To answer your earlier question, Sharon, I think the majority of the open clues fall into the realm of the story. The coma is the best example. We know virtually nothing about it. We don't know if Ty had a car accident or a stroke. We don't know if he was alone or with others when he fell sick.

Me   If we assume that Joan intended that the coma be a fact surrounded by mystery, then we can ask why she wanted it that way. If Ty's coma had resulted from a car accident with Lilly or Rafe driving, blame would become a factor. If Ty had had a stroke while asleep or at work, it might invoke a theme about fate or luck or stress or something like that. But Joan leaves these realistic concerns entirely out of her play. Juliana may be correct, when she calls the coma an image of how lies affect people's lives, because the very fact that we know so little about it strikes me as important. I also think that Geo was sensing something crucial, when he called the threatricalist transformations in the play "magic realism." In my opinion, Joan's handling of the coma, along with her non-realist treatment of time, verges on symbolism. *The Lie* reminds me of Maeterlinck's microdramas, which are full of mysterious and suggestive, but unexplained imagery. In fact, the more I re-read *The Lie*, the more I am convinced that Joan has written a symbolist play.

Keith   No wonder I didn't get this play the first time through. It's like poetry in prose.

Rose   But we haven't yet described the plot, which begins and ends with Ty's coma. Let me give it a try. If I'm reading accurately, scenes 1, 2 and 4 take place in a single day. First, Rafe visits Ty in the hospital, as he often does, staying until he's kicked out. We know that this is Rafe's routine, because the nurse remarks on his frequent visits. Then …

Geo (*Scanning the text.*)   Rafe is at the hospital, intending to put Ty out of his misery but leaves without doing it. Is the play about mercy killing?

Rose (*Continuing without answering Geo.*)   Next Rafe goes directly to Lilly, which is also part of his normal routine. This sequence is clear when she asks how Ty is doing "today."

Louisa   Rafe and Lilly discuss mercy killing in this scene too, making it a main theme in the play. Lilly clearly objects to the idea and shifts the conversation to the larger idea of mercy.

Geo   Rafe upholds the other side of the debate by arguing for Ty's mercy killing. He's a doctor, a man of science, and has seen his patients suffer.

Joan   Religion and science—two ways of seeing life. And don't forget, Ty is also a doctor.

Geo   So he would probably side with Rafe.

Rose   But we don't know. Anyway, the second scene ends, when Rafe leaves and locks the door at Lilly's request. Then in scene 4, Polly arrives to get dinner for her mother and clean up. Her visit is also routine. She calls it "her duty."

Geo   Aha! I bet Lilly insists on being locked in, so that Polly will have to unlock the door when she arrives. Lilly does not want to give Polly any reason to suspect that Rafe has been visiting.

Louisa   That may be, but Polly is smart. When she sees the flowers, she knows. That's why she rants about her mother letting the devil in.

Me   I agree with your chronology, Rose. I would also call scenes 1, 2 and 4 "emblematic," because they function as emblems of the characters' usual behaviors and attitudes.

Juliana   Scene 3 is entirely different. It takes place about thirty years earlier, when Ty comes home from the war and learns that Lilly has had a child. We get to watch Lilly and Rafe tell the lie that will haunt the characters forever.

Hannah   Come to think of it, the positioning of the flashback is interesting. It happens right after Rafe leaves and before Polly arrives, when Lilly is alone. I can easily imagine her thinking about the past, or dozing off, making scene 3 Lilly's memory or a recurrent dream. If we imagine that scene 3 takes us inside her mind, then the chain of events in the play becomes chronological.

Geo   Would that then mean that this play is "A Day in the Life of Lilly"?

Sargis   But Lilly is not in scene 1, so maybe it's "A Day in the Lives of Lilly and Rafe."

Anisha   It's a triangle, guys! How about "A Day in the Lives of Lilly, Rafe and Ty"?

Hannah   And what about Polly?

Sargis   And why leave the nurse out?

Me   It may be that the events will confirm that Lilly is the apex of the triangle and therefore the leading character, but we are not yet far enough along in our examination of the text to say.

Keith (*Searching through a small notebook.*)   Wait, wait … I'm thinking back to our first lesson. Sharon, you were talking about how an action is like a baseball flying, and a counteraction is like gravity pulling against it. Then, when the ball finally hits the ground, an event occurs that is … Here it is … "historic in the life of the baseball. This is now a ball with a past" (Lesson 1).

Me   Yes, events that change the trajectory of the characters' stories and their relationships to one another are not emblematic but historic.

Keith   That would make scene 3 historic in my book. It may be a memory or a dream, but the lie that Lilly and Rafe tell definitely changes everything.

Rose   I would argue that scene 4 is also historic, because Lilly gets the news that Ty is coming out of his coma. His homecoming would definitely change their lives.

Anisha   Let me sum this up to see if I understand. The story spans many years and many events, some of which remain shrouded in mystery, which makes the play more symbolist than realist in style. The plot focuses on one day in the present and includes a flashback to the past, which might be staged as Lilly's memory or dream. In addition, most of the scenes in the plot are emblematic of the characters' usual habits and attitudes, with the only historic events being the lie in scene 3 and the phone calls in scene 4.

Me   You got it, Anisha. A chain of events that tells the story of *The Lie* is beginning to emerge, which brings me to the third and last of my mini-lectures.

The Theory behind the Chain of Events

Stanislavsky defined a play's plot as a chain of events, which, like "a compass," keeps a company moving in the correct direction (Knebel' 1976: 300). I have already defined "event" as the result of an action colliding with a counteraction, and you have experienced such collisions in your etudes on *Macbeth* and *Three Sisters*. Stanislavsky called events the "fabric" from which drama is "woven," and Knebel likened them to "the foundation upon which the author builds the play" (Knebel' [1959] 1982: 26). However, before settling upon the word "event," Stanislavsky used other terms, among them "episodes" (a word still in use in Russia) and "active facts."[7] The latter phrase strikes me as particularly revealing of how he viewed events as facts that convey, not static information, but rather information about what must occur within performances. When acting, actors must account for "active facts" as accurately as they must for other kinds of facts or risk performing off-key.

"Chain" implies that one event is linked to the next in a sequence constructed by the author. Stanislavsky compares a play's chain to a train journey from Moscow to St. Petersburg, with each event like a station stop along the route. The overnight train stops at the two Russian capitols, allowing access only to the start and finish of the journey. The express train stops at the larger cities, offering passengers a better perspective on the changing terrain covered by the route. The mail train stops at every single station, including the smallest, most remote villages (Knebel' [1954] 2009: 26–7).[8] While a cast can use all three trains as models to establish a chain of events, Active Analysis prefers the express.

As an analytical model, the overnight train can be unexpectedly helpful. For example, *The Cherry Orchard* begins with a reluctant Ranyevskaya being brought back home by her young daughter from her lover in Paris in order that she deal with the fact that her estate will soon be sold to pay the mortgage. Ranyevskaya had fled to Paris and took a lover to escape memories of her son's drowning and her profligate husband's behavior. Upon her arrival home, she covers up the pain of her return with expansive expressions of joy. The play ends with the property being sold and leaving enough money in her purse for her to return to her lover in Paris. By comparing the opening with the end, we can see Ranyevskaya's tears and sad words as a mask to hide from her family her relief at unburdening herself of her painful past. By identifying these two points, Chekhov's insistence that his play is a comedy makes sense. For Ranyevskaya at least the play has a happy ending. However, the actor playing the role has far too little information to make the journey from start to finish. By noticing that *The Lie* begins and ends with Ty's coma, we sense its importance, but don't have enough information to understand why that might be.

The mail train represents the opposite extreme. Its slow route simulates the rehearsal process used by Stanislavsky prior to Active Analysis, when he spent months around a table with his cast, studying all facets of the play. Such work can be inherently fascinating. For example, actors might study the cuisine of Russia in the early 1900s in order to imagine the taste of the food served on the train from Paris, the particular dishes enjoyed by Ranyevskaya and her brother at the provincial restaurant mentioned in Act II, and how Varya might have prepared the peas she serves to the estate's peasants in order to save money. But too many stops on the train can try the patience of the passengers and overload them with more than they need to know about the surrounding countryside. Unless such research illuminates what actually happens in the play, it can waste precious rehearsal time. Worse still, actors risk coming on stage with "a stuffed head and an empty heart" (*SS* IV 1991: 325–6). If I we were to investigate every aspect of *The Lie*—including the history of war, the medical conditions of a coma, Lilly's Yankee upbringing, religious cults, etc.—we would need months of rehearsals around the table before ever getting up to try an etude.

Like the express train that marks the route with stops at the big cities, Active Analysis begins by targeting information that is most pertinent to performance. As Knebel explains, "actors learn to identify the big events so that they can understand how the author constructs the plot" (Knebel' [1954] 2009: 25). Therefore, "the main problem to solve during initial rehearsals is to understand the main events in the play. [...] Smaller events can be set aside initially, so as not to distract the actors" from the bigger picture (Knebel' [1959] 1982: 27). Knebel uses three different adjectives interchangeably to name these big events: "main" (*glavnie*), "major" (*krupnie*), and "fundamental" (*osnovnie*) (Knebel' [1959] 1982: 23–7). I only use "main event" for consistency's sake. She teaches that there can be as few or as many main events as the play dictates. She also differentiates main events from the "inciting" (*iskhodnoe*) event that sets the entire play in motion, which may occur in the plot or in the story. By identifying these events, the cast creates an outline or "abstract" that can serve as a "a magnet that attracts all the complexity and multiplicitous aspects that are potential within the play" (Knebel' 1976: 300). To give you an idea of what a chain of events might look like, I'll offer one simple example. Knebel saw the inciting event for *The Cherry Orchard* as the threat of the auction, followed by four main events: Ranyevskaya's return home, the setting of a date for the auction, the selling of the estate, and finally the family's departure (Knebel' 1976: 337). While this particular chain closely parallels Chekhov's four acts, not all chains of events follow the author's acts and scenes. For example, we might find that *The Lie* has more main events than scenes.

Simply put, the point of establishing a chain of events is to provide enough information to get a cast started, but not so much as to drown the actors' enthusiasm for discovery. As Knebel explains, actors get to "know their roles' substance by following the development of the plot, which then actively plunges them into the play's conflicting actions and coun-teractions," making "events the shortest route into the world of the play" (Knebel' [1959] 1982: 26).

Tovstonogov's Alternative Chain of Events

Before I end this mini-lecture, however, I want to alert you to the fact that there are variations in the practice of Active Analysis, just as there are variations in the American Method. One particularly important version that has attracted attention in the West is taught at the St. Petersburg Academy of Theatrical Art by followers of Georgy Aleksandrovich Tovstonogov, a great director whose work defined the Bolshoi Dramatic Theatre from 1956 to his death in 1989.[9] Proponents of his teachings view Stanislavsky as having created Active Analysis, Knebel as having promoted it, and Tovstonogov as having perfected it. For my tastes, this view is deceptively teleological. Tovstonogov did not so much perfect Active Analysis, as adapt it to his own artistry and personal proclivities. He is to Active Analysis as George Balanchine is to classical ballet. Just as Balanchine's changes to dance technique fostered the speed and style of his choreography, so too did Tovstonogov's adaptations to Active Analysis support his directorial goals.

Some of Tovstonogov's changes to Active Analysis make the theory more specific. For example, he categorizes given circumstances into small, medium, and large circles, based upon their importance to the play. Other changes reflect his views on dramatic writing. For example, he prefers the word "conflict" to "counteraction" in order to call attention to the "fight" for status and power in human interactions. Thus, the collision between action and counteraction is reconceived as one character "leading" the scene and the other being "led."[10] Aside from such specific adjustments, however, two principal differences distinguish his practice from Knebel's.

First, he thought of the director as a "benevolent dictator" whose "analysis of the play (complete before the first meeting with the actors) serves as the true basis for awakening the intuitions of the company during the etude process" (Malochevskaia 2003: 138; 83). Those who follow his practice generally divide preparation for production into two parts: the director's analysis of events and the actors' embodiment of that analysis through exploratory etudes. This division of labor can affect the translation of Knebel's term for the technique. "Active Analysis" conveys her understanding that analysis occurs in the active process of exploration that the director and actors experience together in the rehearsal hall. In contrast, Tovstonogov's proponents in the West prefer "Action Analysis," which prioritizes the direc-tor's analysis that precedes rehearsals with the cast. The actors' later embodiment of the director's plan through etudes is then sometimes called "the Method of Physical Actions" or "the Etude Method."[11] The relationship between director and actor reverts to the author- itarianism, with which Stanislavsky had begun his career. Because I love acting and the collaborative work with actors that can create surprise and awe, I prefer Knebel's view of the director as leader of an ensemble of like-minded artists, engaged together in the active analysis of plays.

The second principal difference between Tovstonogov and Knebel is more pertinent to the topic of this mini-lecture. He established a sequence of five events for all plays, criticiz- ing Knebel during a 1973 class for her resistance toward standardization (Gorfunkel' 2007: 110). Like Knebel, he includes an "inciting" event, but always places it prior to the beginning of the play. He then describes the play as unfolding through the "fundamental" event, which sparks the major conflict in the play; the "central" event, which marks the play's climax; a "final" event that resolves the conflict; and at last the "main" event, which illuminates both the author's and the director's perspectives (*sverkhzadacha*) (Gorfunkel' 2007: 110–12 and Malochevskaia 2003: 59–60). Tovstonogov's chain of five events captures the tradi- tional conventions of and can therefore be a valuable analytical tool for dramas that follow Aristotelian structures. However, when plays break with tradition, Tovstonogov's formula will not necessarily hold. Just as I prefer the word "counteraction" to "conflict" because it affords greater flexibility in dealing with dramatic interactions, so too do I prefer Knebel's simpler approach, which allows for as many main events as are needed. Such flexibility is especially important, when working with new plays and new media which often break with past dramaturgical models.

A Cast and Set for *The Lie*

After lunch we will work out *The Lie*'s chain of events and test what we think by means of etudes. Therefore, it's time to cast the play. Louisa and Geo, will you bring your wise perspectives to the roles of Lilly and Rafe? (*They both nod.*) Grigor, your infectious enthu- siasm will suit Ty perfectly. Hannah, please take Polly. (*She smiles broadly.*) Sargis, you will play the nurse, so that you can again "put your foot down" but under quite different circumstances.

Now for our set. Let's use two playing areas. The hospital room will be up on our small stage, so that the audience will remain aware of the comatose Ty during the whole perfor- mance. Lilly's apartment will be on the floor with living, dining, and kitchen areas. Her easy chair is upstage left, a small dining set can be in the center, and the right edge of the stage can serve as a kitchen counter. The theatre's center aisle will lead to Lilly's imaginary entrance door. This means that everyone who enters Lilly's space must walk through the audience. As for costumes and props, use only what you absolutely need. I have brought a box of random things for you to trawl through for ideas. Keith, please take charge of the lights. Use the stage lights only for the hospital scene, the party lights for the flashback to mark it as a memory, and the regular lights for everything else. In short, the visual aesthetics of our production will be theatricalist (with two sites visible at all times and an imaginary door), as well as minimalist (with little furniture and few props). Yes, Geo, such a set suits the pragmatics of our venue well, as you pointed out in an earlier session, but it also suits the non-realist impulse in Joan's play.

Keith   Before we break, can I make a specific suggestion? If, as Joan says, we can choose whatever war we want, I vote for the Persian Gulf War of 1991. That would set the play in 2020, when Joan wrote it.

Hannah   That also means that we can wear our own clothes and use our belongings, including our cell phones.

Me   It may be that the fact of war, like that of the coma, is more important than its realistic details. However, since *The Lie* is a contemporary play, I will accept your suggestion, Keith.

Everyone applauds.

Louisa   Come have some lunch!

Interlude

As the actors gather around the table, they continue to discuss the play with each other and Joan. I take some food and go outside for a moment alone to re-read and think about the play. When I return to the hall, I find the table cleared, the room set up for an etude, and the actors quietly reading the play. I sit down among them and explain that, because we are working with a full play there will be two additional steps in the now-familiar process of rehearsing through Active Analysis: (1) identifying the play's chain of events and (2) examining the character's development (the role's *sverkhzadacha*) within that chain.

In Practice: A Preliminary Chain of Events

Me   This morning, I watched Keith fill his notebook with new information, but as Stanislavsky always said, when it comes to acting, "to know" is "to know how." So, let's get started. I have brought a whiteboard with me to record our ideas. How would you title each of the main events that occur in the plot of Joan's play?

The actors flip through the text, until Sargis raises his hand.

Sargis   Since an event is what happens between an action and a counteraction to bring each interaction to an end, I'll start at the end of each scene. (*He takes the marker and writes.*)

> Event 1: The nurse kicks Rafe out of the hospital.
> Event 2: Lilly requests that Rafe lock her in when he leaves.
> Event 3 FLASHBACK: Lilly and Rafe lie to Ty.

In the last scene, I see two events, so …

> Event 4: The hospital calls with news that Ty is waking up.
> Event 5: Polly locks Lilly in with her demons.

Oh, I almost forgot, the inciting event. Could it be Ty falling into coma? I'm not sure.

Anisha   How about the birth of Polly?

Grigor   I vote for the lie that Lilly and Rafe tell about Polly's birth. If there were no lie, there would be no play.

Keith   Wow. Joan really breaks the mold by putting the first, inciting event smack in the middle of play! What writing!

Me   Sargis, please mark 3 as the inciting event. Any other revisions?

Shari (*Looking at the whiteboard and laughing.*)   This list looks like the chain for an absurdist play, where things just happen for no reason!

Me   That's true. A cursory list of events in most plays, including those by Shakespeare and Chekhov, usually yields a pretty good outline of the overall plot. Knebel would suggest that, when establishing the play's chain of events, it is not enough to ask *what* is happening? One must also ask *why* (Knebel' [1959] 1982: 27). What if we were to revise this list with her suggestion in mind? (*I take the marker and prepare to edit the list.*)

Geo   The reason the nurse throws Rafe out is because he can't do what he has come there to do, which is to put Ty out of his misery. He seems so ambivalent about the mercy killing that he is paralyzed. So, let's say, "Rafe can't make a move."

Me   Does that title actually capture what you just said?

Geo   Let's say instead: "Rafe can't bring himself to go through with Ty's mercy killing." (*I make the change on the whiteboard.*)

Louisa   Lilly doesn't see any sort of killing as merciful, so when scene 2 starts, she first wants to know that Ty is still alive. Then she tries to talk Rafe out of his plan. They go over all the pros and cons of ending Ty's life, as they have done many times before. Lilly concedes nothing and neither does Rafe, so their debate ends in a stalemate. Let's call the second event "Lilly sits tight." No, let me change that: "Lilly can't talk Rafe out of his plan." (*I make the change.*)

Juliana   I think scene 3 is fine as it is.

Hannah   On to the last scene in the play! Two events, is it? If so, then one is nested inside the other, because Polly starts and ends the scene. Let's say, number 4 begins with Polly coming to check on her mother. Event number 5 is the news that Ty is conscious. Then we go back to 4, which ends with Polly locking her mother in with her demons. (*I write.*)

Me   Here's what we've got now. (*Turning the board so that everyone can see.*)

> Event 1: Rafe can't bring himself to go through with Ty's mercy killing.
> Event 2: Lilly can't talk Rafe out of his plan.
> Event 3 FLASHBACK/INCITING EVENT: Lilly and Rafe lie to Ty.
> Event 4: BEGINS with Polly arriving to do her duty ….
> Event 5 EMBEDDED SCENE: Lilly learns that Ty is waking up.
> Event 4: ENDS with Polly locking her mother in with her demons.

Me   Do you see any patterns in this revised chain?

Juliana   I like the way that the first two events lack movement, mirroring the paralysis of the coma. When the hospital calls to say Ty is waking up in the fifth event, that fact might get all three of the main characters moving again. (*Pause.*) But I'm not sure.

Hannah   There is still something off about the end. Polly thinks she's locking her mother in, but the audience knows that Lilly will go to the hospital in the morning, so the last event seems totally ineffectual.

Me   Is that what you think about the end?

Hannah   Yes. (*Taking the marker and writing.*) How about this?

> Event 4: BEGINS with Polly arriving to do her duty ….
> Event 5 EMBEDDED SCENE: Lilly makes a plan to leave for the hospital the next day.
> Event 4: ENDS with Polly locking her mother in with her demons.

Shari   Something still feels off, but I can't get my head around it.

Me   I agree with you, Shari, but maybe our cast can get their bodies and spirits around it by trying an etude. As Knebel' writes: "It might seem that the chain of events concerns only […] the externals of the story, but this is not so. In plays, everything is subject to internal developments as well and thus, the actor's living connection to the play's events elicits feelings and thoughts that can explain the character's deeds" (Knebel' [1959] 1982: 26).

Shari   So is an etude next?

Juliana   Don't we still need to read for the facts?

Me   Yes, and we also need to map the facts, not only against the interactive principles of Active Analysis, but also against this preliminary chain of events.

The Facts and Dynamics in *The Lie*'s Preliminary Chain of Events

Everyone spends the next minutes reading the play again for the facts, until Geo raises his hand.

Geo   Rafe keeps visiting the hospital without carrying out his mercy killing. As a doctor, he certainly knows how to do it "simply," as he tells Lilly in scene 2, probably with a shot of morphine. This time through, I realized that he wants Ty's permission and, of course, Ty can't give it. Look at this line! (*Reading.*) "Wouldn't you like me to praise the Lord and pass the ammunition?" He's talking about the morphine there. I am the action in the scene. Without my visit, there would be no scene and my verb is "to get permission."

Sargis   The line about "God kicking in" and my saying "I trust you" makes me think that the nurse knows what Rafe wants to do, but decides to trust him anyway. After all, he has visited many times before without incident. I thought I was the action, because I'm the one in charge of my patient, but Geo has just persuaded me that I am his counteraction. My verb can be "to discharge" my duties toward my patient and also "to discharge" Rafe, who has overstayed his welcome. (*Everyone laughs.*) I like the double meaning of "discharge," too. I know you told me to put my foot down again, Sharon, but I think doing my duty as a nurse makes more sense.

Grigor   As the comatose patient, who cannot give anybody permission to do anything, I am the real counteraction and the nurse is my alliance. (*Everyone laughs.*) Seriously, doesn't that interpretation make sense? My verb is "to do nothing."

Geo   In short, scene 1 ends with event 1. (*Sargis nods.*)

Louisa   Turning to scene 2, Lilly does not condone the idea of mercy killing. She says it right here   "Blowing out someone else's candle won't make yours shine any brighter." But, what strikes me most is how many times Lilly quotes the Bible. "We know what is good, but we don't do it" comes from Romans 7:15. Then "the tongue will always betray you" refers to Judas whose tongue betrays Jesus in Matthew 26:71–2.

Joan (*Delighted*.)   You saw that! I went to a convent school as a child, you know.

Louisa   Lilly seems to be a religious and morally upright person.

Geo   Maybe Rafe is thinking about Lilly's moral upbringing—the unbending backbone of the pilgrims—when he refers to her "New England childhood."

Hannah   Maybe Polly becomes a religious fanatic to outdo her mother!

Geo   In any case, I don't think Rafe is religious. He's a man of science, a doctor. That's why he undercuts Lilly's biblical references with a French proverb: "A fool's tongue is long enough to cut his throat." Grigor looked it up for me.

Louisa   That line could also refer to Satan's forked tongue.

Sargis   Morality is all well and good, but don't forget, Lilly also objects to the mercy killing on pragmatic grounds. If Rafe is arrested for murder, she will lose the most supportive person in her life. (*Geo and Louisa nod in agreement*.) Maybe she's not really as religious as she thinks she is.

Geo   In any case, Rafe tries to defend his plan.

Louisa   But how strongly? I also notice a pattern in the scene: Lilly brings up an idea, and after a few comments Rafe changes the subject by asking about her eyes, offering to make tea, helping with the hot cup …. You see what I mean? (*Geo nods.*)

Me   Do you have an interactive map for scene 2?

Louisa   Rafe has to be the action, because he comes to visit. I can't debate him unless he's there.

Geo   I assume that I am coming to check in on Lilly, as I always do. It's my routine.

Me   Could there be any other reason for coming?

Geo   Let me think about that … I'm not sure.

Louisa   I'm the counteraction, because Rafe's visit gives me the perfect opportunity to go back to our debate about mercy killing. My verb is "to tell it like it is" and, as far as I'm concerned, there's no arguing with "what is." No wonder we end in a stalemate with neither of us giving in to the other! That's the second event. Hmm. I wonder whether Lilly likes the way things are. With Ty out of the way, Rafe can take care of her the way he did so many years ago.

Grigor   The flashback scene is simple. I am the action because I come home to pick up the pieces of my life. My verb is "to mark my territory." (*Everyone laughs*.) Thank you, thank you. It seemed appropriately clever!

Louisa   I'm the counteraction again. I try to provide him exactly what he wants by acting like the wife he remembers. In fact, that is my verb!

Geo   When I show up, I align myself with Louisa, but with a twist. I "welcome Ty home" with the news that he is a father!

Me I'm not entirely sure that what you describe will lead you to the inciting event of the play, but let's see what happens in the etude. There are, however, other facts in scene 3: Ty picks Lilly up and they begin to make love. Etudes tend to be most productive when actors follow their impulses while working. At the same time, a cardinal rule in acting, whether you are using this method or any other, is never to hurt your fellow actors. Therefore, treat this sexually charged scene no differently than you would treat a violent one, like Othello's smothering of Desdemona. Discuss your verbs, as did Setrak and Rose last time, and work out some physical ground rules to insure each other's safety before you begin.

Hannah Moving on to scene 4, I am the action and I will "rebuke" both my mother and her demons. And since Joan's play is non-realistic, I want to see what happens, if I let my imagination go wild. What if Polly actually sees demons and believes her mother is possessed.

Louisa I am the counteraction. I think that Lilly has never known how to deal with her daughter, and by the time of this play she has stopped trying. My verb will be "to endure" Polly's visit. As for the phone conversations, my verb will be "to plan for Ty's homecoming." I first take in the news from the hospital and then I take action by calling Rafe.

A First Etude: Paraphrase

Me Well, I am not yet convinced about the third and fifth events, but let's try an etude anyway and see what happens. Plan to travel the entire route of the play, moving from station to station, that is from event to event. Also remember, plan *what* you will do but not *how*.

Geo grabs the whiteboard and the cast circles their chairs at the back of the hall. After a while, I see that they are ready. Keith takes his place at the row of light switches, the actors take their places on the set, and the rest of us settle down to watch.

The First Etude on *The Lie*

As the stage lights come up Grigor lies immobile on the stage with Geo sitting next to him. Geo looks around and then puts his hand gently on Grigor's shoulder, as if to get his attention. As Geo begins to speak, Sargis enters with a firm gait and proceeds to tend to his patient. He maneuvers awkwardly around Geo, who seems glued to his chair. Sargis stops and looks squarely at Geo, trying to convince him to go home and get some sleep. Geo stands but does not move toward the door. Sargis exits with a warning not to stay much longer. Geo immediately sits down again and whispers in Grigor's ear: "Do you want me to end it for you, old friend?" Sargis comes back, sees Geo, holds the door open and reprimands the tardy visitor for overstaying his welcome. Geo stands again, pauses for another look at his friend, and then shuffles out the door.

Scene 2 begins with the stage lights going off and the regular lights coming on, revealing Louisa in her easy chair. She wears a gray wig and shawl. Her eyes are covered with a compress and she appears to be dozing. Geo has already descended the stairs, circled around behind the audience, and now stands in the center aisle in front of Lilly's imaginary door. He holds a bouquet of flowers, pulls a key out of his pocket, and lets himself in. Louisa peers out from under her compress to see Geo holding up the flowers. She smiles and puts the compress back over her eyes, as Geo places the bouquet in the vase on the table. As the etude unfolds, the two actors closely follow the pattern that Louisa had identified in the text: she raises a topic; Geo spars with her for a moment; then changes the subject to tea. (I notice that, while their conversation hits all the correct notes, it is punctuated with many lengthy pauses, as if each were searching for just the right thing to say to the other.) *Eventually, Geo drops all efforts at reasoning and sticks out his tongue as if to strangle himself with it, making Louisa laugh out loud. While Geo had clearly initiated the scene, Louisa's strong and persistent counteraction results in the dead-end that is the scene's main event. Geo glances at his watch:* "Well it's time for me to go." *As he takes the tea set to the kitchen area, Louisa calls after him:* "Don't forget to lock the door!" *He exits, locking the imaginary door behind him.*

As Keith switches from the regular lights to the party lights in preparation for scene 3, Louisa removes her gray wig and shawl, transforming into the younger Lilly. She begins tidying the room. Meanwhile, Grigor silently rises from the hospital bed, wearing a white shirt and pants to simulate a naval uniform. He follows the route that Geo had taken earlier to Lilly's door, also carrying a bouquet of flowers. When he knocks, Louisa is at first startled, then takes a deep breath, fixes her hair, and opens the door. Grigor hands her the bouquet and then embraces her so suddenly that she is nearly knocked off her feet. She giggles. In response he leads her to the dining room table, his arm around her waist, while she adds his flowers to the others in the vase and sits. He then circles the room, as if sniffing out what has changed and what remains as it was. Satisfied with his survey, he returns to Louisa, pulls her to her feet and into his arms. At first, she resists ever so slightly, but then gives way to his desire. As Grigor's kisses become more urgent, Geo interrupts with a loud knock at the imaginary door. Louisa breaks away, almost as if relieved, and rushes to open the door. As Geo steps into the room, Grigor smiles broadly and takes his best friend firmly by the hand in greeting. Louisa steps back to give the men a moment together. (I notice that they have inadvertently formed a triangle with Louisa at the apex. Everything in the scene has been going very well, but then there is a pause that seems far too long. Something is wrong. Grigor has entirely forgotten about Ty's exhaustion and his need for a nap. Geo seems unsure of what to say or do.) *After a long pause, Louisa confesses to Grigor that there is a baby, his baby, and that he is a father. Following some celebratory congratulations, all three exit to go see the baby.*

As Keith turns off the party lights, the actors take their positions for the last scene. When the regular lights come on, Grigor lies immobile in the hospital bed and Louisa sits at Lilly's dining table, wearing her gray wig and shawl. Hannah now stands in the center aisle, pulls a key from her bag, and unlocks Lilly's imaginary door. Hannah stands still on the threshold for a moment, her hands on her hips, surveying the room. She notices the flowers in the vase, but says nothing. Instead, she goes over to an orange boom box on the kitchen counter and flips a switch. Acid rock fills the air. (The audience laughs.) *Louisa covers her ears and retreats to her easy chair, which is as far away as she can get from the sound. Hannah begins to move and sway to the music, as if it were the soundtrack of her life. She puts two biscuits on a plate, brings them to the table, and invites Louisa to eat. When Louisa says that she's not hungry, Hannah takes the biscuits back into the kitchen, where she eats* them. *She storms back to the table, picks up the vase, and scolds her mother as she takes the flowers into the kitchen. She then roams around the apartment, testing for dust and looking under objects and furniture for what might be hiding. All the while, she alternates between muttered chants to the music and insults flung across the room at Louisa. At one point she stops moving and lifts her eyes and arms upward:* "Demons, I rebuke you! I cast you out! I excoriate you!" *Louisa peers at Hannah and then toward the audience with a long-suffering gaze. She is clearly waiting for Hannah to finish what she's doing and leave.*

Suddenly Louisa's cell phone rings. It is the hospital with news of Ty's improvement. Her energy now visibly changes as she takes in the news about Ty's condition. She seems excited as she dials Rafe and whispers into the phone: "Pick me up tomorrow, please." *With his answer, she breathes a sigh of relief and hangs up. During the phone calls, Hannah had retreated to the kitchen, cleaning, chanting, and reprimanding, but when Louisa dialed Rafe, Hannah went suddenly still, as if eavesdropping. As Louisa puts down the phone, Hannah begins to tear each flower apart, petal by petal. Then she changes her mind, dumps the flowers in the bin, saying:* "I'll take these with me and burn them later." *In exiting, Hannah deliberately locks the door, as if she has no intention of ever returning. As the door closes Louisa slowly turns her head toward the audience and smiles, as if we were her conspirators. The lights go off. The spectators applaud.*

Assessment in Order to Repeat:

Joan (*Applauding along with the others.*)   I hadn't thought of the nurse as male, but it makes perfect sense! Polly was just as I had imagined her, funny and horrible at the same time.

Keith (*Applauding.*)   I was shocked when Hannah locked the door so deliberately. But, then, when I remembered that Rafe would come for Lilly the next day, I relaxed. (*Everyone laughs.*)

Juliana   Hannah's Polly seemed to enjoy the opportunity to punish her mother for a lifetime of lies. That gave me a chill.

Geo   You already know that my verb in the first scene was "to get Ty's permission." When I felt Grigor's counteraction in his immobility, I naturally turned to Sargis for permission, and he would not give me an inch. I genuinely felt frustrated when I left without getting what I wanted. That frustration carried over into scene 2 and made me change my verb. Instead of checking in on Lilly, I decided "to secure her blessing for the mercy killing." Every time she advanced another reason against it, I got all the more frustrated. I just wanted to shut her up with the tea! When she's drinking, she can't talk! The scene naturally ended in a stalemate!

Me   Did the first event we identified occur?

Geo   Yes, without permission I couldn't make a move.

Me   And did the second event occur?

Geo   Louisa would not be moved! (*Laughing.*) I brought flowers, tea, and love, and none of it got me the blessing I wanted. Actually, I think everything in the overall etude went rather smoothly except for scene 3, when ....

Juliana   Sorry to interrupt, Geo, but I think scene 2 was excruciatingly slow. I love how your first verb took you to your second, but you and Louisa took such long pauses between each thought, that I found myself getting bored.

Rose   You both forgot that the scene is emblematic. You were playing it as if it were the first time that the Lilly and Rafe had ever considered mercy killing.

Me   Rose is correct. I suggest that in the next etude, you make one technical change. Speed it up! You don't need pauses in which to think. All the thinking has happened long ago.

Geo   Wow, good point. But to go back to scene 3, something there went off-track. Everything was fine until I realized that Louisa and Grigor were just standing there, and I was lost. I hit a wall and went blank. Louisa saved the day by jumping forward in the scene.

Grigor   "To mark my territory" didn't work once Geo arrived. I didn't know how to carry on.

Keith   You also forgot all about how tired you are and that you need a nap! (*Grigor nods.*)

Louisa   Once Rafe arrived, my verb didn't work either. Playing wife no longer made sense, because he could see right through my act.

Geo   When I came in, I expected to align myself with Louisa, but I couldn't figure out how to do that because it went against everything I was supposed to say.

Me   I agree that scene 3 fell apart, but you made two interesting discoveries. First, when both men chose to bring bouquets to Lilly, you made the triangular relationship in the play visible. Please continue to use the bouquets. Then later, when Geo entered and Grigor rushed over to shake his hand, Louisa stepped upstage forming an actual triangle on stage. Please keep that expressive blocking in your next etude!

Grigor (*Saluting.*)   Ay, ay, captain!

Rose   I think I know why scene 3 went wrong. Might there be two events in it? The first is Ty coming home, and the second starts when Rafe urges Lilly to tell Ty about the baby. That's why the verbs stopped working when Geo showed up.

Me   Rose is absolutely correct. Let's revise the chain of events. (*I write and turn the whiteboard toward the group.*) How's this?

THE PRESENT
Event 1: Rafe can't bring himself to go through with Ty's mercy killing.
Event 2: Lilly can't talk Rafe out of his plan.
FLASHBACK
Event 3a: Ty's homecoming.
The Inciting Event 3b: Lilly and Rafe lie to Ty.
THE PRESENT
Event 4: BEGINS with Polly arriving to do her duty ....
Event 5 EMBEDDED SCENE: Lilly makes a plan to leave for the hospital the next day.
Event 4: ENDS with Polly locking her mother in with her demons.
THE END

Shari Better and better!

Me Is it really? I still have a major problem with the end of the whole play. Here's the last bit. (*Reading aloud*.) "Polly exits and we hear the key in the lock. Lilly weakly gets up and turns off the music, sits down, starts to rock slowly, wiping the tears from her eyes." I know that we actors do not always attend closely to stage directions, but Louisa's final smile to the audience was so radically different in tone from the ending described by Joan that it violated a key fact in the play: Lilly's final keening.

Anisha What's that?

Me It's a kind of mourning for the dead that involves rocking and crying. We have to dig more deeply into this play in order to understand this last fact, and I suggest we do so by taking a hard look at how Lilly develops as a character from first event to last—her s*verkhzadacha* or arc, if you prefer that term.

The Role's Perspective: Lilly

Me Linking a character's verbs to the play's chain of events can bring valuable, new angles of vision to bear on what Knebel calls the "substance" or "essence" of each role (Knebel' [1959] 1982: 26). (*Handing the whiteboard to Louisa*.) For each event in which Lilly participates, would you please write down whether you are an action, counteraction or alliance and what verb you plan to try next time.

Louisa All right.

> Event 2: Counteraction to Rafe; "to tell it like it is"
> Event 3a FLASHBACK: Counteraction to Ty; "to act like the wife Ty remembers"

Since 3b is newly added to the chain, I have to think about it. (*She reads the interchange between Lilly and Rafe.*) Rafe wants me to tell the truth not only about the baby, but also about our affair …

Geo You bet he does. If they tell Ty the truth, then maybe Rafe and Lilly can make a new life together. So, he's the action and he keeps pushing hard for her to confront Ty …

Louisa But Lilly tries to end their affair. "It'll never happen again." She won't do what Rafe wants, beats around the bush, and eventually lies about the baby being Ty's.

Geo You see, it is she who lies.

Louisa And Rafe lies too by keeping silent. He could have said something if he had wanted to. Don't blame Lilly. They both lie. Let's see … (*Writing.*)

> The Inciting Event 3b FLASHBACK: Counteraction to Rafe; "to control the story"

Juliana Of course she wants to control the story. That's what it means to lie. That's brilliant!

Louisa Going on to scene 4 with its two events …

> Event 4: Counteraction to Polly from beginning to end: "to endure her visit"
> Event 5: Action; "to plan Ty's homecoming"

Me   Do you find any patterns in what you have written?

Louisa   I am the counteraction in every scene except for the phone conversation with Rafe. How can that be? I thought Lilly was the main mover and shaker in this play. I thought that everything she does is to protect her marriage. Could that be her "super-problem"? I'm not sure. But instead of taking action, this list shows that she resists both the men in her life. At the same time, she's no pushover. All my verbs are fulfilled: I do tell it like it is, I do act like a good wife, I do tell my version of the truth to Ty, I do endure, and I do make a plan for Ty's homecoming. (*Looking quizzically at me.*) Maybe it's not the right plan, but still ....

Me   Let's try an experiment.

Grigor   If Stanislavsky and Knebel experimented, then so should we!

Louisa   I'm game.

Rethinking the Role through Knebel's Inner Monologue Exercise

After working on a role for a while, I often find it productive to do a classic exercise developed by Knebel to help actors get inside their characters' heads.[12] My instinct tells me that it might help uncover something new in Lilly. You select as your focus a decision made by your character in the play. Sit down and take a few deep breaths before beginning in order to clear your mind. Once you begin, think as your character throughout the exercise. First,

Fig. 8 Sharon Marie Carnicke (standing) and Louisa Abernathy (sitting) in rehearsal at the Studio of the Stanislavsky Institute for the Twenty-First Century, the American Legion Post, Eagle Rock California, 2014. Teena Pugliese, photographer.

weigh all the facts and circumstances that argue in favor of the decision you are making, In short, mentally talk yourself into it! Once you have made the decision, say "yes" aloud, stand up, and walk toward the door in order to put your decision into motion. Next, as you walk, consider all the facts and circumstances that argue against the decision. In short, mentally talk yourself out of it! The exercise ends when you change your mind, say "no" aloud, and return to the chair.

Me (*Turning to Louisa.*) Since the end of the etude does not align with the end of the play, I would like you to use this chair exercise to investigate Lilly's request that Rafe take her to the hospital in the morning. Please read the text of Lilly's phone call to Rafe!

Louisa-Lilly Hello? Rafe? It's me. They just called from the hospital. He voided. Yes. All by himself. The nurse said without a catheter. See what that means? He's alive. He's going to get better. Come home again. Where will I put him? But he won't live with her. You know how that is. He never wanted her to live with us. What is so urgent? Can't you see my predicament? He's getting better. (*Long pause.*) Yes, that's right. Tomorrow. Eight sharp? Okay. I'll be ready. Yes, dear. Goodnight Rafe. You still have your key?

Me Can you articulate a decision that Lilly needs to make at this moment?

Louisa (*Tentatively.*) She needs to decide exactly how to bring Ty home, where to put his bed, how to arrange for his care, all of that. Let me try.

LILLY'S DECISION

Louisa leans back into Lilly's easy chair, takes three deep breaths, and closes her eyes as she thinks. She becomes very still. After a while she looks up at the hospital bed. She then sits taller in her chair and looks around the apartment. Her eyes fall on various objects, finally resting on the vase. She smiles warmly, as if some sweet memory of Ty has come to her. At this point, she says "yes," stands, and walks toward Lilly's imaginary door. At first, her step is quick and firm, but then her pace slows as if her thoughts were holding her back. She stops cold when she reaches the door and stands for a long time, her eyes focused on the horizon. Unexpectedly she hits her fists into her thighs with a "no," turns abruptly on her heels, and returns to the chair. She sinks down, wraps her arms protectively around her chest, hunches over, and bursts into tears.

ASSESSMENT

Louisa (*Struggling to compose herself.*) How could I have missed something so big?

Geo What, what is it?

Louisa (*Taking the tissue offered to her by Rose.*) I always assumed that Lilly would go to the hospital and arrange for Ty to come home. It wouldn't be easy. He would need a lot of care, but she's his wife. What else could she do? When I said "yes," I was thinking about the time when we were first married. He gave me a single perfect iris, my favorite flower, and he looked at me with such love that I felt some- how embarrassed. But then, as I imagined myself walking into the hospital to make arrangements, I began to think about how he used to look at Polly with hate and at me with suspicion. I found myself thinking that once he came home he would probably punish me with his eyes every day. And he wouldn't leave, like Polly does. I would have to endure him for the rest of my life. I also thought that Rafe would stop coming to make me tea. Suddenly I knew that I could not allow Ty to wake up, let alone to come home. Rafe had been right all along, and mercy had nothing to do with it. We have to do away with Ty before it is too late. Rafe will help me. I have to protect myself no matter what it takes!

Juliana   And so you cried.

Louisa   I cried for myself. I had betrayed my husband by sleeping with his best friend. I had betrayed my lover by not telling my husband the truth. I had betrayed my daughter by keeping her real identity from her. Now, I am betraying my belief that killing is morally wrong.

Keith (*Audibly gasps.*)   This play is a murder mystery!

Juliana   It's more than that. It is an examination of the corrosive effect of lying.

Louisa (*Pulling out her script.*)   Lilly's decision to go through with Ty's mercy killing is right here in this long pause. (*Reading.*) "What is so urgent? Can't you see my predicament? He's getting better." (*Long pause.*)

Geo   I bet that during that pause Rafe calmly explains how they will go to the hospital, ask for a moment alone with Ty, give him an undetectable shot, and wait for "God to kick in."

Louisa   And she answers, "Yes, that's right." (*Laughing.*) But it's the devil, not God, who kicks in. Polly is right, there is a demon here. and it is Lilly.

Juliana   The coma keeps Ty from exposing the truth. How and when he fell into the coma is beside the point. Lilly's "super-problem," her *sverkhzadacha*, from start to finish is how to bury the truth. When Ty begins to wake up, she solves her problem by burying him for real.

Geo   And mercy too is beside the point. While you were listing your verbs, Louisa, I did the same for Rafe. (*He holds up a sheet of paper.*) Here it is:

> Event 1: Action; "to get Ty's permission"
> Event 2: Action; "to get Lilly's blessing"
> The Inciting Event 3b: Action; "to come clean"

Rafe's development is exactly the opposite of Lilly's. I am always the action and all my verbs go unfulfilled. When I looked at this list, I realized that Rafe may talk about mercy and truth, but he does nothing that is merciful or truthful. He's struggling with a single overarching problem too: how to live with himself after having betrayed his best friend. It is easier to blame Ty for not giving him permission, to blame Lilly for not giving her blessing, and, most of all, to blame her for not coming clean, than it is for him to admit his own failings. He wants to bury his own guilt.

Joan   As I said this morning, this is an ugly little play.

Me   I disagree. It is a remarkable play about the ugliness of lies and hypocrisy. (*Turning toward the ensemble.*) I believe that the author's perspective has created a play about how lies kill love.

A Second Etude: Silent

Given what Louisa and Geo have uncovered, we need a revised chain of events and a revised list of Lilly's verbs before we can test our understanding of *The Lie* in another etude.

Revising the Chain of Events

Me   As your director, I will now establish a finalized chain of events for our production:

> THE PRESENT
> Event 1: Rafe can't bring himself to go through with his plan for Ty's mercy killing.
> Event 2: Lilly can't talk Rafe out of his plan.
> FLASHBACK
> Event 3a: Ty's homecoming.
> The Inciting Event 3b: Lilly and Rafe lie to Ty.
> THE PRESENT
> Event 4: BEGINS with Polly arriving to do her duty ….
> Event 5 EMBEDDED SCENE: Lilly sets in motion Ty's killing.
> Event 4: ENDS with Polly locking her mother in with her demons.
> Event 6: Lilly grieves the loss of her soul.
> THE END

Me   I am separating Lilly's decision from her final keening, because two events, however brief, will better structure the play's final moments and better create the play's devastating conclusion.

Revising Lilly's Perspective

Louisa   If Lilly's main problem is to keep the truth of her adultery buried, then she must continue to live the lie throughout the play. Here is my revised list of verbs:

> Event 2: Counteraction to Rafe; "to protect the status quo"
> Event 3a: Counteraction to Ty; "to act like the wife that Ty remembers"
> The Inciting Event 3b: Counteraction to Rafe; "to dance around the truth"

I honestly like "dancing" better than "controlling the story," because it captures the way Lilly plays both sides against the middle and the roundabout way she talks about the baby.

> Event 4: From beginning to end—Counteraction to Polly: "to endure the visit"
> Event 5: Action; "to do whatever it takes"
> Event 6: Action: "to face the truth of my decision"

Me   Let's try another etude, a silent one this time.

The actors again withdraw to the back of the hall with their scripts in hand. Geo grabs the whiteboard for reference. Within ten minutes, they are ready.

The Second Etude on *The Lie*

The performance starts with Geo-Rafe gently placing his hand on Grigor-Ty's shoulder and studying the immobile form for any sign of awareness. In the second scene, the rapid pace of Louisa-Lilly's and Geo-Rafe's sparing with each other creates a sense of intimacy that comes from their long and complex relationship. They seem inextricably bound to each other. Against the background of these first two scenes, I watch Grigor-Ty's home-coming and Louisa-Lilly's lie, told in the presence of her silent lover, as I might watch an accident—knowing that it is about to happen and yet knowing that I can do nothing to stop it. In the last scene, Hannah-Polly's madness creates an atmosphere of ironic absurdity that both frames and punishes Louisa-Lilly for her decision to trade away the last vestiges of her integrity. The etude ends as did Louisa's exercise, with Lilly keening inconsolably for the loss of her soul.

Everybody remains silent for a long time. Finally, Keith applauds and the others join in.

Assess in Order to Determine the Next Step:

Joan (*As the applause begins to die down.*)   Did I write this beautiful, bone-chilling play? I have been watching you every step of the way and yet you managed to surprise me.

Louisa   When I re-read the play in preparation for this etude, I noticed a line of Lilly's in scene 2 for the first time. (*She searches in her script.*) "It's going to rain. Hear that thunder far off? Finally a break." Lilly's last decision is like that impending storm, but the rain doesn't bring relief. It breaks her completely.

Grigor   When the weather reflects how characters feel, it's called the "pathetic fallacy" from the Greek word "pathos" for "emotion." It's a fallacy because we all know that nature does not react to human feelings.

Juliana   That line is like the coma. It's another of Joan's images.

Geo   One of Rafe's lines in the first scene struck me as important for the first time. When the nurse asks why he visits Ty so much, Rafe says, "I do it for my sake." Only after I listed Rafe's verbs, did I understand that he's telling the truth in that line. Rafe's not there, because he cares about his friend, but to absolve himself of guilt.

Grigor   This time, I also noticed that in scene 3, Ty sees Lilly as all "grown up" when he first gets home, but as soon as Rafe arrives, suddenly she's "kid," "baby," and "babe." Even Rafe calls her "a swell kid."

Hannah (*Laughing.*)   Don't they understand that the only "little one" is Polly!

Shari   Here we are, still discovering new things in Joan's text! We started with Shakespeare's difficult verse and now I see that the same care has to be taken with plays that mirror how we normally speak. Reading closely for the facts is not only for old plays, but for new ones too.

Grigor   I don't know if you could tell, but I changed my verb to "rewind time." That choice made me see all kinds of new things in the text. When Ty says "I can't sleep my life away," I felt in my gut how precious little time we all have. And, wham, Joan, you did it again. That line also foreshadows Ty's comatose future.

Me (*Turning to the cast.*)   You now have a strong chain of events to guide you through the rest of your process. Each main event results from a collision between an action and counteraction. You have strong playable verbs. Those of you with more than one scene have verbs that trace your character's development productively. In this etude you have enacted the play for us, using your bodies, minds and spirits. You are ready to memorize the text.

Keith   Well, I for one am ready to buy a ticket!

The Ensemble's Perspective

Me (*Turning toward the whole group.*)   But, before we break for dinner, let's take a moment "to understand how the various elements of the play, how its actions and counteractions, how all this flows together into a single stream that takes us to our overarching perspective" on the play (Knebel' 1976: 264). Why stage *The Lie* today?

Rose   Because this play is a devastating exposé of how lying kills love …

Setrak   and how lies are told to protect the liars.

Juliana   The play follows Lilly to the ultimate betrayal of her own integrity, so we should indeed stage it as "A Day in the Life of Lilly."

Anisha   Much as I wanted to admire her, I now see that she is no heroine. In fact, there are no heroes in this play, no hearts and flowers, no mercy …

Louisa   We should stage this play in order to examine how easily hypocrisy can take root in any of us. (*A long pause.*) Now let's eat.

Epilogue

Juliana, Rose, and Anisha fuss over an unusually luxurious feast of chicken, salad, and pastas, which they arrange artistically on a colorful tablecloth. The rest of us gather around to help ourselves, but Louisa has disappeared. Joan pulls me aside for a moment. "Watching you and your actors work reminds me of a painter, who makes a rough outline, then fills it in with colors and details, until the picture becomes vivid." Before I can respond, the lights go off, plunging the hall into darkness. Then there is a faint flickering of candles at the door, as Louisa enters carrying a cake. Keith turns on the party lights and the ensemble bursts into a robust rendition of "Happy Birthday to Joan." She sinks into a chair, overcome with surprise. "My goodness, how did you know it's my birthday today?" Louisa winks and says, "A little bird told me!" She places the cake in the center of the table and Joan blows out the candles.

Notes

1. "St. Mary of the Angels Church, Hollywood," accessed on April 7, 2021, at https://en.wikipedia.org/wiki/St._Mary_of_the_Angels_Church,_Hollywood.
2. Joan Eyles Johnson has published in *Scream When You Burn* [(1997). San Diego: Incommunicado Press] and in the journals *Reed*, *Sou'wester*, *Mediterranean Review*, *Montserrat Review*, *Footprints*, and *Fiction Southeast*.
3. Personal email from Johnson, April 4, 2021.
4. In his concern over biased reading based on others' perceptions Stanislavsky anticipates Julia Kristeva's postmodern theory of intertextuality.

5. Following Benedetti's lead, Irina Brown in Knebel (2021) uses "supertask."
6. Personal email from Johnson, June 27, 2006.
7. For "episode" see Novitskaia (1984: 217) and Thomas (2016: chapter 5); for "active fact" see Knebel' ([1959] 1982: 27). Irina Brown translates "active fact" as "operative fact" (Knebel 2021: 40 and throughout), thus making the event's distinctive relationship to action less obvious.
8. Stanislavsky first describes this metaphor in his 1927–1928 artistic notebooks.
9. For more on Tovstonogov's career see Smeliansky (1999: xxxv, 13–15, 46–9, 136–40). Another variation as taught at Moscow's State Institute of Cinematography is described by Merlin (2001 and 2007: 185–216). See also Jackson (2011: 166–80).
10. For fuller explanations on these changes see Tovstonogov, "*Rabota c akterom*" [Work with the Actor] (in 1980 vol. 1: 218–34), and "*O Metode*" [About the Method] (in 1980 vol. 1: 235–67); Malochevskaia (2003: 35–7, 47, 64). For English explanations see Irina and Igor Levin (1992 and 2002).
11. I observed this approach at the University of Helsinki (Finland), 2009, in workshops conducted by Veniamin Filshtinskii (The St. Petersburg Academy of Theatrical Arts). In my view, using "the method of physical actions" to distinguish the actor's work from the director's does not reflect the historical reality of Stanislavsky's use of this term or its adoption for the Sovietized version of his work (Chapter 1).
12. I learned this exercise from Natalya Zverova (GITIS) at *MetodiFestival* (Italy), 2008.

Lesson 5 The System in Active Analysis

"With the passage of the years," Knebel writes, "I understood that [Stanislavsky] did not cross out or discard anything, but rather summarized and brought together" all his discoveries about acting. Active Analysis "absorbs his entire life and work. Without understanding this, you cannot understand what is new in his last discovery" (Knebel' 1968: 47–8). I look up from my notes and explain to the actors seated around me that Stanislavsky's broader System is both the foundation upon which his last rehearsal technique is built and also what "enters into your flesh and blood" when you practice it (Novitskaia 1984: 223). I see Hannah biting her lower lip in thought, but continue with the plan for this lesson.

> **Me**   After working intensively with Active Analysis in the last few weeks, it is time to pause and reflect on what you have learned. Is Knebel correct when she says that you cannot understand this rehearsal approach without understanding the work of Stanislavsky's whole life? In other words, by reading for the facts and testing those facts through etudes, have you found the System within yourselves?

> **Geo** (*Anxiously waving his hand*.)   How can we answer that question, if we are not sure what the System is? As I am not!

> **Me**   That's a fair question! You rightfully remind me that there have been so many different interpretations and misinterpretations of Stanislavsky's work that few actors share a common and accurate understanding of his ideas. So I will start with the story of how the System began.

In Search of the Actor's Creative State

In 1906 Stanislavsky experienced a personal crisis during a performance of Ibsen's *An Enemy of the People*. He was playing Dr. Stockmann, one of his favorite roles, when he realized that all his joy in acting had disappeared. What had once been his passion had now become a job.

> Why was it that I used to be bored whenever I was not acting, and now, on the contrary, I am happy when I have a day off? Everyone told me that's the way it always is for professionals who perform every day and often repeat the same roles. But that explanation did not satisfy me.

> (*SS* I 1988: 371)

To find a better answer he analyzed everything he had done to create Dr. Stockmann and then everything that had happened during his many performances of the role. By conducting this research on himself, Stanislavsky detected a subtle, but palpable shift that had occurred between his initial rehearsals and his now routine performances. "I began to realize more and more clearly that the inner content, which I had put into the role when I had first created it, and the outer form that had developed over time were as far from one another as heaven and earth" (SS I 1988: 371).

This erosion of his ability to express in physical form what he had created as "the human spirit of the role" prompted him to think about the nature of creativity. During rehearsals he had been "seized" by a "creative state" that was joyful and productive, but during performances he entered an "actor's state," in which the desire to please the audience predominated. He now understood how essential it is for an actor to maintain a "creative state" while performing in front of audiences.

> I understood that this creative state in all its fullness almost always comes of itself when a genius is on the stage. It comes to less talented people less often, for example on Sundays. It comes even less often to those who are even less talented, for example on holidays. It comes to mediocre actors very rarely, say on February 29. Everyone from the genius to the mediocre actor can intuitively summon forth this creative state to a greater or lesser degree without knowing how they did it, but they cannot use their wills to control it. [...] So I asked myself, "are there no technical paths to control the creative state?"
>
> (SS I 1988: 371)[1]

That single question spurred his lifelong search for anything and everything that can help actors harness their creativity. "My System must serve as a threshold into the creative state, and one must learn to open, not close, the door" (Stanislavskii 1986 vol 2: 193). He analyzed the work of the actors whom he most admired. He compared acting to other art forms like music, dance, and sculpture. He studied the pedagogy of notable teachers of acting, the vocal arts, and dance. He sought ideas in the new science of psychology and in spiritual practices, including Russian Orthodoxy and Yoga.

Initially, he thought about assembling a "grammar" of acting's constituent elements, much as standard grammar identifies the way that sentences consist of subjects, verbs, objects, etc. Stanislavsky also included exercises, drawn from a wide variety of sources, that would train each of the elements. By 1918 Stanislavsky was instead speaking of a "system" for acting, rather than a grammar. This change came about after Stanislavsky had read books by William Walker Atkinson, an American lawyer, who was determined to bring the practice of Yoga to the West. Writing under the pen-name of Yogi Ramacharaka, he lays out "a system of exercises, drills, etc." (Ramacharaka 1906: 88)[2] that served as a model for Stanislavsky. Like Ramacharaka, Stanislavsky reminds his students that his "system" should be envisioned as "an entire culture in which one must grow up and be raised over the course of many years," rather than as a set of hard and fast rules (SS II 1990: 371–2). Modeling himself on "Yogi teachers [who] constantly lead the candidates toward [their] goal [...] first by this path and then by that one, [...] until finally the student finds a path best suited for his feet" (Ramacharaka 1906: 35), Stanislavsky advises his directing students that "one must give actors various paths. One of these is the path of physical action. But there is also another path [... that starts from] feeling" (Vinogradskaia 2000: 498). For me, as for Knebel, Active Analysis brings multiple paths together into a single, harmonious whole.

If Stanislavsky were to answer Geo's question, he might say:

The System is a guide. Open and read. […] Examine the System at home, but forget about it when on stage. You can't play the System. There is no System. There is only nature. My lifelong concern has been how to get ever closer to the so-called "System," that is to get ever closer to the nature of creativity.

(*SS* III 1990: 371)

Geo If the System is whatever helps me as an actor to harness my creative state, then the real question is whether Active Analysis can help me become a better actor.

Me But "better" in what sense? "Good," "better," "best" are nice words, but in art, when styles and tastes change over time and when artists' social and political environments change, there are no absolutes. So I would put the question differently. How does Active Analysis help create performances that convey through our bodies and voices what is in our hearts and minds? If we can do that, then we have harnessed our creative wills.

Keith Heady stuff, guys! (*He makes a note.*)

Anisha But what about the Method? Isn't that the same thing as the System?

Rose I think a system is broader and more inclusive than a single method (Pitches 1999: 112).

Shari (*Harumphing.*) It doesn't really matter what you call it—"grammar," "system," "method," "approach," or whatever.

Me True, Shari. Stanislavsky would agree that we get far too invested in words, as if they were talismans. "About art one must speak and write simply and clearly" (*SS* II 1989: 42), he explains. Unfortunately, many of his words have established a professional jargon that can be mystifying.

Rose Like "objective" from our second lesson and "super-problem" from our fourth.

Anisha But I'm not asking about the word! I want to know if what everyone calls the "Method" is the same thing as the "System."

Me No, they are not. I follow Stanislavsky's lead by calling his work a "System" in order to distinguish it from the "Method," which was developed in New York during the 1930s at the Group Theatre where Lee Strasberg was directing and teaching an ensemble of young, largely inexperienced American actors. One member of the Group, Stella Adler, a far more experienced actor than the others, strenuously objected to Strasberg's use of personal emotion. She traveled to France to find Stanislavsky, where he was recovering from a heart attack, in order to study with him directly. She learned that he emphasized the analysis of text and the importance of imagination, not the substitution of personal emotion for the character's. When she returned, she accused Strasberg of misinterpreting Stanislavsky at a meeting of the Group in 1934. The next day, Strasberg reassembled everyone to announce that he was teaching the Strasberg Method, and not the Stanislavsky System (Carnicke 2009: 65–8).

Keith Can we go back to Stanislavsky and the difference he noticed between "the creative state" and "the actor's state" that's about pleasing the audience? You all know that I struggle with my verbs. When I first started Active Analysis, I was shocked to find out how much I was lying to myself on stage. My etudes were constantly going off track, because I was telling myself that I was doing this or that, when all I was actually doing was bringing attention to myself. I realized that acting for me was a way of being seen. That's "the actor's state," right? To get my etudes to work, I had to stop paying so much attention to myself and start paying attention to my scene partners. I think that "the actor's state" is selfish and "the creative state" is generous.

Me That is an interesting comment! It reminds me of something that Michael Chekhov once said. (*Searching through my notes.*) Ah, here it is:

> The essence of our profession is to give, constantly to give. We give our body, voice, feelings, will, imaginations—everything—we give to our characters.[...] We give the whole of this, our creation to the spectator. [...] And nothing, absolutely nothing remains for ourselves. [...] We are people who are born to give, and not to hold anything back for ourselves.[...] Our pleasure is the result of this giving. [...] If we hold anything back we are egotists, and an egotist on the stage is always torn apart by restlessness.
>
> (Chekhov 1955)

Keith When I dropped the actor's state, I understood what another of my teachers had been saying about acting truthfully under imaginary circumstances. I no longer felt like I was lying.

Shari Why are you so worried about whether you are lying or not? Let's face it. Acting is always a lie. It's a fiction, a construct.

Grigor True. And yet, what we do in an etude feels real while doing it. At least it does when we commit to doing the work of our verbs. I keep hearing Sharon's voice, telling me not to force, but simply to do my verb. I think that when I "force" I'm in the actor's state. "Simply doing my verb" takes me to the creative state.

Shari It's a paradox—finding the truth in the lie.

Grigor Could be, although I think the etudes do keep us honest with regard to the text. (*Laughs.*) I suppose that's a paradox too, since we don't use the playwright's words in etudes.

Keith For me, etudes open the door to the texts. Before Active Analysis, I used to say a lot of things when I was acting that I didn't really understand. I just memorized the lines. Now, when I memorize, I always know what I am saying and what's going on in the scene. One of the other members of this Studio—she's not here now—once told me that she has a kind of dyslexia that makes reading plays hard. But this technique helped her get past that difficulty. (*Chuckling to himself.*) It has certainly helped me with Chekhov!

Me This discussion already touches upon some of the ways in which Active Analysis absorbs Stanislavsky's work. I'd like to take a more systematic look at three particular topics that relate Active Analysis to the System. I'll start by sharing a quandary of my own.

Belief from Knowledge

When many actors hear the name Stanislavsky, they think of an unsatisfied teacher, shouting in disappointment, "I don't believe you!" "I don't believe you" registers as a stereotypical sign of Stanislavsky's training, at times in support and at times in mockery of his

System. This stereotype carries some truth. Stanislavsky did indeed place *belief* (*vera* in Russian) at the heart of his acting System. "You can't create what you can't believe" (*SS* II 1989: 233), he often said. In his eyes, theatrical art at its best activates the innately human ability to believe that dramatic fictions could be possible. "Everything on stage must instill belief in the possibility that it could exist in life as actual feelings and sensations" (*SS* II 1989: 227).[3]

Notice the word "possibility"! Stanislavsky understood *vera* as a belief in possibility. He did not promote the self-delusional process that was later developed in some versions of the Method, that trains actors to become their characters by substituting their real and personal emotions for the fictional ones depicted in a play. Stanislavsky explains that using personal emotion, which is often strong and uncontrollable on stage, can threaten actors' "mental hygiene," because thinking yourself to be the character is like inducing pathological "hallucinations." Beginning actors often "expend all their energy" on pointless efforts "to hallucinate," he writes, thus ruining their ability "to concentrate on stage" (*SS* II 1989: 102; 327). He asks only that actors treat fiction "as if" it could be real, hence his famous term, "the magic if." In the first part of his acting manual, after he describes an especially emotional improvisation, his fictionalized alter-ego Tortsov reminds his students that he had never asked them to hallucinate a madman breaking in at the front door. He asked them only what they would do *if* that circumstance were true (*SS* II 1989: 453–4). When Stanislavsky writes that "You never lose yourself on stage; you always act in your own person as artist; there's no walking away from yourself" while performing (*SS* II 1989: 294), he means that the actor is always present in the character. You don't disappear by becoming someone else, but rather your belief in the character's possibility allows you to step imaginatively into the role and create a hybrid of yourself and the character. That is why Stanislavsky uses a hyphen to refer to the actor-role in his writings.

In short, the actor's reality is the performance. "On stage, truth is whatever you believe and in life, truth is what actually is" (*SS* VI 1994: 81–2). Even when working within the illusionistic style of realism, Stanislavsky did not confuse art with life, as some assume. The theatre scholar Timothy Wiles puts his finger on this point exactly when he writes that for Stanislavsky "what is essentially 'real' about theatrical realism lies as much in the reality of performance itself as in the true-to-life quality of the play's details" (Wiles 1980: 14). Knebel put it even more simply: "The play is our creative reality" (Knebel' 1976: 366).

Think back on what you accomplished in our last few sessions. You measured your success against your ability to believe in the possibilities within your scene and to treat them as your present reality. When you embodied these possibilities, we who watched became absorbed in every little thing you did and believed you. As Stanislavsky observes, audiences "want more than anything to believe in everything in the theatre [and] want stage invention to be persuasive" (*SS* II 1989: 253–4). When this desire to suspend our disbelief is met, we spectators will "sympathize," "empathize," "feel for" the characters you perform. But, when this desire goes unmet, we can admire only your technical virtuosity, "the same way [we] trust a gymnast not to fall from a trapeze" (*SS* II 1989: 267).

Yes, Stanislavsky did interrupt actors' work with "I don't believe you!" because he insisted that actors develop belief in the possibilities within the stories they tell. This critique rang out so often in his classrooms and rehearsal halls that anecdotes about it abound. For example, Knebel recalls a 1931 rehearsal for *Dead Souls* at the Moscow Art Theatre, during which Stanislavsky kept stopping the scene because the crowd (of which she was a part) did not sufficiently convince him that they were amazed, when one of the principal characters (played by his wife Lilina) announced that dead souls were now walking amongst them. Stanislavsky cried out from the auditorium time and again, "I don't believe you," until everyone on stage was at a complete loss as how to proceed. Lilina finally saved the day by announcing that pickles were walking amongst them, an improvised line that genuinely surprised the crowd and earned them Stanislavsky's praise (Knebel' 1967: 251–3).

All right, I thought, I understand how belief works in the System, but I realized that I couldn't remember Knebel mentioning it. So, if Active Analysis absorbs everything in Stanislavsky's work, where did his insistence on the actor's "belief in possibility" go in Knebel's practice? This quandary sent me back to her writings, where I finally found two rare references to "belief" that suggest an answer.

First, in a discussion on the power of the artist's imagination, Knebel mentions in passing that belief lays "the foundation of foundations" (Knebel' 1976: 125) for the creative process. In this fleeting moment she affirms its centrality to the System and also to Active Analysis. At the same time, it strikes me as significant that she says no more about it. Her brevity implies that the actor's ability to believe in fictional possibilities may be a form of tacit knowledge (Lesson 2). The term was coined by the philosopher Michael Polanyi to name the kind of embodied knowledge (like riding a bicycle) that resists verbalization (Polanyi 1966). Since acting is a form of such knowledge, words can only approximate what we know in our bones.

When I turned back to Stanislavsky, I noticed that he expects belief to operate automatically in actors without conscious thought. While he insists that "you can't create what you can't believe" (SS II 1989: 233), so too does he caution actors against consciously thinking about whether they believe or not. "You can't come on stage to create with the nagging thought that 'I can't act as if I'm pretending'" (SS II 1989: 231). Such worry pulls the actor's attention away from the play's circumstances and fosters instead an unhelpful state of self-consciousness, which only induces stage-fright. Actors need to trust that with the help of their unconscious they will develop faith (*doverie* in Russian) in what they do on stage, much as they trust that they will breathe without paying conscious attention. Suddenly, I understood that he was describing "belief" as tacit knowledge before the coining of the modern term by using the word "unconscious" to name what is tacit within us. As he told the actors at an initial meeting of his newly formed Opera-Dramatic Studio on November 15, 1935, his new rehearsal technique will "take you to where your muscles *believe*, so that they themselves will seek *truth* in the story" (Vinogradskaia 2000: 448).

Knebel's second reference to "belief" involves her crucial conversation with Stanislavsky in the mid-1930s, after he had abruptly removed her from a role that she liked playing (Chapter 2). When he replaced her with his wife Lilina, whose interpretation was in the realist style, Knebel assumed that he had objected to the stylized performance that she had developed for the character. When asked to take up the role again, Knebel refused:

[You] yourself taught us that we must do only what we can believe, otherwise we embark upon a path that leads to the copying of others' work. [...] I don't yet have [Lilina's] experience or her technique, but all the same I will not copy her.

(Knebel' 1967: 259)

Stanislavsky responded by asking her to show him exactly how she understood the role by means of an improvised monologue that, in turn, opened the door to a discussion that took Knebel to "the very essence of [Stanislavsky's] artistic convictions" (Knebel' 1967: 259). He had not objected to the style she had used, but only to her having put it on as if it were a coat. She now understood that he expected an actor's belief in a fictional role, whatever its performance style or form might be, to be "justified from within" (Knebel' 1967: 260). By juggling with the play's facts and given circumstances in her etude, she also became viscerally aware that justifying one's belief is actually a process of embodied analysis that triggers the actor's unconscious, or tacit, knowledge. In effect, in Active Analysis belief comes from knowing the role so deeply that your muscles do indeed believe.

Knebel's insight is supported by Stanislavsky's most extended discussion of "belief" in acting, in which he describes the "process of justifying" fictional circumstances as a multi-layered investigation that "appraises the value of every fact and every given circumstance, one by one," in a dramatic work (SS II 1989: 260).

- The process begins in the mind with the actor's "faithful perception" of the play's given circumstances through deep study of the text (SS II 1989: 225).
- Next, the "magic if" serves as the "lever" to move what is imagined by the actor into the physical reality of stage performance (SS II 1989: 225).
- As actors then physicalize all the small details involved with creating the simple physical activities necessary for the performance of a scene—lighting a fire, pouring a drink, writing a letter, or counting money—the more likely belief will come, because "it is easiest to summon truth and belief in the body" (SS II 1989: 234):
- These small physical details in turn "act upon the feelings" (SS II 1989: 245) and lead the actor to the mental, emotional, and even spiritual dimensions of the role.
- Finally, when actors can see that what they do registers in the reactions of "the flesh and blood person standing opposite [them]" on stage, they know that they have found an appropriate sense of belief in their roles' fictional possibilities (SS II 1989: 231).

All these things, working in concert with each other, Stanislavsky writes, "will crowd out acting clichés, overacting, and lies" (SS II 1989: 232). Keith, when you told us that your etudes went off-track because you were lying to yourself, you had effectively made the same discovery that Stanislavsky had.

Keith pats himself on the back. I also see Anisha with a wide grin on her face and call upon her.

Anisha   That process you just described for justifying the circumstances in a play comes very close to what we did in Active Analysis, when we were setting up our etudes! First, we read for the facts ….

Sargis   *Razbor* … (*Laughing at the recollection of his grandfather's use of that word.*) We did indeed get to the bottom of things. Sometimes it was easy to figure out what was really happening like in *Macbeth*. Sometimes it was difficult like in *The Lie*.

Anisha   Then we physicalized the scene through our etudes. Doing that forced us to do all the little things that the scene needs …

Rose   When our partners reacted to what we did, we learned even more about the scene. I'm thinking about the way that Setrak flirted with me in *Three Sisters* right under Keith's nose.

Anisha   The only thing missing is our mapping of the facts to the interactive principles of action, counteraction, alliance, and event!

Me   That's because Stanislavsky hadn't yet articulated them …

Juliana   Missing too is the assessment that takes place after the etude in order to determine whether the scene needs further probing and additional etudes or whether we know enough to memorize the text and set the blocking.

Setrak (*Soberly.*)   Without that step, I might never have noticed Vershinin's hidden flirtation in *Three Sisters*.

Louisa   And I never would have seen the last event in *The Lie*.

Me   Let me sum it up! The addition of the interactive principles and the assessing of etudes do not change, only clarify, the complex endeavor of embodying a dramatic text. (*Reading from my notes.*) "Only this method of analysis can inject a real sense of the play's life into the actor's inner stage consciousness" (Knebel' [1954] 2009:34). By asking myself where belief had gone in Active Analysis, I uncovered one major way in which the System and Active Analysis are two sides of the same coin. Both depend upon Stanislavsky's insight that in acting "knowing" (*znat'*) means "knowing how" (*umet'*). Put another way, Active Analysis brings together your intellectual and tacit knowledge in a holistic inquiry that takes you to where your muscles can believe.

Hannah (*Still biting her lip in thought.*)   You say that Knebel never talks about belief, and yet, by reading for the facts and unleashing our imaginations, we come to believe in the possibility of the fictional circumstances in our scene. Right? (*I nod.*) Then, by doing our etudes, our instincts and even our muscles begin to believe. Right? (*I nod again.*) So, belief results from the deepest kind of knowledge that is simultaneously conscious and tacit, or "unconscious."

Me   That's right.

Keith   When I saw Sargis and Juliana in their last etude on *Macbeth*, I believed that they were married. I also understood exactly why Sargis gave in to Juliana. (*Chuckling.*) I'm married myself and it's all just so familiar.

Shari   And I believed you, Keith, when you stuck to that last verb in *Three Sisters* and you told your truth! But I have to be honest. I didn't believe you before that, when you were floundering around without conviction.

Geo (*Laughing out loud.*)   Do you all remember that play by Molière? I was in it some time ago, but I don't remember the title. I played a rich man who wants to become more educated, so he hires a tutor only to learn that he's been speaking prose all his life without knowing it!

Grigor (*Pulling out his phone and searching.*)   *Le Bourgeois gentilhomme.*

Geo   That's right! I played Monsieur Jourdain! Well, I think that's how we all feel right now. We've been practicing the System all these weeks and never even knew it!

Setrak   That's the way it should be. We don't need to label it, but only do it.

Emotion as the Sixth Sense

Hannah (*After a long moment of silence.*)   In all the time I've known you, Sharon, you almost never talk about our characters' feelings or what emotions we should prepare for a scene. You are as silent about emotion as Knebel was about belief. Yet, whenever I do an etude, I almost always find myself feeling all sorts of things that seem right for the character and scene. If Knebel treats belief as a result of knowing, can we also say that emotion results from doing the work of our verbs?

Keith   That's exactly it. That's why finding the right verb and sticking with it during the etude is so important!

Anisha   Maybe Active Analysis is like professional wrestling. (*Everyone laughs.*) I'm serious. Actors doing a play are not that different from professional wrestlers, who know how the fight will turn out because they are putting on a show. But, even so, wrestlers fight until they are bloodied. And that's how we have to stick with our verbs, until we are bloodied too.[4]

Keith   Not a bad analogy, Anisha!

Grigor   Do you mean to say that emotion is like getting bloodied?

Hannah   It's not always so extreme. Sometimes in an etude my feelings are just ordinary, like the normal feeling of being happy when you see a friend. It was like that in *Three Sisters*, when Louisa and I played Rodé and Fedotik. While we were rehearsing our song, I was genuinely looking forward to performing for the upcoming party. Then, when I looked up and saw what was going on between Setrak and Rose and the confused look on Keith's face, I enjoyed their shenanigans. That's why I switched to that passionate gypsy song. I felt like commenting on what I saw—a kind of musical smirk, I'd say!

Rose   When you did that, I suddenly realized that you had seen us flirting, and I felt embarrassed.

Setrak   No wonder you stood up and walked away from me!

Hannah   At other times, a strong emotion takes me by surprise. That happened in *The Lie*, when Louisa tuned me out. I got so frustrated and angry that I felt like punishing her. Then when I locked the door, vowing never to return, I felt happy leaving her there. (*Looking at Louisa.*) But it was nothing personal, you understand. It was Polly's hurt, not mine.

Louisa   I was your partner for both those scenes, Hannah, and you are right. I felt the same simple emotions as you did in *Three Sisters*. As for *The Lie* (*shaking her head*), I just focused on tuning you out so that I could endure Polly's visit. That's all I did. I kept thinking that when you left, I would breathe a sigh of relief. But when I was finally alone, the horror of what I was planning to do with Rafe the next morning came flooding back to me. Ty had to die. But, at what cost? I was sacrificing everything that I had once held sacred, my integrity and my religious beliefs, all for the sake of a dirty lie. My body rocked and I cried without consciously willing it.

Keith   Your muscles believed!

Louisa   I guess so.

Me   The emotions that Hannah and Louisa describe are wonderful instances of the holistic operations of Active Analysis. When you pursue a verb with as much commitment as you can muster within the dynamics of a scene, an emotion can arise of itself. The more your action meets resistance from your partner's counteraction, the more emotion you might feel as the etude develops.

Louisa   And when the etude is over, thankfully so is the emotion.

Shari   I want to share something personal with all of you, but especially with you Anisha, because you have a whole career ahead of you. When I was your age, my teachers taught me to use emotional recall. I don't remember them saying that they were teaching the Method, but no matter … They taught me to think about something terrible that had happened to me and then substitute that memory for what was going on emotionally with my character. Sometimes it helped me give a good performance and sometimes not. But, whether the performance turned out good or bad, I always left the theatre or sound set with that awful emotion from my past haunting me. It would hang on for hours and days. It was exhausting. It wore me down. I didn't want to keep doing that.

Keith   What you are describing sounds like PTSD (McFerren 2003). When we got back from Desert Storm, a lot of my buddies from the Marines suffered flashbacks. (*Shaking his head*.) They are still suffering.

Shari   That's why I came here. I wanted to learn a different way.[5] Since my feelings in Active Analysis come from what's happening between me and my scene partners, it feels real, but, when the work is over, the feelings go away. Like when I fell in love with you, Geo, because you thought we should move to France, and then after our little devised scene was over, well … Sorry. (*Geo smiles*.)

Me   You are describing one main difference between Stanislavsky's System and the Method. The story goes like this:

Many theatre practitioners assume that Stanislavsky used emotional memory liberally in his early work on the System, but that assumption is mistaken. In his book his alter-ego Tortsov is appalled when he learns that he has unknowingly asked an actor, whose baby recently died, to play a woman who has lost her child (*SS* II 1989: 450–4). After experimenting with personal memories to activate emotions at the First Studio, Stanislavsky began to notice that "restrain[ing] actors from dropping into pathology was becoming very difficult" (Markov 1934: 23). Even cautious use of personal feelings can induce a kind of "stage hysteria," which conveys only "the sick nerves of the actor and not the character's" (Markov 1934: 16). Then, when his most talented protégé, Michael Chekhov, suffered a nervous breakdown, Stanislavsky came face to face with the potential danger of mining one's personal life for the sake of one's character (Chekhov 2005: 4). He shifted his attention away from personal memories and toward empathy and imagination as more reliable and safe sources for creating emotional performances. Shari, Stanislavsky would never have insisted that you use personal emotion, as did your teachers.

Strasberg was not similarly hesitant. At the Group Theatre he judged actors by their willingness to expose their personal emotions and vulnerabilities. As actress Margaret Barker said, "Strasberg was so intent on what he called 'real emotion' that he reduced us to a pulp" (Chinoy 1976: 523). When Sanford Meisner resisted performing an emotional memory exercise in preparation for a role, Strasberg told him that he would be left "without total emotion" and snidely added "if you want to settle for that, that's fine" (Chinoy 1976: 546). In part, Strasberg was influenced by America's fascination with Freudian psychology in the 1920s and 1930s that conceived of the subconscious as a repository of painful and repressed memories. In the twenty-first century Strasberg's approach continues to be taught by gurus such as Ivana Chubbuck. "Every actor knows that discovering and understanding your personal pain is an inherent part of the acting process," she writes, erroneously adding that "this has been true since Stanislavski [sic]" (Chubbuck 2004: vii–x).[6]

By contrast, Stanislavsky seemed uninterested in Freud's dark conception of the subconscious. Instead, Stanislavsky taught that "we are great friends with our subconscious," because it provides an infinite source for our creative imaginations (SS II: 1989: 434–6).[7] His fictionalized self Tortsov demonstrates his understanding of the subconscious by asking two students to mention any objects not present in the room. Their answers—a shaft and a pineapple—appear random and dispassionate, yet sprang effortlessly from their subconscious minds, according to Tortsov, who then asks another student to describe what he is thinking. Before answering, the student mechanically wipes his hands against his trousers, pulls out a folded piece of paper from his pocket and unfolds it. When Tortsov asks the student to repeat his physical behavior, he cannot remember having done anything, proving that his handling of the paper is yet another instance of how easily the subconscious works in normal life (SS II 1989: 435–6).

As for emotion, Stanislavsky treats it as a sixth sense, which can be activated as easily as any of the other five (SS II 1989: 280). He underlines this treatment of emotion by using the Russian word, *chuvstva*, which refers simultaneously to "feelings" and "sensations." "If the result of scholarly and scientific analysis is *thought*," he explains, "then the result of artistic analysis should be feelings and sensations. In art, not reason but feelings and sensations prompt artistic creation" (SS IV 1991). From this perspective, when an etude elicits an emotion from you, it suggests that all your senses are heightened and working. Stanislavsky's concern for the actor's mental health, his notion that the subconscious is the actor's friend, and his envisioning of emotion as a sixth sense should, I hope, reassure you that the emotions you feel when you work with Active Analysis are evidence of your having entered into the elusive creative state that the System seeks to nurture.

Experiencing the Present Reality of Performance

Me   The System is designed to harness the actor's creative state, which in turn depends upon a belief in the fiction's possibilities, so deeply grounded in knowledge of the play that, at times, real feelings and emotions can arise during performance. Stanislavsky calls this creative state "experiencing," during which time all sorts of sensations, not only those we call emotions, become heightened. Therefore, I want to ask one last question today. What do you experience, other than emotions, when you are performing etudes?

Sargis   I feel free to play. As long as I follow the interactive principles and the facts in the text, I can go wherever I want. That freedom took me to a dead-end in my first etude on *Macbeth*. But if I hadn't allowed that mistake to happen, I might never have found the scene.

Setrak   An etude feels to me like a ping-pong match, in which I am constantly respond-ing to what my partners do. During the etudes on *Three Sisters*, I became intensely curious about what Rose and Keith would do next.

Geo   I have never been as attentive to what my partners were saying and doing, as I was when working on *The Lie*. I felt totally present and invested in what was going on at every moment.

Juliana   Whenever anyone asks me why they should learn Active Analysis, I tell them that it gives me a quick entry into a scene. You read the text, you map the principles, and you already know enough to get started. In just twenty minutes, I was playing Shakespeare. It wasn't perfect, but it was a good start. When it was time to act, I wasn't nervous. I just focused on the facts and my verb. By the end of the evening, even Shakespeare's poetry was on my tongue!

Rose   For me, an etude is a visceral experience. Learning Active Analysis is a bit like learning to dance or do gymnastics. You are told to engage your core, but until you do it, you don't know what that means. During etudes, I always feel like I am engag-ing the core of my acting.[8]

Grigor   It's hard to answer this last question. (*Laughing*.) I know it's because we're talking about tacit knowledge and using words to describe what's beyond words, but, if pushed, I would say that I feel like I'm surrendering or maybe letting go of my ego and putting my character first. Like I said earlier, it's not about being clever, but about doing simply what you have to for the sake of the scene.

Shari   I like that word "surrendering." I used to have a habit of trying to direct any scene that I was in, but in etudes, you can't control anything in advance. You have to take what comes and adjust to it.

Keith   You know me, I like to keep things simple, so I'd sum it all up this way: I know what's really going on, I'm present with my partners, and I commit fully to my verbs.

Juliana   Good, summary, Keith, but I would also add that this technique is really "active analysis," because you are constantly and actively processing what's going on in the scene whenever you are working.

Me   Your answers tell me that you all have had moments when you were "experiencing your roles." Stanislavsky would call such moments "happy" but "rare" (*SS* V Part II 1994: 363). As he developed his System, he came to realize that "the art of experi-encing" is exactly the kind of acting that he wanted to "cultivate in [his] theatre and teach in its school" (*SS* II 1989: 59).

Stanislavsky compared the actor's "experiencing" to that of a yogi who has reached the "ecstasy" of the "superconscious"—a higher state in which all your senses are sharpened and you are intensely aware of everything (*SS* V Part II 1994: 348). Drawing from Russian Orthodoxy, Stanislavsky also likens this heightened sense of presence to the spiritual state of "I am" (*ya yesm'*) (*SS* II 1989: 439). "The art of experiencing," Stanislavsky writes, "strives to act upon the audience directly by means of the presence of the actor during the act of creating the role" (Stanislavskii 1958: 483). If you prefer more contemporary analogies, consider the term "flow," coined by the psychologist Mihaly Csikszentmihalyi who studies subjective accounts by athletes and artists at peak performance, when everything for which they have trained comes easily (Csikszentmihalyi 1990).

The Russian word that Stanislavsky chooses is *perezhivanie*. Normally translated as "experience," he uses the word so eccentrically that *The Dictionary of Contemporary Russian Literary Language* attributes one of its meanings to him alone: "the genuine penetration of a psychic state in a represented character" (Hobgood 1973: 149). The prefix *pere-* ("re-") reflects Stanislavsky's understanding that repetition is a distinguishing feature of performance. In fact, it was the routinized repetition of his role in *An Enemy of the People* that had triggered the acting crisis that prompted him to search for a system. The root *zhit'* ("to live") reflects Stanislavsky's desire for the creative state to come alive at every performance. His entire System became a way of collecting technical means that would help him achieve this desire. Literally *perezhivanie* means "re-living," but another Latin root referring to life, as found in "vital" and "vitality," offers another more accurate option: the "reviving" of the creative state during performance. In the first English translations of Stanislavsky's acting manuals, Elizabeth Reynolds Hapgood translated *perezhivanie* so inconsistently that she effectively hid it in plain sight. Her choices include "the art of living a part," "to live the scene," "sensations," "living and experiencing," "experience," and "emotional experience" (Stanislavski 1936: 15; 121; 172; 15; 44; 44). Most of these translations unfortunately support the Method's overemphasis on personal emotion and the expectation that an actor become the character. In my work, I twist the usual translation into "experiencing" in order to convey both Stanislavsky's process-oriented understanding of acting and his eccentric usage.[9]

Stanislavsky defined "experiencing" by contrast with two other prevalent types of acting. First, craftsmanship (or stock-in-trade acting in Benedetti's translation) relies primarily on the use of theatrical conventions or "clichés" to present form without content "like a shell without the nut" (Stanislavskii n. d.: 11; 49; 21). Stanislavsky primarily blames commercial pressure for promoting this type of unartistic acting by forcing actors to produce results quickly and without sufficient rehearsal. As he laments, "Hurried work is a dangerous obstacle to creativity and art" (Stanislavskii n.d.: 52). Second, gestural acting was practiced by successful local actors and international stars like Benoît-Constant Coquelin and Sarah Bernhardt. Stanislavsky calls this type of acting representation, following the lead of Coquelin, who had written that "art is not identification, but representation" (Coquelin 1970: 199). Actors of this type are gripped by the creative state only during rehearsals. When performing, they utilize their technical virtuosities to present the results of their earlier creativity. Something akin to this split between rehearsal and performance had occurred in Stanislavsky's work on the role of Dr. Stockmann. While Stanislavsky recognized representation as artistic, he rejected the school's skewed emphasis on the person of the actor as star. "We love the individuality and art of these actors more than we do their creations," he explains (Stanislavskii n. d.: 110).

By contrast, "experiencing" demands that actors put their characters' stories above their own egos. By inviting the audience into the actor's laboratory and by treating the creative act and the performance as one and the same, the art of experiencing remains essentially active and improvisatory, no matter how well-rehearsed and polished the performances. If you strive for "experiencing your role," then Active Analysis will provide you a simple pathway that will likely take you there.

In Practice: The Exercise as a "Little Piece of Art"

But we have talked long enough. In our short course we dove directly into Active Analysis, skipping over the kinds of exercises that derive from Stanislavsky's System and that help build good acting habits. By practicing the same exercises regularly you become in time an actor who automatically relaxes, concentrates, and observes, making it easier for you to attend to your role and its interactive dynamics while performing.

Exercises deconstruct acting, treating each of its elements separately. At the Opera-Dramatic Studio, Stanislavsky required all his assistants to create for their students a range of exercises on relaxation, concentration, observation, and the like. These were further enhanced by requiring all students to study voice and dance, so that they could better express outwardly their understanding of their characters' inner lives. Exercises are valuable for a number of reasons. For one, carefully chosen exercises can help actors overcome their specific difficulties. For another, a short series can serve as a warm-up for work, much as dancers use a barre. Stanislavsky first used exercises as preparation in 1937 for what he called the actor's *toilette* which is French for getting dressed (Chapter 2). I urge each of you to develop your own personal actor's barre or *toilette* to warm up daily and whenever you need to ready yourself for an audition, class, or rehearsal.

Once acting has been deconstructed, however, it can be a challenge to put its elements back together again. Acting is a holistic activity that uses all of you simultaneously from the hair on your head down to your feet planted on the floor. As Stanislavsky explains, the sum is always more than the parts:

> How astounding a creation is our nature! How everything in it is bound together, blended, and interdependent! Take, for example, the state of the actor on stage. The slightest dislocation in something planned destroys the whole.

> (SS III 1991: 314)

As in a musical chord, one false note can cause disharmony. By treating the various elements in acting as if they were separable from the whole, exercises can create an artificial gap between acting skills and the acting process. I have met actors, who became experts in exercises without being able to transfer their skills to the performance of texts. In order to avoid this gap, I started our course with etudes and scenes. To do an etude well you need to relax, concentrate, and observe closely all at the same time. Your skills develop because you need them. As Knebel's protégé, Anatoly Efros, always told his students, if you know *what* to do, you will figure out *how*.[10] Having experienced the holistic process of acting, you can now better leverage exercises to help sharpen your skills.

The Russian teacher, Natalya Zvereva, once told me that she had always thought exercises tedious, until Knebel offered her the following advice: If you perform every exercise "as if it were a little piece of art," you will never get bored and will always find value in what you do.[11] As I lead you through these exercises now, I ask that you treat each one as "a little piece of art."

Three Classic Exercises from Stanislavsky's System

Let's begin with some historical exercises that derive from Stanislavsky's First Studio, which he founded in 1911 for the systematic study of acting. They derive from Ramacharaka's books on Hatha and Raja Yoga and from the classes on Hindu philosophy that Stanislavsky attended at the Moscow Art Theatre in 1916 in connection with a planned production of a play by the Nobel Prize-winning Indian author Rabindranath Tagore (Stroeva 1973 vol. 1: 19 and 1977 vol. 2: 330).

THE REPOSE OF THE CAT

Creative work needs relaxation, which like "the repose of the waiting cat" does not ready you for sleep, but rather for making your "every motion count" (Ramacharaka 1904: 175; 169). As Ramacharaka explains, "The person understanding relaxation and the conserving of energy accomplishes the best work. He uses a pound of effort to do the pound of work, and does not waste or allow his strength to trickle away" (Ramacharaka 1904: 174). Close your eyes and follow my voice.

- Sit upright in your chair, spine erect. Rock your feet back and forth in order to feel the floor beneath you. Take a moment to sense the ceiling through the top of your head. Feel yourself suspended between floor and ceiling. Start by paying conscious attention to the normally unconscious functioning of your breath.
- Inhale deeply through your nose and send the breath down into your toes; hold the breath; and then exhale out through your mouth, sending the breath up through the top of your head. Hold for a few seconds before taking your next breath.
- Repeat this pattern several times, adding a rhythm: count 4 to inhale, 7 to hold, and 8 to exhale. Allow this rhythm to slow you down and bring you to the present moment.

Now focus on your body:

- As you inhale, raise your right arm up over your head and extend your fingers toward the ceiling. Keep extending your arm and fingers upwards while you exhale. If you raised your right shoulder along with your arm, drop it back into place during the exhale.
- Inhale and extend; then exhale swiftly, allowing your arm to drop down over your head. Your right hand should now connect with your left ear.
- Inhale again. As you exhale, use your arm to pull your head gently toward your right shoulder, stretching the left side of your neck.
- Inhale again and on the exhale pull your head gently downward on a diagonal toward the floor, stretching the back of your neck.
- Use every inhale to deepen your stretch and every exhale to relax the stretch.
- Inhale again and this time, as you exhale, bring your head back to center, square your shoulders, and raise your hand back up toward the ceiling. Hold this pose and your breath for a few seconds, as you feel yourself suspended between floor and ceiling.
- Inhale again and, as you exhale, let your arm "drop of [its] own weight." Ramacharaka reminds us that "this is a hard thing for most persons to do at first trial […] so firmly has the habit of involuntary muscular contraction fastened itself upon them" (Ramacharaka 1904: 180–1).

Repeat this entire pattern to the left.

- Turn your attention now to your legs. Inhale, becoming aware of your right leg. As you exhale, stretch the leg along the floor as if it were being pulled forward by an invisible force.

- Inhale again and this time, as you exhale, raise your leg up to a horizontal position. Hold this pose as you take your next inhalation. Become aware of the weight of the air pushing down against your leg, as you use your muscles to hold it steady.
- Inhale again and, as you exhale, let your right leg drop of its own accord.

Repeat this pattern with your left leg.

- Now shift attention away from yourself to the floor. Learning to exercise your ability to turn attention away from yourself seems especially important, because we work in a medium that so often prompts self-consciousness.
- Think about how gravity pulls you down into the floor. Without the floor pushing up against your weight, you would fall through into the earth.
- Place all your attention on the force coming from the floor, as it pushes up against the legs of your chair and the bottoms of your feet. Allow your body to surrender to the force exerted by the floor.
- Think about the texture of the floor, the materials from which it is made, how old it is, when it was laid, and by whom.
- Finally, consider what you share with the floor. Is it enough to say that you are both in the same room? Can you imagine how the atoms which make up your body and the floor might be similar?
- "In doing this [exercise]," Ramacharaka writes, "you will find that here and there are certain muscles still in a tense condition—let go of them" (Ramacharaka 1904: 180). Stanislavsky imagined that each of us has an "internal monitor" that we can imaginatively send through our bodies, looking for areas of tension (SS II: 1989: 188). Do this now, and whenever you find a tense muscle, exhale and say to it, "Let go." Ramacharaka writes, "If you do this thoroughly (you will improve by practice) you will end by having every muscle in the body fully relaxed and the nerves at rest" (Ramacharaka 1904: 180).
- To bring this exercise to its conclusion, allow the sound of *om*—containing within it all the vowels—to vibrate throughout your body. Take a long inhale through your nose, and on the exhale hum *a-e-i-o-u-mmm*, extending the sound of each vowel and feeling its unique vibration. Repeat three times.

CIRCLES OF ATTENTION

Knebel observes, "Attention is the antennae that we human beings have for communicating with the world around us. The stronger our attention and the more we notice in life, the deeper we penetrate into the heart of things" (Knebel' 1976: 57). You can learn to control your attention, to bend it to your will, and to select what to tune in and what to tune out from the massive amount of details that constantly vie for your attention. As some of you have observed, your scene partners are often your most important objects of attention. Can you attend to the subtlest signals given out by them, while paying little or no attention to spectators, who are unwrapping candy and coughing or to the technicians on a film set who are adjusting the cameras? This exercise trains you to attend to whatever you choose (SS II: 1989: 158–63):[12]

- Keeping your eyes closed, listen to whatever you can hear in this hall. Do you hear others breathing or moving? Is there the whir of a heater or air conditioner? The hum of the lighting? Is there a cricket in the corner? This is a medium-sized circle of attention. Choose and remember three distinct sounds.

- Now narrow your focus to a small circle of attention that includes only your body. Can you hear your own breathing? Your heartbeat? Your pulse? Does your watch or jewelry make any sound? Choose in order to remember one clear sound in this circle.
- Shift back to the medium circle of attention and see if the three sounds you identified a moment ago are still there. Then immediately shift back to your small circle.
- Now broaden your circle of attention to what lays beyond this hall. Make it the largest circle that you can. Listen and identify three sounds in this large circle. Does a motorcycle pass by? Is there a car starting? Are there voices of passers-by on the street? Do they sound happy or angry? Choose to remember at least three sounds.
- Shift your circle several times, randomly going from large to small or medium, and back again.
- Finally, recall each sound you identified and weave them together in a story. Allow the story to be as realistic or as fantastic as you like.

THE TREE

Stanislavsky was fascinated by the ways in which meditation techniques can strengthen an actor's six senses and imagination through the process of visualization. The following meditation (*SS* II 1989: 133–6) is intended to bring your attention to nature and thus activate your higher consciousness, called the "superconscious" by Ramacharaka (1906: 120). Unlike the "unconscious" that functions automatically (like breath and tacit knowledge) or the "subconscious" part of the mind that stores memories and associations, the "superconscious" transcends the material world and connects to the spiritual plane. Stanislavsky saw it as the true seat of creativity and defines it as what "most of all elevates a person's soul and thus must be valued and preserved in our art" (Vinogradskaia 2000: 58).

In this exercise there is only one rule. When I ask a question, go with your first association whatever springs to your mind, because each answer becomes a choice upon which other choices are then built. For example, if you decide that your visualization takes place at night, you cannot then shift to day. Going forward, whatever you see, hear or smell is conditioned by the fact that it is night.

To prepare, close your eyes and imagine that you are sitting in a cocoon of light, which represents your creative space. See with your mind's eye where the edges drop off into darkness. Imagine that the light has color and warmth. See the color and feel the warmth on your skin. It is as if you are caught in a spotlight that isolates you in time and space, allowing you freedom to create. The visualization proper now begins.

- Imagine that you are a tree. See it in your mind's eye. What species are you? How tall have you grown? How straight or bent? What do your leaves or needles look like? Notice that you have already made choices in your answers, some conscious and other not. For example, if you imagined your leaves as green, you may have set your vision in spring or summer. Attend to everything that surrounds each choice you make.
- See more. See the texture of your bark. Add the number and shape of your branches.

- Now imagine yourself looking out and observing your location. Are you growing near a beach or a highway? Are you in a backyard or a forest? Study the specifics of your environment. Embroider each detail that springs to mind.
- Add the sense of touch. How does the light feel as it hits your branches and trunk? Is it strong and warm like the sun at mid-day or soft and cool as at twilight? Notice that your answers may also suggest a time of day, a season of the year, or a geographical location.
- Now send your roots down into the dark ground. How do they feel as they go deeper? Is the soil sandy or moist? Rocky or dry? Warm or cold? How grounded do you feel?
- Shift your attention to your branches and imagine how they feel as they extend up toward the sky. Is the air warm or cold? Does rain or hail hit them? Do you feel wind through your branches, or is the air still?
- Bring together the sensations of your roots reaching down and your branches upward. Feel suspended between earth and sky.
- Breathe deeply and slowly as you review all the specific choices you have made so far in your visualization. You are a particular tree, growing in a particular place, at a particular time. Bring all these choices together into a single image before continuing.
- Now add sound to your environment. What do you hear based on where you are? Are there birds, waves, or cars traveling by? Keep building detail upon detail.
- Add the sense of smell. Is there a perfume in the air or the foul odor of garbage?
- Does anything come to you as a taste? Perhaps the sap, running through you is sweet or tart? Can you taste something in the air?
- Breathe deeply, review your choices, and then sharpen and consolidate all your impressions. Dwell for a time in your imagination.
- Suddenly you are aware that something is happening right in front of you. Observe it closely. Perhaps it is a lover's tryst, children playing, a battle, the start of a forest fire, a robbery, or an act of generosity toward another. Watch this event unfold step by step and narrate the story to yourself, as it unfolds. Take your time. Allow yourself to become involved in what you see.

When you reach the end of the event, let your visualization dissolve. You are back in your cocoon of light. Take a few deep breaths and continue to listen to my voice.

- Notice that I did not ask you to imagine a tree that you know in life. Perhaps you chose a familiar tree. Perhaps you created a fantastic one. The choice was yours. I did not insist that you mine either your personal life or your imagination.
- Next, think about what you felt as the event that you imagined was unfolding. Did your heart race? Did you feel compassion for those caught up in the story? Did you feel happy at others' happiness? Did you feel fear from an approaching danger? The story was the prompt to your sixth sense, which is often best triggered by compassion for others. If an emotion came to you, Stanislavsky would say that you successfully activated your sixth sense as you had earlier activated the other five. If not, then perhaps emotion will come the next time you try a visualization.
- To end, take another deep breath. Wiggle your toes, fingers, and eyelashes. Open your eyes and come back into our hall.

Everyone seems mellow and confident. Geo leans over to tell Shari about how he pictured himself as a redwood. At first, he noticed animals rushing past him and felt curious to know why they were running. Not until he smelled smoke did he realize that a fire was sweeping through the forest and approaching him. Then he became afraid for the animals and for himself. I also hear Juliana telling Setrak about how peaceful she felt, as she watched a picnic being laid out beneath her branches. The smell of strawberries made her mouth water. Speaking to his brother, Sargis describes the tree in their grandfather's backyard, while Grigor responds with a laugh, saying that he saw himself on a faraway planet as an alien tree with fuchsia-colored leaves and bright blue bark. I step into the conversation to suggest that, when they try this meditation technique again, they imagine something else entirely—sitting on a beach; flying on a magic carpet or in a space ship; eating a magical apple—or use it to work on a role by creating their character's home or daily routine.

Knebel's Favorite Exercise: Devising a Story through Gestures

I have one more exercise to share. Knebel developed and taught this one at the State Institute for Theatrical Arts (Zvereva 2021: 103). I use it whenever I want to turn a group of individuals into a collaborative ensemble. It goes like this:

- The group sits in a semicircle around a single chair or stool, where a story will unfold silently through gestures.
- The group closes their eyes and takes three deep breaths to clear their minds.
- The exercise begins with the first actor on either side of the semicircle going to the central chair. She makes the story's first simple gesture. For example, she might raise her right hand to her forehead and peer off to the left, as if looking for some-one. After holding the gesture for a moment, she then returns to her place in the semicircle.
- The person sitting next to her then takes the central chair, repeats the first gesture exactly as it was performed, then adds a new one of his own that advances the story. For example, after peering under his hand off to the left, he might drop his arm and look at the watch on his left wrist, thinking, "Where is my friend?" He then returns to his place.
- The next person in line goes to the central chair, repeats the first two gestures exactly as they were initially performed, then adds a third. Perhaps, after checking the time, he stands impatiently, tapping his right foot and folding his arms across his chest.
- The exercise proceeds in this fashion, with each actor in turn adding a gesture, until the last person concludes the story.

This exercise is deceptively simple but takes a great deal of practice to perform correctly. The actors must repeat every gesture exactly as its originator first executed it. Did she use her right hand or left? Did they move slowly or quickly? What was happening in the lower body when the arms were crossed? The actors also need to follow the internal logic of the story by imagining the thoughts behind each gesture. Did these thoughts emerge clearly? Was there a story? Did it have a beginning, middle, and end? The first time you do this exercise, you will likely forget many things that you have observed. Was it her right hand or left? Did the third gesture include tapping of the foot or not? Once you master this exercise, however, you will find that it strengthens most of the good habits you need as actors: relaxed attention, careful observation, efficient memory, the will to collaborate with others, and the ability to connect thought to gesture and tell stories through your body. This exercise also provides valuable training for screen acting, which demands that in reaction shots and close-ups actors must repeat exactly what they did in the earlier master shot. If they cannot, they may be edited out of the final film.

I turn to Rose, who knows this exercise well and ask her to lead the group in a few rounds, as I clear the table. Rose resets the chairs and begins. Knowing that this exercise can become addictive when each story emerges as "a little piece of art," I finish cleaning up and settle down to watch.

Notes

1. The reference to February 29 was included in Stanislavsky's initial draft, but removed from the first Soviet publication. I have kept it, because I find it amusing.
2. Stanislavsky owned Russian translations of Ramacharaka's *Raja Yoga* (1906) and *Hatha Yoga* (1904). Both books are still in print. For more on Stanislavsky's interest in Ramacharaka see Carnicke (2009: 170–83) and White (2005: 73–2).
3. Some have argued that Stanislavsky's call for belief links him to the romantic school, as does Worthen, who writes: "Much like the Romantic artist, Stanislavsky's actor must overcome the invalidating restrictions of his milieu to achieve a genuine, self-creating art form—a life in art" (1984: 145).
4. I thank Natalie Peyser, my intern for the National Science Foundation sponsored project on emotional expressivity, conducted at the University of Southern California's Viterbi School of Engineering (Lesson 6), for this analogy.
5. This anecdote was shared with me by a well-known actor in Puerto Rico during my intensive course on Active Analysis at the Victoria Espinoza Theatre in San Juan, 2009.
6. Chubbuck adds that her technique grew "out of my search to overcome my own personal traumas" and that she can teach "even a non-actor […] to learn how to use your pain and win your goals" (2004: vii–x).
7. Freud was translated into Russian in 1910 and recommended to Stanislavsky in 1911, but there is no firm evidence that he took the recommendation. When required by Soviet censors, he looked into Ivan Pavlov's research on conditioning. The only psychologist whom Stanislavsky studied deeply was the French behaviorist, Théodule Ribot (Carnicke 2009: 155; 162–3).
8. I thank Francesca Calvo, an actor who is a member of my Studio and has assisted me in my classes at the University of Southern California, for this metaphor.
9. Jean Benedetti follows suit in his translation of *An Actor's Work* (2008).
10. As recalled by the Russian actor, Lyubov Zabolotskaia Weidner, in a personal discussion on August 22, 2021.
11. From a private conversation in Italy at the *MetodiFestival*, 2008. In Zvereva's latest book, she quotes Knebel as attributing this idea to Michael Chekhov (2021: 103).
12. Reminiscent of this exercise is Tovstonogov's division of a play's given circumstances into three circles: the small includes anything that creates conflict within the plot; the medium embraces conditions that affect the characters' lives; and the large circle refers to the story's social, historical, and cultural conditions (Malochevskaia 2003: 37–8).

Lesson 6 Working with Active Analysis in the Real World

Prelude

We are gathering today for the last session of our intensive course on Active Analysis. I look over at the table, laden with desserts that Louisa has baked and spy my favorite rum cake. Clearly, the group is ready to celebrate. However, I am left wondering whether I have conveyed the technique's full richness and range. The more I have worked with its simple principles the more I understand how they embrace human complexity. I also understand why Knebel warned that when the simple is "reduced to the simplistic, that which is complex loses its true scope" (Chekhov 1995 vol. 2: 22). Such reductive thinking had allowed Soviet loyalists to distort Stanislavsky's last ideas by limiting them to the realm of physical action.

Time and time again I have seen how flexibly Active Analysis applies to plays in different aesthetic styles and for new performance media. When I directed *Uncle Vanya* at the National Academy of the Arts in Norway, I used the technique to develop a theatricalist production with each act beginning in a percussive composition, created by the actors to convey Chekhov's use of sound effects as the music of everyday life (Carnicke 2013: 122–4).[1] During a three-year scientific investigation into the ways that emotion is expressed through physical gesture, I used the technique for performance capture, a cinematic technology that denies actors the trappings of costumes and sets, while recording their motion as computer data, not their images (Carnicke 2012: 321–38). I have also investigated the technique's use at special sessions in my Studio for postdramatic, expository-heavy works that do away with characters in any traditional sense of the word and as a guide for devising new content for stage and new media (Carnicke 2016). Active Analysis is a living legacy, precisely because it readily adapts to works and media that its creators could never have imagined.

The actors are milling around, hugging each other, and patting themselves on their backs. Shari is wandering around with a grab bag full of gifts, inviting everyone to select one. When I picked her up, she placed the bag in the back of my car and handed me a package. "I wanted you to have this one," she said as I unwrapped a lovely, old-fashioned feather pen. "I know you are writing a book," she smiled. Now I see that Grigor has chosen a small picture frame and Hannah is paging through her new mini-planner.

As I watch them, I feel fairly confident that all have advanced in their acting. Those who are new to Active Analysis have grasped its dynamic principles sufficiently to keep working with it. The others have added new dimensions to their practice. The more Geo put aside his previous ways of working and trusted to the etude process, the freer he became in his acting choices. Keith experienced for the first time the difference between mentally and viscerally feeling what it is to play an active verb. Even Louisa, whose career in film and television is extensive, deepened her practice, when she discovered how traveling along a false path in an etude can suddenly illuminate another, richer way.

Rose has managed to get all the actors into their seats. As I join them, I ask a simple question: "How will you use Active Analysis in your future work?" I look at them. They look back at me without responding. I am considering whether I should explain the reason behind my question, when I hear the door behind me open. Tiffany Cole has snuck in and is standing just inside the door with Liliana Carillo. "When we decided to meet for dinner, we chose the restaurant around the corner, hoping that that you would be here in the Studio," says Tiffany. "We'll just sit quietly to the side and observe, if you don't mind," Liliana adds. Both have been long-time members of the Studio. Tiffany acts on stage and screen and supplements her income with teaching at a local college. For her 2019 breakthrough performance, she played the title character in *Fefu and Her Friends* by the Cuban born playwright, María Irene Fornés, at the Odyssey Theatre in Los Angeles. Liliana appears in the regional theatres of southern California, while also working as an educator in the public schools. Keith and Juliana get chairs for them.

"What good luck to have you drop by today," I say. "We were just about to begin a discussion about taking Active Analysis outside this Studio. You and Louisa Abernathy have been doing just that for some time, and so I insist that you three tell us your stories before this session is over." But first, I turn to the group and explain why I consider this session's topic to be the necessary conclusion to our course. My reasons are twofold, involving the production conditions under which actors work and the various career paths open to them.

The Ideal Meets the Real

After conducting one of my first workshops on Active Analysis in Finland, a number of actors shared with me their experience of having gone to study in Russia. They returned, inspired by the technique, but soon realized that they could not import the training without also importing the Russian repertory system. In short, they felt unable to practice Active Analysis in their native land. From that moment, I decided to focus my teaching on the simple, interactive principles behind Active Analysis that are widely applicable in all sorts of situations and always to include a roundtable on how these principles can be productively used in the work-a-day world of acting.[2]

Stanislavsky once called his System "a culture in which to grow" (*SS* III 1990: 371–2). He could have said the same of Active Analysis as a discrete rehearsal technique, since it consolidates everything in his overall system. Like a culture, any practice in the arts demands years to master and Active Analysis is no exception. My understanding and practice of it have evolved and continue to evolve whenever I take on a challenging, new project. In the last few weeks, we have spent relatively little time together in this hall. Nonetheless, we forged an ensemble by exploring some texts in a like-minded, collaborative fashion, much as Stanislavsky's and Knebel's students would have done decades ago. We set aside our egos, trusted and respected each other, and honestly assessed what we had achieved and where we had failed. In effect, we created an ideal Petri dish in which to nurture the culture of Active Analysis.

But let's not kid ourselves! Outside this hall, you will rarely find such ideal conditions, unless you are in the fortunate position to make them yourselves. This clash between the ideal and the real is nothing new. Let me share a letter sent to Knebel by a former directing student who had graduated from her course about ten years earlier:

> You taught us to be artists, and we understood and valued that. You made us thirst for creative work. We wanted to build a new kind of theatre. […] But, then we found ourselves in a real-life theatre. We clashed with the peculiarities and problems that exist there. We saw how other directors worked […] We were ready to collaborate with our actors, but they said, 'Just tell me what to do and I will do it. Don't wear us out with etudes!' […] So, I taught myself to work like a craftsman instead.
>
> (Knebel' 1976: 292–3)

You will remember that craftsmanship is Stanislavsky's term for the kind of unartistic acting that emerges from hastily prepared, commercial productions (Lesson 5). By giving in to the expectations of those around him, Knebel's student confessed, "I no longer felt the joy that goes with being an artist. Besides that, I saw how quickly theatrical conventions become clichés that are stale, old-fashioned, and tasteless" (Knebel' 1976: 292–3).

Louisa I can understand the letter-writer's feelings, but if we want to work as professional actors, we have to face the fact that acting is a business. Once we do that, we don't get so easily discouraged.

Rose But facing that fact shouldn't mean that we also have to betray what it is we value.

Me That is what Knebel's student finally realized. After stumbling, he regained his footing by reconnecting with the values that are implicit in the technique. He ends his letter this way:

> You nurtured my taste, kept me from small-mindedness and crudeness. […] Most importantly, you fostered tact and decency, honesty, and boldness without arrogance in us. All this—in art and in life, gives us the chance to overcome our failures, without losing belief in ourselves and our work. This is the base, that is solid, that gives me confidence and perspective.
>
> (Knebel' 1976: 293–4)

Tiffany "Boldness without arrogance!" That reminds me of what Michael Chekhov said about actors needing generosity and humility (Lesson 5). Ego gets us only so far.

Louisa "The chance to overcome our failures!" We all need that for sure. I certainly made my share of mistakes along the way.

Grigor I'm sorry to inject a note of negativity, but I don't quite see how this letter applies to us. Knebel's student crashed into a wall of reality, got up and started again. But he was a director whose job is to take charge of rehearsals. As actors we are not in the same position. We cannot insist on others using Active Analysis.

Anisha Grigor is right. What control do we have? After our lesson on *Three Sisters*, I was so smitten with Active Analysis that all I wanted to do was work this way forever. I started talking to everyone about it. I called up my former acting teachers. I asked my new agent about it. I talked to other actors. I was shocked at how few people had heard of it, and those who had just snickered and told me that it is too much trouble to use. Then I phoned my friend, Caroline Sanchez, who urged me to join this Studio. She loves Active Analysis too. She said that for a while she thought of Active Analysis as a kind of unicorn—an ideal, beautiful, wonderful, but also a fantastic fiction.

Keith   Nope, Active Analysis is real all right. I'm out there. I book a commercial now and again, nothing fancy. I would put it this way. I came to class, and Sharon said, "let's make a table." To do that, I had to learn how to use a hammer and knock in some nails. So now, we've made the table, and I'm walking out with the ability to use a hammer for a lot of other things. I can put nails in walls, floors, bookshelves, whatever you want.[3] That's how I see what's happening here. We work on a scene, and I come away knowing how to use actions, counteractions, and verbs—yes, verbs!—for anything I damn well chose to do. Pardon my French, ladies.

Geo   Just be careful not to use a hammer on a screw! (*Everyone laughs.*)

Hannah   If you are saying that Active Analysis is a set of tools, don't forget about *razbor*—reading for the facts. I learned how to dig deep and get beyond the obvious to figure out what is really going on in the text. And then there's *zadacha*, the character's problem. When I get stuck in a scene, I step back and ask myself, "what's my problem?" If I can answer that question, everything tends to fall into place.

Keith   Do you guys remember Francesca Calvo? (*Louisa, Shari, and our three guests nod enthusiastically.*) She's been picking up quite a bit of voice-over work lately. She once told me that recent commercials are just little scenes. They are all about problems and solutions. If you can identify the *zadacha* and then come up with a verb to solve it, you are all set.

Tiffany   But Active Analysis is more than a set of tools. It's also a mindset, a way of thinking about plays and performance.

Sargis   In other words, it's a culture, like Stanislavsky said.

Rose   It has certainly changed the way I think. When I'm using Active Analysis, I'm like a fish, swimming in water. I no longer notice the water, but it's there. The same way a fish takes the water for granted, I now take it for granted that a play is a score for performance and scenes are collisions between actions and counteractions. Once I understand how each role in a scene contributes to its dynamics, I feel grounded in my acting.

Keith   And verbs—the nails that hold everything together! Oh, I almost forgot! (*Pulling a book from his jacket pocket and holding it up for all to see.*) I found this at our local library sale—*501 English Verbs* by Thomas S Beyer, Jr. (*Reading from the copyright page.*) Barron's Educational Series from Hauppauge, New York, 1998. (*Looking up.*) Perfect, don't you think? I'm happy to share it.

Grigor   I use the thesaurus on my phone, Keith. It's more convenient.

Geo   So, is Active Analysis a mindset or a set of tools?

Setrak   It's both.

Me   And how you use it depends on what you are trying to do. Which brings me to my next point …

Various Paths in Acting

There are as many paths to a career in acting as there are actors. When I was working in New York, I admired the Puerto Rican actor, Raúl Juliá. He played Edmund to James Earl Jones' King Lear with an intensity that was riveting to watch at Joseph Papp's Shakespeare in the Park. I remember standing in line for hours at Lincoln Center for the Performing Arts to get a ticket to see his Lopakhin in *The Cherry Orchard*. When Juliá was asked to describe how he became an actor at the American Theatre Wing's Seminar on "Working in the Theatre," he prefaced his remarks by saying, "I can tell you about what happened to me as a matter of curiosity," but "don't think that it might happen for others" in the same way, because "you cannot make rules out of this game. All circumstances are different," and every career necessarily develops in its own way.[4] Whether you think about Active Analysis as a culture, in which to grow your passion for acting, or as a set of pragmatic tools, it can serve as your guide. How you will use it is ultimately up to you and your aspirations.

Stage and Screen

Just look around you.[5] Liliana prefers theatre. Louisa has worked primarily in film and television. Tiffany has combined screen acting with live performance. Their stories will suggest how Active Analysis can be used in these familiar venues.

Liliana Carrillo: The Art of Regional Theatre

I have always preferred working on stage, where I feel connected not only to my partners, but also to the audience. This is my art. That's why I love Knebel's advice that we treat everything we do as "a little piece of art" (Chapter 2 and Lesson 5). If that's how we think as human beings and actors, then what we do *is* art.

I have utilized Active Analysis for live theatre productively. It has been especially beneficial when I have had to make an acting choice quickly. For example, I have often been thrown into a show as a replacement after three or four weeks of rehearsals. The rest of the actors have been working together and then I pop in as a last minute substitution, because something happened to someone. That's what happened when I played Cassandra for the Torrance Theater Company's production of *Vanya and Sonia and Masha and Spike* by Christopher Durang. At my audition, I was expected to step into an already rehearsed scene with the cast. The director asked me what I needed to prepare and I said that I wanted to watch a scene that Cassandra is not in. "I just want to watch you rehearse, so that I can figure out how to insert myself into what you have already created," I told him. You see, I didn't have the time to build a role. I had to see what was happening, pick something, and then just do it. Active Analysis really lends itself to that kind of thinking, because in the Studio we often repeat etudes in order to try out different verbs. I watched. They handed me the text of a scene. I made a choice on the spot. I reminded myself that I don't need to be particularly attached to the choice, I just have to be able to do it. Based on my observations, I thought Cassandra was full of life unlike the other depressed characters. So I chose "to inject life into this house" as my verb. That's how I blasted into the scene.

After the audition was over, I asked the director if he wanted to see it another way. "No," he said, "You've got the part. Just keep doing it that way." But this is what I love about Active Analysis. If he had said that he didn't like what I did, it would not have been a big deal. I could easily have said, "okay, let me try something else." With this way of working, if something doesn't work, then it doesn't work. Try the next thing! You're not hurting my feelings. My soul is not crushed. I'm not a destroyed actor, because my verb didn't work. Let me find another one. With Active Analysis our choices can change and fluctuate. That helps me, even if I'm the only person on the stage utilizing this process.

I think that what Hannah just said about reading for the facts as a tool is right. When I audition, I like to read the entire play beforehand, if it is available. In fact, when I read the play, I can almost always guess correctly what scene they will likely ask me to do for the audition. Reading for the facts is beneficial, because I can bring an idea into the room with me. I make my choice and I play my verb. If they want something else, I can change.

Another thing that I do is translate whatever is asked of me into the terms of Active Analysis. Directors use so very many words. I get lost in all those words. A director might say, "That was good, but ... " Then after five more sentences, she finally ends up telling me what mood or emotion she wants from me. But these things are not tangible. I cannot play a mood. I cannot "be angry." So I filter everything they say through Active Analysis. I can't play a mood, but I can do something that might suggest one. I cannot give you anger, but I can do something that will lead me to explode. Playing anger or a mood will only lead to clichéd results.

Speaking of results, I keep getting cast as a woman who breaks down and cries. When I get a new script and I see that on page 26 I'm going to have to cry, I know what my ultimate end will have to be. But, as Stanislavsky warns, if you worry about the results at the outset, you will only end up with worn-out clichés. When I trust the process in Active Analysis, the crying comes. By knowing if I'm the action or the counteraction, I know what reality my character desires for herself. Then, when circumstances or another character denies me that reality, I get frustrated and the tears come. So for me it's about connecting with the circumstances in the play that frustrate your character. By doing that, it's easier to cry near, if not exactly on, page 26!

I want to end by talking about memorization, because so many jobs require that you come letter perfect to rehearsals. Since studying Active Analysis, I have found that if I remain focused on what I'm doing, memorization is no longer an issue for me. I know *what* the lines mean to the character and that is *why* I remember them. What I cannot remember tells me what I don't yet understand about the scene. My lapse helps me revisit the facts in a productive way. I don't sit there memorizing. It's about understanding how what I'm saying is connected to the event.

This approach to memorization, together with the way that we do etudes, has also helped me know what to do when my partners forget their lines, because I am comfortable thinking on my feet. They just keep talking. They throw in lines from the end of the scene. And I think to myself, "Wait, we can't go to the end yet. We're going to miss chunks of the story. The scene won't make any sense." So I maneuver around and guide them back. I can do this because I understand what's happening and why we're saying the things that need to be said. Once, when this happened to me, I thought my partner would be angry. Instead, she said, "Oh my God, you saved me." These things I'm able to do, because of the flexibility that Active Analysis allows. I'm not tied to a memorized script. Yes, my job as an actor is to say what is written on the page and to hold to the integrity of the play. But before I can do that, I have to understand why these words are given to me. For me, this process of work has been very beneficial. After all, the actor's job is ultimately to tell the story that the playwright intends to be told, not to say memorized lines.

Louisa Abernathy: The Business of Screen Acting

Everything that all of you have said so far sounds right. Active Analysis has changed my point of view on my characters. It has given me new tools. And I do use it to prepare for auditions and roles. But, as I said earlier, if you don't understand the way the industry works, nothing, not even Active Analysis, can keep your spirits high. Once you know and accept the business end of things, you don't get hurt as much. So whenever you come to me, I'm going to talk about this as a business with some art in there somewhere.

I was a theatre major in college, but I came to LA to work in the film and television industry. While I had a lot to learn at the start, I have had a blessed career, working with so many great actors, even my idol James Earl Jones in his television series, *Gabriel's Fire,* for which I had a recurring role! I've done so many television shows that I can't remember all the titles. I have a fair number of films under my belt too. I remember a nice scene with Walter Matthau in *Out to Sea* (dir. Martha Coolidge, 1997) and working on the Tyler Perry film *Diary of a Mad Black Woman* (dir. Darren Grant, 2005). I have no regrets.

I consider myself mostly a day-player. That's when you get hired for a small part, and you get called to the set for a day—usually a very long day—maybe two if you're lucky. Before the merger of the Screen Actors Guild and AFTRA, which represented actors on radio and television, there was a standard contract for "under five," that's under five lines. And some still use that cut off for soap operas and sit coms and such. So that's me—a day-player and an "under five," and that's okay. I'm here to make a living. I don't need to be anybody's star.

It has often been said that the hardest thing is to be a day-player. You don't get a lot of help, because you are not the star. The project is not about you. You are hired to do your job without any fuss. Besides that, the pace of work is very fast. They have no time for you to work on your art. But don't put this kind of work down. You are supporting the project. What you are doing is important. What was it that Stanislavsky said? There are no small roles, only small actors? I live by that saying and have been fortunate.

The challenge is to develop your character out of very little. Your lines might be "hello," "goodbye," or "whatever." That doesn't give you much time on screen. Some characters are easier to play than others. For example, it can be easier when you get a role that is a little closer to who you are. Call it "type-casting!" But, even then, you have to remember that you're still a character. They may say, "just be yourself," but they still want you to play the character that they think you are. So, again, you have to remember that you are always playing a character.

To meet the challenge, you have to bring something memorable to your roles and I have found that the verbs in Active Analysis are especially useful in doing that. What you bring is the only control you've got. Not to mention the fact that, if you don't bring something they find interesting, they can edit you right out of the project. Having a few verbs in my pocket allows me to change direction whenever they want something else. If the casting director doesn't like what I do, I just shift my verb. Active Analysis also trains you to be bold and try things that could turn out to be memorable. Even before I knew about this technique, I always had an instinct to try something memorable in my auditions. For example, I once had an audition and the script said that my character runs out of the room screaming, and so I did that. Most people don't do such things, but I got the part! Active Analysis supports that instinct of mine.

When I first got to LA, I had to learn a lot about the technical aspects of film and television. So I took work anywhere I could, even as an extra. I was always glad to be on a set, letting them pay me to learn. I wasn't there to make friends. I have a lot of those. I was there to watch and observe. I remember my first job as a principal, playing the role of a game show contestant. Well, I did my scene. The director says, "that's wonderful." I say, "can I go now?" At that time I didn't know that if there are ten people in the scene, then after they shoot you, they have to shoot the close-ups of all the others, reacting to you. It was so tedious, a very long, long day. Of course, the director does let the main stars go home, leaving you to work the close-ups with the assistant director reading your partner's lines off-camera. So, when you look past the camera, all you see is somebody walking by, maybe eating, or whatever. It's hard, so I always do stick around and read with my partners, because I know that people appreciate it. But when your partner has gone, Active Analysis helps fill in what's missing. I put myself in the imaginary circumstances, think about my verb, and doing that I can even cry easily. I don't think about it as a technique really, but that's what we are always doing here in the Studio.

I also want to say something about a short I did called *Cross Words Together* (dir. Shubham Sanjay Shevade, 2018), because shorts often give you more time on screen to develop a character. This one is about how love weaves in and out of three women's lives. I play Muriel, who is described as a "witty old woman," and I was the lead. (*Chuckling*.) I'm still not used to saying that! Anyway, the film has won a lot of awards, but the awards are beside the point. I loved that project, because I really got to develop my character as we do here in the studio.

I'll just end by saying that I'm still out there auditioning for supporting roles. And Active Analysis does help me bring that little something that is necessary to stand out in this very competitive industry.

Tiffany Cole: Stage and Screen

The very first time I used Active Analysis outside this Studio, I was cast in a two-person film. I was surprised to learn that my acting partner had also studied the technique with a Russian émigré. The screenplay was written as one long scene, something like *The Russian Ark* (dir. Aleksander Sokurov, 2002), which made history because it was filmed in one take. That meant we had to rehearse before filming. My partner and I convinced the director to allow us to use etudes, even though he had no idea what we were doing. Later, I noticed the director switching up his game plan by repositioning the cameras based on our work. It was a great experience, but the film never got picked up for distribution. As Louisa would say, it's just part of the business.

Then when I played Fefu at the Odyssey, we explored relationships and movement at some of our secondary rehearsals, while the director focused on other scenes. Naturally, I decided to use Active Analysis, but I didn't tell the other actors what we were doing or ask them to identify actions, counteractions, verbs. Nothing like that. I just said that I wanted to try something different. I got away with it because my character has a natural take-control energy. We got a lot out of our etudes. We found logical movements around the stage and additional moments between the characters. We made the connections between the characters strong. With the relationships more fleshed out, I felt grounded by the time we got to the play's surreal ending, and not only able to go there myself, but also able to bring the audience there as well.

I've recently been teaching text analysis as my day job, and Active Analysis is the only acting perspective that I use, because it's the shortest way to get students to see how a play is not only about the words but about what's happening underneath the words. Like Liliana said: when you know *why* a character speaks, *what* is going on becomes clear. In class, the students can see the link between how things unfold in the dialogue and the actions that drive the characters.

There is one other technical aspect of filmmaking that I'd like to address. Imagine that it's a twelve-hour day. You were called in six hours ago and you still haven't gone on set. Active Analysis helps me get up and work whenever I am called, no matter how long I've been waiting or how climactic the scene might be. I follow my imagination into the given circumstances. I reconnect with them as if they were a bridge into whatever moment that I need to create. Of course, it's also important to manage your energy while you are waiting around. I am careful to keep my energy for myself. As Louisa said, you're not there to make friends. You have to be able to turn your energy on like a machine, because that is your job. So I look for ways to keep my body moving or engaged throughout the day, so that when I'm needed, my body is already prepared. Then, as I just said, I go to the imaginative circumstances, commit to those, and my body is ready to go along with the ride, because I've bridged my body and imagination.

Working Solo with Active Analysis

Keith (*Raising his hand*.)   I have a question. How do you use Active Analysis solo for auditions? I find it tough when it's just me, myself and I preparing a monologue or a self-tape. I miss all the ideas I get from interacting with other actors.

Hannah   Don't forget, there are a lot of monologues in plays too!

Louisa   I certainly had a difficult one at the end of *The Lie*.

Hannah   In fact, some new plays are just long solo performances. I can't imagine that preparing solo for an audition is that much different from working on an actual monologue.

Me   Performing a monologue is admittedly more difficult than interacting with a partner in a scene, because you need to create not only your own character, but also the illusion of the character with whom you are speaking. In effect, you have to work in the same way that a pantomime artist creates the illusion of a wall by pressing and leaning into space.

Louisa   That's why you need to build your imagination and put yourself into the circumstances.

Tiffany   And that's why I always go back to the imagined circumstances and commit to those when I am working on set.

Me   Knebel emphasized that "our problem as artists is always to develop our imaginations" so that they become "flexible and free" (Knebel' 1976: 219).

Rose   Nonetheless, the basic process of rehearsing is the same. When I audition or get a job, I prepare at home. I read for the facts. I figure out if I am the action, counteraction, or an alliance. Then I play with a number of different verbs that might fit.

Tiffany   I generally assume that I am the impelling action in auditions. That way I can take better control of the scene, especially when I am paired with people who—and I say this without any ego—don't seem to know what they are doing. In cases like that, you have to stay on point and do your job. You can't afford to let them spoil your audition. The problem is similar to the ones that Liliana and Louisa described when your partners forget their lines or when you are reacting to an absent partner in a close-up. Active Analysis trains you to trust what you are doing, so you don't drown, even if the other person is pulling you under, or if there is no other person there.

Rose   Having more than one verb when you walk in to audition is especially crucial in adjusting to whatever the casting director asks of you.

Keith   Again, the verbs! The text gives you the actions, counteractions and events, but we actors have a lot of freedom in choosing our verbs.

Tiffany   I also like to get up and move around in order to test out a verb by physicalizing it. Moving helps me know whether or not I am actually doing what I say I'm doing.

Rose   Once I've done all that, I memorize the text. After that, I step away from it for a while and trust that when I get up to work everything I need will be there for me.

Trailblazing

While many of you will aspire to careers on stage and screen, others of you will discover different paths. During the 2020 pandemic, when many of us moved our work to video platforms, the solo performer Deborah Margolin and I were invited to participate in a virtual class given by Milton Justice, a close assistant to Stella Adler. The topic was how to prepare for auditions. When Milton asked Deborah to speak, she said that she had auditioned only once, when invited to do so by a director who had seen her perform the role of Hamlet for the 1989 Women's One World (WOW) Theatre Festival in New York. The audition went so poorly that the casting director asked her whether she had ever been in a play before.[6]

This anecdote, when placed beside Margolin's long and influential career, underlines the fact that there are as many ways to act as there are actors. As Margolin often repeats, "I work because I work. I don't ask permission and I don't wait to be granted permission to do my work." Margolin co-founded the feminist company, Split Britches, in 1980 with Lois Weaver and Peggy Shaw, two founders of WOW. At first, Margolin focused on writing until the others pulled her into performing as well. She studied acting with the Russian-born Polina Klimovitskaya, who was well known among New York's avant-garde companies and a graduate of the directing program established by Knebel in Moscow. Split Britches devised their works through improvisations that Margolin would then capture in writing. "We would make lists of stuff we always wanted to do on stage, and then we would do it." Their initial performances began at WOW and the company was subsequently offered the use of the auditorium in Bellevue mental hospital, where, as Margolin recalls, their audience sometimes consisted of a few drunks and homeless people who had come in from the cold, until a local newspaper published "a rave review of our play."

Recalling her *Hamlet*, Margolin writes that "I always wanted to play the role and I did," but the production "was never conceived as a play done in drag; neither was it conceived as a play that in any way altered the genders of Shakespeare's characters. [...] The enactments of these characters fell into a sacred and liminal space [...] in which gender [...] needed no explanation or defense" (Margolin 2015: 77). Margolin's words remind me of Irina Rozanova's desire to play Hamlet and Stanislavsky's advice to her in 1937 to approach the role, not as a man, but in the same way that she would approach any role (Chapter 2).

During fifteen years with Split Britches, Margolin began to tour throughout the United States performing self-scripted works. Her eleven solo pieces and numerous full-length multicharacter plays won her an OBIE Award for Sustained Excellence of Performance in 1999–2000. She continues her active career and can serve as a model trailblazer for all of us. "You find a group of people with whom you are morally and aesthetically consonant, you make work, and eventually people will watch,"[7] she advises.

Among our Studio members, Teena Pugliese has been clearing her own path by using Active Analysis to make socially engaged films that connect her spiritual values with her art. "For me acting has always been a very spiritual experience," she says, and this type of work "brings me joy and love."[8] She found her calling when she was hired to edit and record content for the award-winning Netflix documentary, *Awake: A Dream from Standing Rock* (dir. Josh Fox, James Spione and Myron Dewey, 2017). She soon realized that her training as an actor and filmmaker could be a valuable tool in extending her work as an activist for indigenous rights and as a youth mentor. She moved to the Standing Rock Reservation and began making shorts that used etudes to structure stories told by thirteen-year-old Native American girls, thus devising new content for new purposes by relying on Stanislavsky's and Knebel's legacy. When Teena reflects on her role as director, she echoes Knebel's sense that directors are not the bosses but rather the leaders of like-minded ensembles. "If we were in the industry," Teena says, "they would call me the director of my shorts, but really I was just a guide" to their stories. "I didn't want to do anything scripted, so I focused on etudes and captured them on camera." Teena represents the next generation of performing artists who, like Deborah Margolin, do not ask permission to make the works they desire.

Therefore, I want to end by suggesting how Active Analysis can morph from a means of accessing pre-written texts to a guide for structuring new works.

Devising New Works through Active Analysis

Rather than reading for the facts and exploring texts through etudes, actors can reverse engineer the process by using etudes to select and arrange facts in performances of their own making. At the Opera-Dramatic Studio Stanislavsky experimented with devising new plays in just this way. In one project, he prompted his assistants to take inspiration from the news in order to develop a science fiction play (Chapter 2). Decades later, at the

Central Children's Theatre Knebel produced two devised works, *The Little Humpbacked Horse* and *The Magic Blossom*. For the one, her actors' etudes guided the hand of a professional playwright and for the other, the actors themselves crafted their performance text (Chapter 3).

While there exists little information about these experiments, Lidia Novitskaya includes one page of advice, which reads like a checklist for devising through Active Analysis, in her book on the Opera-Dramatic Studio. First, every etude that contributes to the plot of the work should develop as if it were "a little play in and of itself." It should include a collision between an action and a counteraction, "realized through creative problems" that the characters seek to solve through their verbs and culminate in an event that advances the story. Additionally, each actor within the etude should cultivate "a line of inner thoughts, supported by a filmstrip of images" when interacting with their partners in order to ensure that the dialogue reflects the inner dynamics behind human interactions (Novitskaia 1984: 360). Second, the chain of events that structure the work's plot must be grounded in "a main, overarching aim (a *sverkhzadacha*)" that conveys the ensemble's perspective (Lesson 4). This perspective should develop as a dynamic trajectory with "a beginning, culmination, and resolution" that will capture and then retain the audience's attention (Novitskaia 1984: 360). Third, each character within the devised story should have "a detectable line of development" (the role's perspective in Lesson 4) that can also be traced from beginning to end in a trajectory that captures and retains the audience's attention (Novitskaia 1984: 360).

Juliana That description pretty much matches what we did in the Studio last year when we devised short plays through etudes. We all came in with something that we had taken from the news as a starting point for some monologues. We then worked on our pieces, much as Rose just described. We had to identify to whom we were speaking, why we said what we did, and what event or decision might occur within the frame of our speech. As we worked, we tried different verbs, until we found something that conveyed what we wanted to create. The more we refined what we were doing, the more fictionalized our work became. That fictional impulse surprised me, since we had begun with real news. In fact, the fiction took over and hooked us into imagining more and more possibilities.

Me What you are saying reminds me of Knebel's belief that art is a generative force in the world. She writes:

> Theatrical art does not simply copy life; art creates its own forms, its own lines, colors and thoughts. [...] The talented person, who takes life in, does not copy life in art, but unfailingly forges it anew in the crucible of his or her own thoughts, feelings, sufferings, and dreams.
>
> (Knebel' 1976: 209–10)

Anisha Were you developing solo performances?

Juliana At first we were, until one day Sharon noticed some interesting parallels in a few of our monologues. She then suggested a circumstance under which four of us might find ourselves in the same room at the same time, and that led us to devise a full scenario. At that point, the fictional framework became even more interesting, because one of us was working with a news story about a person who had died and another was speculating about her person's future. I was strictly in the present, I admit. Yet, in the world we were creating the past, present and future could interact through our imaginations.

Keith (*Looking through his notes.*)   Sounds like you found the "belief in fictional possibilities" that Stanislavsky put at the heart of his System (Lesson 5).

Juliana   Yes, I would say so.

There is a pause in the room, until Shari raises her hand.

Shari   I think Anisha has something more to say. Don't you? (*Nudging Anisha.*) Go on …

Anisha   Well … The truth is … I started experimenting with Active Analysis even before I joined this group. I had read about it last year and it sounded interesting. I got a group of friends together and I convinced them to try using it to create a web series. The idea was for each of us to come up with an idea for an episode, something like a short story, each month.[9] We started by filming improvisations, not real etudes, because I didn't yet understand about actions, counteractions, and events at that time. The improvs were fun to do, but, when we watched them later, we thought they were, well … boring. All these weeks, I've been taking what we've been learning here back to the group. The Active Analysis map is definitely making our experiments more interesting. I am starting to think that we might actually do some good work …. But I'm not yet sure.

Me   Keep at it, Anisha! The more you experiment and then assess what you have accomplished and where you need to work harder, the clearer your path will become. My hope is that people like you will take this legacy and use it to create dynamic performances for now and for the future, cleaning the dust off classics and making new works too.

Louisa   But the future can wait, because the present demands celebration. The table is set and "today, now, here," to quote Stanislavsky, there is time enough to enjoy some cake!

Notes

1. Performed in Norwegian with scenography by Christina Lindgren, the production premiered on October 20, 2015, with the actors Rustam Louis Foss, Kristine Cornelie Margrete Hartgen, Maria Omarsdottir Austgulen, Ragnhild Jørgensen Tysse, Kim J. Olsen, Leo Magnus de la Nuez, Olavus Frostad Udbye, and Ragnhild Meiling Enoksen.
2. The following discussion is adapted from a Roundtable on "Working in the Profession," the Stanislavsky Institute for the 21st Century, September 20, 2021.
3. Lyubov Zabolotskaia Weidner shared this metaphor in a personal video conversation on September 18, 2021.
4. American Theatre Wing's "Working in the Theatre Seminar," 1978, accessed on October 31, 2021, at https://www.youtube.com/watch?v=k61NKqGKvqQ.
5. Liliana Carillo's, Louisa Abernathy's, and Tiffany Cole's remarks are transcribed and edited from the Studio's Roundtable, September 20, 2021, and included here with their permissions.

6. The online class took place on June 22, 2021. Justice has a podcast series and a book (2021), both titled *I Don't Need an Acting Class*. All quotations from Margolin in this section are taken from a follow-up video conversation on October 30, 2021, and are used with her permission.
7. Private video conversation, October 30, 2021.
8. Teena Pugliese is quoted from the Studio Roundtable on September 20, 2020, with her permission.
9. This fictional project was inspired by Bianca Dovarro's "Project 321," which released one short film per month for a year, accessed on November 13, 2021, at https://www.biancadovarro.com/project321.

Appendix

The Lie (2020)

by Joan Eyles Johnson[1]

Characters

Dr. Tyrone Reed, *"Ty," young and old*
Lilly, *his wife, young and old*
Dr. Raphael Melville, *"Rafe," young and old*
Nurse
Polly, *Lilly's middle-aged daughter*

Scene One

A hospital room. **Ty** *labors to breathe under a white shroud that almost covers his face. His eyes are closed.* **Rafe***, on old man, sits quietly beside the bed for a few seconds, then speaks softly, afraid to be heard.*

Rafe   You can't hear me. Can you? (*He looks around suspiciously.*) Nobody's here but us. Ty. Ty. (*Whispers.*) Can you hear me? (*Sighs.*) Lilly's doing fine. I mean. Everyone gets cataracts. She's fine.

The **Nurse** *enters hurriedly.*

Nurse   That will be it for today Doctor Melville. Time to go home and rest yourself.

Rafe   Visiting hours are …

Nurse (*Interrupts him with a stern glare.*)   Doctor. What's the good of it? I mean …

Rafe   It's for my sake. Don't you see that? I'm the one …

Nurse   Next thing, you'll be my patient if you don't sleep.

Rafe   He's my dearest friend. My colleague.

Nurse   Even his wife doesn't visit as much.

Rafe   She's got her own troubles.

Nurse (*With a long stare at* **Ty**.)   He has no troubles. Beyond all that.

Rafe What's going to happen?

Nurse You're a physician. You know the ropes. Nothing will happen now. This is it until God kicks in.

Rafe Nurse … Never mind. I'll be going. (*Takes his hat from the end of the bed.*) In just a minute. Just one more minute.

Nurse (*Leaving.*) I trust you. Keep your word. Go home.

Rafe I'm going now. (*Bending near* **Ty**.) Wouldn't you like me to praise the Lord and pass the ammunition, old boy? If you're suffering. (*Pause.*) I know we are, all of us. Well, Lilly and me. Can't stand it.

Nurse (*Entering.*) Now! I thought you were a man of your word! Goodnight Doctor!

Rafe *puts his hat on his head. Pauses and exits slowly.*

Scene Two

Lilly. *Her eyes under a washcloth, sits in an old, overstuffed arm chair under an antique floor lamp.* **Rafe** *enters.*

Lilly Is that you?

Rafe Yes.

Lilly How was it today?

Rafe Like yesterday. The day before. Two years ago.

Lilly What's the reason?

Rafe There is no understanding who's in charge.

Lilly You're a doctor.

Rafe Retired.

Lilly Ty never retired. Doctors can't stop being doctors, any more than teachers can stop …

Rafe How's the eye?

Lilly Fuzzy.

Rafe I can't help think he's suffering.

Lilly Me too. To be alive and dead at the same time.

Rafe What happened to the quality of mercy?

Lilly He had no mercy when he had patients.

Rafe That's not true.

Lilly In the war.

Rafe Are you suggesting …

Lilly (*Interrupting*.)   You know what I mean. Had to be tough. No time for bedside manners.

Rafe   Want some tea?

Lilly   Too lazy to hold the cup.

Rafe   Come now. We should be grateful we can still hold a cup.

Lilly   Was he changed in any way? Are they keeping him clean?

Rafe   Rhetorical questions?

Lilly   Get the tea.

Rafe *exits.*

Lilly (*To offstage*.)   Just plain. (*Pause*.) He's suffering. I know it.

Rafe (*From offstage*.)   We mustn't project.

Lilly   We're suffering.

Rafe   This whole thing will die with him. We won't have to feel guilty anymore. I owe him something.

Lilly   We have suffered enough. Look at us! A life of irony. A life of one big lie and all its consequences.

Rafe *enters with tea on a tray and sets it between them on a small table he kicks along with his foot.*

Rafe   What are you jawing about now? Here then. Slowly. You'll have to look! There. There.

Lilly   OOH! It's hot.

Rafe   The sky's blue. Tea's hot.

Lilly (*Sipping carefully*.)   I suppose you thought about it again when you saw him.

Rafe   I always think about it.

Lilly   Blowing out someone else's candle won't make yours shine any brighter.

Rafe   Lilly and her New England childhood! No one is exempt from talking nonsense!

Lilly   How would you do it?

Rafe   Simply.

Lilly   You'd be tried and hanged.

Rafe   They don't hang old men any more.

Lilly   It's going to rain. Hear that thunder far off? Finally, a break.

Rafe   I'll be left to live the horror of memory.

Lilly   We know what is good, but we don't do it.

Rafe   I'm going to. I'm going to.

Lilly   The tongue will always betray you.

Rafe   A fool's tongue is long enough to cut his throat.

They both laugh, when they see they are speaking in clichés.

Lilly   If we didn't want to live under these conditions, we should have been born into a different world. (*Her hands shake. The cup rattles.*)

Rafe   We were born in a different world. The rules changed on us.

Lilly   What's a few years? Maybe months? Days.

Rafe   That's the truth.

Lilly   Now you're a man who always tells the truth. (*Hands him her teacup.*) Here. Put it up.

Rafe *gets up slowly and returns the tea things to the kitchen.*

Lilly   Who'll keep me company when they take you away?

Rafe *comes back and takes his hat from the hall table.*

Lilly   Lock me in, will you?

Rafe   Polly will still visit you.

Lilly   Polly is not company. She's my daughter.

Rafe   Maybe you can force her to choose between home and away. When it's done.

Lilly   No matter what choice you make, he's still going to die.

Rafe   Take care. Little one.

Rafe *exits slowly. We hear him lock the door from the outside.*

Scene Three

Almost immediately after the key stops, **Ty** *enters the room as a young man in a white naval uniform. He goes over to* **Lilly** *and kisses her forehead. She begins to throw off her "old" clothes and white wig and stands, a young pretty woman!*

Ty   So glad! So glad to be home!

Lilly   They said "today." Oh Ty. You're so handsome! Almost hate to have you remove this.

Ty   Liar! (*Kisses her.*) I never want to see it again. (*Walks around.*) Ah. Home! Nothing's changed.

Lilly   Not even me?

Ty   You're prettier. What did you do to your hair?

Lilly   Rafe called. He's coming for supper.

Ty   He's home too?

Lilly   Last month.

Ty   Just like old times again! I'm starving.

Lilly   I'm insulted.

Ty   Oh baby! (*He lifts her in his arms and walks to the couch*.)

Lilly   You'll drop me.

Ty   Can't even trust your mate?

Lilly   Don't be silly, Ty. Put me down.

Ty   You have changed. You've grown up.

Lilly   Anyone would. Worrying about you all the time.

Ty   Were you faithful to me, honey?

Lilly   It took a lot of willpower.

Ty (*Depositing her on the couch*.)   Willpower is trying hard not to do something you really want to do.

Lilly   Oh you big lug!

They laugh and kiss and begin to make love. There is a knock on the door.

Ty   You invite somebody else?

Lilly (*Getting up*.)   Yes?

Rafe (*From behind the door*.)   It's Rafe. Lilly. I … (*She interrupts him by swinging the door open suddenly*.) Oh! Surprise! (*Seeing* **Ty**.) Thought you were coming home on Monday.

Ty   Yeah? Have you been keeping my girl company?

Rafe (*Making a joke out of it*.)   Sure. She's a swell kid. Brave. Loyal.

Lilly   Let's get some coffee.

Ty (*Going to the liquor cabinet*.)   No. This calls for a celebration! How are you, Rafe?

Rafe   Tired. Grateful. You're okay! (*Hits his shoulder*.) Say! You've come through!

Ty (*Pouring whisky all around*.)   We all have. (*Drinks in one gulp*.) Whew! Gotta catch some shut-eye. Let me catch forty winks, baby. Then let's all go out on the town!

Rafe   Don't let me get in the way of your homecoming, pal.

Lilly   Rafe's only been home a little longer than you, darling.

Ty (*To* **Rafe**.)   Still the gorgeous kid I married, isn't she?

Lilly   We've been waiting for this day, darling.

Ty   Nothing's changed. Has it, babe?

Lilly   Everything is just like you left it.

Ty   See you two later. If you'll excuse me.

The two stand staring after **Ty** *as he exits to the bedroom.*

Rafe (*After a brief silence.*)   Well?

Lilly   I'm his wife.

Rafe   I always knew that.

Lilly   It'll never happen again.

Rafe   How can you say that?

Lilly   Like this. It'll never happen again.

Rafe   I'll take that job in Albany.

Lilly   Whatever it takes.

Rafe   Have you told him about …

Lilly   He'll rest. Then I'll tell him.

Rafe   We're always putting things off. Tell him now. While I'm here. (*He goes to the door of the bedroom.*) Ty! Could you wait one more minute before you sleep?

Ty *enters from the bedroom.*

Ty   I'm home for good now. No need to panic.

Rafe   We have something to tell you.

Ty   Oh. Oh?

Lilly   No, darling, it's good news!

Ty   Yes?

Rafe   It's your place to tell, Lilly.

Lilly   While you were away …

Ty   This is going to make me happy?

Lilly   I'm not alone anymore.

Ty   What?

Lilly   I … (*Laughs.*) Oh this is so melodramatic. I don't mean it to be … The truth is I had a baby … you and I … you left me … a little girl ….

Ty   What? Where? Why didn't I know? It takes almost a year to have a baby. Why didn't I get news of this?

Lilly   Silly. Remember. You were on the other side of the world. Secret stuff. We were completely cut off from each other. Darling. Rafe here … He helped me every step of the way …

Ty (*Elated.*)   What's her name? Where is she? (*Suddenly frightened.*) She's not … I mean there's nothing wrong with her …

Rafe   She's perfect! At my mother's house. Lilly wanted to greet you all by herself … You know …

Lilly   I thought we should get acquainted again … Pick up where we left off …

Ty   This is ridiculous. I'm a father! I've got a baby girl! How old is she?

Lilly   Her birthday is in two weeks. She'll be one.

Ty   Oh my God! I can't wait! Let's go.

Rafe   Well …

Lilly   Ty. There's time to rest first.

Ty   Almost two years. I can't sleep my life away. Come on. Rafe! Thanks, old friend, for seeing this through for me.

Rafe   Don't mention it.

Lilly *and* **Rafe** *follow after* **Ty**, *who grabs his coat and exits.*

Scene Four

Knock on the door of **Lilly's** *room.*

Lilly (*Eyes covered again.*)   Come.

Lilly *removes the cloth to see her daughter,* **Polly,** *enter and go into the kitchen without a word.*

Polly (*After a pause. From offstage.*)   Yes. It's "just" me. (*Enters with a tray of tea and biscuits*.) Eat today? (*Pause.*) I said, "eat today," old lady?

Lilly   Yes. Thank you.

Polly   Good. Then you don't need me here.

Lilly   No. I don't. Didn't ask you to come.

Polly   It's my duty.

Lilly   Since when have you thought that way?

Polly (*Losing her temper.*)   You better respect me, old woman, or you're going to starve to death! Hear me? You're going to respect me! Oh it's the devil again! (*Shrieking.*) You've let the devil in here again. The minute my back is turned you let demons enter this place. (*Changed tone.*) I rebuke you, demon of religiosity! Get away from me. I rebuke you demon of rituality! Leave my presence! (*To* **Lilly**.) Hear me, old woman? I told you to play that music I brought from church last week. That music will keep the devil out of here. Hear me? (*Screams.*) Hear me? You will answer me! Do what I say!

Lilly (*With resignation.*)   Yes. Yes. Yes.

Polly   Oh don't play the martyr! Where did you get these flowers? They look like something the devil would bring in here. Better take them with me and burn them.

Polly *starts the music. A shrill rock-style religious group sings about "Every knee shall bow." The phone rings over the music!*

Lilly (*Answering.*)   Yes. This is she. He what? He what? What should I do? Well, my insurance is supposed to cover most of it. I've sold all my belongings that were worth anything. I'll get somebody to bring me down to see you tomorrow. (*Hangs up the phone and dials again.*) Hello? Rafe? It's me. They just called from the hospital. He voided. Yes. All by himself. The nurse said without a catheter. See what that means? He's alive. He's going to get better. Come home again. Where will I put him? But he won't live with her. You know how that is. He never wanted her to live with us. What is so urgent? Can't you see my predicament? He's getting better. (*Long pause.*) Yes, that's right. Tomorrow. Eight sharp? Okay. I'll be ready. Yes, dear. Goodnight Rafe. You still have your key?

She hangs up the phone. She sits down on the rocker, as **Polly** *enters.*

Polly   I'm leaving now. I'm locking you in here. I can't trust you for one minute. You are a demon-lover. You'll be letting them in here the minute my back is turned.

Polly *exits and we hear the key in the lock. Lilly weakly gets up and turns off the music, sits down and starts to rock slowly, wiping the tears from her eyes.*

End of Play

Note

1. Published by permission of Joan Eyles Johnson, July 9, 2020.

Bibliography

Abbey Theatre Oral History Project (1968), *The Cherry Orchard*. Available online: https://www.youtube.com/watch?v=MtdObMWiO0w.

Abensour, G. (2019), *Une vie pour le théâtre: Maria Knöbel [sic] et la formation du metteur en scène au XXe siècle en Russie* [A Life for the Theatre: Knebel and the Director's Education in 20th Century Russia], Paris: Panthéon.

Adler, S. (1988), *The Technique of Acting*, New York: Bantam Books.

Aquilina, S. (2020), *Modern Theatre in Russia: Tradition Building and Transmission Processes*, London: Methuen Drama.

Aristotle (1958), *On Poetry and Style*, trans. G. M. A. Grube, New York: Bobbs-Merrill Co.

Autant-Mathieu, M. C. (2003), "Stalin and the Moscow Art Theatre," *Slavic and East European Performance*, 23 (3): 70–85.

Balukhaty, S. D. (1967), "*The Cherry Orchard*: A Formalist Approach," in R. L. Jackson (ed), *Chekhov: A Collection of Critical Essays*, Englewood Cliffs: Prentice-Hall, Inc: 136–46.

Baron, C. and S. M. Carnicke (2008), *Reframing Screen Performance*, Ann Arbor: The University of Michigan Press.

Beckerman, B. (1970), *Dynamics of Drama: Theory and Method of Analysis*, New York: Drama Book Specialists.

Belknap, R. L. (2016), *Plots*, New York: Columbia University Press.

Benedetti, J. (1990), *Stanislavski: A Biography*, New York: Routledge.

Benedetti, J. (1998), *Stanislavski and the Actor*, London: Bloomsbury Methuen.

Beumers, B. and M. Lipovetsky (2009), *Performing Violence: Literary and Theatrical Experiments of New Russian Drama*, Bristol: Intellect.

Bown, M. C. (1998), *Socialist Realist Painting*, New Haven: Yale University Press.

Braun, E. (1995), *Meyerhold: A Revolution in Theatre*, Iowa City: University of Iowa Press.

Caldarone, M. and M. Lloyd-Williams (2004), *Action: The Actors' Thesaurus*, Hollywood: Drama Publishers.

Carnicke, S. M. (2004), "Screen Performance and Directors' Visions," in C. Baron, D. Carson, and F. Tomasulo (eds), *More than a Method: Trends and Traditions in Contemporary Film Performance*, Detroit: Wayne State University Press: 42–67.

Carnicke, S. M. (2009), *Stanislavsky in Focus: An Acting Master for the Twenty-First Century*, 2nd edn, New York: Routledge.

Carnicke, S. M. (2010a), "The Knebel Technique: Active Analysis in Practice," in A. Hodge (ed), *Actor Training*, 2nd edn, New York: Routledge: 99–116.

Carnicke, S. M. (2010b), "Stanislavsky and Politics: Active Analysis and The American Legacy of Soviet Oppression," in E. Margolis and L. Tyler-Renaud (eds), *The Politics of American Actor Training*, New York: Routledge: 15–30.

Carnicke, S. M. (2010c), "Stanislavsky's System: Pathways for the Actor," in A. Hodge (ed), *Actor Training*, 2nd edn, New York: Routledge: 1–25.

Carnicke, S. M. (2012), "Emotional Expressivity in Motion Picture Capture Technology," in J. Sternagel, D. Levitt, and D. Mersch (eds), *Acting and Performance in Moving Image Culture: Bodies, Screens, Renderings*, Blelefeld: Transcript: 321–38. Available online: https://doi. org/10.14361/transcript.9783839416488.321.

Carnicke, S. M. (2013), *Checking out Chekhov: A Guide to the Plays for Actors, Directors, and Readers*, Brighton: Academic Studies Press.

Carnicke, S. M. (2014), "The Effects of Russian and Soviet Censorship on the Practice of Stanislavsky's System," in R. A. White (ed), *The Routledge Companion to Stanislavsky*, New York: Routledge: 249–64.

Carnicke, S. M. (2015), "Michael Chekhov's Legacy in Soviet Russia: A Story about Coming Home," in M. C. Autant-Mathieu and Y. Meerson (eds), *The Michael Chekhov Companion*, London: Routledge: 191–206.

Carnicke, S. M. (2016), "Stanislavsky's Active Analysis for Twenty-First Century Actors: Be Flexible," [Filmed Lecture for Digital Theatre Plus at Rose Bruford College, U.K.] Available online https://www.digitaltheatreplus.com.

Carnicke, S. M. (2017), "Duse and the Stanislavsky System of Acting," in M. P. Pagani and P. Fryer (eds), *Eleonora Duse and* Cenere (Ashes)*: Centennial Essays*, Jefferson: McFarland and Co.: 57–71.

Carnicke, S. M. (2019a), "Improvisations and Etudes: An Experiment in Active Analysis," *Stanislavski Studies*, 7 (1): 17–35. Available online: https://www.tandfonline.com/doi/full/10.108 0/20567790.2019.1576109.

Carnicke, S. M. (2019b), "Rethinking 'Stanislavskian' Directing," in P. Tait (ed), *The Great European Directors: Antoine, Stanislavski, Saint Denis*, London: Bloomsbury Methuen: 91–112.

Carnicke, S. M. and D. Rosen (2014), "A Singer Prepares: Stanislavsky and Opera," in R. A. White (ed), *The Routledge Companion to Stanislavsky*, New York: Routledge: 120–38.

Chamberlain, F. (2004), *Michael Chekhov*, London: Routledge.

Chekhov, A. (2009), *Chekhov: 4 Plays and 3 Jokes*, trans. S. M. Carnicke, Indianapolis: Hackett Publishing Co., Inc.

Chekhov, M. (1955), "Lecture 11," [Audio Taped Lecture Recorded in Hollywood], New York: The New York Public Library for the Performing Arts.

Chekhov, M. A. (1995), *Literaturnoe nasledie* [Literary Heritage], ed. M. O. Knebel', 2nd edn, 2 vols, Moscow: Iskusstvo.

Chekhov, M. (2005), *The Path of the Actor*, ed. A. Kirillov and B. Merlin, trans. D. Ball, London: Routledge.

Chinoy, H. K., ed. (1976), "Reunion: A Self-Portrait of the Group Theatre," A special issue of *Educational Theatre Journal*, 27 (4).

Chubbuck, I. (2004), *The Power of the Actor: the Chubbuck Technique*, New York: Gotham Books.

Chushkin, N. N. (1968), *Gamlet-Kachalov* [Hamlet-Kachalov], Moscow: Iskusstvo.

Clay, C. J. (2014), "Vector Theory and the Plot Structures of Literature and Drama," *The Dramatist*, January/February: 53–5.

Clurman, H. (1994), *The Collected Works of Harold Clurman: Six Decades of Commentary on Theatre, Dance, Music, Film Arts and Letters*, ed. M. Loggia and G. Young, New York: Applause Books.

Coquelin, B. (1970), "The Dual Personality of the Actor," in T. Cole and H. K. Chinoy (eds), *Actors on Acting*, New York: Crown Publishers: 190–202.

Csikszentmihalyi, M. (1990), *Flow: The Psychology of Optimal Experience*, New York: Harper and Row.

Durylin, S. N. and P. A. Markov, eds. (1955), *K. S. Stanislavskii: Teatral'noe nasledstvo: materialy, pis'ma, issledovaniia* [Stanislavsky's Theatrical Legacy], vol. 1, Moscow: Akademia Nauk SSSR.

Dybovskii, V. (1992), "V plenu predlagaemykh obstoiatel'stv" [Imprisoned by the Given Circumstances], *Minuvshee*, vol. 10: author's typescript.

Efros, A. (2006), *The Joy of Rehearsal: Reflections on Interpretation and Practice*, trans. J. Thomas, New York: Peter Lang.

Efros, A. (2007), *The Craft of Rehearsal: Further Reflections on Interpretation and Practice*, trans. J. Thomas, New York: Peter Lang.

Erlich, V. (1969), *Russian Formalism*, The Hague: Mouton.

Ezrabi, C. (2012), *Swans of the Kremlin: Ballet and Power in Soviet Russia*, Pittsburgh: University of Pittsburgh Press.

Filippov, B. (1977), *Actors without Make-Up*, Moscow: Progress Publishers.

Gauss, R. B. (1999), *Lear's Daughters: The Studios of the Moscow Art Theatre, 1905–1927*, New York: Peter Lang.

Germanova, M. N. (n. d.), "Vospominaniia" [Unpublished Memoirs], New York: Bakhmetieff Archives at Columbia University.

Goldhill, S. (2007), *How to Stage Greek Tragedy Today*, Chicago: University of Chicago Press.

Gorfunkel', E. I., ed. (2007), *Georgii Tovstonogov: Repetiruet i uchit* [Tovstongonov: Transcripts of Rehearsals and Classes], vol. 2., St. Petersburg: Baltiiskie sezony.

Gurevich, L. Ia., ed. (1948), *O Stanislavskom: Sbornik vospominanii* [About Stanislavsky], Moscow: VTO.

Hay, P. (1987), *Theatrical Anecdotes*, New York: Oxford University Press.

Hobgood, B. M. (1973), "Central Conceptions in Stanislavsky's System," *Educational Theatre Journal*, 25 (2): 147–59.

Hristić, J. (1995), "'Thinking with Chekhov': The Evidence of Stanislavsky's Notebooks," *New Theatre Quarterly*, 11 (42): 175–83.

Ignatieva, M. (1998), "Stanislavsky's Second *Othello*: The Great Director's Last Revelation," *Murcia's Cuadernos de Filologia Inglesa*, 7 (2): 1–10.

Ignatieva, M. (2008a), "Stanislavsky's Death: August 7, 1938," *Slavic and East European Performance*, 28 (3): 52–4.

Ignatieva, M. (2008b), *Stanislavsky and Female Actors: Women in Stanislavsky's Life and Art*, New York: University Press of America.

Ignatieva, M. (2016), "Stanislavski's Best Student Directs: Maria Lilina's First and Last Production," *Stanislavski Studies*, 4 (1): 3–12. Available online: https://www.tandfonline.com/doi/full/10.1080/20567790.2016.1155362.

Istoriia sovetskogo dramaticheskogo teatra (1966–1971), [History of Soviet Theatre], 6 vols., Moscow: Nauka.

Jackson, D. (2011), "Twenty-first-century Russian Actor Training: Active Analysis in the UK," *Theatre, Drama, and Performance Training*, 2 (2): 166–80. Available online: https://www.tandfonline.com/doi/abs/10.1080/19443927.2011.602704.

Justice, M. (2021), *I Don't Need an Acting Class*, Lanham: Applause.

Kheifits, L. E. (2001), *Prizvanie* [Vocation], Moscow: GITIS.

Knebel', M. O. ([1954] 2009), *Slovo v tvorchestve aktera* [The Word in an Actor's Creative Work], Moscow: GITIS.

Knebel', M. O. (1955), "O deistvennom analize p'esy i roli" [On the Active Analysis of the Play and the Role], *Teatr*, 1: 74–91 and 2: 105–123. [See Thomas 2016.]

Knebel', M. O. ([1959] 1982), *O deistvennom analize p'esy i roli* [On the Active Analysis of the Play and the Role], Moscow: Iskusstvo.

Knebel', M. O. (1967), *Vsia zhizn'* [All of Life], Moscow: VTO. [Also published in St. Petersburg: Planeta Musyki, 2020.]

Knebel', M. O. (1968), "Vysokaia prostota" [High Simplicity], *Teatr*, 9: 46–9.

Knebel', M. O. (1969), "*Vyshnevyi sad* v Irlandii" [*The Cherry Orchard* in Ireland], *Teatr*, 5: 158–66.

Knebel', M. O. (1971), *O tom, chto mne kazhetsia osobenno vazhnym: Stat'i, ocherki, portrety* [What Seems Most Important to Me], Moscow: Iskusstvo.

Knebel', M. O. (1976), *Poeziia pedagogiki* [The Poetry of Pedagogy], Moscow: VTO. [Also published together with her 1955 article on Active Analysis in Moscow: GITIS, 2010.]

Knebel', M. O. (1979), "Vital Work with My Eminent Students," in M. Morton (ed and trans), *Through the Magic Curtain: Theatre for Children, Adolescents and Youth in the USSR*, New Orleans: Anchorage Press: 107–35.

Knebel, M. (2006), *L'Analyse-Action: En deux livres et quelques annexes* [Analysis-Action: In Two Books and Some Addenda], compiled by A. Vassiliev (ed), trans. N. Struve, S. Vladimirov, and S. Poliakov, Paris: Actes Sud-Papiers.

Knebel, M. (2021), *Active Analysis*, compiled by A. Vassiliev (ed), trans. I. Brown, London: Routledge. [This volume is an English translation of Knebel 2006.]

Kort, M. (2010), *The Soviet Colossus: History and Aftermath*, 7th edn, London: M. E. Sharpe.

Kovalskaya, E. (2012), "New Drama: Plays for Nonexistent Theater," [Paper presented at the symposium, *Literary Theatricality: Theatrical Text*], Princeton: Princeton University.

Krechetova, R. (2013), *Stanislavskii*, Moscow: Molodoi gvardiia.

Kristi, G. (1952), *Rabota Stanislavskogo v opernom teatre* [Stanislavsky's Work with Opera], Moscow: Iskusstvo.

Leach, R. and V. Borovsky, eds. (1999), *A History of Russian Theatre*, Cambridge: Cambridge University Press.

Lehmann, H. (2006), *Postdramatic Theatre*, trans. K. Jürs-Munby, London: Routledge.

Lemon, L. T. and M. J. Reis, eds. and trans. (1965), *Russian Formalist Criticism: Four Essays*, Lincoln: University of Nebraska Press.

Letopis', abbreviation for Vinogradskaia (2003).

Levin, I. and I. Levin (1992), *Working on the Play and the Role: The Stanislavsky Method for Analyzing the Characters in a Drama*, Chicago: Ivan R. Dee.

Levin, I. and I. Levin (2002), *The Stanislavsky Secret: Not a System, Not a Method, but a Way of Thinking*, Colorado Springs: Meriwether Publishing, Ltd.

Lewis, R. (1958), *Method or Madness?* New York: Samuel French, Inc.

Liadov, V. I., ed. (1998), *O M. O. Knebel'* [About Knebel], Moscow: no publisher.

Listengarten, J. (2014), "Stanislavsky and the Avant-Garde," in R. A. White (ed), *The Routledge Companion to Stanislavsky*, New York: Routledge: 67–81.

Magarshack, D. (1952), *Chekhov the Dramatist*, London: John Lehmann.

Magarshack, D., ed. and trans. (1961), *Stanislavsky on the Art of the Stage*, New York: Hill and Wang.

Malochevskaia, I. (2003), *Rezhisserskaia shkola Tovstonogova* [Tovstonogov's School for Directors], St. Petersburg: St. Petersburg Academy of Theatrical Art.

Margolin, D. (2015), "*Hamlet* (1989): Scripted after Shakespeare's *Hamlet*," in H. Hughes, C. Tropicana, and J. Dolan (eds), *Memories of the Revolution: The First Ten Years of the WOW Café Theater*, Ann Arbor: University of Michigan: 75–82.

Markov, P. A. (1934), *The First Studio*, [typescript of translation by M. Schmidt] New York: The New York Public Library for the Performing Arts.

McFerren, C. (2003), "Rethinking Affective Memory: Background, Method and Challenge for Contemporary Actor Training," Ph.D. diss., University of Colorado at Boulder.

Meisner, S. and D. Longwell (1987), *Sanford Meisner on Acting*, New York: Vintage Books.

Melik-Pashaeva, K. L. and V. M. Turchkin, eds. (1999), *GITIS v portretakh i litsakh* [GITIS in Portraits and Personages], vol. 1, Moscow: GITIS.

Merlin, B. (2001), *Beyond Stanislavsky: The Psycho-Physical Approach to Actor Training*, London: Nick Hern Books.

Merlin, B. (2003), *Konstantin Stanislavsky*, New York: Routledge.

Merlin, B. (2007), *The Complete Stanislavsky Toolkit*, Hollywood: Drama Publishers.

Moore, S., ed. and trans. (1973), S*tanislavski Today: Commentaries on K. S. Stanislavski*, New York: American Center for Stanislavski Theatre Art, Inc.

Muse, J. H. (2017), *Microdramas: Crucibles for Theater and Time*, Ann Arbor: University of Michigan Press.

Nemirovitch-Dantchenko [*sic*], V. (1956), *My Life in the Russian Theatre*, trans. J. Cournos, Boston: Little, Brown, and Co.

Nemirovich-Danchenko, Vl. I. (2003), *Tvorcheskoe nasledie* [Creative Heritage], vol. 4, Moscow: Moskovskoe khudozhestvenyi teatr.

Novitskaia, L. P. (1984), *Uroki vdokhnoveniia: sistema K. S. Stanislavskogo v deistvii* [Inspirational Lessons: Stanislavsky's System in Action], Moscow: VTO.

Pashennaia, V. (1954), *Iskusstvo aktrisy* [The Actress' Art], Moscow: Iskusstvo.

Pavis, P. (2003), *Analyzing Performance: Theater, Dance, and Film*, Ann Arbor: University of Michigan Press.

Pitches, J. (1999), *Science and the Stanislavsky Tradition*, New York: Routledge.

Polanyi, M. (1966), *The Tacit Dimension*, Garden City: Doubleday and Co., Inc.

Radishcheva, O. A. (1999), *Stanislavskii i Nemirovich-Danchenko: Istoriia teatral'nykh otnoshenii: 1917–1938* [The History of Stanislavsky's and Nemirovich-Danchenko's Relationship], Moscow: Artist, Rezhisser, Teatr.

Ramacharaka (1904), *Hatha Yoga: Or the Yogi Philosophy of Physical Well-Being*, Chicago: Yogi Publication Society.

Ramacharaka (1906), *Raja Yoga; Of Mental Development*, Chicago: Yogi Publication Society.

Robinson, V. (2021), "Roundtable: The Fourth Wall and the Iron Curtain—Theatre and Politics 1950–60s," *Conference of the American Association of Slavic*, East European and Eurasian Studies: November 8.

Rosenstein, S., L. A. Haydon and W. Sparrow (1936), *Modern Acting: A Manual*, Los Angeles: Samuel French.

Rozov, V. S. (1977), "Rezhisser, kotorogo ia liubliu" [A Director I Love], *Avrora*, 1: 60–6.

Rudnitskii, K. (1974), *Spektakli raznykh let* [Shows from Various Years], Moscow: Iskusstvo.

Rumiantsev, P. I. (1969), *Stanislavskii i opera* [Stanislavsky and Opera], Moscow: Iskusstvo.

Ryzhova, V. F. (1967), *Put' k spektaliu* [Journey to Production], Moscow: Iskusstvo.

Sakwa, R. (1999), *The Rise and Fall of the Soviet Union: 1917–1991*, London: Routledge.

Scott, J. W. (1999), *Gender and the Politics of History*, New York: Columbia University Press.

Shapiro, A. (1999), *Kak zakryvalsia zanaves* [How the Curtain Opens], Moscow: Novoe literaturnoe obozrenie.

Shevtsova, M. (2020), *Rediscovering Stanislavsky*, Cambridge: Cambridge University Press.

Simmons, E. J. (1961), *Through the Glass of Soviet Literature: Views on Russian Society*, New York: Columbia University Press.

Smeliansky, A. (1991), "The Last Decade: Stanislavsky and Stalinism," trans. S. Larsen and E. Thoron, *Theater*, 23 (2): 7–13.

Smeliansky, A. (1996), "Assimilation: How Stalin, the Moscow Art Theatre Founder Stanislavsky and the Playwright Bulgakov Got Along or Didn't," *The New Theater Review*, 15: 41–5.

Smeliansky, A. (1999), *The Russian Theatre after Stalin*, Cambridge: Cambridge University Press.

Smeliansky, A. M., I. N. Solov'eva, and O. V. Egoshin, eds. (1998), *Moskovskii khudozhestvennyi teatr: Sto let* [The Moscow Art Theatre: 100 Years], 2 vols., Moscow: Moskovskii khudozhestvennyi teatr.

Smith, M. G. (2015), "A Race to the Stratosphere in 1933," *Daily Planet: Air and Space Magazine*, August 24. Available online: https://www.airspacemag.com/daily-planet/race-stratosphe re-1933-180956387/.

Sobolevskaia, O. S. (1988), *K. S. Stanislavskii rabotaet, beseduet, otdykhaet* [Stanislavsky at Work, in Conversation, at Rest], Moscow: STD.

Solov'eva, I. N. (1966), *Spektakl' idet segodnia* [Today's Show], Moscow: Iskusstvo.

Soloviova [*sic*], I. (1992), "Do You Have a Relative Living Abroad? Emigration as a Cultural Problem," in L. Senelick (ed), *Wandering Stars: Russian Émigré Theatre, 1905–1940*, Iowa City: University of Iowa: 69–83.

Solov'eva, I. N., ed. (2005) *Pis'ma O. S. Bokshanskaia i V. I. Nemirovich-Danchenko* [Correspondence between Bokshanskaya and Nemirovich-Danchenko], vol. 2, Moscow: Moskovskii khudozhestvennyi teatr.

Solzhenitsyn, A. (1973), *The Gulag Archipelago, 1918–1956: An Experiment in Literary Investigation*, trans. T. Whitney, 2 vols., New York: Harper and Row.

SS, abbreviation for Stanislavskii (1988–1999).

Stanislavski [*sic*], C. (1936), *An Actor Prepares*, trans. E. R. Hapgood, New York: Theatre Arts Books. [Abridged version of an early typescript of *Rabota aktera nad soboi, chast' 1* (An Actor's Work on the Self, Part I) in SS II ([1938] 1989).]

Stanislavskii, K. S. (1943), *Rezhisserskii plan: Otello* [Promptbook for *Othello*], ed. R. K. Tamantsova, Moscow: Iskusstvo.

Stanislavsky, K. S. (1948), *Stanislavsky Produces Othello*, trans. H. Nowak, London: Geoffrey Bles.

Stanislavski [*sic*], C. (1949), *Building a Character*, trans. E. R. Hapgood, New York: Theatre Arts Books. [Abridged translation of *Rabota aktera nad soboi, chast' 2* (An Actor's Work on the Self, Part II) in *SS* III ([1938] 1990).]

Stanislavskii, K. S. (1958), *Sobranie sochinenii* [Collected Works], vol. 5 [Essays, Speeches, Commentaries, Diaries, Reminiscences], Moscow: Iskusstvo.

Stanislavski [*sic*], C. (1961), *Creating a Role*, trans. E. R. Hapgood, New York: Theatre Arts Books. [A compilation of selected archival drafts published as *Rabota aktera nad roliu* (An Actor's Work on a Role) in *SS* IV ([1957]1991).]

Stanislavskii, K. S. (1981), *Rezhisserskie ekzempliary K. S. Stanislavskogo* [Directorial Plan for *The Seagull*], vol. 2., Moscow: Iskusstvo.

Stanislavskii, K. S. (1986), *Iz zapisnykh knizhek* [From the Artistic Notebooks], 2 vols., Moscow: VTO.

Stanislavskii, K. S. (1988–1999), *Sobranie sochinenii* [Collected Works], 9 vols., Moscow: Iskusstvo. [See the List of Abbreviations of Frequently Cited Sources.]

Stanislavski [*sic*], K. (2008), *An Actor's Work: A Student's Diary*, trans. and ed. J. Benedetti, London: Routledge. [Translation of *Rabota aktera nad soboi, chast' 1* and *chast' 2* (An Actor's Work on the Self, Parts I and II) in *SS* II (1989) and *SS* III (1990).]

Stanislavski [*sic*], K. (2010), *An Actor's Work on a Role*, trans. and ed. J. Benedetti, London: Routledge. [Translation of *Rabota aktera nad roliu* [An Actor's Work on the Role] in *SS* IV (1991).]

Stanislavsky, K. S. (2014), *Stanislavsky—A Life in Letters*, ed. and trans. L. Senelick. New York: Routledge. [A selection from Stanislavsky's Letters in *SS* VIII (1998) and *SS* IX (1999).]

Stanislavskii, K. S. (n. d.) Typescript, [Untitled draft of an acting manual with handwritten notes] Berkeley: Bancroft Library, University of California.

Steiner, P. (1984), *Russian Formalism: A Metapoetics*, Ithaca: Cornell University Press.

Strasberg, L. (1956–1969), "The Actors Studio," Sound Recordings No. 339A, Madison: Wisconsin Center for Film and Theater Research, An Archive of the University of Wisconsin and the State Historical Society of Wisconsin.

Stroeva, M. N. (1973 and 1977), *Rezhisserskie iskaniia Stanislavskogo*, 2 vols., Moscow: Izdatel'vstvo Nauk.

Syssoyeva, K. M. (2013), "Revolution I: Meyerhold, Stanislavsky, and Collective Creation, 1905," in K. M. Syssoyeva and S. Proudfit (eds), *A History of Collective Creation*, New York: Palgrave: 37–58.

Tcherkasski, S. (2016), *Stanislavsky and Yoga*, trans. Vreneli Farber, London: Routledge.

Thomas, J. (2016), *A Director's Guide to Stanislavsky's Active Analysis*, London: Bloomsbury. [Includes Thomas' translation of Knebel 1955.]

Toporkov, V. O. (1950), *K. S. Stanislavskii na repetitsii* [Stanislavsky in Rehearsal], Moscow: Iskusstvo.

Toporkov, V. (1979), *Stanislavski In Rehearsal*, trans. C. E. Edwards, New York: Theatre Arts Books.

Toporkov, V. (2004), *Stanislavski In Rehearsal: The Final Years*, trans. J. Benedetti, New York: Routledge.

Tovstonogov, G. A. (1980), *Zerkalo stseny* [The Stage Mirror], vol. 1, Leningrad: Iskusstvo.

Vassiliev, A. (1999), *Sept ili huit leçons de théâtre* [Seven or Eight Lessons in Theatre], Paris: P.O.L.

Vinogradskaia, I., ed. (2000), *Stanislavskii repetiruet: Zapisi i stenogrammy repetitsii* [Stanislavsky Rehearses], Moscow: Moskovskii khudozhestvennyi teatr.

Vinogradskaia, I., ed. (2003), *Zhizn' i tvorchestvo K. S. Stanislavskogo: Letopis'* [A Chronicle of the Life and Creative Work of Stanislavsky], 4 vols., Moscow: Moskovskii khudozhestvennyi teatr. [See the List of Abbreviations of Frequently Cited Sources.]

Vladimirova, Z. V. (1991), *M. O. Knebel'*, Moscow: Iskusstvo.

White, R. A. (2005), "Stanislavsky and Ramacharaka: The Influence of Yoga and Turn-of-the-Century Occultism on the System," *Theatre Survey*, 47 (1): 73–92.

Whyman, R. (2008), *The Stanislavsky System: Legacy and Influence in Modern Performance*, Cambridge: Cambridge University Press.

Wiles, T. (1980), *The Theater Event*, Chicago: University of Chicago Press.

Worrall, N. (1989), *Modernism to Realism on the Soviet Stage: Tairov, Vakhtangov, Okhlopkov*, Cambridge: Cambridge University Press.

Worthen, W. B. (1984), *The Idea of the Actor*, Princeton: Princeton University Press.

Zvereva, N. A. (2014), *Vospominaia Mariiu Osipovnu Knebel': Uroki, repetitii, spektakli* [Remembering Knebel: Classes, Rehearsals, Shows], Moscow: GITIS.

Zvereva, N. A., ed. (2021), *Obretenie shkoly: M. O. Knebel', Teatral'naia pedagogika* [Attainment in School: Knebel's Theatrical Pedagogy], Moscow: GITIS.

Index